FROM LEFT: PAVELO68/SHUTTERSTOCK, MONIKA MINT/SHUTTERSTOCK, BTWIMAGES/SHUTTERSTOCK

Medina (p100), Hammamet

Toolkit

Storybook

DELPIXEL/SHUTTERSTOCK

The Sahara (p229)

TUNISIA

THE JOURNEY BEGINS HERE

It's interesting times in Tunisia, a country that feels like it's transitioning from colonialism, vintage beach resorts and dated Noughties autocracy, to a new world of possibilities birthed by the Arab Spring in 2011. With its easy charm, it's easy to forget the import of those events, which gave voice to an intense desire to construct a different future for the country. This new era is being forged by a growing community of cultural activists, entrepreneurs and artists who are surfacing Tunisia's fascinating multiethnic history, creating fresh experiences in its startlingly varied landscapes, and evolving its music, art and craft traditions. It's these grassroots efforts and the passion of the people putting Tunisia back on the map that make visiting the country now so interesting and rewarding.

Paula Hardy

@paulahardy

Paula has been an Africa-focused travel journalist for over 20 years.

My favourite experience is watching a fiery sun set over the **Grand Erg Oriental** (p239) only to be replaced by a silver moon that makes the desert floor glitter like the waves of an ancient sea.

lonely planet

Tunisia

Paula Hardy, Lauren Keith, Virginia Maxwell, Owen Morton, Isabel Putinja, Paul Stafford, Dr Jenny Walker

CONTENTS

Amphitheatre of Thysdrus (p199)

The Sahara (p229)

WHO GOES WHERE

Our writers and experts choose the places that, for them, define Tunisia.

LAUREN KEITH/LONELY PLANET

The **Tunis medina** (p58) is a jewel in the country's crown. Don't try to rush through – the twisting, narrow alleyways ensure that's not possible. Meandering lanes filled with markets, hole-in-the wall shops and fast-food joints are worthy distractions, as are what you find behind the colourful metal-studded doors that brighten the bougainvillea-draped alleys. The medina is the best of the Tunisian capital, all squished together.

Lauren Keith

@noplacelike_it

Lauren is a guidebook author and travel writer often found somewhere between the Midwest and the Middle East.

ANDREAS WOLOCHOW/SHUTTERSTOCK

As the only surviving example of an ancient Punic city that was never built over by the Romans, the UNESCO-listed archaeological site of **Kerkouane** (p111) is exceptional. There's something about standing among its maze of ancient stones on the edge of a rocky coastline and trying to imagine what life looked like here more than 2000 years ago.

Isabel Putinja

@isabelswindow

Isabel is a travel writer, solo walker and slow traveller.

LEV LEVIN/SHUTTERSTOCK

The subterranean villas of **Bulla Regia** (p140) are more than just ruins in the soil; they show the capacity for cultures to unite to create something unique and beautiful. Roman building ingenuity meeting the nous of the Amazigh. While we tend to overlook the negatives that came with the older empires wielding control, the fact that something positive has endured for 2000 years sends a hopeful message about the possibilities of unity in these times of division.

Paul Stafford

@paulrstafford

Paul is based in Birmingham, UK. When not entangled in a web of words and pictures, he is one half of the alternative indie rock duo PHWOAR.

CHRISTOPHE CAPPELLI/SHUTTERSTOCK

I love exploring medinas, so I was spoiled for choice while researching Tunisia's central coast. What fascinates me is how each medina has its own distinct character – the medina in **Kairouan** (pictured; p188) is geared to its residents, Sfax's seems totally mercantile and 100% local, and the medina in Sousse seems to seamlessly balance traditional and tourist functions. When I walk through these medinas, their history manifests. It's totally magical.

Virginia Maxwell

@maxwellvirginia

Though based in Australia, Virginia spends as much time as she can in the Mediterranean, but still has 12 countries there on her to-do list.

KONSTANTIN AKSENOV/SHUTTERSTOCK

Dougga (p158) is one of northern Africa's finest Roman sites: its ruins, straggling down a hillside, contain a theatre, two monumental arches, a magnificent ensemble of temples, and a most unusual mausoleum. Alongside these splendid public buildings, however, you'll find the remains of houses and shops, giving you an insight into daily life 2000 years ago.

Owen Morton

@owenmortonmanul

Owen is a UK-based travel writer who specialises in the Middle East and the Caucasus. Follow him (and his rotund Pallas Cat toy) on Instagram.

LEV LEVIN/SHUTTERSTOCK

Stand at the base of a honey-combed granary in Ksour Country and feel the wind nipping at a hilltop site and you're reminded that Amazigh life in the arid reaches of the Saharan fringe was a battle against the elements. I'm in awe of the ingenuity of isolated communities to make the best of the harsh hand nature has dealt them. **Ouled Soltane** (p212), with vaulted cell upon cell scrambling up to the sky, is a rebellion against the grasp of the desert.

Dr Jenny Walker

@jennywalkertravel

Dr Jenny Walker is a higher education consultant and author.

CONTRIBUTING WRITERS

Tharik Hussain

tharikhussain.co.uk

Author of the award-winning Minarets in the Mountains: a Journey into Muslim Europe, *Tharik has contributed to various Lonely Planet guidebooks and to* National Geographic, The Guardian *and the BBC. Tharik wrote 'Religion in Tunisia'.*

Sanad Tabbaa

sanadtab.net

Sanad is a former historian and short story and travel writer based in Amman. He specialises in stories about the melancholy, mystical and mundane. Sanad wrote 'History of Tunisia in 15 Places' and 'Pirates of the Mediterranean'.

Hanane Zahrouni

@byhananezahrouni

Hanane is a British-Tunisian writer who has lived across the world, always seeking her next great escape. With a background in Environmental Science, she loves sustainable and adventurous travel. She wrote 'Meet the Tunisians' and 'Kairouan: City of Knowledge & Fatima Al-Fihri'.

Tunis
A charming cosmopolitan capital with an ancient medina (p53)
Lake Ichkeul
A lagoon landscape favoured by birds and water buffalo (p127)
Bizerte
Forts, ports and spectacular sunsets (p120)
Cap Bon
Vineyards, hot springs and lots of spicy harissa (p92)
Dougga
One of the best-preserved Roman towns in Africa (p158)
Hammamet
A summer cultural hub beside golden beaches (p96)
Kairouan
One of Islam's holiest pilgrimage destinations (p185)
Sousse
A World Heritage–listed fortified medina (p172)
El Jem
A sensational colosseum and mosaic collection (p197)
Mahdia
An authentic fishing port on a pretty peninsula (p192)
Palermo
Sicily
ITALY
Pantelleria
Mediterranean Sea
Lake Bizerte
Lake Ichkeul
Bizerte
Raf Raf
Menzel Bourguiba
Mateur
Sejnane
Nefza
Tabarka
La Calle
Annaba
Gulf of Tunis
El Haouaria
Cap Bon
Kelibia
Menzel Temine
TUNIS
La Marsa
Tebourba
Soliman
Menzel Bou Zelfa
Korba
Aïn Draham
Beni Mtir
Béja
Medjez el Bab
Grombalia
Nabeul
Bou Salem
Ghardimaou
Jendouba
El Aroussa
El Fahs
Zaghouan
Hammamet
Bou Ficha
Souk Ahras
Al Karib
El Kef
Siliana
Al Sars
Nadour
Enfidha
Gulf of Hammamet
ALGERIA
Tajerouine
Ad Dahmani
As-Subayhah
Maktar
Ousseltia
Sousse
Monastir
Msaken
Kairouan
Téboulba
Kalaat Khasba
Tebessa
Sebkhet Sidi el-Hani
Kerker
Mahdia
Hajeb El Ayoun
Sidi Amor Bou Hadjila
El Jem
Sbeitla
Chebba
Kasserine
Sidi Bouzid
Sebkhet el Gharra
El Hencha
Djebeniana
Thelepte
Bir Al Huffay
Regueb
Sfax
Chergui
Bir Ali Ben Khlifa
Gharbi
Kerkennah Islands
Moulares
Al-Mazzunah
Mahares
Tamerza
Metlaoui
Gafsa
Sebkhet en Noual
Skhira

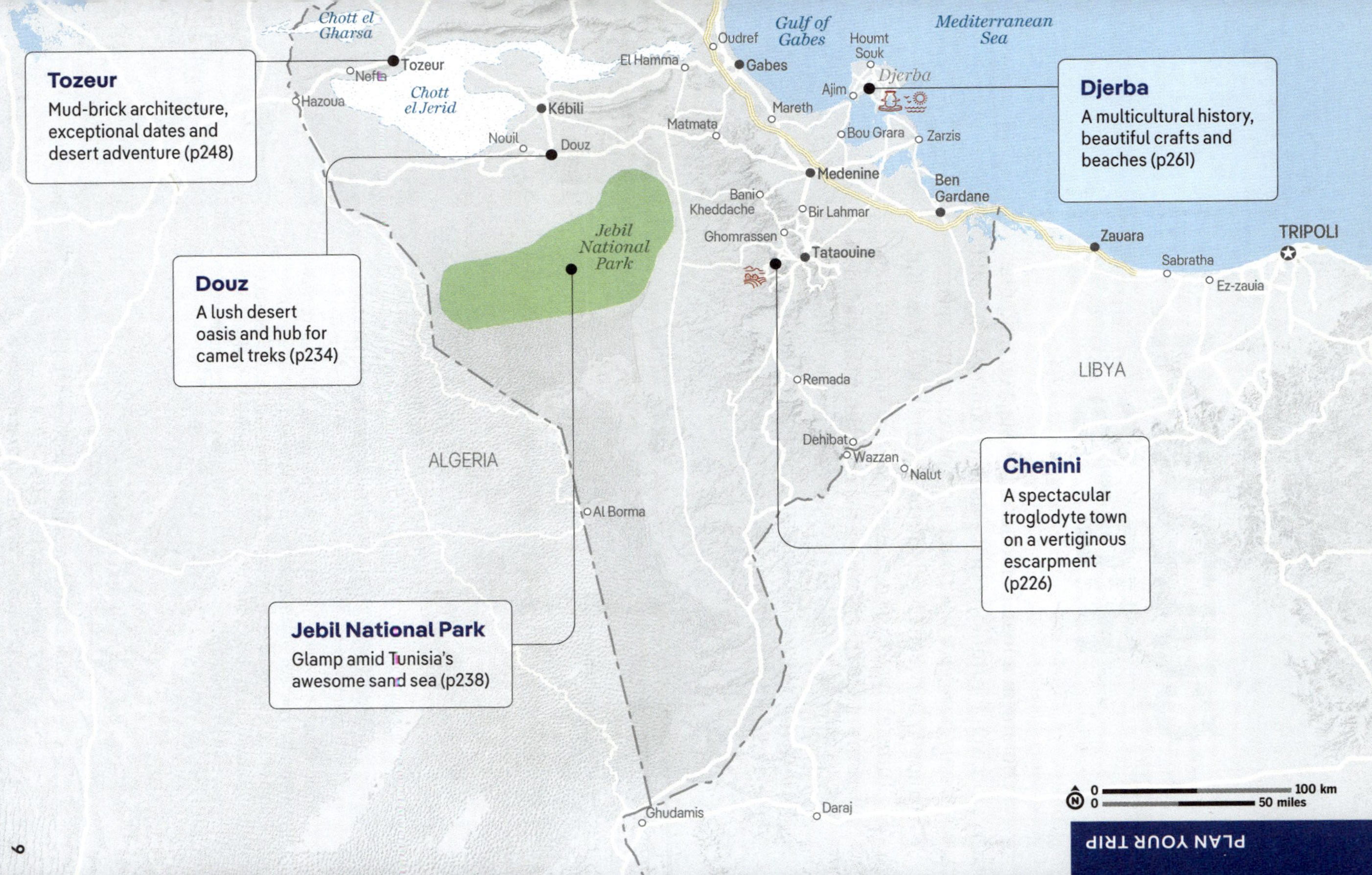
Tozeur
Mud-brick architecture, exceptional dates and desert adventure (p248)
Douz
A lush desert oasis and hub for camel treks (p234)
Jebil National Park
Glamp amid Tunisia's awesome sand sea (p238)
Djerba
A multicultural history, beautiful crafts and beaches (p261)
Chenini
A spectacular troglodyte town on a vertiginous escarpment (p226)
Mediterranean Sea
Gulf of Gabes
Chott el Gharsa
Chott el Jerid
Jebil National Park
ALGERIA
LIBYA
TRIPOLI
Tozeur
Nefta
Hazoua
El Hamma
Oudref
Gabes
Houmt Souk
Djerba
Ajim
Mareth
Matmata
Kébili
Nouil
Douz
Bou Grara
Zarzis
Medenine
Ben Gardane
Bani
Kheddache
Bir Lahmar
Ghomrassen
Tataouine
Zauara
Sabratha
Ez-zauia
Remada
Dehibat
Wazzan
Nalut
Al Borma
Ghudamis
Daraj
0 100 km
0 50 miles

CULTURAL HIGHS

Looking at a map of modern Tunisia, you might be forgiven for thinking that this is a country that could only have ever been a bit-part player, a tiny speck trapped between the giants of Algeria and Libya. But Tunisia's history is a rich and storied one, from the ruins of Carthage, whose general Hannibal dared to challenge Rome, to the glories of medieval Islam, through years of Turkish and French colonisation, and into the forward-facing modern period.

FROM LEFT: DI GREGORIO GIULIO/SHUTTERSTOCK, KATARZYNAZAKOWSKA/SHUTTERSTOCK, ANIBAL TREJO/SHUTTERSTOCK

Local Lingo

The official language of Tunisia is Arabic, but French is widely spoken and will help you get by. Day-to-day, however, locals speak Tūnsi (or Derja), Tunisian Arabic.

Appropriate Dress

Keep shoulders and knees covered in town and particularly when visiting mosques and religious monuments. Also refrain from wearing singlets and shorts.

Festival Season

June, July and August are prime festival time in Tunisia with notable festivals taking place in Carthage, Bizerte, Hammamet, Testour, Sousse and El Jem.

Great Mosque (p186), Kairouan

BEST CULTURAL EXPERIENCES

See the world's finest collection of Roman mosaics, including a contemporary portrait of the poet Virgil, at the 1 **Bardo Museum** (p68) in Tunis.

Discover Tunisia's myriad multicultural influences with a food tour or cookery workshop with 2 **Sawa Taste** (p105).

Contemplate Islamic history at Kairouan's 3 **Great Mosque** (p199), the oldest in North Africa and considered by some to be one of the holiest sites in Islam.

Make port at 4 **Djerba** (p261), a maverick island with a unique Jewish-Tunisian history, an ancient synagogue and a deep tradition of artisan crafts.

Experience an archetypal oasis in 5 **Tozeur** (p248), with its ancient brick-built medina and vast *palmeraie* planted with date palms, pomegranate, fig and citrus trees.

URBAN PLEASURES

Tunisia is one of the most urbanised countries in North Africa and its northern seaboard is lined with characterful cities. They have been moulded by multicultural influences over the centuries, lending them each a distinct personality. Combine this with a deep-seated tradition of hospitality and a penchant for enjoying life's quotidian pleasures and you'll discover much to enjoy in urban Tunisia.

BEST URBAN EXPERIENCES

Get a feel for medina life and enjoy personalised hospitality by staying in a historic dar (courtyard house) in ❶ **Tunis** (p90).

Enjoy top-class theatre, film and music concerts at holiday haven Hammamet's ❷ **International Festival** (p98).

Come for a wander round the souq then a feast in ❸ **Sfax** (p201), Tunisia's largest fishing port, where the medina is full of fantastic seafood restaurants.

Enjoy modern medina life, cafe culture and a food tour in Sousse's stunningly well-preserved ❹ **medina** (p174), a World Heritage Site.

Go off piste to ❺ **Djerbahood** (p271) in the tiny village of Erriadh, where every house is a work of art thanks to a unique collective art project.

FROM LEFT: KATIEKK/SHUTTERSTOCK, BIESZCZADY_WILDLIFE/SHUTTERSTOCK

Smoking

Smoking is one of Tunisia's great national pleasures with men making up the majority of smokers. Non-smoking areas in hotels and restaurants are rare.

Ramadan

The main holiday is Ramadan, the Muslim fasting month, when the country switches to a different rhythm. Cities come alive at night after the sunset meal, *iftar*.

Cafe Culture

Cafes deck every corner of every major city. Drinks of choice include Turkish coffee, espresso, cappuccino, tea with mint or pine nuts, and refreshing citronnade.

VADIM_N/SHUTTERSTOCK

Amphitheatre of Thysdrus (p199), El Jem

❸❷ ❹❺ ❶

BEST ANTIQUITY EXPERIENCES

Admire El Jem's ❶ **Amphitheatre of Thysdrus** (p199) – the fourth largest colosseum in the Roman world after the ones in Rome and Capua.

Discover ❷ **Dougga** (p158), one of Africa's most complete Roman sites, set in the picturesque Kalled Valley surrounded by olive groves.

Wander well-preserved, mosaic-clad rooms complete with colonnaded courtyards in the subterranean Roman villas of ❸ **Bulla Regia** (p140).

Spend hours admiring the world's largest collection of Roman mosaics, as well as Punic sculpture and jewellery and Greek artefacts at the palatial ❹ **Bardo Museum** (p68).

See remnants of Carthage in the monumental ruins of the ❺ **Baths of Antoninus** (p78), still awesome in scale.

ANTIQUE SPLENDOURS

Carthage dominates Tunisia's history. Now a well-heeled northern suburb of Tunis, this once-great power dominated the western Mediterranean in the 6th century BCE. But Rome could not abide the competition and after a hundred years of war laid it low. They built their colonial cities on Punic ruins, some of which are stunningly well preserved.

Clothing Tips

Antiquity sites aren't flip-flops and beachwear territory. The sites are often huge, very exposed and full of tumbled down stones. Wear decent shoes and SPF.

Notable Museums

Tunisia's best archaeological museums are the **Bardo** (p68) in Tunis, the **Archaeological Museum in El Jem** (p197), and the **Sousse Archaeological Museum** (p172).

NATURAL WONDERS

Tunisia's size belies the diversity of its natural attractions, from a balmy Mediterranean coastline, the spitting image of Italy, to the oak-forested slopes of the Kroumirie Mountains, the semi-desert hinterland of Dahar and the stunning sand seas of the Grand Erg Oriental. What's more, it takes just six hours to travel from the coast to the desert, meaning you can enjoy vastly different experiences and atmospheres without excessive time spent travelling.

FROM LEFT: MIKE HOERI/SHUTTERSTOCK, DENIS KABANOV/SHUTTERSTOCK, SOFIENE X/SHUTTERSTOCK

Migration Season

Tunisia sits on a strategic bird migration route between Africa and Europe and in spring and autumn tens of thousands of storks, cranes and raptors pass through.

Climate Change

Tunisia is highly vulnerable to the impact of climate change and faces rising summer temperatures and reduced precipitation. Use water wisely.

National Parks

Although Tunisia has eight national parks and 16 reserves, the only one with visitor facilities is Ichkeul National Park near Bizerte.

BEST NATURAL EXPERIENCES

See flamingos, herons, egrets and water buffalo grazing in the blue-green marshland of ❶ **Lake Ichkeul** (p127).

Hike the verdant green trails in the cork oak forests of the ❷ **Kroumirie Mountains**, then bed down in the mountain town of Aïn Draham (p134).

Take a slow drive around Cap Bon to ❸ **El Haouaria** (p112), where you can swim in rock pools and enjoy the spectacular views and wild beaches.

Drive the 2m-high causeway across ❹ **Chott El Jerid** (p254), a great glittering salt pan that conjures amazing mirages.

Spend the night among the silent, shifting dunes of the ❺ **Jebil National Park** (p238) and satisfy every desert fantasy you've ever had.

LIVING CRAFT TRADITIONS

Wander any Tunisian souq and you'll mmediately see that Tunisia has a vibrant, living craft tradition. Centuries of technical know-how have made Tunisian artisans experts in ceramics, textiles, leatherwork, embroidery, carpet weaving, carpentry, coral and silver jewellery, and basketry. While many of these traditions are now threatened, young digital-savvy artists are determined to find new markets to sustain the country's age-old crafts.

BEST CRAFT EXPERIENCES

Get a hands-on appreciation of the skill required to be a bookbinder, leatherworker, potter or calligrapher by joining one of ❶ **Mdinti's workshops** in Tunis (p60).

Purchase a memorable keepsake direct from the women artisans at their roadside stalls in ❷ **Sejnane** (p129), the home of UNESCO-listed Amazigh pottery.

Find ❸ **Nabeul's** famed colourful glazed ceramics in its souqs, and much else including *foutas*, basketry, jewellery, floral water and spicy harissa (p103).

Buy a fine Persian-style knotted carpet at ❹ **Société Tapis Allani** (p190) in Kairouan, where they were first introduced to Tunisia.

Go shopping or take a workshop on ❺ **Djerba** (p267), another craft hub famous for its basket and mat weaving, embroidery and Guellala pottery.

FROM LEFT: JOHN WREFORD/SHUTTERSTOCK, HICHEM KAOUANE/SHUTTERSTOCK

Capital Finds

In the Tunis souqs look out for embroidered textiles, *babouche* (slippers), engraved silverware and *chechias*, Tunisia's traditional red felt hats.

Qartaj

Qartaj.com is a Fair Trade website showcasing and selling the best Tunisian artisanal crafts, including textiles, ceramics and rugs. They also ship internationally.

Foutas

Handloomed *foutas* are the original hammam towels and are a Tunisian household staple. They can be used as shawls, beach wraps, tablecloths or bedspreads.

LCHPHOTOGALLERY/SHUTTERSTOCK

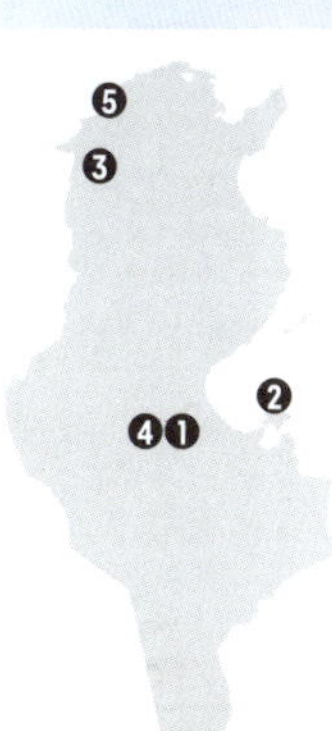

Matmata (p214)

VILLAGE VIBES

Away from the capital and big coastal cities, life in Tunisia's villages continues to follow traditional rhythms and a largely agricultural lifestyle as depicted in the film *Under the Fig Trees*. There's astonishing variety here, too, from coastal villages focused on fishing and tourism to ancient Amazigh troglodyte towns in the Dahar Mountains and Bedouin villages sustained by oasis palm groves.

Manners

Be considerate of the fact that rural communities are more conservative and dress respectfully. Also, be sure to greet everyone you meet.

Access

To reach remote hilltop towns, mountain strongholds and desert oases, having your own set of wheels is best rather than relying on taxis.

BEST VILLAGE EXPERIENCES

Don't miss the troglodyte town of ❶ **Matmata** (p214) in the Dahar mountains, where Amazigh ancestors dug into the mountain to create unique subterranean homes.

Watch local life carry on regardless of tourism at the bustling Monday and Thursday souq at Djerba's charming cobbled port of ❷ **Houmt Souk** (p264).

Discover remnants of Roman, Christian, Jewish and Islamic eras and settle into a slow pace of life in the ancient streets of ❸ **El Kef** (p154), one of Tunisia's oldest villages.

Celebrate desert culture in December at the fantastic ❹ **International Festival of the Sahara** (p236) in the desert oasis of Douz.

Stumble upon ❺ **Beni Mtir** (p136) and you might think you've arrived in an Alpine village with its red-roofed French architecture, deconsecrated church and surrounding forest.

COASTAL BEAUTY

Tunisia has a stunning 1400km coastline that alternates between dramatic rocky shoreline covered in macchia and Aleppo pines, and long sandy beaches. The most popular – and busy – beaches are those that run south of Cap Bon all the way to Djerba. Here, there are resorts to suit all tastes from bougie, adult-only boltholes to chic dars (courtyard houses), villas and farmhouses, as well as large, family-friendly resorts with every imaginable facility.

FROM LEFT: TRAVEL-FR/SHUTTERSTOCK, FLANEURXELMUNDO/SHUTTERSTOCK, IURI DZIVINSKYI/SHUTTERSTOCK

Beach Season

The beach season in Tunisia is between June and October when the water is warm enough for swimming. Outside this time, most resorts close.

Thalassotherapy

Thalassotherapy is a feature of many Tunisian resorts and you can expect a whole range of wraps, baths, showers and treatments using mud and essential oils.

Diving

There's limited diving in Tunisia with the best sites in Tabarka (p139), where you'll find coral gardens, and Djerba (p271), with wrecks to explore.

Sidi Bou Said (p81), Tunis

BEST COASTAL EXPERIENCES

Wander the bijou beach and marina and take in dreamy sea views from clifftop cafe terraces in Tunis' seaside suburb of ❶ **Sidi Bou Said** (p81).

Lunch at a table set among rock pools far from the crowds at ❷ **El Mansourah** (p109), the prettiest of Cap Bon's beaches.

Hop over to ❸ **Djerba** (p261), an island that has everything you could desire: sandy beaches, a charming cobblestone town and a history of ethnic diversity.

Stroll around the peninsula for lovely sea views among ancient ruins on Mahdia's pretty ❹ **Cap Afrique** (p195).

Escape the summer crowds by heading north to ❺ **Plage Cap Serrat** (p130), where you'll find clear water and the friendly Auberge Le Pirate (p145).

ADVENTURES OUTDOORS

Tunisia may be famous for 'sun, sand and sea' holidays, but get beyond the beaches and you'll discover the country is well adapted for an adventure holiday. Despite being just a little bigger than England, the diversity of landscapes is striking, which means you can go diving and kayaking one day, then hiking and mountain biking the next and finish on the back of a camel in one of the largest sand seas in the Sahara.

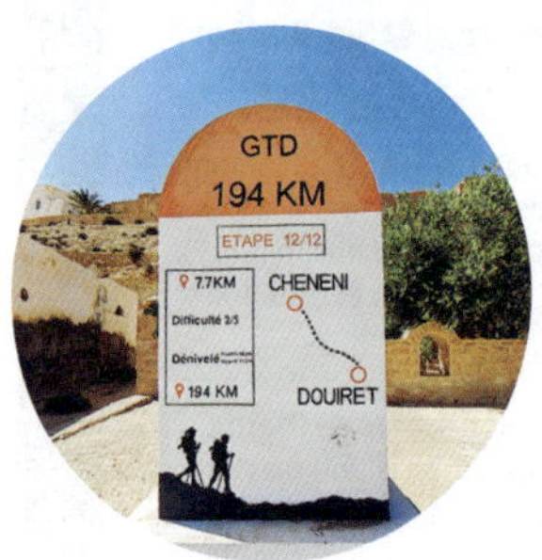

FROM LEFT: DIMA007/SHUTTERSTOCK, MAURO PASSARELLA/SHUTTERSTOCK, DMITRY EAGLE ORLOV/SHUTTERSTOCK

Hiking Highs

In 2024 two new hiking trails were established: the Trans Tunisia Trail (p153) in the northwest and the 194km Dahar Hiking Trail in the southeast.

Winter in the Desert

First-time desert visitors may be surprised at how cold it gets on winter nights, sometimes dropping to 3°C. Bring thermals and decent outer layers.

Pit Villages

If you stay overnight in Matmata or other troglodyte villages in Ksour Country, arrive before dark so you can find your accommodation.

Grand Canyon of Tunisia (p257)

BEST ADVENTURE EXPERIENCES

Head out with a camel caravan or a 4WD into the Grand Erg Oriental dunefield in the ❶ **Jebil National Park** (p238) – a trip highlight for many.

Explore the green forests of Kroumirie Mountains around Aïn Draham on foot or mountain bikes with ❷ **Dar El Ain** (p139)'s well-devised tours.

Hike the ancient, arid landscape of the Dahar Mountains around ❸ **Ghomrassen** (p224), Douiret and Chenini.

Go cycling, horse riding, diving, wind- and kitesurfing on the little island of ❹ **Djerba**, an outdoor playground (p271).

Take the most spectacular hike in the country: the sinuous, 4.5km trail through Tunisia's ❺ **Grand Canyon** (p257) connecting the ghost villages of Midès and Tamerza.

REGIONS & CITIES

Find the places that tick all your boxes.

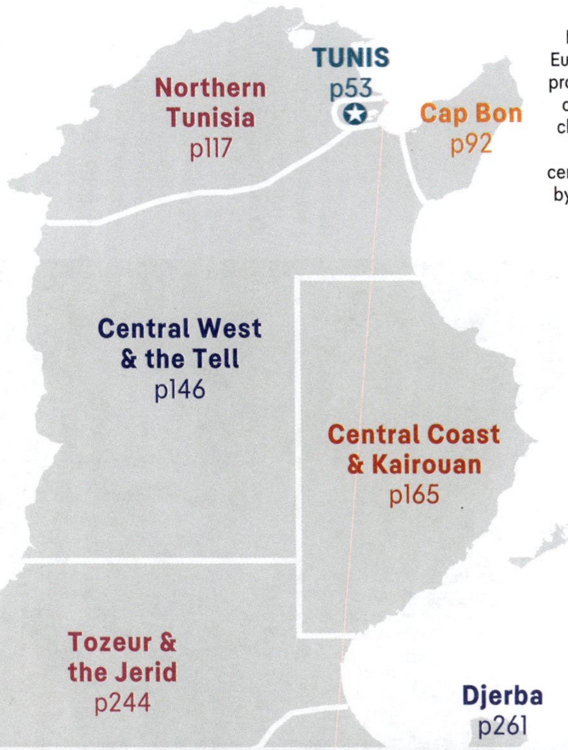

Northern Tunisia

WILD BEACHES AND MOUNTAIN ESCAPES

Beloved by Tunisians but overlooked by everyone else, northern Tunisia is the country's most under-appreciated region. It has some of Tunisia's finest beaches surrounding the port towns of Bizerte and Tabarka, and it's also home to the extensive forests of Aïn Draham, UNESCO-listed Lake Ichkeul, and rolling, golden farmland hiding intriguing Roman sites such as Bulla Regia, Chemtou and Utica.

p117

Central West & the Tell

ANCIENT RUINS AND BUSTLING MEDINAS

The plains and mountains of the Tell and Dorsale that trace Tunisia's western border are where Amazigh tribes held the line against ambitious Roman Imperialism in hilltop towns like El Kef and on the inviolate Jugurtha's Table. In its shadow, the ruins of once proud Roman colonies, such as epic Dougga and evocative Uthina, offer a lesson in the rise and fall of mighty empires.

p146

Northern Tunisia p117
TUNIS p53
Cap Bon p92
Central West & the Tell p146
Central Coast & Kairouan p165
Tozeur & the Jerid p244
Djerba p261

Tunis

TUNISIA'S QUIETLY COOL CAPITAL

Maghrebi, Mediterranean, Levantine and European: Tunis is a complex but charmingly provincial capital today, and once the capital of Carthage, the North African power that challenged Rome. It has two distinct faces, one determined by its souq-filled, 8th-century Arab medina; the other characterised by its French Colonial–era expansion, full of museums, cafes, restaurants and clubs.

p53

Cap Bon

SANDY BEACHES, ANCIENT RUINS AND ORCHARDS

Cap Bon is a crooked peninsula that points towards Sicily, 150km across the Mediterranean. It has close ties with Europe and shares the same lovely pine- and citrus-clad coastline. Summer action centres on the resort of Hammamet, although the real beauty lies in the market-town of Nabeul, the fishing port of Kelibia and the ruined Carthaginian settlement of Kerkouane.

p92

The Central Coast & Kairouan

LIVING HISTORY IN VARIED LANDSCAPES

This is postcard Tunisia, where the past meets the present in a string of fascinating cities and sites. They include august Sousse with its historic medina and fine collection of Roman mosaics, the centuries-old souqs of Sfax, pretty sea-facing Mahdia and desert city Kairouan. El Jem's colosseum, meanwhile, is just a fraction smaller than the one in Rome.

p165

Tozeur & the Jerid

OASIS TOWNS IN AN ARID LANDSCAPE

The Jerid sits between two major salt lakes, Chott El Jerid and Chott El Gharsa, and is an agricultural hub famous for its dates. The moonlike environment is best explored from the vibrant frontier town of Tozeur, which is bounded by a lush green palm grove on one side and a snow-white expanse of salt on the other.

p244

The Sahara

INSPIRING DESERT LANDSCAPES, HOME TO NOMADS

In the south and west rise the shifting sand dunes of the Grand Erg Oriental, one of the Sahara's most expansive sand seas. Here you can venture out of the dusty oasis town of Douz on camel or by 4WD to explore one of the country's most remarkable and breathtaking landscapes.

p229

Matmata & the Ksour

EXTRAORDINARY DWELLINGS – UNDERGROUND AND TOWERING ABOVE

Southern Tunisia is a place of stark, alien landscapes and isolated Amazigh villages perched on mountains or dug into the earth like in famous Matmata, the film shoot for Star Wars. Ancient *ksour* (traditional fortified granaries) also dot the countryside, the best of which is Chenini, spectacularly sited on a mountain ridge.

p208

Djerba

ARCHITECTURAL HERITAGE, TRADITIONAL HANDICRAFTS, SANDY BEACHES

To the classically inclined, the name Djerba conjures images of Homer's Land of the Lotus-Eaters, an island so seductive that it's impossible to leave. While many visitors sequester themselves at resort hotels along beautiful Plage Sidi Mahrès, exploring the island's countryside and historic towns reveals a fascinating multicultural history.

p261

ARTAXERXES_LONGHAND/SHUTTERSTOCK

Place de la Kasbah, Tunis (p53)

ITINERARIES

The Capital & Cap Bon

Allow: 5 days **Distance:** 188km

There's a huge amount to see around Tunis and this itinerary combines a bit of everything, blending the history, culture and museums of the capital with the beach resorts and food-focused market towns of Cap Bon. Distances are short and can be covered by public transport, although having your own car offers more freedom.

1

TUNIS 2 DAYS

Start in cosmopolitan **Tunis** (p53) meandering around the UNESCO Heritage medina (pictured above), shopping in the souqs, marvelling at the food market and joining artisans in calligraphy or bookbinding workshops. Devote a morning to the exceptional Roman mosaics in the Bardo Museum, an afternoon to the beaches of La Marsa and Gammarth and an evening to a traditional hammam. Stay in a dar (courtyard house) in the medina for maximum atmosphere.

2

CARTHAGE 1 DAY

Engage a good guide to explore the ancient ruins of **Carthage** (p74). Seek out the once monumental Baths of Antoninus (pictured above), the Roman villas and the spectacular view from the top of the Brysa Hill. It's a huge site, so consider an e-bike tour. Then walk or take a taxi to picturesque Sidi Bou Said, one of the prettiest villages in Tunisia, with lots of great galleries and seaview restaurants.

FROM LEFT: TRAVEL-FR/SHUTTERSTOCK, EMILY MARIE WILSON/SHUTTERSTOCK

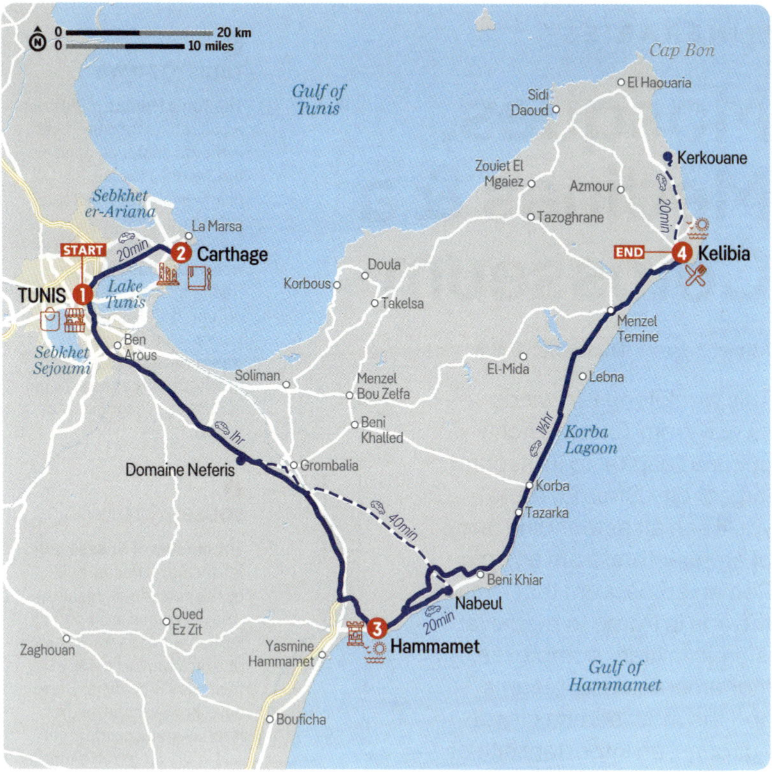

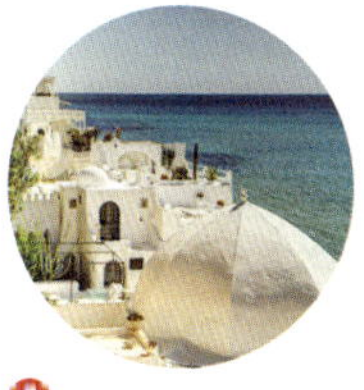

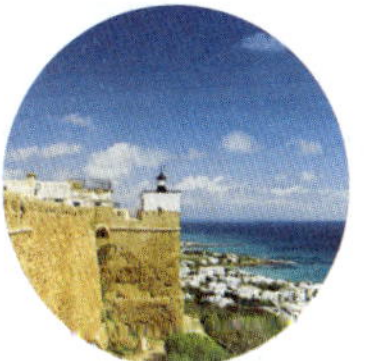

3 HAMMAMET 1 DAY

Once a sleepy fishing village, **Hammamet** (p96, pictured above) is now Cap Bon's main resort town and buzzes with summer holidaymakers. They come for the charming medina, picturesque fort and miles of golden beaches, off which you can go boating, kayaking and windsurfing.

***Detour:** On Thursdays head to nearby **Nabeul** (p103) to browse the market for a couple of hours. Then head on to **Domaine Neferis** (p291) for a wine-tasting before circling back to Hammamet in the evening.*

4 KELIBIA 1 DAY

Finally, make your way north to the ancient fishing town of **Kelibia** (p110), a mere 70km from the Italian island of Pantelleria. It has an awesome crenellated citadel (pictured above), fine sandy beaches and some of the country's best fish restaurants such as **El Mansourah** (p109).

***Detour:** Drive to **Kerkouane** (p111) and spend two hours exploring the only surviving remains of a Punic city, located on a windswept peninsula.*

MEHDI33300/SHUTTERSTOCK, WITR/SHUTTERSTOCK

ITINERARIES

Mosques, Medinas & a Colosseum

Allow: 7 days **Distance:** 471km

This week-long trip winds its way from Tunisia's richly cultured capital to its second largest city, Sfax. En route you'll see an astounding array of architecture, from an epic Roman colosseum that rivals the one in Rome to medieval Islamic military complexes, monumental mausoleums and the most serene city of Kairouan, an important site of Islamic pilgrimage.

Great Mosque (p175), Sousse

1 TUNIS 2 DAYS

The **Tunis Medina** (p58) is an architectural treasure, built in the 7th century around the Zitouna Mosque. It is full of artisanal souqs, historic palaces, *madrasas* (religious schools) and royal tombs as well as boutique hotels in traditional dars. The other face of Tunis is the 19th-century, French-built Centre Ville, where you'll find surprising hybrid structures such as the cathedral, synagogue and theatre.

2 SOUSSE 1 DAY

The **medina of Sousse** (p174) is a medieval marvel built by the powerful Aghlabids, who integrated an imposing kasbah within its walls as well as a rare *ribat,* a hostelry for their Islamic soldiers. These days, however, the medina is full of atmospheric cafes and interesting craft shops as well as a great archaeological museum. Take our **DIY walking tour** (p177) and be sure to overnight in a historic home.

3 KAIROUAN 1 DAY

Kairouan (p185) was the Aghlabids' 9th-century capital, and it retains a lost-in-time feel. Some Muslims consider it the most holy city after Mecca, Medina and Jerusalem and come on pilgrimage to the Great Mosque and *zaouias* (Sufi lodge complexes) that are hidden in the characterful medina. Explore them and graze on the city's good street food, then contemplate the rugs on sale – they're the best in Tunisia.

Gulf of Tunis
Zouiet El Mgaiez
Azmour
START
La Marsa
Kelibia
TUNIS
Korbous
Takelsa
Menzel Temine
Ben Arous
Soliman
Menzel Bou Zelfa
El-Mida
Beni Khalled
Grombalia
Korba
Tazarka
Nabeul
Zaghouan
Hammamet
Yasmine Hammamet
1½hr
Bouficha
Enfidha
Nadour
Gulf of Hammamet
As-Subayhah
Kelaa Kebira
Sousse
Monastir
Kairouan
1hr
Msaken
Téboulba
1¾hr
Sebkhet Sidi el-Hani
Sebkhet Moknine
Mahdia
Kerker
Bou Merdes
Ksour-essaf
Sidi Amor Bou Hadjila
El Jem
Chebba
Sebkhet el Jem
Sebkhet el Gharra
2hr
El Hencha
Djebeniana
Triaga
Jebkhet Bou Jemel
END
Sfax
Kerkennah Islands
Bir Ali Ben Khlifa
1hr
Gharbi
Mahares
Graiba
0 20 km
0 10 miles

4 MAHDIA 2 DAYS

Mahdia (p192) is located on a spectacular peninsula and retains its authentic character as Tunisia's biggest fishing port. Eating fish here is a highlight and the town is famous for its handloomed textiles. Also be sure to explore the pretty promontory, Cap Afrique, either on foot or underwater.

***Detour:** Spend half a day admiring the amazing **Amphitheatre of Thysdrus** (p199), El Jem's epic colosseum.*

5 SFAX 1 DAY

Sfax (p201) has another impressive 9th-century medina (pictured below), but this time there's barely a souvenir shop in sight. Instead, you'll find fantastically cinematic souqs that have been used in various films, and an authentic vision of how past and present can harmoniously coexist.

***Detour:** Take a ferry to Gharbi, the largest of the lovely **Kerkennah Islands** (p205), for a day of cycling, bird-watching and plates of local octopus.*

ANGELA N PERRYMAN/SHUTTERSTOCK

Camels, near Douz (p234)

ITINERARIES

A Grand Tour

Allow 2 weeks **Distance** 1242km

Tunisia is small enough that you can plan a tour of almost the whole country in two weeks. It's a fabulous ride covering a huge variety of culture and landscape. Start with your toes in the Mediterranean sea in the cosmopolitan capital Tunis, then trace the golden coastline through Roman ruins and olive groves to end in the silence of the Sahara.

1

TUNIS 3 DAYS

To experience **Tunis** (p53) fully, allow three or four days. This gives you time to explore the medina's mosques, palaces and souqs, visit the **Bardo Museum** (p68, pictured) and **Carthage** (p74), do a cooking course and have a hammam. Then spend a day on the beach at **Gammarth** (p86) and book dinner on one of the pretty terraces in **Sidi Bou Said** (p83).

2

SOUSSE 1 DAY

Stay beside Bou Jaffer beach or in Sousse's World Heritage medina. **Sousse** (p172) is a popular seaside hub with great street food, an excellent archaeological museum and craft shops with high-quality, locally made souvenirs.

Detour: *Day trip to holy* ***Kairouan*** *(p185) to contemplate its marvellous mosque and shrines, or alternatively head to the fishing port of* ***Mahdia*** *(p192) for lunch and a beautiful seaside walk.*

3

SFAX 1 DAY

To immerse yourself in Tunisian life unmediated by tourism, you have to spend a day in **Sfax** (p201). With nary a souvenir shop in sight, the medina (pictured) buzzes with daily life and still harbours a blacksmith's quarter, which looks like a place from another time.

Detour: *Nearby is the epic Roman colosseum in the town of* ***El Jem*** *(p197) and a museum full of mosaics, which warrant half a day.*

FROM LEFT: FRANCESCO LORENZETTI/SHUTTERSTOCK, EMILY MARIE WILSON/SHUTTERSTOCK, CHRISTOPHE CAPPELLI/SHUTTERSTOCK

4

DJERBA ⏱3 DAYS

Take a break on the island of **Djerba** (p261), with its beautiful sandy beaches, the cobblestoned town of Houmt Souk and a long history of ethnic diversity. Hang out with the potters of Guellala (pictured), bike around the olive groves and tour its UNESCO heritage sites.

Detour: *South of Djerba is Ksour Country, a mountainous Amazigh area. Explore the fortified granaries, starting with* ***Ouled Soltane*** *(p212).*

5

DOUZ ⏱3 DAYS

Plan for a few days in **Douz** (p234) so you have time to try your hand at camel riding before heading off into the desert to stay at a Bedouin camp in the Jebil National Park. Here you'll bed down in the Grand Erg Oriental, Tunisia's stunning sand sea where huge dunefields rise and fall as far as the eye can see.

6

TOZEUR ⏱2 DAYS

Finally, take the causeway across the surreal Chott el Jerid saltpan to land in **Tozeur** (p248), a lively oasis town enveloped in a huge palm grove, which you should explore, as well as the labyrinthine old quarter, Ouled el Hadef. Then set off for a sunset camel ride to Ong Jemal, guided hikes through the Midès Canyon and visits to villages like **Nefta** (pictured).

VALERY BARETA/SHUTTERSTOCK

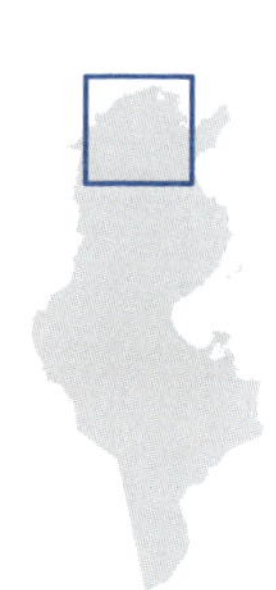

Bizerte (p120)

ITINERARIES

Off the Beaten Path

Allow: 10 days **Distance:** 525km

Travelling off the beaten path in Tunisia is surprisingly easy, particularly if you head north of the capital. Here you'll find some fantastically rugged coastline, deserted beaches, unique freshwater lakes where water buffalo roam, and forest-clad mountains hiding Amazigh towns. Dotted in between are a series of atmospheric Roman ruins.

1

TUNIS 1 DAY

Plug into medina life by staying in a traditional dar. Meet the locals by attending an artisanal workshop with cultural organisation **Mdinti** (p60) or visiting the central market for a cooking class with **Sawa Taste** (p72). Also consider visiting during Ramadan or the Festival de la Médina for a unique insight into local community, and don't leave without having a scrub at the local hammam.

2

BIZERTE 2 DAYS

Set off to **Bizerte** (p120), Africa's northernmost city and a quaint fishing port flanked by lovely beaches. Here you can wander the 3km-long Corniche, watch the fish being hauled ashore, eat excellent seafood and go boating in the bay where dolphins are still abundant.

***Detour:** At the protected **Ichkeul National Park** (p127), you can spend half a day exploring a lagoon full of migrating birds and water buffalo.*

3

TABARKA 2 DAYS

Tabarka (p137) has a Genoese fortress (pictured) and more golden beaches. It's also a popular place for diving given that its reefs are famous for their carmine coral and fish-filled underwater grottoes.

***Detour:** **Sejnane** (p129) is worth a couple of hours to see the artisanal potteries where Amazigh women fashion terracotta wares. Recognised by UNESCO as an intangible cultural heritage, they make fabulous keepsakes.*

FROM LEFT: KATIEKK/SHUTTERSTOCK, HICHEM KAOUANE/SHUTTERSTOCK, LOULOUPHOTOS/SHUTTERSTOCK

0 20 km
0 10 miles
START
1 TUNIS
2 Bizerte
3 Tabarka
4 Aïn Draham
5 El Kef
6 Zaghouan
END
Sidi Ferdjani
Ichkeul National Park
Lac Bizerte
Menzel Bourguiba
Raf Raf
Gulf of Tunis
Sejnane
Mateur
2¼hr
50min
Nefza
La Marsa
40min
ALGERIA
Zirba
Tebourba
Béja
Medjez el Bab
Oulad Cheikh Ayed
Uthina
Bulla Regia
Bou Salem
30min
Jendouba
Dougga
20min
El Aroussa
2¼hr
El Fahs
Al Karib
1¼hr
Enfidha
Siliana
Bargou
Nadour
Al Sars

4

AÏN DRAHAM ⏱ 2 DAYS

In Tabarka arrange a tour with **Dar El Ain** (p139) to discover the lush cork forests of the Kroumirie Mountains that surround the hill station of **Aïn Draham** (p133, pictured). The mountains are the eastern edge of the Atlas range and the town is a popular weekend bolthole.

***Detour:** Definitely don't miss the remarkably well-preserved Roman ruins of **Bulla Regia** (p140), which deserve half a day.*

5

EL KEF ⏱ 2 DAYS

El Kef (p154) is an ancient Amazigh stronghold and Tunisia's highest city. It's full of character and has charming boutique hotels and guesthouses. Stay a while to enjoy the tranquillity, explore the Ottoman kasbah and visit the **Museum of Popular Arts and Traditions** (p155).

***Detour:** Drive to the ruins of **Dougga** (p158), a Roman city that deserves several hours of exploration.*

6

ZAGHOUAN ⏱ 1 DAY

Pretty **Zaghouan** (p150) is a low-key place with a Roman water temple (pictured) integrated into the attractive whitewashed medina. It's a place to kick back and relax, meander the medina's flower-filled alleys and park yourself in a restaurant and people watch.

***Detour:** Spend three hours admiring the elegant sandstone amphitheatre and mosaic-filled villas of **Uthina** (p151).*

SKAZARPHOTO/SHUTTERSTOCK, LEONID ANDRONOV/SHUTTERSTOCK, KHALID TALBI/SHUTTERSTOCK

ITINERARIES

An Island, Mountains & Desert

Allow 1 week **Distance** 666km

Tunisia's unique landscapes and rich, rollicking history have long attracted storytellers, from the Greek epic author, Homer, to Star Wars creator George Lucas. The charming island of Djerba and its extraordinary rocky hinterland are littered with film location sites, incredible troglodyte villages and ancient *ksour* (granaries). Beyond them the cinematic dunefields of the desert await.

1

DJERBA ⏱ 2 DAYS

Fly into **Djerba** (p261), the sand-fringed island of Homer's Lotus-Eaters in the *Odyssey*. It's a microcosm of the country with a unique multicultural heritage where you can visit the oldest synagogue (pictured) in Africa, as well as Catholic and Orthodox churches alongside Muslim shrines and mosques. The small town of Houmt Souk is full of artisan crafts, while Erriadh is an open-air gallery showcasing the street art of 150 muralists.

2

MATMATA ⏱ 1 DAY

Next it's south to a galaxy far, far away. In **Matmata** (p214) is the famous Hotel Sidi Driss, site of Star Wars hero Luke Skywalker's childhood home on the planet Tatooine. A stay in one of the town's 'pit dwellings' (pictured) is a must. Engage a local guide to explore the semi-subterranean city and visit the small ethnographic museums, **Maison Troglodyte Matmata** (p293) and **Musée Berber** (p217).

3

KSAR OULED DEBBAB ⏱ 1 DAY

Just 10km west from the real Tataouine is the fabulous **Ksar Ouled Debbab** (p224, pictured), an Amazigh granary converted into a hotel. It sits in the heart of Ksour Country where you can tour more of these structures like **Ksar Ouled Soltane** (p212) and **Ksar Haddada** (p227), used as locations in Star Wars.

Detour: *Don't miss the stunning mountain top town of* ***Chenini*** *(p226), clinging to an escarpment, where you can easily spend an hour or two.*

Star Wars prop, Matmata (p217)

4

KSAR GHILANE 1 DAY

Ksar Ghilane (p240) literally sits at the end of the road and is the southernmost oasis in Tunisia, perched at the edge of Great Sand Sea. It's home to now-settled nomad families who farm dates thanks to the plentiful hot springs. They also guide tourists on exciting camel and quad bike rides in the dunefields and to the ruined Roman granary of Tisavar.

5

DOUZ 2 DAYS

Finally arrive in **Douz** (p234) at the edge of the desert for thriling adventures. Douz has a huge date *palmeraie* (palm grove, pictured), a lively Thursday market and dozens of experienced desert outfits that can organise excursions by quad, 4WD or camel.

***Detour:** On Douz's doorstep is the surreal **Chott el Jerid** (p254), a shimmering white salt pan where mirages abound. Take a two-hour drive across the causeway to experience the surreal effects.*

WHEN TO GO

Tunisia has two climatic zones: the maritime Mediterranean coast, with hot summers and wet winters, and the Saharan south.

Tunisia's varied landscape incorporates a classic Mediterranean coastline with forested mountains, coastal wetlands and estuaries, rocky hammada, and the huge Saharan dunefield of the Erg Oriental. This creates diverse microclimates and makes Tunisia a year-round destination with warm summers and autumns on the coast and pleasant winters and spring in the desert, when daytime temperatures hover around 30°C.

The prevailing wind is from the west, and the mountainous coast is wet in winter, with northern Tabarka receiving the most rain, although temperatures rarely fall below 12°C. The best time for hiking is spring and early summer, when the forests are a deep, lush green and flowers bloom among Roman ruins. Beach resorts fill up during summer, so if you want to enjoy the same balmy temperatures without the crowds aim to travel in autumn. Turn south to the Saharan towns of Douz and Tozeur for winter adventure. Be conscious of reduced opening hours and etiquette (p293) if travelling to Tunisia during Ramadan or one of the Eids.

The Sahara (p229)

FROM LEFT: FILIP FUXA/SHUTTERSTOCK, JOYCE YPP/SHUTTERSTOCK

I LIVE HERE

RAMADAN NIGHTS

Leila Ben Gacem is the president of cultural organisation Mdinti *mdinti.org*

Tunis' medina is totally transformed during the fasting month of Ramadan. In the morning it's quiet and perfect for a tour to admire the fusion of Mediterranean architectural styles and visit the artisan souqs. In the evenings it comes to life, with concerts, alley cafes buzzing with people, local art shows in public spaces and families dressed up in their smartest clothes for *Iftar* – the meal breaking the fast.

HEATWAVES

Since 2021, Tunisia has suffered a series of severe summer heatwaves, which caused wildfires and pushed temperatures to 50°C in August 2024. Rainfall has fallen 3% annually over the past three decades, exacerbating water scarcity issues. In summer, stay hydrated and use water mindfully.

Weather Through the Year

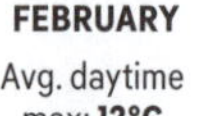

JANUARY	FEBRUARY	MARCH	APRIL	MAY	JUNE
Avg. daytime max: **12°C**	Avg. daytime max: **12°C**	Avg. daytime max: **14°C**	Avg. daytime max: **17°C**	Avg. daytime max: **21°C**	Avg. daytime max: **25°C**
Days of rainfall: **4**	Days of rainfall: **4**	Days of rainfall: **3**	Days of rainfall: **4**	Days of rainfall: **2**	Days of rainfall: **1**

SHIHILI (OR CHICHILI)

Tunisia's *shihili* wind roars out of the desert into the Gulf of Gabès, sending temperatures soaring and filling the air with fine sand. The storms usually last 10 to 12 hours, but can last two to three days. They happen year-round, but are most common in spring.

Biggest Tunisian Events

International Festival of Hammamet (p98) Tunisia's biggest cultural event, hosting music, theatre, dance and art in an amphitheatre facing the sea. **July and August**

Festival International De Sousse (p180) Another significant summer festival, this time in Sousse. It attracts famous local singers and bands as well as the occasional international guest star. **Dates vary**

El-Jem International Symphonic Music Festival (p199) Fills the extraordinary colosseum of Thysdrus with thousands of spectators. **Summer**

International Festival of the Sahara (p236) This big Saharan shindig, hosted in Douz, involves camel pageants and Saluki dog races and brings a party atmosphere to the small oasis town. **November**

Authentic Local Festivals

Festival de la Médina (p65) At this niche festival dedicated to celebrating medina life in Tunis you'll enjoy Andalusian poetry readings and lively local bands in beautiful heritage venues. **End of Ramadan**

La Ghriba Festival Begins 33 days after the start of Passover and draws Jewish pilgrims from around the world to celebrate in Djerba's ancient synagogue (p271) and participate in two days of religious festivities. **May or June**

Tozeur International Oasis Festival (p253) A showcase of desert culture in Tozeur, where you'll hear storytelling and traditional music and witness camel and horse racing. **December**

Harissa Festival Nabeul (p103) is the home of harissa, Tunisia's famous chilli paste, which the town celebrates with a three-day food festival featuring tastings, workshops and cookery competitions. **January**

I LIVE HERE

AUTUMN IN THE DESERT

Mehdi Baccouche is founder of IN NEFTA *@in_nefta*

In Nefta, autumn is a magical time, especially October and November, when the city comes alive as families gather to harvest and process dates. The weather is perfect, ideal for enjoying a sunset over the desert dunes. This is also when the Rouhaniyet Sufi Music Festival occurs, a beautiful experience that captures the essence of the region's spiritual and artistic traditions.

Tozeur International Oasis Festival (p253)

RAINY CITY

The northern port city of Tabarka, surrounded by cork and oak forests, receives the most rainfall in Tunisia, on average 1000mm per annum. The southern coastal city of Gabès receives just 223mm.

JULY	AUGUST	SEPTEMBER	OCTOBER	NOVEMBER	DECEMBER
Avg. daytime max: **28°C**	Avg. daytime max: **29°C**	Avg. daytime max: **26°C**	Avg. daytime max: **22°C**	Avg. daytime max: **17°C**	Avg. daytime max: **13°C**
Days of rainfall: **0**	Days of rainfall: **1**	Days of rainfall: **2**	Days of rainfall: **4**	Days of rainfall: **4**	Days of rainfall: **4**

CHRISTOPHE CAPPELLI/SHUTTERSTOCK

Prayer hall (p187), Great Mosque, Kairouan

TRIP PLANNER

RELIGION IN TUNISIA

Tunisia is 98% Muslim, and Islam is the dominant religion. Jews and Christians make up the other 2%. Most Tunisian Muslims are Sunnis and belong to the Maliki school of theology and many follow a Sufi *tarikah* (school) as well. There are also small numbers of Ibadis, based on the island of Djerba.

Tunisian Islam

Most Tunisians belong to the Sunni Maliki *madhab* – one of the four major schools of Sunnism – brought to the region by the Umayyad Caliphate in the 7th century. Tunisia is also home to many adherents of Sufism, the mystical branch of Islam with *tarikahs* like the ancient Shadilli order and the modern Madaniyyah order still active in the country. As one of the more liberal North African nations, Islam is observed in varying degrees in Tunisia, and seemingly very little in the more urban, middle-class places like Tunis.

Tunisian Muslim Festivals

Dates for Tunisia's main Muslim religious holidays are dependent on the lunar-based Hejira calendar, which is approximately 11 days shorter than the Western calendar; this means the holidays seem to occur at different times each year.

Mawlid an-Nabi or Eid El Mawlid is a lesser Eid celebrated most emphatically by the Sufis of Tunisia. This celebrates the birth of the Prophet Muhammad and sees cities like Kairouan put on extravagant festivals of Sufi music and *dhikr* (remembrance), whilst mosques and *zaouias* (Sufi lodges) across the country do the same on a smaller scale.

Ramadan is the month in which the Quran was revealed and when Tunisian Muslims refrain from eating, drinking, smoking and having sex between dawn and dusk (see sidebar for more). Eid El Fitr, also known as Eid El Saghir, or the Small Feast, marks the end of Ramadan and lasts

MOSQUE & ZAOUIA ETIQUETTE

Non-Muslims are welcome to enter mosques and *zaouias* in Tunisia, with the exception of one or two of the holiest *zaouias*. It is important to remember that as spectacular as some of these spaces are, they remain active places of worship.

If you do enter a mosque, men and women should enter via their respective entrances, bearing in mind that many smaller mosques, especially in rural areas, will not have female areas. When entering a mosque or a *zaouia*, dress modestly (no shorts or sleeveless tops), and if you are a woman cover your head with a scarf.

ROBERTONENCINI/SHUTTERSTOCK

Women in Bizerte (p120)

three days. Eid El Fitr and Eid El Adha, known locally as Eid El Kabir, observed on the 10th of the month of Dhu El Hijjah, are the two Eids celebrated across the globe by most Muslims. On these Eids Tunisians dress in their finest outfits; attend a special Eid prayer; and visit the cemeteries to pay their respects to deceased family members before spending the day exchanging gifts and feasting with family and friends. Across Tunisia Eid markets pop up where children go to spend their Eid money, as society starts to slowly return to normality. The second Eid is also when across Tunisia there is the mass slaughter of sacrificial sheep, goats and camels by families who feast on them and distribute them to the less fortunate in society.

PHILIPPE LISSAC/SHUTTERSTOCK

Prayer beads

RAMADAN IN TUNISIA

- This is the month non-Muslim travellers are weary of, with Tunisian society really slowing down. Even in the most touristy areas, businesses and visitor sites reduce their hours or close. That said, many Muslim travellers love to visit Tunisia during Ramadan, especially the holiest places like Kairouan, to spend time in acts of piety, seclusion and worship.
- Most Tunisians will be fasting from sunrise until sunset during Ramadan. No traveller is expected to fast (even for Muslim travellers fasting is optional) but during the month, apart from cosmopolitan urban areas and tourist traps, eating in public is frowned upon. If you intend to travel to Tunisia in Ramadan, it would be wise to adopt a local schedule; sleep in late and enjoy the nocturnal festivities when restaurants and coffee shops stay open late into the night. If you do head out in the daytime, be sure to plan ahead and check opening hours, as well as packing a lunch to eat indoors. In the evenings, make the most of the special *iftar* (meal to break fast) menus at restaurants or even a free *iftar* at one of the mosques.
- Typically, Tunisian *iftar* is light and will include dates, water and *chorba*, the much loved bulgur soup, made with beef or chicken and served with *kesra* (bread).

FROM LEFT: ANISBOUKHRIS/SHUTTERSTOCK, BFA /ALAMY STOCK PHOTO

Hiker near Guermassa (p225)

GET PREPARED FOR TUNISIA

Useful things to load in your bag, your ears and your brain.

Clothes

Beachware is best confined to resorts. Outside these areas, wear tops that cover shoulders and chest. Pants (not shorts) are best in conservative rural areas.

Hats are essential in summer and always in the desert.

Scarves, required to cover women's hair in mosques, are also useful in the desert where temperatures drop rapidly at night.

Trainers or good walking shoes are best for walking around medinas and rocky Roman ruins. Hiking boots or trail shoes are best for hikes along coastal and forest trails.

Rainjackets are useful on the coast in winter and spring when the weather is variable and wind is brisk.

Smart casual clothes will be appreciated when going out for dinner or meeting people, as Tunisian culture is very courteous.

Manners

Greetings are important so wish people a good day. Men should wait for women to offer handshakes.

The left hand is considered unclean as it's used for personal hygiene. Don't use it to handle food from a communal dish.

Mosque etiquette requires everyone to remove their shoes before entering and for women to wear a headscarf.

During Ramadan it's impolite to eat or drink in public between sunrise and sunset.

READ

The Colonizer and the Colonized (Albert Memmi; 1965) An examination of the interrelated psychological effects of colonialism.

Behind Closed Doors: Women's Oral Narratives in Tunis (Monia Hejaiej; 1996) Insights into Tunisian women's lives from a female perspective.

The Italian (Shukri Mabkhout; 2017) A tale of two lovers, leftist Abdel Nasser and philosophy student Zeina, struggling with their clashing ideologies.

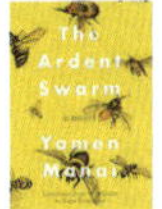

The Ardent Swarm (Yamen Manai; 2021) An allegory based on a beekeeper depicts Tunisia's sociopolitical landscape following the Arab Spring.

Words

Tunisia is bilingual: Arabic is the official language, and French its second. English is also widely spoken in the capital and resort areas.

Sabah el khir – Good morning.

Msa el khir – Good evening.

Brabi or **s'il vous plait** – Please.

Aychek, shokran, merci alayk or **inshallah merci** – Thank you.

Ismi... or **je m'appelle...** – My name is...

Ey – Yes.

Le – No.

Chnouwa? (for men) or **ismik?** (for women) – What is your name?

Je voudrais un billet aller simpler/un billet retour – I would like a one-way/return ticket.

Bkadech? or **c'est combien?** – How much does it cost?

Twakhar or **en retardé** – Delayed.

Annuler/en annulé – Cancelled.

Faites-le plein, s'il vous plait or **brabi âabeha** – Say this if you're at a service station and want to fill up.

Diesel – Diesel.

Sans plomb – Unleaded petrol.

Ana nabati or **je suis végétarien** – I am vegetarian.

Âandi hassasiya... or **allergique...** – I'm allergic to...

Tikblou carta? or **acceptez-vous des cartes de crédits?** – Do you accept credit card?

Azul – Hello. (Amazigh)

Artufat – Goodbye. (Amazigh)

Tanmert – Thank you. (Amazigh)

WATCH

Silences of the Palace (Moufida Tlatli; 1994) Award-winning drama set in 1960s Tunis, as the country throws off French rule.

As I Open My Eyes (Leyla Bouzid; 2015) The best fiction film about the Arab Spring.

Arab Blues (Manele Labidi; 2019) Comedy about psychotherapist Selma, who exposes local anxieties in her Tunis practice.

Under the Fig Trees (Erige Sehiri; 2022; pictured) A drama ripe with romance for young fruit pickers released from the confines of their villages.

Four Daughters (Kaouther Ben Hania; 2023) Docudrama of Olfa Hamrouni, who lost two daughters to Islamic extremism.

LISTEN

Ghalbek Ghalbek (Lotfi Bouchnak; 2013) An album from Tunisia's Pavarotti and the perfect intro to Tunisia's national musical style, *malouf*.

Kelmti Horra (Emil Mathlouthi; 2012) The debut studio album by Tunisian singer Mathlouthi, which became the anthem of the 2011 revolution.

Revolution 1 (Erin Clare Brown; 2020) A podcast telling the story of the Tunisian Uprising through the people who lived it by the Tunis editor at New Lines Magazine.

Frigya (Imed Alibi; 2021) A stunning exploration of North African percussion from an electronic perspective. Meanwhile, his album *Safar* explores Sufi influences.

LIZAVETTA/SHUTTERSTOCK

The Sahara (p229)

HOW TO... Do Desert Travel

The southern quarter of Tunisia is a small, but varied, portion of the Sahara encompassing *hamada* (stony plateaus), *regs* (dry plains), *wadis* (dry river valleys), chotts (saltpans), *oueds* (ephemeral lakes) and *ergs*, the dunefields that compose 'sand seas'. Although it's tempting to think that the desert is a vast expanse of nothing, it is full of life and has long been inhabited by Amazigh and Bedouin tribes.

Get Ready

The best time to travel in the desert is between October and May. The sun is no joke, so bring high-SPF sunscreen, sunglasses, a hat and a water bottle. At night temperatures plummet so you'll need a sweater or fleece, long trousers, woolly socks and a wind jacket. A scarf keeps the sun and sand at bay and is a good neck warmer. Protect your camera and phone – the fine sand gets everywhere.

Tozeur or Douz?

Tozeur is notable for its architecture, authentic oasis culture and delicious dates. The town sits at the foot of the Atlas Mountains and you can hike in slot canyons and to oasis springs. Also near here is the vintage Star Wars set of Mos Espa. Most people come for one or two days, but we recommend three.

Douz has a frontier town feel and is inhabited by Bedouin tribes who lead tourists on 4WD and camel treks into the Grand Erg Oriental. This is the quintessential desert experience where you overnight in a tent and hear stories of desert life. You'll need three days to enjoy the experience comfortably.

Self-Drive or Tour?

Tozeur and Douz are accessible by hire car. The drive from Tunis to Tozeur is six hours and from Djerba to Douz is 3½ hours. The drive between the two oases across the Chott el-Jerid saltpan is two hours. If you drive across the chott, don't drive on the saltpan as the crust can break and your car will sink into sulphurous mud.

To get into the desert proper you'll need to book a tour. Arrange these in Tozeur and Douz. Tours into the Jebil National Park require an overnight stay in a camp and prices range from around €50 for an overnighter by camel to €250 for a half-board camping experience with long 4WD access.

CAMEL RIDING TECHNIQUE

- To mount, approach from the side and climb on.
- Hold on to the pommel as the camel rises.
- The hind legs go up first, so lean back and then forward.
- Cross your legs around the front of the saddle for comfort.
- Relax your body into the slow rocking gait while you ride.
- To dismount, lean back first as the camel's front legs go down first. Then lean forwards.
- Once seated, swing your leg around the front of the saddle and slide off.

ANDRZEJ LISOWSKI TRAVEL/SHUTTERSTOCK

Hammam, Houmt Souk (p264)

HOW TO... Hammam

The Antoninus Baths of Carthage were the third largest bathhouse in the Roman Empire, signifying the central role of bathing in early North African urban life. The Romans gifted us the traditional bathhouse complex, while Muslims infused the ritual with a spiritual dimension given the centrality of water and cleanliness in Islam. Over time the hammam evolved into a cornerstone of daily life in Tunisia.

Get Prepared

If going for a DIY experience in a local hammam, bring along a towel or a *fouta* (a lightweight hammam cloth), some flip flops, a bathing suit or extra underwear (locals don't bathe naked), your toiletries and hair products. You can buy the traditional *saboun beldi* (a blend of olive oil and eucalyptus) and coarse crepe *kessa* (scrubbing glove) at the hammam, and borrow a bucket or bowl for dousing yourself with water. Avoid bringing jewellery and excess money.

The Steam Room

Then head to the steamy *harara* (hot room) where the air is full of moisture. Sit or lie on the heated benches for 10-15 minutes to allow your pores to open and the skin to soften. The steam also relaxes the muscles, preparing you for exfoliation.

The Scrub

After your steam comes the traditional exfoliation using the *kessa* glove and *saboun beldi*. Locals do this themselves or for each other, as most people come to the hammam with other family members or friends. However, hammam attendants are available to do it for you for a small fee. You'll then be rinsed off with warm water to wash away all the dead skin.

Clay Mask or Massage

Some hammams offer either a mineral-rich clay or seaweed mask, to detoxify the skin, or a massage with jasmine oil, which helps stimulate circulation and nourishes the skin, locking in hydration.

Rest and Relaxation

The ritual ends by spending some time resting in a cooler room wrapped in your *fouta*, sipping mint tea or water to rehydrate and nibbling on dried fruit and nuts.

ISLAMIC ABLUTIONS

In Islam, it's customary to perform ablutions before praying. The two cleansing rituals are *ghusl*, a full-body purification, and *wudu*, washing the face, hands and feet. Hammams are, therefore, usually located near mosques as they are used for ablutions. And, they are never mixed sex – women come during the day and men at night. Regular visits to the hammam aren't only a way to prepare for prayer, but are essential for all major events like weddings and religious festivals. Over the centuries, the hammam became an integral part of North African Muslim culture, creating an important social space, especially for women, and providing a retreat for physical and spiritual purification.

NEMIR2000/SHUTTERSTOCK

Seafood dish

THE FOOD SCENE

This Mediterranean cuisine is packed with sun-focused flavours, and based around grains, vegetables, seafood, olive oil and the spicy national condiment, harissa.

Sitting at a crossroads between Europe, the Levant and Africa, Tunisia's kitchen is a tasty mix of a myriad flavours contributed to by the Amazigh, Romans, Arabs, Sephardic Jews, Turks, Andalusians, French and Italians. The indigenous Amazigh bequeathed couscous, the Maghreb staple, while Tunisia's key coastal position during the early spice trade brought cumin, caraway, saffron, mustard, cayenne, ginger, cinnamon, dried rosebuds, black pepper and sugar to the table. The Phoenicians brought citrus, stone fruit and olive trees, the Romans grains and an obsession with mullet, the Arabs spices and the Ottomans sticky and flaky pastries and nuts. Chillies and tomatoes then arrived from the Americas with the Spanish, and the French introduced wine, cheese and bread along with new cooking techniques. Fish, of course, has always been a staple, running the gamut from mackerel to mussels, octopus and enormous groupers and tuna. Bread is eaten at every meal and harissa (spicy chilli paste) is a national obsession. In fact, tiny Tunisia has one of the richest and most creative cuisines in the Maghreb.

Tunisian Food in General

Tunisians are as likely to start the day with a coffee and *pain au chocolat* as they are to eat fritters or *sohlob* (sorghum, sugar, cinnamon and ginger). It's this variety that makes food here so exciting. Generally, the

Best Tunisian Dishes

Kammounia
Meat stew with cumin.

Koucha
Lamb, potatoes and tomatoes, seasoned with spices cooked in a clay pot.

Loup à la Sfaxienne
Perch baked with tomatoes, onions, peppers, garlic and capers.

Mechouia
A grilled salad of cooked tomatoes, green peppers, onions, olive oil, spices.

further south you go the 'drier' the cuisine, with less fish, fewer vegetables and more lentils, couscous and red meat. On the coast, fish and vegetables dominate with lunch and dinners involving soups, salads, *tajine* (a frittata-like egg dish with meat, fish or vegetable fillings) or fish, followed by couscous or pasta.

Kemia: Small Plates

Kemia means 'small quantity' in Arabic and refers to an assortment of mezze appetisers, often served as an aperitif. As well as nibbles such as nuts, olives, *poutargue* (mullet roe) and spiced octopus, particular delights include crushed vegetables mixed with spices or pickled.

Otherwise, Tunisia's most famous starter is the smoky-tasting *salade mechouia*, a delicious blend of roasted peppers, garlic and harissa, which is served with white bread. *Salade Tunisienne* is another hit: comprising finely chopped tomatoes, onion and peppers seasoned with lemon juice, olive oil and mint. In winter, have *chorba*, a punchy, oily, tomato-based soup. Finally, don't pass up the chance to try *brik*, a deep-fried filo pastry stuffed with onions, parsley, potato, capers, tuna, egg, seafood, chicken or meat. There's a sweet version of them, too, filled with almond or sesame paste and drenched in honey.

Mechouia

Fish, Fish, Fish

With 1400km of coastline, Tunisia has excellent seafood, including sole, red mullet, mackerel, grouper, perch, octopus, squid and shellfish, with lobster a feature around Tabarka. Favoured seasonings are garlic, saffron, cumin, paprika, turmeric or dried rosebuds, though often fish is simply grilled with lemon and olive oil, or baked. The traditional accompaniment to fried fish is *tastira*, a delicate mixture of chopped fried tomatoes and eggs, seasoned with

Harissa

HOT, HOT HARISSA

Tunisian cooking revolves around harissa, a fire-red concoction made from crushed dried chilli, garlic, salt and caraway seeds. It's also served neat with a pool of olive oil – you dip your bread into the mix – as an appetiser.

It was the Spanish who introduced hot peppers to Tunisia and now most chillies are grown in Nabeul, where harissa is celebrated in a three-day festival each January (p35), and Gabès (p219). The word harissa comes from the Arabic, meaning 'break into pieces', as the paste is traditionally made by pounding red chillies in a mortar. An old tale says that a man can judge his wife's affections by the spice in his food – if it's bland then love is dead.

FROM LEFT: ANASTASIA KAMYSHEVA/SHUTTERSTOCK, VIKTORIA HODOS/SHUTTERSTOCK

Ojja
Tomatoes, onions, chillis and harissa combined with scrambled eggs.

Shakshuka
A tomato, onion, potato, chilli pepper and paprika stew, with optional eggs.

Ragoût de gnaouia
A rich beef and okra stew spiced with paprika and served with bread.

Chorba frik
A spiced meat, freekeh (green wheat) and chickpea soup.

Pastries
Baklava, densely nut-stacked *bjeouia* and orange blossom-scented nut-paste *boules*.

FRANCK LEGROS/SHUTTERSTOCK

Couscous, vegetables and meatballs

caraway seeds and salt. Look out for succulent prawns simmered in a *gargoulette* (clay cooking pot).

Vegetarians & Vegans

Fruit, vegetables, grains and nuts are staples here, so those looking for meat-free options should be able to navigate the menu. *Kemia*, mezze-like appetisers, also offer a good range of vegetarian options. Otherwise, your best bet will be starters: *salade Tunisienne* or *salade mechouia* are delicious and ubiquitous. The *brik* is sometimes meat-free, and *ojja* (fresh tomatoes and chillies blended into a spicy sauce – be aware that prawns, merguez or brains are often added, and eggs stirred in at the last minute). There are vegetarian versions of *chorba*, a chickpea soup, although the most common recipe includes meat. You can find vegetarian couscous and pizza is popular on the coast. *Shakshuka*, *lablabi* and *tajine* are other options if you eat eggs. Just ask to hold the meat additions. Vegans will find eating out much harder, as eggs are used in many dishes, but self-catering with local produce will be a pleasure.

Alcohol

Although Tunisia is a Muslim country, it is a producer of wine and beer and alcohol is widely available. Most towns will have a bar or two, but only upmarket restaurants serve alcohol.

Beer is popular. Celtia is the local brand and is also available in a nonalcoholic variety called Celestia.

In antiquity, Tunisia was known as the vineyard of Rome and today has a number of high-quality vineyards near the coast. Vineyards to look out for are Kurubis, Neferis, Domaine Shadrapa and Les Vignerons de Carthage.

A popular aperitif is *boukha*, a gloopily sweet, aromatic spirit made from distilled figs often mixed with Coca-Cola. Aniseed-based *pastis* (a French relic) is also popular.

Most street bars are smoky, all-male affairs. In resort areas there's a wider selection of places to drink, including hotel bars and upmarket restaurants. Shops and supermarkets sell alcohol, but be considerate of local culture and put your bottles in bags when carrying them in public.

Local specialities

Couscous

There are more than 300 ways of serving up the national dish, couscous, a grainy, soft cereal. It's the dish to eat at celebrations, usually communally, with people delving into a single bowl. Couscous is prepared by steaming it in a *couscoussière* (two-piece pot). The sieve-lined upper part holds the couscous, while the sauce (vegetables, chickpeas, beef, chicken, lamb or fish) cooks underneath. Fish with couscous is unique to Tunisia, and on Djerba and the Kerkennah Islands it is served with stuffed squid.

Street Food

Brik A deep-fried pastry stuffed with tuna, potatoes, and a runny egg. Djerba is famous for them.
Fricassé A small, fluffy bread sandwich stuffed with tuna, potatoes, egg, and olives
Kafteji Deep-fried vegetables served with an egg and potatoes. Can be eaten as a dish or stuffed in a sandwich.
Lablebi A brothy soup of chickpeas and sometimes meat poured over bread to form a stew. Egg and harissa optional.
Makloub A pizza dough sandwich folded over with vegetables, chicken, mayonnaise and harissa.
Mlawi A flatbread wrap filled with cheese, egg, meat, veggies and harissa, and eaten like a burrito.

Fruits & Sweets

Assidat zgougou A pine nut porridge/cream, often prepared to celebrate the Mawlid (holiday marking the birth of the Prophet Muhammad).
Baklava Layers of filo pastry and finely chopped nuts, soaked in honey.
Bambalouni The beloved deep-fried Tunisian doughnut.
Bouza A mousse-y hazelnut cream.
Deglat Ennour Of its 100 varieties of date, this is the finest.
Figuier d'Inde Barbary figs or prickly pears are in season from October.
Garn Ghzal (or Meshi Tataouine) A deep-fried dough stuffed with sesame, almonds and walnuts.
Harissa hlowa A semolina almond cake soaked in syrup.
Makhroud Date-stuffed, honey-soaked wheat cakes from Kairouan.
Samsa A sweet *brik* pastry filled with almonds, pistachios or hazelnuts.

MEMORABLE MEALS

Sawa Taste (p72) Tunis' Marche Centrale is a fantastic food gallery. Discover it on Sawa's food tours with local chefs, who'll show you the best stalls and most authentic locales.
Dar el Jeld (p62) Tunisian food gets the fine-dining treatment and is served in a handsome 18th-century courtyard mansion.
Le Barberousse (p98) Dazzling sunlight, refined fish dishes and views of the moonlit sea from Hammamet's ramparts make meals at Barberousse unforgettable.
El Mansourah (p109) Tables set on a rocky headland with turquoise sea lapping at your feet set the scene for delicious seafood and a bottle of white muscat.

THE YEAR IN FOOD

SPRING

Warming lentil or grain soups and *loubia* (white bean stew) are heartwarming in the cold, early months of the year. Spring *tajine* with potatoes, peas and chicken is also popular.

SUMMER

Strawberries, apricots and peaches ripen in early summer, followed by almonds, melons, watermelon and succulent grapes. Salads and fish grace the tables, while street stalls sell *fricassé*.

AUTUMN

Pomegranates, figs and prickly pears are ripe in September. Red and yellow peppers are at their peak, and couscous comes with pumpkin and squash. The olive and date harvest begins in late October.

WINTER

Soups reappear, particularly *lablebi* and *chorba*, both with chickpeas. Date season continues in the south and citrus comes into season, including blood oranges, mandarins and bergamot.

FROM LEFT: ANNA PUZATYKH/SHUTTERSTOCK, INNA REZNIK/SHUTTERSTOCK, NEW AFRICA/SHUTTERSTOCK, STANISLAV71/SHUTTERSTOCK

FROM LEFT: HICHEM KAOUANE/SHUTTERSTOCK, ANETTA STAROWICZ/SHUTTERSTOCK

Cap Farina (p125)

THE OUTDOORS

Tunisia is famous for its beaches, but there is plenty of adventure to be had on the pine-clad coast, in the Kroumirie Mountains and deep in the Sahara.

Tunisia is similar in size to England, but the diversity of landscape is truly amazing. One day you might find yourself diving amid the coral gardens of Tabarka and the next cycling around the olive groves of Djerba. In the west, hiking trails hide in the lush, green forests of the Kroumirie Mountains, while in the east is the arid, otherworldly landscape of Dahar with its troglodyte villages and *ksour* (fortified granaries). Then there are the spectacular dunefields of the Sahara, which you can explore by camel or 4WD.

Beaches & Water Sport

Beaches remain Tunisia's main tourist draw. Stretches of golden sand ring Cap Bon, including the remarkably clear waters at Plage de la Mansoura and Sidi Mansour in **Kelibia** (p110), with another great summer option at **Ras Ed Drek** (p113) in El Haouaria. **Hammamet** (p96) has grown up around its glorious curve of beach, which stretches for miles along the coast. Here you'll find all manner of water sports fun supplied by **Club Nautique Hammamet** (p99). The best beach in the south is **Plage Sidi Mahrès** (p269) on Djerba. Also here is the 10km-long Ras Rmel sandbar, which is a protected wetland and home to pink flamingos. **Cap Serrat** (p130), at the centre of the rugged north coast, shelters a lovely, small sandy bay that's all but deserted for most of the year.

DIVING

Tabarka (p139) is a popular dive site with red coral. Otherwise, **Djerba** (p271) offers wrecks and fish-filled underwater canyons.

BIRD-WATCHING

UNESCO-listed **Ichkeul National Park** (p127) attracts waterfowl from all over Europe, and flamingos gather on **Tazarka Lagoon** (p107).

CYCLING

You can mountain bike in the forests around **Aïn Draham** (p135). For gentle rides through olive groves contact **Djerba Cyclo** (p269).

FAMILY ADVENTURES

Find an endless amount of waterbased fun at **Club Nautique Hammamet** (p99) and on Djerba at **Les Dauphins** (p271). The **Iberostar Selection Royal El Mansour** (p207) in Mahdia is also a great resort base.

Visit the troglodyte museum and bed down in a cave hotel in **Matmata** (p214).

Time travel through the era of dinosaurs and elephants in the desert at Tozeur's **Chak Wak Park** (p251) and the **Dar Charaït Museum** (p253).

Hop aboard a camel at **Mos Espa** (p255) for a ride amid Star Wars props or let teens loose on a quad bike at **Ksar Ghilane** (p242).

Head out for a night or two in a Bedouin tent among the dunes of the **Jebil National Park** (p238).

Hiking

Hiking is a newly developing pastime in Tunisia. The northern coast offers some pretty coastal trails around **Cap Farina** (p125) and **El Gléâa** (p130), while the Kroumirie Mountains around **Aïn Draham** (p133) offer trails in thick pine and oak forests. The potential is limited by the lack of detailed maps required to venture off the beaten track independently. However, local hotels and Tabarka-based travel agency, **Dar El Ain** (p139), can organise guides.

Meanwhile agencies in **Tataouine** (p221) organise hiking between the *ksour* of the Dahar region. The **Great Dahar Crossing** (or Dahar Hiking Trail) is a new 220km, 12-stage hike across the remote southeast. It can be broken down into smaller stages, one of the most interesting being the 8km hike between Douiret and Chenini. Other hikes centre on the town of **Ghomrassen** (p224) where you'll find dinosaur footprints and petroglyphs.

Dahar region

Finally, in the south, you'll find the stunning Midès Canyon, aka **Tunisia's Grand Canyon** (p257). You can walk in its shaded depths between Tamerza and Midès, while the trail around **Chebika** (p258) will bring you to a true desert oasis with a little waterfall.

Desert Adventure

No trip to Tunisia would be complete without experiencing the Sahara Desert. We recommend the Grand Oriental Erg in the **Jebil National Park** (p238), which is known for its striking wind-sculpted dunes, which extend to the horizon. From **Douz** (p234), you can trek by camel into the desert, then set up camp and enjoy the solitude of the dunes. While there is an undeniable romance about riding a camel into the Saharan dunes, you can range further and faster in a 4WD. Overnight trips are possible and involve camping in a traditional Amazigh tent. The most popular one-day trip is over the dunes from Douz to **Ksar Ghilane** (p240), returning via the sealed road.

THALASSOTHERAPY
Take seawater treatments in Hammamet spas like **Bio Azur Thalasso** (p98), or soak in the ancient hot springs of Korbous.

KITESURFING
Djerba is a great place for kitesurfing thanks to its shallow lagoons and guaranteed wind. **Les Dauphins** (p271) runs courses.

HORSE RIDING
Nothing beats a sunset ride on the beach and **Club Equus Hammamet** (p98) offers rides on beautiful Amazigh and Arabian horses.

QUAD BIKING
Ksar Ghilane (p242) is the quad bike capital of the desert. Jump aboard and head out into the desert sands.

Water Sports

1. Diving, Tabarka (p139)
2. Kitesurfing & kayaking, Djerba (p271)
3. Sailing & windsurfing, Hammamet (p99)
4. SUPs and kayaking, Sidi Bou Said (p84)
5. Hot springs, Korbous (p102)

Hiking & Cycling

1. Cap Farina (p125)
2. Aïn Draham, Kroumirie Mountains (p133)
3. Ichkeul National Park (p127)
4. Ghomrassen, Dahar region (p224)
5. Midès Canyon, Tozeur (p257)
6. Djerba (p269)

Beaches

1. El Mansourah Beach (p110)
2. Maamoura Beach (p107)
3. Ras Ed Drek (p113)
4. Plage Sidi Mahrès (p269)
5. Plage Cap Serrat (p130)
6. Gammarth Beach (p86)

Mediterranean Sea
Palermo
Sicily
ITALY
Pantelleria
ALGERIA
Lake Bizerte
Bizerte
Lake Ichkeul
Raf Raf
Menzel Bourguiba
Sejnane
Nefza
Tabarka
La Calle
Mateur
Tebourba
TUNIS
Gulf of Tunis
El Haouaria
Kelibia
Menzel Temine
Soliman
Grombalia
Korba
Aïn Draham
Béja
Medjez el Bab
Bou Salem
Ghardimaou
Jendouba
El Aroussa
Zaghouan
Nabeul
Hammamet
Bouficha
Souk Ahras
Al Karib
El Fahs
El Kef
Siliana
Nadour
Enfidha
Gulf of Hammamet
Al Sars
As-Subayhah
Tajerouine
Ad Dahmani
Maktar
Ousseltia
Sousse
Msaken
Monastir
Kairouan
Téboulba
Kalaat Khasba
Sebkhet Sidi el-Hani
Kerker
Mahdia
Tebessa
Hajeb El Ayoun
Sidi Amor Bou Hadjila
El Jem
Sbeitla
Chebba
Kasserine
Sidi Bouzid
Sebkhet el Gharra
El Hencha
Djebeniana
Thelepte
Bir Al Huffay
Regueb
Sfax
Chergui
Bir Ali Ben Khlifa
Gharbi
Kerkennah Islands
Moulares
Al-Mazzunah
Mahares
Tamerza
Metlaoui
Gafsa
Sebkhet en Noual
Skhira

ACTION AREAS

Where to find Tunisia's best outdoor activities.

TUNISIA

THE GUIDE

Northern Tunisia p117
TUNIS P53
Cap Bon p92
Central West & the Tell p146
Central Coast & Kairouan p165
Tozeur & the Jerid p244
Djerba p261
Matmata & the Ksour p208
The Sahara p229

Chapters in this section are organised by hubs and their surrounding areas. We see the hub as your base in the destination, where you'll find unique experiences, local insights, insider tips and expert recommendations. It's also your gateway to the surrounding area, where you'll see what and how much you can do from there.

Door in Sidi Bou Said (p81), Tunis

PIXACHI/SHUTTERSTOCK

For places to stay in Tunis, see p90

LIFE FOCUS/SHUTTERSTOCK

Above: Zitouna Mosque (p58); right: Sidi Bou Said (p81)

Researched by
Lauren Keith

Tunis

TUNISIA'S QUIETLY COOL CAPITAL

Maghrebi, Mediterranean and European: waves of migration – starting in ancient times – have endowed the fabric of Tunis with a rich flavour.

In Tunis, the term 'living history' really does apply. Take the magnificent medieval medina (the old walled city), sidelined by the French after their 19th-century occupation of the country but now emerging from decades of neglect and revealing its vibrant character once again. Boutique guesthouses called dars have taken over grand but crumbling mansions, bringing back their former beauty after years-long restoration projects.

But the story of colonisation starts much earlier, in the historic seaside settlement of Carthage: founded by the Phoenicians, destroyed and then rebuilt by the Romans, and now the province of well-to-do residents. Razed by the Romans in 146 BCE, following the Punic Wars, the city was re-established by Julius Caesar in 44 BCE, and it soon became a provincial capital of Roman Africa. Within 200 years, it was the third-largest imperial city behind Rome and Alexandria, with 300,000 residents, three forums, a circus holding 70,000 spectators, a mammoth bathhouse and an amphitheatre – the ruins of which you can still visit.

VALERY BARETA/SHUTTERSTOCK

After the ousting of the Byzantines, successive Islamic empires both built up and neglected Tunis, even moving the capital elsewhere in Tunisia for a time. The city flourished and trade boomed under the Hafsids, who ruled from 1229 to 1574, until the Ottomans arrived on the scene. Adding to the city's population were Muslims and Jews fleeing religious persecution in Spain and Italy. Many were fine artisans and gave Tunis a stunning architectural style that survives today.

Tunis is now a contemporary capital with 2.7 million inhabitants, but it has an unhurried air and doesn't feel as full-on as the more visited cities in nearby Morocco and Egypt. Tunis is defined by the Mediterranean Sea, and nearly year-round its whitewashed boulevards are bathed in sunshine. Brightly coloured bougainvillea froths over the medina walls, and plastic chairs line the narrow alleys, inviting passersby to stop for a mint tea. Tunis has long been a resilient and forward-looking city, one that makes an excellent starting point for any exploration of Tunisia.

THE MAIN AREAS

MEDINA
The historic heart of Tunis.
p58

CENTRE VILLE & THE BARDO
Main food market and museum.
p66

CARTHAGE
Famous Punic and Roman ruins.
p74

SIDI BOU SAID
Picture-perfect clifftop village.
p81

LA MARSA & GAMMARTH
Beachside 'burbs.
p86

Find Your Way

Beyond the medina, Tunis is spread out. From Bab El Bhar, the eastern gate that separates the medina from the modern city, to the clifftop village of Sidi Bou Said is 21km, which takes about 30 minutes in a car. Public transport is inexpensive but crowded.

FROM THE AIRPORT

Book an airport transfer through your accommodation to avoid the scrum of taxi touts. This is especially important if you're staying in the medina, as drivers sent by your accommodation can get you to the hotel door instead of dropping you off at the outer medina gates.

TAXI

You can hail taxis on the street, but an easier option is to book on the Bolt app, which gives you a fare estimation. You cannot pay through the app, so bring cash. Ride-hailing apps like Uber and Careem do not operate in Tunis. Try Bolt or InDrive.

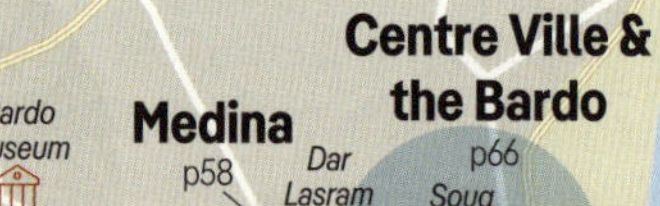

TRAIN

The TGM (which stands for Tunis-Goulette-Marsa) is a suburban train line connecting central Tunis with the beachside suburbs. It's cheap (1DT one way), though crowded, and there's no timetable. In early 2025, the section between Tunis Marine and Kheireddine was closed for repairs with no set reopening date.

TRAM

Tunis' tram network, called *métro léger,* has six lines, but the only one of interest to visitors is Line 4 to reach the Bardo Museum. Tickets are sold at station kiosks and must be bought before you travel. The carriages are seriously dilapidated.

Sebkhet er-Ariana

La Marsa & Gammarth
p86

Supersouk

La Villa Bleue

Ennejma Ezzahra

Sidi Bou Said
p81

Roman Villas

Baths of Antoninus

Carthage
p74

Lake Tunis

Gulf of Tunis

0 5 km
0 2.5 miles

Plan Your Time

Tunis' top sights are spread throughout the city and its suburbs, so if you're spending more than a few days here, devote each day to a different area to save transport time.

TRAVEL-FR/SHUTTERSTOCK ©

Cafe Panorama (p64)

Day 1

Morning

- The **Bardo Museum** (p68) is one of North Africa's biggest cultural treasures. Set in a lavishly decorated 15th-century palace, this institution houses the incredible repository of mosaics collected from all over Tunisia, including several roomfuls from Carthage.

Afternoon

- Ready to get lost in the medina? Grab a delicious Tunisian lunch at **Bab Tounès** (p62), close to the Bab El Bhar entrance, and then explore its souqs and tiled dars on a tour with **Mdinti** (p60).

Evening

- Wind down over dinner at **Dar El Jeld** (p62), one of the city's top restaurants, housed in a handsome dar in the medina.

You'll Also Want To...

Tunis has big sights, but visiting this city is often much more about unwinding and kicking back in true Mediterranean style.

STAY IN A DAR

One of the biggest charms of visiting Tunisia is reserving a room in a dar, a guesthouse similar to a Moroccan riad. Spend a few nights in the medina at **Dar Ben Gacem** (p90) or **La Chambre Bleue** (p90).

VISIT ZITOUNA MOSQUE

Non-Muslims aren't allowed to enter most mosques in Tunisia. This is also true for **Zitouna Mosque** (p58) at the heart of the medina, but travellers not here to pray can still walk around the courtyard.

RELAX IN A HAMMAM

The hammam experience is just about vigorous enough to qualify as an activity. Go local with a scrub in a neighbourhood **hammam** (p65) in the medina or upmarket at a high-end hotel or **dar** (p85).

Day 2

Morning

- Check out the ancient sites of Carthage, walking through the ruins of the massive **Baths of Antoninus** (p78), admiring the in-situ mosaics at the **Roman Villas** (p78) and taking in the view from the top of **Byrsa Hill** (p77).

Afternoon

- Enjoy a late-afternoon wander through the picturesque blue and white village of **Sidi Bou Said** (p81) - it's practically illegal to go for a stroll here without a *bambalouni* (fried doughnut) in hand.

Evening

- Reserve a table for dinner at **La Villa Bleue** (p83), an upmarket restaurant in a beautifully restored dar that sits on a high point in Sidi Bou Said overlooking the Mediterranean.

Day 3

Morning

- Now that you have your bearings a bit better, return to the medina to shop for souvenirs in the **souqs** (p60). At rooftop **Cafe Panorama** (p64), you can rest your feet (though maybe not your wallet - you have to walk through a shop to get here) while enjoying views of Zitouna Mosque and the medina rooftops.

Afternoon

- Decamp to the upmarket seaside suburb of La Marsa to continue the shopping spree at its local **boutiques** (p89). Pause for a drink at the rooftop of **Dar El Marsa** (p88).

Evening

- Go all out on a seafood dinner with Med-blue views at **Le Grand Bleu** (p88) or **Le Golfe** (p88).

GET COOKING

Sign up for a tour of **Marché Centrale** (p71) with Sawa Taste of Tunisia and then head to the kitchen with a chef to change your foodie finds into some of Tunisia's best-loved dishes.

WORK ALONGSIDE A MASTER ARTISAN

The traditional crafts of the medina, such as **bookbinding**, **ceramics** and **leather working**, haven't died out, and you can try your hand at these old-school skills under the watchful eye of an expert (p60).

TOUR A PALACE

Sidi Bou Said is as pretty as a painting, and its star building, **Ennejma Ezzahra** (p81), is a 20th-century masterpiece of Orientalist design, commissioned by a French-born painter and musicologist.

HIT THE BEACH

Tunis is the best place in the country to combine culture with time on the strand. Get the full relaxing resort experience at **La Residence** (p91), with access to the long stretch of sand in **Gammarth** (p86).

Medina

THE HISTORIC HEART OF TUNIS

GETTING AROUND

The narrow streets mean that sightseeing in the medina must be done on foot. Be sure to wander down Rue Sidi Ben Arous (named after a 13th-century mystic and professor) and its continuations Rue Dar El Jeld and Rue du Pacha. These streets take you through the most attractive section of the medina. Most taxi drivers won't drive inside the medina but instead leave you at set entrance points, such as Bab El Bhar (p66) on the eastern side or near the government buildings of **Dar El Bey** on the west side.

Founded by the Arabs in the 7th century, the medina *was* Tunis for more than 1000 years. The city existed solely within these gates and high walls and extended its geographical boundaries only in the 19th century. A maze of vaulted souqs, alleys lined with massive, brightly painted doors opening to lavishly tiled dars (mansions), and landmark mosques with distinctive octagonal minarets, the medina is deservedly a UNESCO World Heritage Site. This sprawling labyrinth of ancient streets and alleyways is one of the most impressive medieval medinas in North Africa and one of Tunisia's greatest treasures.

It's home to numerous covered markets selling everything from shoes to shisha pipes, as well as bustling cafes, back streets full of artisans at work and a royal mausoleum. Historic palaces, hammams, mosques and madrasas (theological colleges) are scattered throughout, many lavishly decorated – the medina always rewards aimless exploration.

The Magnetism of Zitouna Mosque

The medina revolves around this must-see sight

Everything in the medina leads to or from **Zitouna Mosque** *(free)*, founded around 699 CE but rebuilt and restored several times since. Its name means 'olive', but the source of the moniker is disputed. Some think that the mosque was first built next to an olive tree, while another story says that it was constructed on top of a church that contained the relics of St Olivet.

Non-Muslims can enter the courtyard but not the prayer hall. Women must wear a headscarf, which you can borrow at the northern entrance off Souq El Attarine if you don't have one. All visitors must dress modestly, covering to elbows and knees. The huge, chandeliered prayer hall incorporates more than 200 columns recycled from Carthage (p74); if you're not allowed in, stand at the door threshold to get a good look. The 43m-high rectangular minaret in the northwest corner is a medina landmark.

The mosque's doors aren't always open to non-worshippers. Your best bet is to try in the afternoon between prayer times.

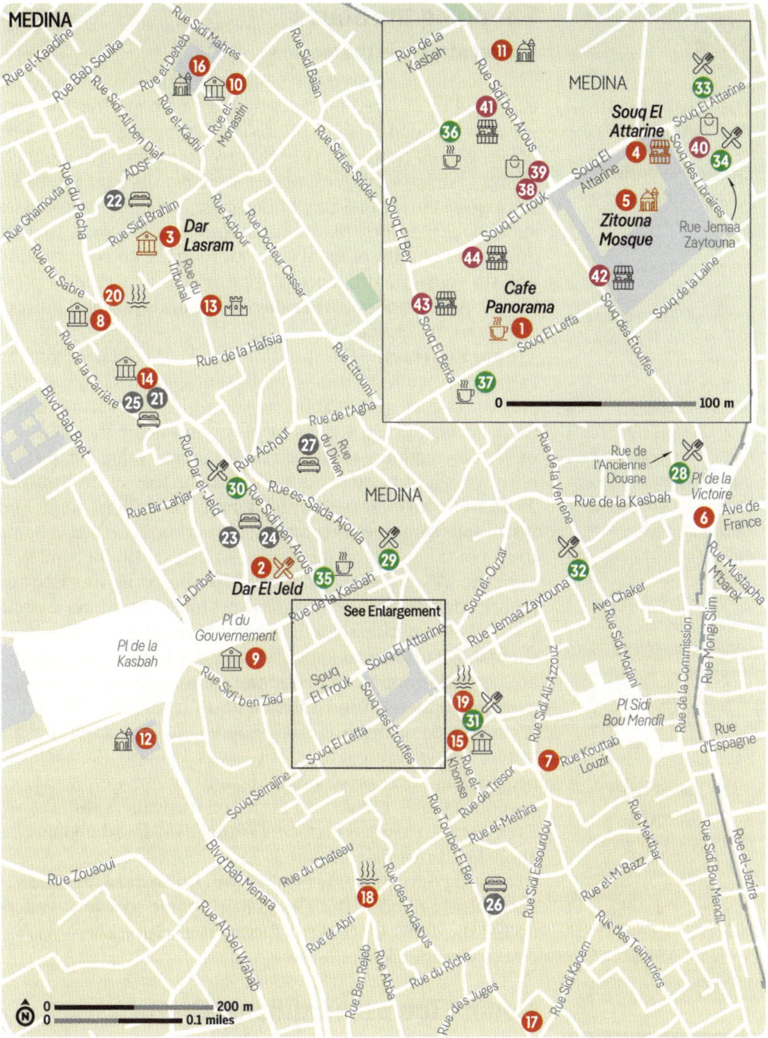

MEDINA

HIGHLIGHTS
1 Cafe Panorama
2 Dar El Jeld
3 Dar Lasram
4 Souq El Attarine
5 Zitouna Mosque

SIGHTS
6 Bab El Bhar
7 Dar Bach Hamba
8 Dar Ben Achour
9 Dar El Bey
10 Dar El Monastiri
11 Hamouda Pacha Mosque
12 Kasbah Mosque
13 Kheireddine Palace
14 Madrasa Bir El Hajjar
15 Madrasa Slimania
16 Sidi Mehrez Mosque
17 Tourbet El Bey

ACTIVITIES
18 Hammam Daouletli
19 Hammam El Kachachine
20 Hammam Sidi Sahbi

SLEEPING
21 Dar Ben Gacem
22 Dar Ben Gacem Kahia
23 Dar El Jeld
24 Dar El Medina
25 Dar Ya
26 El Patio Courtyard House
27 La Chambre Bleue

EATING
28 Bab Tounès
29 Dar Slah
30 Dkik & Zit
31 Doken
32 El Ali
33 Fondouk El Attarine
34 Mahdaoui

DRINKING & NIGHTLIFE
35 Cafe Belkadhi
36 Cafe Chaouachine
37 Cafe du Souk
see 44 M'Rabet

SHOPPING
38 Ed Dar
see 33 Fondouk El Attarine
39 Le Berbere
40 Maison de Senteurs
see 32 Roumouz
41 Souq des Chechias
42 Souq des Étoffes
43 Souq El Berka
44 Souq El Trouk

TOP SHOPS IN THE MEDINA

Ed Dar: Explore five floors of curious antiques, rugs and textiles in this treasure trove in a traditional dar.

Fondouk El Attarine: Top-quality Tunisian handicrafts are artfully displayed in the upstairs and side rooms of this handsome *funduq* (caravanserai).

Maison de Senteurs: Facing the main entrance to Zitouna Mosque, this gorgeous boutique sells perfumes, soaps, cosmetics and toiletries.

Le Berbere: Plenty of shops sell *babouches* (traditional slippers), but this one is a cut above the others in style and quality.

Roumouz: Secreted in a space off the stairway leading to El Ali (p62), this shop sells contemporary artisanal ceramics, textiles and jewellery.

TOP TIP

In the evening, the medina has few eating options, as most restaurants are open for lunch only. If you're staying here, check restaurant opening hours carefully or arrange dinner at your guesthouse. The medina is a traditional neighbourhood and doesn't have any bars. Only a few restaurants serve alcohol.

Shopping the Souqs

Market streets in the medina

The medina is centred on Zitouna Mosque (p58), which is encircled by covered markets that are named after the people who founded them or the goods they specialised in – and often still sell centuries after they were established. 'Refined' trades – shops selling carpets, jewellery, silk and the like – were closest to the mosque, while dirtier and noisier businesses such as carpenters, blacksmiths and tanners were further away. The quality of what's on offer varies, so shop around and do your due diligence. Bargaining is expected in most places. Avoid visiting on Fridays and Sundays when most of the shops are closed.

Souq El Attarine (Perfume Makers' Market) dates from the 13th century and is still home to shops selling fragrant oils and waters, as well as touristy souvenirs and satin baskets used for wedding gifts. Its location on one of the medina's major thoroughfares and next to Zitouna Mosque means that it's always jam-packed. Souq El Attarine leads into **Souq El Trouk** (Turkish Market), traditionally the tailors' souq, and it still sells some clothing among the souvenirs. It's also home to one of the medina's most popular cafes, M'Rabet (p64).

On the western side of Zitouna Mosque, **Souq des Étoffes** (Fabric Market) is one of the medina's most atmospheric pockets, full of traditional ateliers and always abustle with local shoppers. Look up to spot the gate decorated with striped arches and propped up by Roman columns from Carthage.

Barrel-vaulted **Souq El Berka** dates from Ottoman times. It's now a goldsmith's market where courting couples come to pick out wedding jewels, but it was formerly the enslaved people souq where prisoners of Muslim corsairs were sold from a wooden block. Later, with piracy on the wane, sub-Saharan Africans were traded instead. (Trade of enslaved people was abolished in Tunisia in 1846.)

Hanging onto its name by a thread, **Souq des Chechias** is now mostly filled with cafes, but it's home to a few traders plying the dying craft of producing and selling *chechias,* Tunisia's traditional blood-red felt caps.

Medina Tours & Traditional Crafts

Keeping heritage alive

The last bastion of traditional handicrafts in the capital, the medina is the perfect spot to work alongside master artisans teaching their crafts to visitors or to learn about its history from locals who grew up navigating its winding streets. Cultural organisation **Mdinti** *(mdinti.org)* arranges information-filled, eye-opening tours of the medina, which can be themed to your interests, such as food or history. You could also embark on a scavenger hunt with puzzles and challenges to solve as you go. Either way, you're guaranteed to walk down alleys and see places that you would never have found on your own.

Continues on p62

MEDINA MEANDER: HITTING THE HIGHLIGHTS

You could spend days wandering this neighbourhood, but this quick dive into the medina's maze shows off its best sites.

START	END	LENGTH
Tourbet El Bey	Dar Lasram	1.5km; 2 hrs

Start your medina explorations on the southern side of the neighbourhood at 1 **Tourbet El Bey** (p64), the beautifully tiled royal mausoleum that's the final resting place of 165 beys, princes and princesses of the Husainid dynasty, including 14 of the 19 rulers that were in power from 1705 to 1957. Head north on Rue Tourbet El Bey for about 400m, turning right to reach 2 **Madrasa Slimania** (p63), a former theological college with an exquisitely decorated prayer hall. Return to Rue Tourbet El Bey and continue north until you arrive at the junction of Souq El Leffa and Souq de la Laine. Veer left into the former to arrive at 3 **Cafe Panorama** (p64). Climb the stairs through the shops to reach the cafe's mosaic-adorned rooftop terrace, where you can admire a view over the Zitouna Mosque.

Now it's time to visit 4 **Zitouna Mosque** (p58) – make sure you're dressed modestly. Enter from the doors on Souq El Attarine. Non-Muslims cannot go into the prayer hall but can check it out from the courtyard beneath the towering 43m-tall minaret. Backtrack along Souq El Attarine and turn right (north) on Rue Sidi Ben Arous, one of the medina's most attractive streets. After about 450m, turn right (east) on Rue de la Hafsia and then left (north) into Rue du Tribunal to visit 5 **Dar Lasram** (p63), a jewel of a historic mansion.

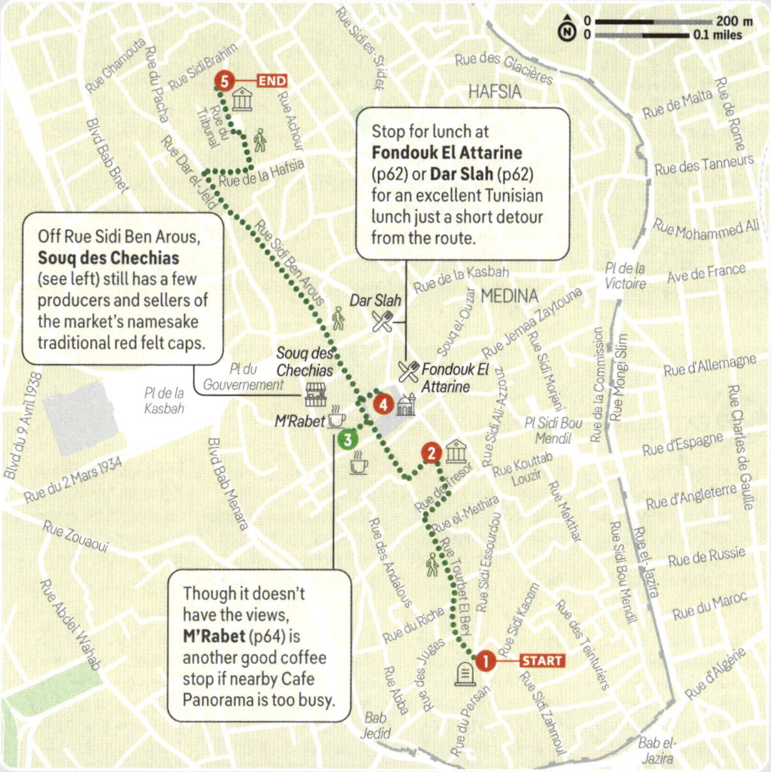

Stop for lunch at **Fondouk El Attarine** (p62) or **Dar Slah** (p62) for an excellent Tunisian lunch just a short detour from the route.

Off Rue Sidi Ben Arous, **Souq des Chechias** (see left) still has a few producers and sellers of the market's namesake traditional red felt caps.

Though it doesn't have the views, **M'Rabet** (p64) is another good coffee stop if nearby Cafe Panorama is too busy.

LOST IN TUNIS

Mourad Ben Cheikh Ahmed is a city explorer and photo blogger from Tunis. *@lostintunis*

Most locals and visitors love the walk from Rue Sidi Ben Arous to Rue de Pacha, but if you want to see more authentic and less touristy parts that make great photos, extend your walk into a longer circuit that stops by the neighbourhood of Bab Souika, the partially surviving medina gate of Bab El Khadra, the market stalls of Sidi El Bahri and the former Jewish quarter of El Hafsia before returning to your starting point.

Along the way, you'll come across many souqs, street-food stands, mausoleums, flea markets and vintage shops that are worth checking out.

CHRISTOPHE CAPPELLI/SHUTTERSTOCK

Dar Lasram

Continued from p60

Delve further into the history of the medina by joining one of the hands-on craft workshops. Learn the historic art of bookbinding, choosing the materials to use for the cover and putting together the interior pages. Make your own wallet, bookmark or another accessory during a leather workshop, or have a go at the potter's wheel to shape your own ceramics. Learn to cook Tunisian dishes in a historic medina house or whip up a bottle of perfume with favourite local scents, such as jasmine, oud and orange. Understand the intricacies of Arabic lettering by joining an expert calligrapher and learn to use traditional paper, pens and ink. The souvenirs you take home from these workshops certainly beat almost anything you'll find in a shop.

EATING IN THE MEDINA: OUR PICKS

Dar El Jeld: The medina's top dar also has one of its best Tunisian restaurants. Bookings essential. *noon-3pm & 7.30-11.30pm Mon-Sat* €€€

Dar Slah: Welcoming Tunisian eatery in an old house on the medina's busiest thoroughfare. *noon-3.30pm Mon-Sat* €€

El Ali: House-turned-restaurant with ceiling beams and stained-glass windows. The talented chef puts twists on local dishes. *8.30am-5.30pm Mon-Sat* €€

Fondouk El Attarine: Authentic Tunisian food is served in the covered courtyard of a restored *funduq. 10am-6pm Mon-Sat* €€

Bab Tounès: Great menu of elevated Tunisian dishes in the arched cellar space of the former French embassy. *noon-10pm Mon-Sat* €€

Doken: Smart, simple bistro serving Tunisian and Mediterranean dishes (many vegetarian) near Zitouna Mosque. *noon-4pm Tue-Sun* €

Dkik & Zit: Hole-in-the-wall spot stuffing deliciously filling Tunisian 'burritos' with tuna, eggs, fries and cheese. *10.30am-9pm* €

Mahdaoui: Tables fill an alley near Zitouna Mosque, and the simple daily menu offers couscous, grilled fish and more. *10am-3pm* €€

Marvellous Medina Mansions

Tiles and traditional architecture

Many of the most beautiful buildings in the medina are historic mansions called dars. While some of them have been transformed into boutique guesthouses (p90), others are museums, art galleries and offices for local foundations.

Once home to the Lasram family, who worked as scribes for the beys (Ottoman provincial governors), the magnificent **Dar Lasram** *(5DT)* dates from the early 19th century and was one of the first historic mansions restored under the auspices of the Association de Sauvegarde de la Médina de Tunis (Association to Safeguard the Medina of Tunis), whose offices are here. The interior features richly tiled rooms and courtyards, painted ceilings, and lace-like stucco moulding. The family lived on the 1st floor, while guests stayed on the upper floor. Leave the house and continue south on Rue du Tribunal to find the entrance to the mansion's *makhzen*, the former stables and warehouse that's now used as a cultural centre and arts space.

South on Rue du Tribunal, the 19th-century **Kheireddine Palace** *(free entry)* is the grandly named Museum of Tunis and hosts occasional free art exhibitions. It has some tiles in the entryway, but unfortunately the rest of the interior has been unsympathetically modernised.

Built at the beginning of the 19th century for the son of Mahmud Bey, the seventh leader of the Husainid dynasty, and then gifted to M'hamed El Monastiri, a prominent trader in *chechias* (traditional felt caps), **Dar El Monastiri** *(free entry)* has a particularly lovely entrance door framed with carved limestone. It's now home to the Centre National des Arts Calligraphiques, which trains specialists in traditional Arabic penmanship. If the door is open, you can wander into the Andalusian-style courtyard featuring tiles and intricate lattice stuccowork.

Poke your head into **Dar Ben Achour** *(free entry)*, which has lovely black-and-white striped arches and a blue tiled courtyard. It was the home of Tunisia's prime minister from 1882 to 1907 and is now the headquarters of the Tunisian Association of Monuments and Sites.

The 17th-century mansion of **Dar Bach Hamba** *(free entry)* beautifully blends traditional tilework with contemporary pieces as the headquarters of arts org **L'Art Rue** *(lartrue.org)*. The rooms surrounding the central open-air courtyard house temporary exhibitions, such as sound installations by creatives who recently moved to a new city.

DAR-CHITECTURE

Similar to riads in Morocco, Tunisian dars (p284) are historic homes in the medina built in a traditional architectural style. Many have been converted into guesthouses, and staying in one is a highlight of a visit to Tunis (p90).

Dars have large wooden doors that are brightly painted and decorated with metal studs. The inner open-air courtyard, often decked out in colourful tiles on the ground floor, is the heart of the home, where multigenerational families met for meals and socialising, but it's never visible from the entrance and is located around the corner from the front door. Traditionally, visitors had to wait in the *skifa* (entry hall) until they were allowed into the family's intimate space.

Learn About Tunisian Architecture

Back to school in the medina's madrasas

Historic theological colleges called madrasas are stunning examples of architectural creativity in the medina. Ali Pasha, ruler of Tunisia from 1735 to 1756, commissioned **Madrasa Slimania** *(free)* as a memorial to his murdered son Suleiman. Entered from the street via an unusual elevated entrance porch, it has a lavishly tiled domed prayer hall. Below the

LANDMARK MOSQUES BEYOND ZITOUNA

Non-Muslims cannot enter most mosques in Tunisia, but even if you're not allowed in, these buildings have fascinating histories and make good navigational landmarks.

Sidi Mehrez Mosque: Named after Tunis' patron saint, this 1692 mosque has something missing – construction of the mosque's minaret was cancelled because of political upheaval.

Kasbah Mosque: The minaret of this 13th-century mosque has a lozenge design in Moroccan Almohad style. The call to prayer is signalled by a white flag on the exterior.

Hamouda Pacha Mosque: This 17th-century mosque reflects the prosperity of that period. Its witch's-hat minaret is octagonal, typical of the Turkish Hanafi strand of Islam.

black-and-white striped horseshoe arches, the 18 rooms that originally housed students are now used as offices.

Ali Pasha also built **Madrasa Bir El Hajjar** *(free)* in 1757. Walk through the beautifully tiled entryway and through a bright yellow door to reach the horseshoe-arch-encircled courtyard.

Sip Mint Tea with a View

Take it all in at Cafe Panorama

The mosaic-adorned rooftop **Cafe Panorama** can be hard to find, but its view over the courtyard of Zitouna Mosque (p58) is the best in the medina. It's off Souq El Leffa and has a sign at ground level. Walk through the ground floor (a souvenir shop), the 1st floor (a rug shop) and then up to the roof. Come during prayer time when you can see Zitouna's muezzin – an actual person – make the call to prayer with his non-amplified voice, a rare occurrence, as most mosques now use loudspeakers or voice recordings.

See Royal Tombs at Tourbet El Bey

An Ottoman-style mausoleum

In the Middle Ages, people were buried outside of the medina walls, but starting from the 16th century, the rulers wanted to spend eternity closer to the medina's holy shrines and theological schools within the walls. Most of the rulers from the Husainid dynasty, which ruled the country from 1705 to 1957, are buried in **Tourbet El Bey** *(5DT)*.

This royal resting place is topped with green fish-scale domes typical of Ottoman mausoleums. Inside is an intricate mix of tiles and stucco built during Ali Pasha II's reign (1758–82). Many subsequent Husseinite beys, princesses, ministers and trusted advisers ended up here. The tombs of men are topped with marble renditions of their preferred headgear, be it turban or *chechia* (traditional felt cap), with the number of tassels showing their importance, while the women have a standing marble slab with an engraved epitaph. The **Hall of Enthroned Beys** is the most elaborate room of the complex and contains the remains of 13 rulers.

Scrub Your Stress Away in a Hammam

Getting in hot water

Hammams (bathhouses) were once the cornerstones of social life in the medina, but like the old-fashioned trades in the souqs, they are fading away. Often recognisable by their

DRINKING IN THE MEDINA: TOP CAFES

M'Rabet: Arches and columns loom over mint-tea drinkers sitting on rug-covered platforms in this characterful cafe. *9am-6pm Mon-Fri, 10am-5pm Sat*

Cafe du Souk: This always busy local spot has a central area packed with tables plus nooks and crannies in which to sip your coffee or tea. *10am-7pm*

Cafe Belkadhi: Outdoor tables line both sides of narrow Rue Sidi Ben Arous. Don't miss the indoor area with a German-made letterpress. *7am-10pm*

Cafe Chaouachine: A mass of tables under the vaulted arches of an atmospheric medina souq, this cafe is popular with all ages and genders. *7am-11pm*

CHRISTOPHE CAPPELLI/SHUTTERSTOCK

Tourbet El Bey

arched doorways painted in colourful stripes (signs are in Arabic only), the hammams that are still in business in the medina feel as if they haven't changed (or been deep cleaned) for hundreds of years.

To sample the local hammam experience, bring a towel (or *fouta,* a cotton bath sheet sold in many medina shops) and a bathing suit or underwear. (Locals don't bathe naked - they wear their underwear in the hammam.) For an inexpensive DIY experience, do as the locals do and bring your own scrubbing mitt and soap, or you can pay for an attendant to take off your top layer of skin, give you a quick massage and rinse you down.

Hammams are never mixed sex; some are for men only, some are for women only and others are open to men for part of the day and women during another part of the day. The local hammam experience doesn't vary much by neighbourhood, so pick the one that's closest to your accommodation. The going rate is about 25DT for a scrub and massage from an attendant, who might also ask for a tip. English is generally not spoken, but the attendants are usually friendly and welcoming. Bring minimal cash and no valuables - lockers are not available, and you store your belongings on an open shelf accessible to all.

Hammam El Kachachine, open to men only, is the medina's oldest still-functioning hammam. Enter through the old-fashioned barbershop. For women only, **Hammam Sidi Sahbi** is within easy walking distance of Dar Ben Gacem (p90) and other guesthouses on Rue du Pacha. On the southern side of the medina, **Hammam Daouletli** is open from 2pm to 7pm for women and after 7pm for men.

For an upmarket (and pricier) hammam in the medina, the high-end hotel of Dar El Jeld (p90) offers a more personalised and private experience.

FESTIVAL DE LA MÉDINA

On Ramadan evenings, the Tunis medina comes to life as locals break their fast after sunset. It's the only time of the year that the medina's shops, cafes and restaurants are open late.

Festival de la Médina *(facebook.com/FestivalMedina)* injects a huge dose of culture into the neighbourhood, staging traditional live music, Andalusian poetry readings and other cultural performances at venues across the medina. It's a particularly atmospheric time to explore the area, and especially so when beautiful venues like Dar Lasram (p63) are once again filled with music and community. Check out the list of events on Facebook, which also has links to buy tickets online.

Centre Ville & the Bardo

MAIN FOOD MARKET AND MUSEUM

GETTING AROUND

To reach the Bardo, take *métro léger* Line 4 from Place de Barcelone (the start of the line) or République and get off at Bardo station. The carriages are in extremely poor condition, often with broken windows and nonfunctioning doors that remain open while the tram is moving.

This neighbourhood is the hub for public transport to elsewhere in the city and the country. TGM trains to the suburbs depart from **Tunis Marine Train Station** (though at the time of writing, the train line was partially closed and replaced by a bus from Tunis), and trains to southern Tunisia leave from **Tunis Ville Train Station**.

Shooting eastward out of the medina, the wide, straight street of Ave Habib Bourguiba speaks volumes about French colonial ambition and ideals. This road is often called the 'Champs-Élysées of Tunis', though about the only thing it has in common with Paris is that they are both tree-lined boulevards.

Known as Centre Ville (City Centre) or the 'European City', this part of town is laid out in a modern grid graced with blocks of once grand but now rundown buildings. Tunisia's best museum – the Bardo, a must-visit – is northwest of the medina, but besides that, this neighbourhood has few attractions. Instead, Centre Ville is the place to book a modern hotel if you don't want to overnight in the medina (but are you *really* sure you don't want to stay in a charming dar?) or if you're dying for a drink of alcohol after days in the dry medina.

Find Your Friends at Bab El Bhar

Gateway to the city

Also called Porte de France or French Gate, the huge arch of **Bab El Bhar** (Gate of the Sea) was the medina's eastern gateway until the French demolished the surrounding walls to create Place de la Victoire. It remains a main entry point with quick access to Zitouna Mosque (p58) and the main souqs.

Bab El Bhar is a common place for people to meet up before heading into the squiggly lanes of the medina, so it's often busy. Kids play in a fountain on the gate's western side, and young men try to tempt the crowds with trays of desserts or light-up plastic toys.

Check Out a Colonial-Era Church

Inside the Cathedral of St Vincent de Paul and St Olive

A short walk from Bab El Bhar, the **Cathedral of St Vincent de Paul and St Olive** *(free)* opened on Christmas in 1897 and is the only Catholic cathedral in the country. It has a striking

Continues on p71

CENTRE VILLE & THE BARDO

HIGHLIGHTS
1 Habibi Downtown
2 Marché Centrale

SIGHTS
3 Bab El Bhar
4 Cathedral of St Vincent de Paul & St Olive
5 Hotel du Lac
6 Pont de la République Street Art

SLEEPING
7 Grand Hôtel de France
8 Hôtel Carlton
9 Hôtel Royal Victoria
10 Kyriad Prestige City Center

EATING
11 Chez Slah
12 El Walima Bent El Bey
13 Kafteji Douiri
14 Restaurant Sfax

DRINKING & NIGHTLIFE
15 Art'Cafe
16 Atom
17 Cafés Ben Yedder
see 20 Cercle des Amis du Théâtre National
18 Le Grand Café du Théâtre
19 Power Coffee

ENTERTAINMENT
20 Le 4ème Art
21 Théâtre Municipal

SHOPPING
22 Deyma

TRANSPORT
23 Tunis Marine Train Station
24 Tunis Ville Train Station

KADAGAN/SHUTTERSTOCK

The Carthage Room

TOP EXPERIENCE

Bardo Museum

Home to the largest collection of Roman mosaics in the world, the Bardo is one of the best museums in North Africa. Its massive and magnificent collection provides a fascinating portrait of southern Mediterranean life in ancient times. The art isn't expressed only in the mosaics – part of the collection is set in a beautiful palace built by the Hafsids (1228–1574).

DON'T MISS

- Mosaic portrait of Virgil (Room 1)
- Marine mosaics (Room 6)
- Carthage Room (Room 9)
- Zodiac mosaic and harem architecture (Room 10)
- Ulysses mosaic (Room 16)

Upper Floors & the Palace

While you can, of course, visit the museum galleries in any order, the room numbering starts upstairs, making it a bit easier to keep track of where you've been – parts of this palace complex can feel like a maze.

After buying a ticket, proceed up the staircase to **Room 1**, home to a famous mosaic portrait of the Roman poet Virgil flanked by two muses: Calliope (epic poetry and eloquence) and Polymnia (pantomime).

PRACTICALITIES

● bardomuseum.tn ● 13DT ● 9am-5pm Tue-Sun Jun–mid-Sep, 9.30am-4.30pm Tue-Sun mid-Sep–May

Proceed to **Room 3**, which displays marble statues and other finds from a shipwreck discovered off the coast of Mahdia in 1907. After sitting underwater for nearly 2000 years, the parts of the pockmarked marble now resemble coral.

The **Punic Room (Room 4)** showcases statuary, including an extraordinary 1st-century-CE statue of a lion-headed goddess wrapped in a costume imitating the wings of a bird. Down the stairs, **Room 5** contains tombs unearthed in Carthage. **Room 6** is a favourite, particularly for kids, for its lively marine mosaics depicting sea critters.

Several parts of Tunisia's history come together in the eastern wing of the museum, originally built as a Hafsid palace built in the Middle Ages and extended by the Ottomans in the 18th century. They are responsible for the grand reception rooms, some frosted with colourful tile-covered, ornate stuccowork and gilding.

The double-height **Carthage Room (Room 9)** has statues from the ancient city and huge floor mosaics. These rooms are must-sees before visiting Carthage (p77), which doesn't have any major mosaic pieces left in situ; all were moved here (and to the Carthage National Museum, closed until 2027) for protection.

From Room 9, head up the marble ramp to the **Treasures Room (Room 10)**, one of the most beautiful places in Tunis. This lavishly decorated former apartment once housed the harem of the Ottoman governor Sadok Bey (r 1859–82), and its carved stucco ceiling is exquisite. The zodiac mosaic on the floor is one of the museum's most famous pieces.

Backtrack through Room 9 to the **Althinburos Room (Room 11)**, once Sadok Bey's music room – it was under renovation when we visited but is set to reopen. One of its mezzanines was for the women of the harem and the other for musicians. Mosaics here depict ships and fishing techniques, as well as a banquet at Carthage.

Continue to the gilded and vaulted **Roman Villas Room (Room 13)**, with its mosaics depicting life in the rural mansions of Roman Africa. Take the stairs up and find the **Ulysses Room (Room 16)**, home to a 4th-century-CE mosaic of the Homeric hero lashed to the mast of his ship to resist the lure of the Sirens. Also here is a lovely mosaic from the same era of Venus being crowned by two female centaurs.

It takes some effort to find, but don't miss the tucked-away **Small Palace (Room 17)**, built in Andalusian style with striped arches, tons of tiles and a central fountain basin (no longer working).

Ground Floor

Return to the ground floor to lap up even more mosaics. Some of the rooms take a slight jump ahead in time through Tunisia's Byzantine and Islamic eras. Track down the Blue Quran of Kairouan in **Room 29**. Written in the 9th or 10th century, the Blue Quran is so named because it's written on rare indigo-coloured parchment. Its blocky Kufic script,

A SOMBRE START

In 2015, 21 foreign visitors – most of them tourists from Europe – and one police officer were killed in a terrorist attack at the Bardo. Isis claimed responsibility for the attack, which occurred as the visitors were getting off a bus to visit the museum. Today, a memorial in the Bardo's entranceway records their names and nationalities, and security at the museum remains high.

ROMAN AFRICA

After their victory over Carthage in the Third Punic War in 146 BCE, the Romans founded the province of Africa – the little country now known as Tunisia once had the name of the entire continent. Roman Africa was the empire's breadbasket, and it shipped olives and grains across the Med, growing fat from the proceeds. Incredibly intact ruins of affluent ancient cities are dotted across Tunisia's landscape, but most of their mosaics are stored in the Bardo.

TOP TIPS

- Groups tour the museum around 10am, so come later and spend the afternoon marvelling.
- Between your visits to the upper floor and the ground floor, take a break in the cafe, which serves decent coffee and pastries in a beautifully tiled covered outdoor space. It's signposted from the ground floor. A coffee or mint tea is sure to bring some of your energy back.
- If you're arriving by tram, you have to cross a couple of busy roads without any assistance from traffic lights. Do not follow navigation apps like Google Maps – the only entrance is on the museum's western side, off Rue Mongi Slim.

written in gold ink and set with egg white, is a masterpiece of Arabic calligraphy.

Other impressive artefacts include the 6th-century Demna Baptistery, a Byzantine-era, hot-tub-sized baptismal font covered in tile depicting scenes of salvation, in **Room 28**. It was unearthed in Tunisia's Cap Bon in 1955.

Bardo Museum

Ground Level

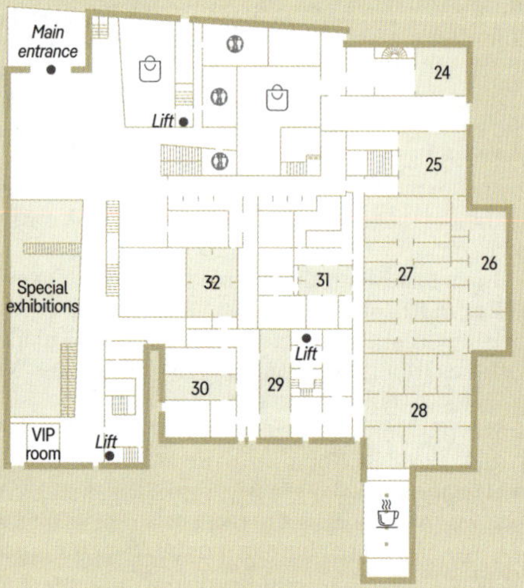

Level 1

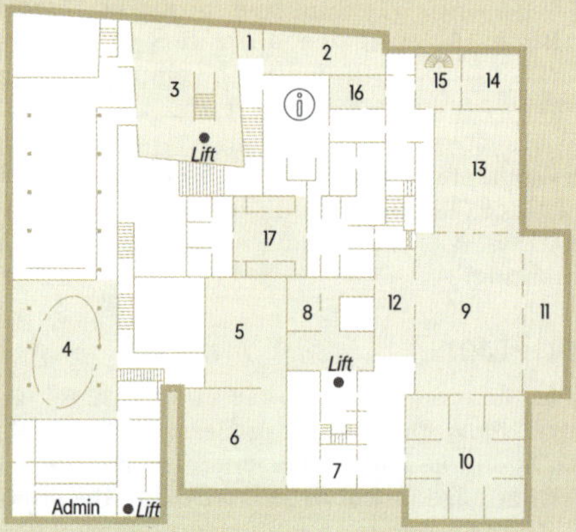

STUDIO/SHUTTERSTOCK

Dates for sale, Marché Centrale

Continued from p66
golden facade facing Ave Habib Bourguiba, but if you want to explore inside, walk around the corner on Rue d'Alger to find the entrance. The architectural style melds Gothic, Byzantine and Moorish elements.

Sights, Smells & Sounds of Marché Centrale

Market mayhem

Tunisians love food, and if you do too, hotfoot it to **Marché Centrale** (Central Market) for a visual and sensory feast. Tunisian food markets offer a great introduction to local culture, and fishmongers, butchers, cheese merchants, fruit and vegetable vendors, and florists compete to catch your eye with extravagant displays of lemons, salads, spices, dried fruits, olives and glistening seafood from all around the coast and country.

The original market building dates from 1891, and the halls behind are later additions. Marché Centrale has three distinct areas: an enormous fish hall where you can watch locally caught creatures of the sea being theatrically weighed, gutted and scaled; a central hall where mounds of spicy harissa, tubs of plump olives and blocks of pungent cheese are sold; and a rear fruit and vegetable section.

One of the best times to visit is early spring, when white bigaradier (bitter orange) and pink pelargonium (geranium)

A TASTE OF TUNISIA

Lamia Temimi co-founded Sawa Taste of Tunisia, a food-focused tour company. *@sawatasteoftunisia*

Fast, cheap but also surprisingly nutritious and healthy, many of the most iconic Tunisian street foods reflect the multifaceted cultural influences that have shaped the country through time, borrowing their names from Turkish, Italian or French.

For example, *leblebi* (the Turkish word for chickpeas) is a chickpea broth served over day-old bread, topped with tuna and a poached egg. Tunisian *fricassé* is a savoury fried pastry stuffed with ingredients like egg, olives, harissa, capers and mashed potato. We offer a street-food tour that's a wonderful entry point for discovering the rhythms and geographies of daily life in the capital.

EATING IN CENTRE VILLE: OUR PICKS

Chez Slah: This restaurant in an unprepossessing pocket of Centre Ville serves super-fresh fish in a 19th-century villa. *noon-3pm & 6-9.30pm Mon-Sat* €€€

Kafteji Douiri: Cram into this tiny space, open since 1931, to get a ticket and wait your turn for fantastic *kafteji* (fried vegetables with egg). *8am-2pm Mon-Sat* €

Restaurant Sfax: Offers a slew of regional specialities, including *kamounia* (cumin-spiced beef stew) and rice or couscous *aux lapin* (with rabbit). *11am-9pm* €

El Walima Bent El Bey: Feast like royalty at this lavishly styled restaurant started by Salwa Bey, granddaughter of Tunisia's last sovereign. *noon-4pm Mon-Sat* €€

THE BRUTALIST HULK OF HOTEL DU LAC

Sitting prominently on the northern side of Ave Habib Bourguiba is the 1970s Brutalist concrete building of **Hotel du Lac**, designed by Italian architect Raffaele Contigiani. This curious 10-floor structure looks like an upside-down flattened pyramid – the top floor is twice as long as the bottom floor – and its shape is said to have inspired the tank-like sandcrawler vehicles in Star Wars, which was first filmed in Tunisia (though artists who worked on the movie say this is not true).

This curious structure has sadly been abandoned since 2000, and it's at risk of demolition; however, architecture preservation groups have so far managed to delay that fate.

TOP TIP

If you're looking for a snack or a lovely gift to take home, **Deyma** *(facebook.com/dattes.deyma)* sells Tamerza dates stuffed with pistachio paste and dried apricots, or covered in sesame seeds. It also has locally produced date soaps, olive oil and olive paste.

flowers are in season. Piles of these are offered in the rear hall, where they perfume the space and are snapped up by locals who use home stills to produce flower water (from pelargonium) and the essential oil known as neroli (from bigaradier). Later in spring, rose petals are harvested and sold for the same purpose, offering a similarly fragrant display.

More produce is offered in the streets surrounding the market. Head to Rue d'Espagne for freshly roasted coffee beans and spices, and Rue du Danemark for olives and pickles.

The best way to visit Marché Centrale is with **Sawa Taste of Tunisia** *(sawataste.com)*, a food-focused tour company that pairs you up with a chef for a market tour. You then head to the kitchen to make authentic Tunisian dishes.

Cheers to the City from Habibi Downtown

Up on the rooftop

Good bars are hard to come by in Tunis, particularly if you're a female traveller or you don't want to bathe in cigarette smoke, but fear not – Centre Ville has a couple of options worth visiting.

Habibi Downtown *(@habibidowntown_)* is an import from the seaside suburb of Gammarth (p87), where the good times roll in summer, but fortunately this Centre Ville space is open year-round. Enter the old-school Soviet-feeling El Hana hotel lobby and take the lift to the 10th floor, still signposted as Jamaica Bar. A complete 180 from the decor downstairs, Habibi brings Instagram vibes of bright colours and strings of small Edison bulbs to its indoor-outdoor rooftop space. Locals complain that the drinks are sold at expensive Gammarth prices, and they aren't wrong. The cocktails are a bit of a let-down, so stick to beer or wine. The main part of the rooftop is south-facing, so you can't fully see the sunset, but the views over the city and the Municipal Theatre are tops.

Another decent Centre Ville bar is **Atom** *(instagram.com/atom_baraudiophile)*, on the 1st floor of Hotel Ibn Khaldoun. It feels like a university-student hangout with vintage furniture and a 1980s peach and maroon colour palette, but it's blissfully smoke-free. It calls itself a 'listening bar', a trend that started in Japan of community-centred places to relax and focus on music, and on some nights a DJ spins tracks. There's no sign, so go into the hotel lobby and up the stairs, turn right and go around the corner.

Capital Culture

On stage in Tunis

A lovely building on Ave Habib Bourguiba, **Théâtre Municipal** seats more than 1000 theatre-goers. French architect Jean-Émile Resplandy designed this eye-catching Art Nouveau edifice at the start of the 20th century, and it would look right at home on any major Parisian boulevard. It hosts theatre, ballet, opera and symphonic music performances. See what's on and buy tickets online at teskerti.tn/category/theatre-municipal-de-tunis.

Théâtre Municipal

Built as a cinema but now functioning as an intimate theatre space, **Le 4ème Art** *(facebook.com/Le4emeArt)* is the epicentre of Tunis' contemporary cultural scene. Home of the Théâtre National Tunisien (Tunisian National Theatre), it puts on performances of theatre, dance and music. The **Cercle des Amis du Théâtre National** cafe in the theatre's foyer is a great place for a coffee or tea during the day.

Street Art in Tunis

Painting the town at Pont de la République

The 2011 revolution brought many changes to Tunisia, one of which was the start of an open street-art culture. Artists initially used their work as a protest mechanism, and today some pieces still mark political events but also celebrate culture and colour. One of the best places to view street art is underneath the **Pont de la République**, where in 2016 local street artists, supported by the Ministry of Cultural Affairs, used some of the 130 pylons of the bridge to create a huge, open-air gallery of works celebrating the fifth anniversary of the revolution. Sadly, the government's Ministry of Equipment painted over these original pieces in 2019. Their erasure caused an uproar, but artists repainted the area a few months later.

CARTHAGE INTERNATIONAL FILM FESTIVAL

The **Carthage International Film Festival** *(@jcctunisie official)* is an annual event that celebrates cinema from Arab, African and European countries. Founded in 1966, it's one of the longest-running festivals of its kind in the region. Though Carthage is in the name, the opening and closing ceremonies take place at Théâtre Municipal (see left) in Centre Ville. The top prize given to winning filmmakers, however, is the Tanit d'Or (Golden Tanit), named after the Carthaginian goddess.

In addition to film screenings, the event also hosts workshops and discussions with the directors and actors. It takes place over a week in late October, November or December – check social media for specifics.

DRINKING IN CENTRE VILLE: BEST CAFES

Cafés Ben Yedder: This much-loved coffee roaster has a modern non-smoking cafe near Marché Centrale. *6am-6pm Mon-Sat, to 2pm Sun*

Le Grand Café du Théâtre: The tables at this popular cafe are arranged on two tiers, and patrons are screened from the pavement by greenery. *7am-11pm*

Art'Cafe: The comfy couches in this cavernous space are popular for work meetings, cakes and coffee, and young locals meeting up with friends. *6am-9pm*

Power Coffee: Slurp a milkshake, juice or espresso in the velvet chairs under the leaves of pothos plants and wicker light fixtures. *8am-10pm*

Carthage

FAMOUS PUNIC AND ROMAN RUINS

GETTING AROUND

Carthage covers a large, hilly area that slopes down towards the sea. Some of the main sites are walkable, but a taxi makes it easier to cover longer distances.

The TGM train makes six stops in Carthage, but services are sporadic and not set to a timetable, so it's unlikely to be a convenient way to get around, but it might make sense if you're going further to Sidi Bou Said or La Marsa. Stations are not well marked on navigation apps like Google Maps.

Carthage is an exclusive residential suburb and retains a sense of historical importance forged over millennia. Few remnants of the Carthaginian settlement and only a few ruins from the Roman period remain, so some visitors are disappointed by their visit. However, with some imagination (and a good guide), the fragments can evoke an epic past.

It's said that Dido, queen of the Phoenician city-state of Tyre, founded Carthage, though the story is almost certainly a fabrication. Dido did a deal with the locals, who agreed to give her a plot of land that could be covered by an oxhide, and she cut the hide into a long, fine string that marks out what is now Byrsa Hill (*byrsa* means 'oxhide' in Greek). She went on to build a great city, but after refusing the hand of a local king, she died by suicide to avoid war. Roman poet Virgil tells a similar tale in the *Aeneid*.

Remember the Sacrifices of WWII

Sombre war cemetery

The **North Africa American Cemetery** *(abmc.gov/cemeteries-memorials/about-north-africa-american-cemetery/; free)* is a striking forest of white crosses that bears testament to the Americans killed in North Africa during World War II. The site covers nearly 11 hectares, with 2841 neatly ordered graves at the cemetery and a wall of remembrance

EATING IN CARTHAGE: OUR PICKS

Les Indécis: One of the best places to eat and hang out in Tunis, with modern takes on Tunisian classics in a coffee shop atmosphere. *4-10pm Tue, from 9am Wed-Sun* €€

Le Restô: Savour the menu of Mediterranean food and sushi against the spectacular glittering water views from this terrace at Villa Didon. *9am-11pm* €€€

Punic'Art: After a busy day of sightseeing, this casual cafe with burgers, pizza, cakes and coffee, and set in a park at the water's edge, is a treat. *8am-midnight* €

Tchevap: Classy Italian restaurant with chandeliers and white tablecloths. Loved by locals, though service isn't always up to snuff. *noon-3pm & 8-11pm* €€€

HIGHLIGHTS
1 Baths of Antoninus
2 Roman Villas

SIGHTS
3 Beit Al Hikma
4 Byrsa Hill
5 Carthage National Museum
6 Cathédrale St-Louis de Carthage
7 La Malga Cisterns
8 Magon Quarter
9 North Africa American Cemetery
10 Punic Ports
11 Roman Amphitheatre
12 Roman Theatre
13 Tophet of Salammbo

ACTIVITIES
14 Le Lemon Tour

SLEEPING
15 Villa Didon

EATING
see 15 Le Restô
16 Les Indécis
17 Punic'Art
18 Tchevap

to commemorate 3724 others missing in action. The open-air map room details in mosaic form the battle that started in 1942 to reclaim North Africa from Nazi Germany.

TOP TIP

Most travellers visit Carthage for the day from their base in the medina or Sidi Bou Said, but this area does have one excellent place to stay (p90), though it comes with a hefty price tag.

ELAKAZAL/SHUTTERSTOCK

Byrsa Hill

TOP EXPERIENCE

Archaeological Site of Carthage

Carthage was once a Mediterranean maritime power and one of the wealthiest cities in the ancient world, inspiring poetry, mythology and envy. It now lies partly excavated among exclusive villas in a swanky Tunis suburb. The vast majority of the ruins date from Roman-era Carthage rather than the earlier Punic period, and what's visible today is scant and requires a bit of imagination.

DON'T MISS

- View from Byrsa Hill
- Baths of Antoninus
- Amphitheatre
- Roman Theatre
- Mosaics in the Villa of the Aviary
- Punic Ports
- Mosaics in Bardo Museum

Carthage History

A Phoenician settlement founded in the 9th century BCE, Carthage was a marvel of the ancient world. Built on a site of great natural beauty, the city boasted walls 34km in length, with houses running from the top of Byrsa Hill down to the waterfront and its ingenious interconnecting harbours. Carthage's source of wealth – and its defining feature, along with its urge to trade – was its navy.

PRACTICALITIES

- One-day pass for eight sites 12DT
- 8.30am-5pm mid-Sep–Apr, 8am-6pm May–mid-Sep

After repeated clashes with the Roman Republic during the Punic Wars, the Phoenicians' colony-turned-capital vanished at the hands of the conquerors from the other side of the Mediterranean, who torched and (eventually) rebuilt Carthage to their own specifications and enslaved the local population.

Carthage existed for more than 500 years before the Romans took over in 146 BCE, but because of the city's brutal destruction, little remains of the original Punic capital. However, the spectacular downfall of such a civilisation still captivates modern minds, and the UNESCO-listed Carthage remains a common stop on Tunisia itineraries.

Byrsa Hill

In Punic times, **Byrsa Hill** was occupied by a temple to the Carthaginian god Eschmoun. The Romans destroyed most of the Punic structures, and all that remains is a small, well-preserved section of a residential quarter dating from the time of Hannibal (around the 3rd century BCE). It's still possible to discern a street grid dotted with carefully planned domestic structures - some of which were once five storeys high - complete with subterranean cisterns and ground-floor shops.

From the terrace in front of the **Carthage National Museum** that now sits atop the hill, it's possible to see the ancient **Punic Ports** (p79) and the intensely blue Gulf of Tunis, a stunning scene. The museum is closed for renovations until at least 2027. It sits on the crest of Byrsa Hill and is housed in an early-20th-century building that once functioned as a Catholic seminary.

Nearby **Cathédrale St-Louis de Carthage** is also shut for restoration. The architect of this now-deconsecrated, 19th-century, French-built cathedral employed an unorthodox mix of Moorish, Byzantine and Gothic architectural styles in its design. When it's open, the interior is used for exhibitions and concerts. The cathedral was dedicated to the 13th-century French saint-king Louis IX, who died on the beach at Carthage in 1270 during the ill-fated Eighth Crusade. He was hoping to convert the Hafsid ruler; instead, his troops wilted in the heat.

Roman Amphitheatre

This **amphitheatre** was once one of the largest in the Roman Empire, with a capacity of 36,000 people who came to watch animal hunts, gladiators, and capital punishment executed by *damnatio ad bestias* ('condemnation to the beasts'). Today, only the overgrown oval of the stage remains, along with a sinister subterranean passage where victims were once led to their fate.

La Malga Cisterns

The restored remnants of the huge 2nd-century-CE **cisterns** that supplied Roman Carthage with water are located near the western edge of the ancient city. The original complex was nearly 1km long and fed by a huge aqueduct carrying mountain spring water from Zaghouan.

PLAN YOUR TIME

The ticket covers all Carthage sights but only for one day. It can be a lot to squeeze in, so start early.

Short on time? Prioritise the Baths of Antoninus, the Roman Villas and Byrsa Hill.

Half-day See Byrsa Hill, the Roman Theatre, Roman Villas and Baths of Antoninus on foot or by bike. If you have two or four wheels, add on the Roman Amphitheatre.

Full-day Check out the main highlights as well as the lesser-visited sites, such as the Punic Ports. Break for lunch at Le Restô (near Byrsa Hill, p74) or Les Indécis (between the Punic Ports and Tophet of Salammbo; p74).

UNDER RENOVATION

Unfortunately, some of the sites listed on the ticket are not currently open and might not be for several years. The government launched a competition for architects to submit plans to revitalise the Carthage National Museum, expected to reopen in 2027. The small Paleochristian Museum has also been closed for years.

Roman Theatre

The **Roman Theatre** has been almost totally reconstructed, so it gives a good sense of what the venue looked like, though the work isn't very historically sympathetic. It's used as the main venue for the annual **International Festival of Carthage** *(festivaldecarthage.tn)*, which stages music and theatre performances in July and August. The theatre is thought to have originally accommodated 5000 spectators.

Roman Villas

A visit to this former **residential enclave** gives a real sense of refined ancient Roman life in Carthage. Walk up the hill to find the reconstructed **Villa of the Aviary**, the main reason for visiting this site. It features a columned portico, a courtyard with a mosaic floor showing birds among plants, hence the villa's name, and a terrace with views over the Gulf of Tunis.

Baths of Antoninus

The Romans chose a sublime seaside setting for the monumental **Baths of Antoninus**. Begun under Hadrian and finished in the 2nd century CE under Antoninus, it was the largest thermae (bath complex) outside Rome, supplied with water by the great Zaghouan aqueduct. Just the foundations remain, but they are awesome in scale. Find an information panel that shows the plan of the baths up the stairs above the main complex, which helps you imagine how it would have functioned in its heyday.

Baths of Antoninus

An octagonal caldarium (hot room) was flanked by smaller saunas and led to a small tepidarium (warm room), which allowed access to the huge 22m-by-42m frigidarium (cold room) at the centre with its eight colossal pillars. Beyond this was a wonderful 17.5m-by-13.5m seaside swimming pool, no trace of which remains. To either side of the frigidarium were palaestras (gymnasiums), where people could indulge in naked wrestling and other sports.

A sole 15m-high frigidarium column gives a sense of its former dimensions – its capital alone weighs 8 tonnes – and huge fragments of marble inscription supply a taste of the decor. To the southwest, a huge semicircular construction with about 80 seats was discovered, which archaeologists at first thought was a theatre. It turned out to be communal latrines. Only the shape and traces of the mosaic floor remain.

The baths were destroyed by the Vandals (doing what they did best) in 439 CE, and the stone was reused by the Arabs during the construction of Tunis.

The overgrown garden contains other archaeological remains, including Punic tombs.

Magon Quarter

Excavations in the **Magon Quarter** have uncovered a small area of Roman workshops superimposed on a 5th-century-BCE Punic residential artisans' quarter. Like the residential quarter on Byrsa Hill, the layout is ordered, and the small houses are endowed with cisterns.

Across the street, have a quick peek at **Beit Al Hikma**, a gleaming white, crenellated building that's now home to the Tunisian Academy of Sciences. It's where French Prime Minister Pierre Mendès-France acknowledged the autonomy of the Tunisian government in 1954, paving the way for decolonisation and the start of the Republic of Tunisia.

Punic Ports

Today, only the shape of the legendary **Punic Ports**, the coveted basis of Carthage's power and prosperity, remains. A narrow channel linked the southern, oblong merchant port to the northern circular naval port. This arrangement meant that the military port was hidden from the outside, but the Carthaginian navy could see out to sea. The military base had moorings for an incredible 220 vessels in dry docks and around the quay-lined edge. The 7-hectare commercial port was bordered by quays and warehouses.

The ports were filled in by Roman general Scipio after Carthage's destruction in 146 BCE, but in the 2nd century CE, the Romans reinvented the islet as a circular forum with two temples and used the port to house their merchant fleet, which shipped wheat to Rome. Rises in the sea level meant the quay walls had to be raised several times. By the end of the 6th century, the harbour had fallen into disuse, and today only small two-person fishing boats can be found in its waters.

HOW TO GET AROUND CARTHAGE

Walking: Starting at Byrsa Hill is a good idea so that most of your trek is downhill to the Baths of Antoninus, passing by the Roman Theatre and Roman Villas.

Bicycle: Le Lemon Tour *(lelemontour.com)* rents standard bikes and e-bikes. You can DIY it or join one of their tours – either way, we recommend an e-bike for the hills. Wear a helmet and be mindful of traffic.

Taxi: Drivers hang around the Baths of Antoninus and will negotiate a price to take you around and wait while you explore.

Tour: Group tours generally only go to Carthage's main sights (Baths of Antoninus, Byrsa Hill, Roman Theatre and Roman Amphitheatre), so if you want to see it all, get a private guide.

Train: You could use the TGM to cover larger distances, but you'll probably end up waiting so long for the train to arrive that it would have been faster to walk.

TOP TIPS

- Visit the Bardo Museum (p68) the day before coming to Carthage. The most impressive mosaics are here, and the on-site Carthage National Museum is closed for renovations until 2027.
- Getting a guide is worthwhile. The ruins are scant and require good stories to bring them to life. Signage is poor to nonexistent.
- You can buy the entry ticket from any of the sites. You must pay in cash, and the site guardian marks off the places you've been with a pen.
- The Baths of Antoninus is the only site with a cafe on the premises, but it's not always open.

KATHARINA SHMATKO/SHUTTERSTOCK

Tophet of Salammbo

Tophet of Salammbo

Originally dedicated to the deities Baal Hammon and Tanit, this Carthaginian **sacrificial site** and burial ground is dotted with stubby stelae engraved with simple geometric shapes and symbols. When the site was excavated by a French team of archaeologists in 1921, more than 20,000 urns, each containing the ashes of a child (mostly newborn, but also children up to age four), were found under the stelae. Wandering through the site is a haunting experience.

The name Tophet is Hebrew for 'place of burning' and comes from biblical references to child sacrifice, such as in Jeremiah: '[the people of Judah] have built the altar called Tophet... and there they burn to death their little sons and daughters'. While ancient sources are unequivocal about the Carthaginians' practice of child sacrifice, various other interpretations try to explain what may have actually taken place. The Romans, despite their righteous horror, couldn't have been too spooked, as they built workshops, warehouses and a temple over the site.

Sidi Bou Said

PICTURE-PERFECT CLIFFTOP VILLAGE

With its distinctive blue and white colour scheme, hilly cobbled streets draped with blooming bougainvillea and captivating glimpses of azure Mediterranean waters, Sidi Bou Said is one of the prettiest spots in the entire country – and this neighbourhood knows it. Named after a 13th-century Sufi saint (the last word in the village's name is pronounced sigh-*eed*), Sidi Bou has a distinctive architectural style that's a mix of Ottoman and Andalusian, a result of the influx of Spanish Muslims fleeing the Reconquista in the 16th century.

For French colonisers, the sleepy fishing village was a perfect depiction of the Orientalism romanticised by Europeans in the 19th century, and they committed to ensuring that its character – both real and imagined – was preserved. (The village was given protected status in 1915.) It still retains a sense of North African fantasia today, both for visitors and, interestingly enough, Tunisians themselves.

GETTING AROUND

The village is divided into two sections: one on the clifftop (upper village) and the other radiating out from the roundabout at the foot of the hill (lower village). Steep Rue Habib Thameur connects the two.

Rue Habib Thameur east of Rue du 2 Mars 1934 is pedestrianised, so taxis drop you off here. If you're arriving with luggage, book through your accommodation or make sure the driver takes the 'back' roads of Rue Taieb Mhiri or Hedi Zarrouk so you arrive closer to the door.

Arabic Music & Orientalist Architecture

A palace of creativity

Built between 1912 and 1922 for French-born Baron Rodolphe d'Erlanger and his Italian countess wife Elisabetta, the palace of **Ennejma Ezzahra** *(cmam.tn; 12DT)* is a European interpretation of traditional Maghrebi and Andalusian design, filled with virtuoso carved stucco and wooden inlay work, marble floors and columns, ornate furniture, and an internationally renowned collection of traditional musical instruments. The magnificent reception hall and richly decorated salons are architectural highlights in a city full of them, and the house was only ever owned by the d'Erlanger family before it was sold to the government in 1989. During World War II, Nazi soldiers occupied its floors, and the Luftwaffe slept in Elisabetta's quarters.

Before stepping inside, take in the Persian Garden, planted with fragrant geranium and sweet basil. When the plants were

HIGHLIGHTS
1 Ennejma Ezzahra
2 La Villa Bleue

SIGHTS
3 Amilcar Beach
4 Dar El Annabi
5 Sidi Bou Said Beach

ACTIVITIES
6 Dar Saïd Spa
see 2 La Villa Bleue

SLEEPING
see 6 Dar Said
7 La Menara Hôtel & Spa
see 2 La Villa Bleue
8 Maison Dedine

EATING
9 Au Bon Vieux Temps
10 Bambalouni Sidi Bou Said
11 Dar Zarrouk
12 Le Pirate

DRINKING & NIGHTLIFE
13 Ben Rahim
14 Bleue
15 Café des Délices
see 10 Café des Nattes
16 Cook's
see 14 Sociale

SHOPPING
17 Aly.C Gallery
18 Galerie A.Gorgi
19 Galerie Saladin
20 Luna Concept Store
21 Renaissance Concept Store

TOP TIP

Wi-fi isn't great in most accommodation in Tunis, so if you need internet, pop into Sociale (p84), a chill coworking space with a roof terrace (day pass standard/student 15/10DT). It also puts on events, including meditations and movie nights.

warmed by the sun, the perfume would waft up into Elisabetta's room. A landscape of prickly pear imported from Mexico and eucalyptus from Australia cascades down the hill, offering a majestic view of the sea and Sidi Bou Said's cliffscape. Sadly, the garden terraces are now off-limits for visitors because of the risk of landslips.

Rodolphe was a painter – don't miss the baron's recreated art studio filled with his early Modern figurative canvases – but he also became a leading authority on traditional Arabic music, particularly the revival of *malouf*, a musical style that comes from Andalusian refugees who settled in Tunisia, Algeria and Libya after the Reconquista. He started writing *La*

Musique Arabe, a work that eventually became a six-volume collection after his death.

The palace and the people who called it home have a rich history, but unfortunately signage in the palace is minimal. You can still get a sense of the palace's musical past by attending a classical music concert. Check the palace's Facebook page for upcoming events *(facebook.com/CentredesMusiquesArabesetMediterraneennes).*

Visit a Former Family Mansion

A home of history and heritage

Sidi Bou Said has long been a neighbourhood of the elite, and **Dar El Annabi** *(5DT)* allows you to step inside a historic family home. From the outside, it doesn't look like much – homes in North Africa are designed this way intentionally to not reveal the family's wealth – but this 18th-century house is vibrantly tiled and centred on courtyards filled with jasmine and bougainvillea, with a cast of kooky wax figures sporting some fabulous traditional clothing downstairs. Upstairs, you'll find a bizarre mix of haute-bourgeois furnishings and 1980s electronics.

It was originally built as the Annabi family's summer retreat, and rooms on display include a prayer hall and a little library stuffed with various local titles and black-and-white family photos. The superb panorama from the top terrace sweeps across the village, the bay and Carthage. The entrance ticket includes a cup of tea, which is often left sitting lukewarm in the Andalusian courtyard.

Sidi Bou Said's Famous Cafes

Mint tea with a view

Perhaps the most iconic photo of Sidi Bou Said shows a series of whitewashed terraces cascading down the cliffside at **Café des Délices**, which offers seating with million-dollar views. As a result, it charges about that much for basic drinks and stock-standard food served by indifferent and inattentive staff – this might be the most expensive mint tea you drink in North Africa (at least 10DT; cafes elsewhere sell mint tea for less than half that price). The steady stream of first-time customers has also led to some questionable practices, such as bringing out the more expensive cups of mint tea with almonds by default instead of the standard mint tea you asked for. That view, though...

BEST GALLERIES & SHOPS

Aly.C Gallery: Paintings, drawings and other creative works by Tunisian artists in a small but bold gallery. Don't forget to look up at the delicately decorated ceiling.

Renaissance Concept Store: Beautiful high-end handcrafted homewares and accessories located in an old home that you'll wish was your own.

Luna Concept Store: The jewellery, clothing and artistic prints of Tunis neighbourhoods make excellent, affordable souvenirs.

Galerie Saladin: This tiny gallery down a small alleyway in the lower village sometimes showcases major local artists.

Galerie A.Gorgi: This highly regarded gallery displays the work of contemporary Tunisian artists in individual and group shows.

EATING IN SIDI BOU SAID: OUR PICKS

La Villa Bleue: A lavishly tiled dining room and an outdoor terrace are an elegant setting for refined Tunisian and French cuisine. *noon-12.30am* **€€€**

Dar Zarrouk: Big on atmosphere, with a large sea-facing terrace filled with cloth-draped tables and diners eating plates of Mediterranean seafood. *noon-10.30pm* **€€€**

Au Bon Vieux Temps: 'In the Good Old Days' has a nostalgic feel, serving French and Tunisian dishes in the view-tastic former home of writer André Gide. *12.30pm-midnight* **€€€**

Bambalouni Sidi Bou Said: You can't walk around town without a freshly fried, sugar-dusted *bambalouni* (doughnut) from this hole-in-the-wall place. *8am-10pm* **€**

PAUL KLEE IN SIDI BOU SAID

Sometimes called the father of abstract art and Surrealism, Swiss-born painter Paul Klee (1879–1940) took a two-week trip with fellow artists August Macke and Louis Moilliet to Tunisia in 1914, spending time in Sidi Bou Said. It's said that the artist discovered his taste for light and colour here and that this Tunis trip forever changed the course of his artistic work.

In dozens of watercolours painted in the decades after his time in Tunisia, he started to paint more abstract forms with bright palettes. 'Colour has taken possession of me,' he wrote. 'No longer do I have to chase after it; I know that it has hold of me forever. Colour and I are one.'

Fronted by steep steps that feature in many photographs, **Café des Nattes** is a long-standing traditional cafe that hosted Sidi Bou Said's bohemian types of yesteryear. The interior has seating on rush-mat-covered platforms, but the spot you want is outside on the small terrace, which is ideal for checking out the cobbled catwalk of the street. Like Délices, the food and drink offering is standard and overpriced. Insist on seeing a menu and check it against your bill.

Swim in the Sea in Sidi Bou Said

Beachy keen

On the southern side of the clifftop village lies **Sidi Bou Said Beach** and a yacht-filled marina. The beach can be accessed from the upper village via Impasse Thameur, which leads to a staircase with 365 steps (be careful – it's not well maintained) or Ave de l'Environnement. It's just a small slice of sand compared to the beaches on offer in La Marsa and Gammarth (p86), but it has a more stunning setting. A beach shack called **Lucky Boy** rents stand-up paddleboards and kayaks. Don't leave any valuables behind while you're out in the water.

Backed by a cliff, the beach faces west, making it a perfect spot for sunset photos from water level. There are kiosks for snacks and drinks, but **Le Pirate** is the only sit-down

DRINKING IN SIDI BOU SAID: BEST CAFES

Ben Rahim: Tiny, hip cafe in the lower village that bills itself as the first and only speciality coffee shop in Tunisia. *10am-midnight*

Bleue: Excellent stop for well-made espresso drinks and tahini hot chocolate, plus breakfast plates, sandwiches and salads. *8am-midnight*

Sociale: For digital nomads, remote workers or travellers who just need to soak up some wi-fi, this quiet coworking space is a godsend. *8am-9pm Mon-Fri, weekend hours vary*

Cook's: Head upstairs and pick from the long menu of creative coffee drinks, such as latte speculoos, made with Belgian cinnamon-flavoured biscuits. *8am-11pm*

SOFIENE X/SHUTTERSTOCK

View towards Sidi Bou Said beach

restaurant, serving seafood and grills with a French slant. It's a nicely relaxed place, though overpriced. Nearby **Amilcar Beach** has loads more space but is often strewn with rubbish.

Soak in the Steam

Best spas in Sidi Bou Said

Sidi Bou Said is a haven of luxe dars, and their spas can make you forget all your worries with Maghrebi-style hammam treatments.

At the spa at **La Villa Bleue** *(lavillableuesidibousaid.com)*, you can add clay masks – green for treating ailments, red for improved blood circulation or yellow for skin toning – to your private hammam and scrub. Other options include a 'Berber ceremony' using *ghassoul* (a natural clay from Morocco) and honey soap.

The relaxing **Dar Saïd Spa** *(darsaid.com.tn)* offers sea-salt scrubs and clay wraps in its lovely white-tiled hammam, as well as 40-minute and hour-long massages.

REMNANTS OF THE REIGN OF BEN ALI

The Arab Spring began in Tunisia, and the uprisings that started in 2010 ousted Zine El Abidine Ben Ali, the country's authoritarian president. Ben Ali was well known to have luxurious leanings, and he had a huge palace in Sidi Bou Said. When he fled the country for Saudi Arabia in 2011, he left behind a presidential pad filled with antiquities, art and his personal belongings, as well as a slew of high-end cars and boats, which were auctioned off by the government to replenish the country's coffers.

The mansion is not open to the public, but Sidi Bou residents go for walks on the steep roads below the palace that wander past the former president's helipad.

La Marsa & Gammarth

BEACHSIDE 'BURBS

GETTING AROUND

The core of La Marsa around the beach and Cafe Le Saf Saf is walkable. Unlike Sidi Bou Said, this area is mostly flat and follows a sort-of straight grid of streets. To go further or to travel around Gammarth, you need to find a taxi or hire a car.

La Marsa has two TGM stations, **La Corniche** and **Marsa Plage**, at the end of the train line from Tunis.

Once the summer base of the Ottoman beys, La Marsa is an exclusive seaside suburb at the end of the TGM train line littered with grand villas and whitewashed 20th-century apartment buildings. The palm-lined beach stretches north around a bay that finishes beneath the cliffs of the resort village and ambassadorial hangout of Gammarth (pronounced with a hard t at the end: gam-*MART*). This area is relatively uncrowded on weekdays, but everyone in Tunis seems to descend at weekends, especially during summer, when beach bars line the sand and partiers dance until the wee hours. Gammarth is the government-designated *Zone Touristique* (tourist area), and its huge hotels and resorts make comfortable stays but leave little room to experience local culture.

These neighbourhoods feel like the polar opposite of the medina – and geographically, they are. At times it's hard to believe they are part of the same urban area.

TOP TIP

Most international travellers don't make time to visit these neighbourhoods, but La Marsa and Gammarth are the perfect antidote to the madness of the medina. Take a break from long days of sightseeing at one of the area's relaxing hotels and head to the beach or decompress in a hammam.

Kick Back at the Local Beaches

Sun, sand and sea

Pack your *fouta* (thin Tunisian towel) and join the local crowds flocking to urban **La Marsa Beach** to escape the summer heat with a dip in the clear waters of the Med. In colder months, this 1km-long stretch of sand becomes a playground for fishermen, footballers, and romantics strolling along the shoreline. It might not be the cleanest of beaches, but the view to Gammarth is charming.

Backed by five-star resorts, the long, curved beach in **Gammarth** offers some of the best spots for a swim, with sunloungers and waiter service for hotel guests.

Staying out Late in Summertime

Nightlife under the stars

In summer, La Marsa and Gammarth groove to their own beat under the twinkling sky at dozens of open-air nightclubs. Many of these bars are transitory, open for only a few months a year

SIGHTS
1 Gammarth Beach
2 La Marsa Beach

ACTIVITIES
see 5 Dar El Marsa
see 7 Four Seasons Hotel Tunis
see 8 Spa by Clarins

SLEEPING
3 Dar Corniche La Marsa
4 Dar El Kif
5 Dar El Marsa
6 Dar Marsa Cubes
7 Four Seasons Hotel Tunis
8 La Residence

EATING
9 Bistro Nippon
10 Ivy
11 Lapero Tapas & Pintxos
12 Le Golfe
13 Le Grand Bleu
14 Les Ombrelles
15 Sakura Pasta
16 The Cliff

DRINKING & NIGHTLIFE
17 Cafe Houasse
18 Cafe Le Saf Saf
see 5 Dar El Marsa
19 Studio Fan
20 Tangerine Rooftop
21 Tiki Bar

SHOPPING
22 Coeur de l'Artisanat
23 El Marsa Gallery
see 10 Indinya
24 Lyoum
25 Supersouk
see 19 Supersouk Pop-Up
26 XYZ Concept Store
27 Yuka

(usually June through September) and otherwise abandoned and sometimes dismantled until the weather warms up again.

A great spot for sunset, **Tangerine Rooftop** is painted in bold pinks and oranges and pours good cocktails that many find worthy of an Instagram post. **Tiki Bar** *(facebook.com/tikigammarth)* is one of the original scene setters for the wave of beach bars that have popped up along the Gammarth coastline. Expect live rap and hip-hop, plus lots of dancing, after 9pm on weekends.

BEST SPAS

Spa by Clarins: From the first whiff of orange blossom here, the luxurious spa in La Residence hotel (p91) is set to seduce. The staff are professional, and the menu includes several thalassotherapy treatments, which use saltwater and seaweed.

Dar El Marsa: Get scrubbed down with sea salt or covered in a *beldi* soap wrap made from henna and algae. Hammam packages include a scrub, wrap, massage, facial and nail polish.

Four Seasons: One of Tunis' most expensive hotels unsurprisingly has one of the city's top spas. You're sure to feel rejuvenated after treatments that feature Turkish coffee, chocolate, orange blossoms or Tunisian incense.

MASHHOUR/SHUTTERSTOCK

La Marsa Beach (p86)

Sweeping views of La Marsa Beach are on offer at **Dar El Marsa** *(darelmarsa.com)*, an all-season bar-restaurant on the roof terrace of a fashionable hotel. Tables surround a small pool, and its long hours mean you can also enjoy breakfast or a quiet afternoon drink.

Chill out at La Marsa's Best Cafes

Espresso, mint tea and more

La Marsa has a strong cafe culture, which leans both historic and hip. The neighbourhood's most famous, best-loved and most traditional cafe is **Cafe Le Saf Saf** *(facebook.com/le.safsaf)*, which has seating in a lovely tiled courtyard shaded by trees, perfect for a leisurely tea or coffee break. Opposite Saf Saf and with just as much atmosphere, **Café Houasse** has a charming interior with high ceilings, tiled walls and plenty of old photographs.

On this other side of the cool spectrum, **Studio Fan** *(instagram.com/studio__fan)* brings La Marsa's cafe scene into the present. Head through the L'Agora cinema doors and turn left to find the space, which often buzzes with espresso-caffeinated Tunisian students working on projects. Upstairs is a pop-up branch of **Supersouk** *(instagram.com/supersoukshop)*, which sells made-in-Tunisia homewares,

EATING IN LA MARSA & GAMMARTH: SAVOURING THE VIEW

Le Golfe: Italian-ish seafood restaurant with a glamorous step-to-the-sand setting. Named Tunisia's best restaurant by World's 50 Best in 2025. *noon-midnight* €€€

The Cliff: This elevated restaurant serves globe-trotting plates at the edge of the sea. Watching the sunset is a must on a summer's evening. *noon-midnight* €€€

Le Grand Bleu: Perched high above the bay, this seafood spot has a terrace that commands truly fabulous views. Order the Sfax-style octopus. *noon-midnight* €€€

Les Ombrelles: The seafront location draws plenty of customers, and the good-quality French-influenced food keeps them happy. *11.30am-midnight* €€€

clothing and jewellery that make excellent souvenirs. The main **Supersouk** shop (see below) is much larger with a bigger and better selection. It's more difficult to get to but worth visiting if you like what you see here.

On a Shopping Spree

Best galleries and boutiques

La Marsa is packed with small boutiques and concept stores where you can source beautiful homewares, fashion and more.

Even if you don't have pockets deep enough for original artworks, **El Marsa Gallery** *(galerielmarsa.com)* is worth a look. Occupying a beautiful vaulted space behind a grand wooden door in the heart of La Marsa, it's one of Tunisia's most respected and internationally focused commercial galleries, with a small but impressive stable of contemporary artists from around the Arab world. Across the street, **Coeur de l'Artisanat** *(instagram.com/coeurdelartisanat)* has a space stuffed full of handicrafts, bags, *foutas* and handmade soaps.

Everything sold in bijou **Yuka** is made in Tunisia. This shop specialises in quality artisan-designed textiles, including rugs, scarves and towels. **XYZ Concept Store** *(instagram.com/xyzconceptstore)* is a favourite international resident shopping haunt close to Marsa Plage train station. It stocks an eclectic range of clothes, jewellery and homewares from French and local designers.

Lyoum *(lyoum.tn)* sells fun shirts and jumpers with English and Arabic phrases ('Yalla', 'Habibi', 'Hendrix Loved Harissa'), while **Indinya** *(instagram.com/indinya_tunisia)* is the place for upcycled products, such as jasmine- and orange-blossom-scented candles poured into reused beer bottles.

It's a taxi ride outside of the core of La Marsa, but **Supersouk** *(instagram.com/supersoukshop)* is a one-stop shop for made-in-Tunisia goodies by contemporary creatives. Have a peek at the pop-up shop above Studio Fan before you make the trip; the main shop is in Soukra, between La Marsa and Tunis.

TUNIS FOR FAMILIES

Having little ones along with you in Tunis will ensure you get lots of smiles and local contact. Because Tunis isn't a huge city, you always have quick access to the beach if kids start to suffer from sightseeing overload.

Children will enjoy the colourful medina markets and can be bribed with stuffed camels or toy drums, though be aware that the main drags can get crowded and pushchairs are difficult to manoeuvre.

Some children will enjoy a short dose of the Bardo Museum with its Roman mosaics – the pictures tell stories and feature lots of animals. Sidi Bou Said has a popular *bambalouni* (doughnut) stand, and La Marsa has a long sandy beach and plentiful ice-cream shops.

EATING IN LA MARSA & GAMMARTH: BEST INTERNATIONAL EATS

Bistro Nippon: Oozes simple Japanese cool and serves tasty and hearty soup and noodle dishes in a small but trendy space. *noon-3pm & 6.30-10pm Mon-Sat* €€

Ivy: This hipster haven hits the brunch spot with avocado toast, eggs Benedict and vegan-friendly smoothie bowls. *9am-11pm Tue-Sun* €€

Lapero Tapas & Pintxos: A welcome addition to the eating scene, this tiny Spanish-Mexican restaurant offers an extensive menu. *noon-11pm Tue-Sat* €€

Sakura Pasta: Spaghetti and sushi are on the same menu at this cute two-level fusion restaurant – stick with the plates from just across the Mediterranean. *noon-4pm & 7-11.30pm* €€

Places We Love to Stay

€ Budget €€ Midrange €€€ Top End

Medina p58

Dar Ya € This historic mansion is as close as Tunis comes to a hostel. Some of the 15 rooms have bunk beds – a good option for groups of friends – and they share clean bathrooms.

Dar Ben Gacem €€ This gorgeous 17th-century building with original features was given a chic makeover that respects its history while offering contemporary comforts.

Dar Ben Gacem Kahia €€ The sibling property of the original Dar Ben Gacem is a lovely traditional former mansion with mint-green accents, colourful tiling and well-chosen traditional furnishings. A tile museum should be open in the basement by the time you read this.

La Chambre Bleue €€ Restoring this insanely charming house is an ongoing labour of love for its owner, who is a welcoming host. He offers two magnificently decorated suites in the 19th-century upstairs section of the building and a second contemporary-chic room in the 12th-century stables below. Breakfast includes local pastries and homemade jams.

El Patio Courtyard House €€ Modern bathrooms and excellent beds are only two of the many attractive features at this boutique B&B, which offers three prettily decorated rooms in a renovated 18th-century dar deep in the Tourbet El Bey quarter of the medina.

Dar El Medina €€ Run by the family that has lived here for generations, this 19th-century courtyard mansion has been decorated in a simple, stylish mix of the traditional and the contemporary. Service can be grudging, and the ground-floor restaurant doesn't quite hit the mark.

Dar El Jeld €€€ A beautifully renovated 18th-century palace that's well known as the cream of the crop of high-end stays in the medina, with huge luxe suites. Amenities include a spa and hammam, a renowned Tunisian restaurant, and a rooftop bar that also serves international plates.

Centre Ville & the Bardo p66

Grand Hôtel de France € This colonial-era hotel next to the Marché Centrale has a faded 1930s elegance. The cheapest rooms don't include air-con, breakfast or showers.

Hôtel Carlton €€ This hotel on Ave Habib Bourguiba offers good-sized rooms. The decor is as hip as Centre Ville gets, with some decent contemporary art on the walls.

Hôtel Royal Victoria €€ Next to Bab El Bhar at the edge of the medina, this hotel has taken over the former British Embassy. It's overpriced but has an excellent location, and the rooms are comfortable, with double-glazed windows and small bathrooms.

Kyriad Prestige City Center €€ A bit removed from the action but overlooking the République tram station, this modern hotel is a solid choice with helpful staff. The 1st-floor terrace is a great spot to relax.

Carthage p74

Villa Didon €€€ This 10-room designer hotel has an enviable location next to the archaeological ruins of Byrsa Hill. Suites are huge and command views of the Gulf of Tunis – we'd say the best in the city – from private balconies. The hotel has an on-site spa and a terrace restaurant, Le Restô (p75).

Sidi Bou Said p81

La Menara Hôtel & Spa €€ Best 'budget' pick in an expensive neighbourhood. Rooms are gorgeously decorated in traditional styles and named after Tunis' historic eras (Ottoman, Husseinite etc). There's no on-site restaurant, and it's a 15-minute walk to the upper village.

La Villa Bleue €€€ The ultimate Sidi Bou Said experience. Excellent facilities include a lovely spa, hammam, two pools, a restaurant and a hybrid library/bar. All 13 rooms are luxe, but suites are particularly desirable because they have balconies with Mediterranean views.

Dar Said €€€ Travellers who are lucky enough to score one of the elegant sea-facing rooms in this converted villa will be thrilled, but the dark rear rooms may disappoint. The huge garden terrace offers phenomenal views of Sidi Bou Said spilling into the sea.

Maison Dedine €€€ In a secluded location beside Sidi Bou Said Beach, this white cubist boutique hotel is on the Small Luxury Hotels of the

World list and offers a handful of sleek rooms that book out far in advance, plus a stunning infinity pool.

La Marsa & Gammarth

p86

Dar El Kif €€ A more budget-friendly stay in upmarket La Marsa, this little B&B sits next to a park and is a 15-minute walk from the beach. The cosy rooms have traditional Tunisian decorations.

Dar Marsa Cubes €€ In a residential area near the beach, this villa with a handful of individually styled rooms oozes traditional charm. It has a bougainvillea-surrounded pool and is steps from the beach.

Dar El Marsa €€€ Sleek design, a location directly opposite the beach and extremely professional staff are a few of the attractions of this modern hotel, but the hammam and rooftop restaurant-bar with a pool seal the deal. It's worth paying a little extra to upgrade to a sea-view room.

Dar Corniche La Marsa €€€ Originally built as a family's beach home, this adults-only bolthole has five rooms, three of which have balconies looking out to the sea. You'll feel even more at home relaxing around the pool and sitting down at a table with a home-cooked meal.

La Residence €€€ This huge, secluded five-star hotel in Gammarth with a resort ambience is well maintained and professionally operated. Sign up for a cooking class that uses produce from the organic garden, stroll to the beach or swim in the large outdoor pool. The spa is top-notch, and its indoor saltwater pool, sauna and steam room are open to all guests.

Four Seasons Hotel Tunis €€€ This brand promises and delivers unparalleled luxury – with a price tag. These rooms in Gammarth feel a bit old fashioned, but their sandy colours are sure to coax you to the beach. It makes a great stay for families, and staff go out of their way to help.

Dar Said, Sidi Bou Said

Researched by Isabel Putinja

Cap Bon

SANDY BEACHES, ANCIENT RUINS AND ORCHARDS

Rugged coastlines and soft curves of sandy beach complement ancient ruins, age-old fortresses and lush orange orchards in the home of harissa.

Tunisia's northeasternmost region is a small peninsula covered in citrus trees and ribboned with neat rows of vineyards and evergreen olive groves. Cap Bon's fertile earth produces much of the country's fruit and vegetables, including the chilli peppers crushed to make harissa, Tunisia's beloved condiment. Lush orchards provide oranges and mandarins in winter, but also peaches, quinces and watermelons in summer; 80% of Tunisia's wine is also produced here.

Cap Bon is also where modern Tunisian tourism had its beginnings, with the mammoth beach resorts that sprung up in Hammamet and its surroundings from the 1960s. Most visitors gravitate to the sandy beaches of the Gulf of Hammamet, but there are many sublime sweeps of strand extending all the way up the coastline. Meanwhile, Cap Bon's northern shoreline on the Bay of Tunis is just as scenic, especially near the jagged cliffs of Korbous where hot springs spill into the sea.

There's also plenty of history, culture and nature to marvel at here. Relics of Punic and Roman times are scattered across the peninsula, with the most significant archaeological remains in Kerkouane distinguished as the only intact Punic city and a UNESCO World Heritage Site. Nabeul is an important centre for glazed pottery and handicrafts, while the northernmost tip of Cap Bon is rugged and remote.

BTWIMAGES/SHUTTERSTOCK

THE MAIN AREAS

HAMMAMET
Sandy beaches and an enchanting medina.
p96

NABEUL
A hub for glazed pottery.
p103

KELIBIA
A fort, a port and beaches.
p108

For places to stay in Cap Bon, see p115

STANA/SHUTTERSTOCK

Left: Nabeul (p103); above: beach, Hammamet (p96)

Find Your Way

Covering an area of only 2840 sq km, Cap Bon is a compact peninsula flanked by the Gulf of Tunis at its northern shore and the Gulf of Hammamet on its southern coastline.

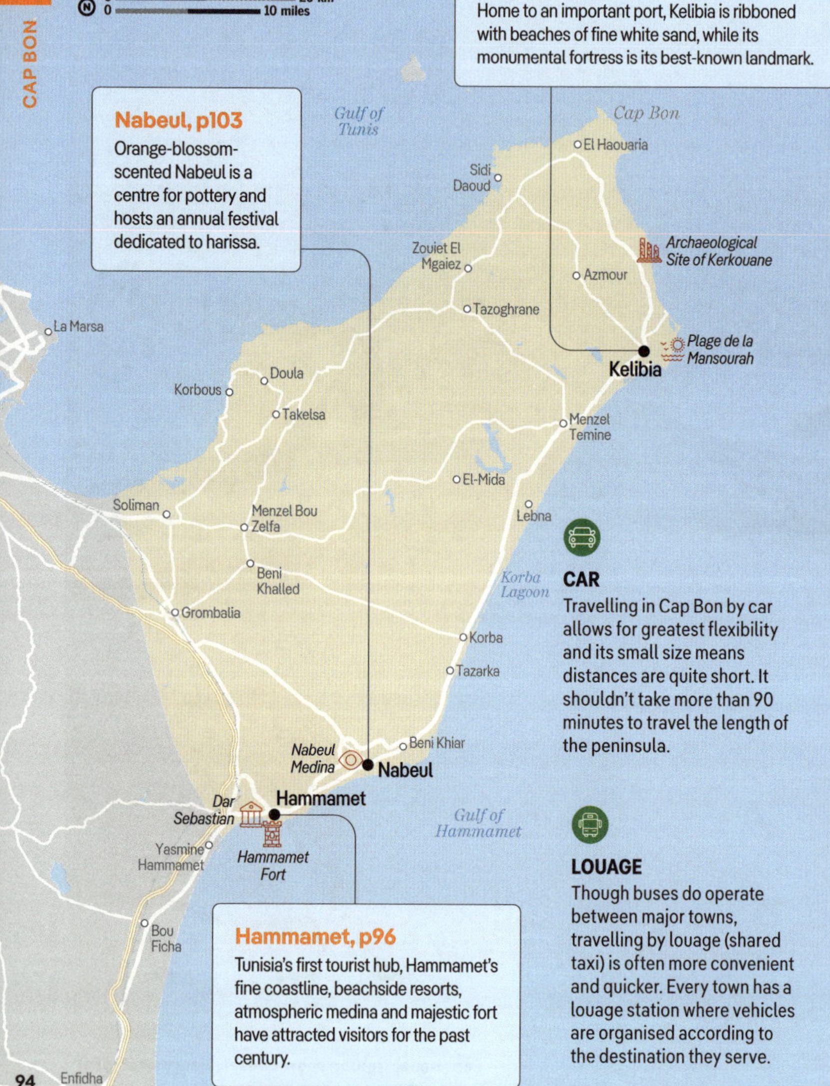

Kelibia, p108

Home to an important port, Kelibia is ribboned with beaches of fine white sand, while its monumental fortress is its best-known landmark.

Nabeul, p103

Orange-blossom-scented Nabeul is a centre for pottery and hosts an annual festival dedicated to harissa.

Hammamet, p96

Tunisia's first tourist hub, Hammamet's fine coastline, beachside resorts, atmospheric medina and majestic fort have attracted visitors for the past century.

CAR

Travelling in Cap Bon by car allows for greatest flexibility and its small size means distances are quite short. It shouldn't take more than 90 minutes to travel the length of the peninsula.

LOUAGE

Though buses do operate between major towns, travelling by louage (shared taxi) is often more convenient and quicker. Every town has a louage station where vehicles are organised according to the destination they serve.

ANDREAS WOLOCHOW/SHUTTERSTOCK

Pottery, Nabeul (p103)

Plan Your Time

Beach lovers and gastronomes will get their fill in Cap Bon. But so will nature enthusiasts, handicraft fans and history buffs.

A Weekend Break

- Wander the labyrinth of narrow lanes in Hammamet's medina and climb the ramparts of **Hammamet Fort** (p96) for sweeping views. Then take the short drive to **Nabeul** (p103) for its **pottery shops** (p105), lively markets and fascinating museum. Round things off with wine tasting in **Grombalia's vineyards** (p101) or with a soak in **Korbous' natural hot springs** (p102).

Five Days in Cap Bon

- Add on a trip to **Kelibia** (p108) for its sublime beaches and a seafood lunch at one of the many waterside bistros here. Then nose around the ruins of the fascinating UNESCO-listed archaeological site of **Kerkouane** (p111), the only surviving example of a Punic city. Finally, press on to the windswept landscape of **El Haouraria** (p112) for a road trip of its best sights.

SEASONAL HIGHLIGHTS

SPRING

The scent of orange blossoms fills the air as warm days draw visitors keen to enjoy Cap Bon without the crowds.

SUMMER

Peak tourist season with high temperatures. The **International Festival of Hammamet** adds a cultural vibe.

AUTUMN

Warm, sunny days continue into October, but the crowds don't. This is an ideal season to explore Cap Bon.

WINTER

Nights can be nippy but there's plenty of daytime sunshine. **Nabeul's harissa festival** spices things up.

Hammamet

HERITAGE ARCHITECTURE | SANDY BEACHES | THALASSOTHERAPHY

GETTING AROUND

Hammamet is served by two airports: Tunis-Carthage International Airport is 72km away, while Enfidha-Hammamet International Airport is more accessible, located 52km from the city centre.

If you're travelling from Tunis, the bus (60 minutes) or direct train (75 minutes) are both comfortable options.

The town itself is compact and easy to navigate on foot. If you want to cover more ground, taxis are affordable and reliable, but some visitors may prefer to rent a car. If you're not in a hurry, buses and share taxis also head up and down the coast.

At the end of the 19th century, Hammamet was not much more than its compact walled medina, home to a few hundred residents. In the 1920s artists and writers flocked here and socialite George Sebastian built his sprawling seaside villa where he hosted dignitaries and the glitterati of the time. By the 1960s mass tourism had firmly arrived with the development of beachside resorts, while the International Festival of Hammamet (p98) put the town on the cultural map.

Hammamet is Cap Bon's biggest destination, with its population exploding fourfold in the summer months. Its beaches of fine sand and turquoise waters are the main tourist draws, but old Hammamet still retains its original allure and charm. As temperatures drop in the winter, the focus shifts to wellness with resorts offering curative thalassotherapy retreats.

A Fort with a View

A visit to Hammamet Fort

The imposing **Hammamet Fort** *(patrimoinedetunisie.com.tn/en/monuments/the-citadel-borj-of-hammamet; entry 8DT)* is the city's most iconic landmark. This commanding 9th-century citadel at the northwestern corner of the medina is also one of Hammamet's oldest structures. A climb up to its ramparts rewards with panoramic 360-degree views – a good way to get your bearings and an idea of the city's size and surroundings.

Buy your entry ticket and venture through the glass door into a courtyard of towering trees and a domed mausoleum of Sidi Bou Ali Mohamed, a holy man. Three hefty cannons and 6m-thick walls hint at the fort's historically important defensive duty to protect from seafaring invaders.

Steps lead up to ramparts circling the entire fort. From the northwest tower you can behold the crescent-shaped gulf

lapped by blue-green waters, with colourful fishing boats resting on the sandy beach. From the opposite tower, take in the medina's dazzling white domes and rooftops and the majestic mountains in the distance. There's a small cafe here for those wanting to linger a bit longer.

A House in Hammamet

Dar Sebastian and gardens

Built in the late 1920s, **Dar Sebastian** *(ccih.gov.tn; entry 5.5DT)* was the beachside home of Romanian-born millionaire and socialite George Sebastian. Here he hosted artists and writers such as Paul Klee and Somerset Maugham and high-level dignitaries including Winston Churchill and Dwight Eisenhower. Sold to the Tunisian state in the 1960s just before his death, this is now the International Cultural Centre of Hammamet.

Poke around the villa's stark white rooms of vaulted ceilings and wide arches now used as a gallery space. Some of its original furnishings are still here. Seek out the long black marble table, a sunken bathtub in the shape of a cross, the marble-tiled swimming pool set in a colonnaded courtyard and a fascinating 1930s refrigerator in the kitchen.

Next, stroll through the jasmine-scented gardens of pine and cacti and orchards of orange, fig and pomegranate trees. The sea-facing Greek-style amphitheatre was built in 1962 as the venue for the International Festival of Hammamet (p98).

TOP TIP

The charm of old Hammamet shines through in the off season when the pace of life slows to a more serene rhythm. Plan a visit after the sun-seeking tourists have gone home to wander the medina's quiet lanes, savour the views from sea-facing cafes and have the beach to yourself.

HAMMAMET THE CULTURAL HUB

The sea-facing neo-Greek amphitheatre set in the leafy grounds of the **International Cultural Centre of Hammamet** – with Dar Sebastian (p97) as its headquarters – is the fabulous venue of Tunisia's biggest cultural fest. Since 1964, the **International Festival of Hammamet** has hosted performances of music, theatre, contemporary dance and art, as well as cinema screenings. Every July and August this celebration of the arts showcases musicians, performers and artists from the Arab and Mediterranean regions as well as other countries from around the world.

In the past decade it has expanded, with free shows at outdoor venues such as Hammamet Fort in an effort to bring the festival to the people. In 2026 the festival is set to celebrate its 60th edition.

Sunset Beach Stroll on Horseback

Horseriding with Club Equus Hammamet

Take in Hammamet's sensational sunsets during a beachside ride with **Club Equus Hammamet** *(clubequus-hammamet.com; 2hr ride 140DT)*. Meet Sami Gaaloul, a competitive endurance rider, and his Swiss-born wife Sonia at their rustic ranch where they lovingly tend to a dozen Amazigh and Arabian racing horses.

Set out on an off-road trail through olive groves and along a dried-out creek to the beach. Ride along the golden sands and watch the sky explode as the sun makes its dramatic descent. If you're up for it, end with a dip in the sea on horseback.

If you're a morning person, ask about sunrise rides. There's also the option to explore mountain trails on half-day or full-day excursions. Riders of all levels of experience are welcome.

A Soak in Healing Waters

Thalassotherapy bliss

Give thalassotherapy a try at **Bio Azur Thalasso** *(bioazurthalasso.com; 20min session 80DT)* and surrender to the curative properties of seawater. Bliss out with a healing soak in

EATING IN HAMMAMET: OUR PICKS

Le Barberousse: Elegant seafood restaurant atop the medina's ramparts. The large bay windows offer panoramic views over the medina and the port. *noon-midnight* €€€

Resto La Plage: Fresh-from-the-boat seafood and many more options at this splendid beachside dining spot with views of the fort. *noon-3.30pm & 7-11.30pm* €€€

Le Petit Pêcheur 1: A firm favourite dishing up classic Tunisian cuisine as well as platters of seafood, pasta and grilled meats. *11.30am-1am* €€€

Restaurant Ettahrir: A simple eatery opening onto a pavement patio, it's widely popular for its plates of Tunisian delights at affordable prices. *noon-midnight* €€

TRAVEL-FR/SHUTTERSTOCK

Bio Azur Thalasso

a whirlpool bathtub filled with mineral-rich seawater and an added boost of essential oils or seaweed serum. Alternatively, book one of their 'regenerating' or 'bio-energetic' **massages** *(50min 140-180DT)* to get complimentary access to the sublime aquatonic pool. Fed with seawater and heated to 33°C, the pool opens onto an open-air section where you can relax in a hot tub while taking in the gorgeous seaviews. Or simply pay 60DT for pool access.

A Spot of Surf & Sun

Water sport adventures

Looking to spend some time in Hammamet's warm waters? Head to **Club Nautique Hammamet** *(98 345 931; 20-49DT per hour)*, smack on the seafront next to Resto La Plage. Here you can rent stand-up paddleboards, one- or two-person kayaks, windsurf boards or sailing dinghies for kids. Private coaching is also available for beginners.

HAMMAMET: FROM FISHING PORT TO RESORT TOWN

Hammamet was a quiet fishing port when it first attracted artists and writers to its sandy shores. Built in 1959, Hotel Miramar symbolised the very beginnings of mass tourism here. By the 1970s hotels numbered to over two dozen, with new constructions gradually taking over the coastlines running north (Hammamet Nord) and south (Hammamet Sud). The tourism boom reached its pinnacle in the late 1990s with the development of Yasmine Hammamet 10km to the southeast. This colossal resort includes sprawling high-end hotels with casinos and spas, a marina, aqua and theme parks, a large conference centre and a brand new but somewhat soulless medina.

DRINKING IN HAMMAMET: CAFES WITH A SEA VIEW

Cafe Sidi Bouhdid: You're lucky if you snag a table at this popular spot tucked between the fort's walls and the water. *6am-midnight*

La Rambla Cafe Resto: A popular stop for brunch with a sea view from the huge sunny patio. Open year-round. *7.30am-midnight*

Pupput le Bar: A trendy hangout serving alcohol with a lounge vibe and beachside bar and restaurant in summer. *hours vary*

Mamaia Beach: This cosy beach bar is the place to enjoy a cocktail with your toes in the sand. *11am-9pm, summer only*

A WANDER THROUGH HAMMAMET'S MEDINA

Venture inside the medina's fortified walls to see what lies amid its labyrinth of narrow alleys, whitewashed walls and painted doorways.

START	END	LENGTH
Bab Bhar	Christian Cemetery	1km, 1 hr

One of six gates, sea-facing **1** **Bab Bhar** opens onto the medina's commercial quarter. Venture into the passageways of the **2** **covered souq** where eager vendors hawk colourful rugs and textiles, leatherwork and mosaic paintings. Pause at **3** **Bab Belghith** to admire the art installation of colourful garlands and plant-filled pots adorning the walls. Retrace your steps and continue to the **4** **Grand Mosque**, the medina's most commanding structure, whose present form dates from the 13th century.

Nearby, look for the bright red and green door of the 17th century **5** **Hammam Sidi Belguith**. Residents still come here for a traditional steam bath, and visitors are welcome. Stop in at the **6** **Dar Khadija Museum** to learn about Hammamet's history and see a detailed 3D model of the medina. Then climb to the terrace for panoramic views over whitewashed rooftops.

Continue along the passageways of the residential quarter, home to 800 residents and perhaps as many cats. Pause at **7** **Gallery Zarrouk** to browse the sublime artwork of artist and polyglot Zarrouk Fehri, a native of the medina.

Exit the medina and look for Hammamet's **8** **Christian Cemetery** abutting the ramparts. It was first conceived in the late 19th century as the final resting place for French soldiers, while just opposite lie the tombs of the Muslim cemetery.

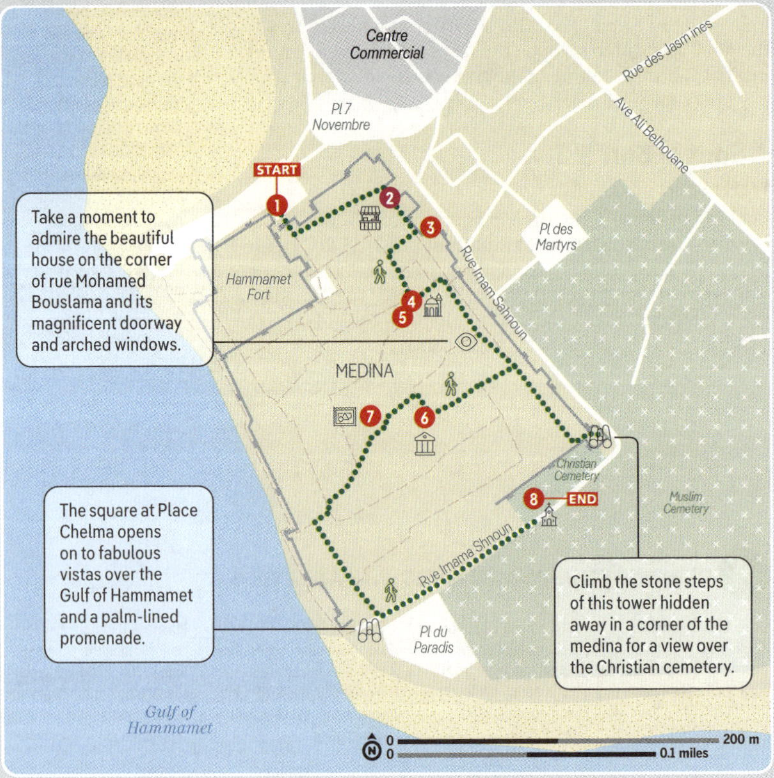

Take a moment to admire the beautiful house on the corner of rue Mohamed Bouslama and its magnificent doorway and arched windows.

The square at Place Chelma opens on to fabulous vistas over the Gulf of Hammamet and a palm-lined promenade.

Climb the stone steps of this tower hidden away in a corner of the medina for a view over the Christian cemetery.

Beyond Hammamet

From Hammamet you can venture into the heart of Cap Bon where lush agricultural fields meet vineyard covered landscapes.

Away from the shiny beachside resorts of Hammamet lies the agricultural heartland of Cap Bon. In summer you'll see piles of watermelon, figs, cactus fruit and tomatoes for sale by the roadsides, while in winter there are crates of oranges, mandarins and lemons. A handful of winemakers produce excellent vintages here and welcome wine lovers into their tasting rooms.

From Hammamet, it's less than an hour's drive to Cap Bon's northern coast on the Gulf of Tunis. The drive along the cliff-side road hugging the coastline to Korbous is particularly picturesque – though a section is currently being repaired following a landslide. The hot springs here draw weekend crowds for a soak in the healing waters.

Places

Grombalia

TIME FROM HAMMAMET: **30 MINS**

Cap Bon in a glass

Swirl and sip your way through some of Tunisia's best varietals during a two-hour winery tour and tasting experience at **Domaine Neferis** *(neferis.com; from 70DT).*

Set in a bucolic valley surrounded by mountains, this is a particularly scenic spot ribboned with 150 hectares of vineyards bordered by olive groves and forestland. A handsome 19th-century chateau is the centrepiece of this estate where 15 varieties of wine are produced. Syrah and Carignan grapes make fruity reds, while Grenache is a delicate rosé. Whites include Chardonnay and Muscat d'Alexandrie – the only native grape growing here.

Rached Kobrosly, winemaker and oenologist, welcomes visitors to the estate with some background on the 2000-year-old history of winemaking in the Grombalia region. He then shares a brief primer on the different stages of the vinification process while leading the way through the winery's state-of-the-art cellars.

The highlight is, of course, a tasting session of four of the estate's award-winning vintages accompanied by a selection of locally produced cheeses, extra virgin olive oil and thick slices of tabouna bread.

GETTING AROUND

If you're looking to explore beyond Hammamet you'll need your own wheels if you want maximum flexibility. Do keep in mind that some rural roads are not well maintained and potholes are common. While there are frequent louages connecting major towns, they don't cover places located anywhere off the main axes. To travel to Korbous by louage, change in Soliman. The only existing train connections are to Nabeul and Tunis.

KORBOUS PAST & FUTURE

Korbous has been a wellness destination since Roman times thanks to its hot springs, but this erstwhile spa town is past its glory days. There's only one sprawling but sad hotel left open and one restaurant, **Le Chalet**. Also, the scenic coastal road between Korbous and the Ain Oktor spring is closed after a section was washed away into the sea following landslides more than a decade ago. Though reconstruction work began in 2020, this has since stalled.

Meanwhile, a massive construction site has taken over the spot where the historic thermal station once stood. Plans are in motion but it may take some time for Korbous to get its groove back.

Korbous

TIME FROM HAMMAMET: **1 HR**

Thermal hot spring bliss

Korbous gets busy at weekends when day-trippers from the capital descend for a dip in the therapeutic natural springs surging from the rocky mountainside. There are seven springs of varying temperatures located in the town and along the coastline, but not all of them are accessible after a landslide washed away part of the road. Each is marked with its name, temperature, mineral content and medical indications.

Ain Echfa is the spring gushing in the town centre, supplying free hot water to the last existing hotel and two hammams in town. Walk a few minutes northwards along the coast to Ain Fakroun while taking in the fabulous views across the Gulf of Tunis of La Goulette and Sidi Bou Said. At only 37°C, this spring is perhaps the least popular.

Press on a bit further up the road to **Aïn Atrous**. This spring swelters at 59°C, filling two small concrete pools before cascading down a few rocks and spilling into the sea. Here you can enjoy the sensation of soaking in seawater warmed by the hot spring.

Hammam soak and steam

Al Arraqah is the town's traditional hammam, operating 24/7 and open to either men or women on alternating days. A steam bath here costs 4DT while a massage can be had for 10DT.

The **Centre Thermal** around the corner is slightly more upmarket with a menu of hammam and spa packages. To experience the curative benefits of spring water, opt for a **75-minute treatment** *(50DT)* that starts with a long soak in a private hot tub. For an extra 5DT you can get an expert rub-down with a loofah glove. This is followed by a slathering of seaweed serum and then a rinse-off before rounding things off with a relaxing essential oil massage.

Other treatment options start at 19DT for a steam bath of 40 minutes, while for 115DT you can enjoy a two-hour splash-out that includes a steam bath, hot-tub soak, massage and facial treatment.

Nabeul

ANCIENT HISTORY | MARKETS | POTTERY HUB

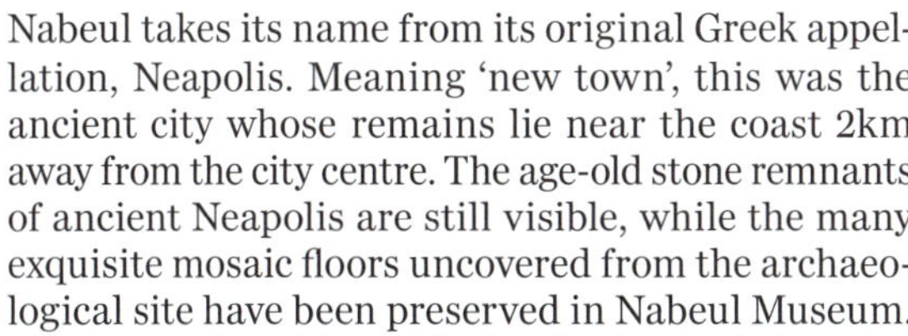

Nabeul takes its name from its original Greek appellation, Neapolis. Meaning 'new town', this was the ancient city whose remains lie near the coast 2km away from the city centre. The age-old stone remnants of ancient Neapolis are still visible, while the many exquisite mosaic floors uncovered from the archaeological site have been preserved in Nabeul Museum.

Today, modern Nabeul is Cap Bon's administrative centre, while its claim to fame is its status as a centre for glazed pottery. This long artisanal tradition also extends to textile weaving and rush mats, which are still handmade by artisans in the medina today.

Nabeul somehow evokes all the senses. With its streets lined with orange trees, the heavenly perfume of orange blossoms reigns in springtime, while in winter the fruits fill the gutters. The tradition of flower distillation continues here, while harissa, Cap Bon's celebrated chilli paste, has its own festival.

GETTING AROUND

Nabeul is well connected by train and bus to Hammamet and Tunis. Yellow shared taxis also operate along the main road between Hammamet and Nabeul and can be flagged at any point on the way. Once you're in town, most attractions can be easily accessed on foot, but the 2km stretch to the beachfront may be a bit of a hike for some. If that's the case, then there are plenty of yellow taxis milling about offering a cheap and hassle-free way to get from A to B.

Markets, Souqs & Shops

Shopping in Nabeul's medina

Nabeul Medina is the centre of the city's commercial heart. This is where everyone shops, from Nabeul natives on a grocery run to day-tripping visitors seeking out souvenirs. The arched gate at the junction of Habib Bourguiba Avenue and Rue Farhat Hached Street is the entryway to the tourist market. Vendors peddle a plethora of goods here, from traditional Tunisian clothing, rugs and pottery to plastic Chinese trinkets and Turkish designer bag knock-offs.

The covered souqs leading to the **Grand Mosque** offer a more local vibe. The smell of leather infuses with incense, and tiny barbershops butt against cubbyhole-sized stores selling everything from spices and sweets to sandalsand cookware.

Head to the alleys behind Martyr's Square to find the humming produce market where locals buy homegrown fruit and veg. For a quick lunch, buy fresh fish at the fish market and have it fried up for you and served with a side of salade mechouia at one of the half-dozen small eateries next door.

TOP TIP

Thursdays are market days in Nabeul, when the shopping throng swells into crowds in the streets branching off eastwards from Martyr's Square and the lanes of the medina.

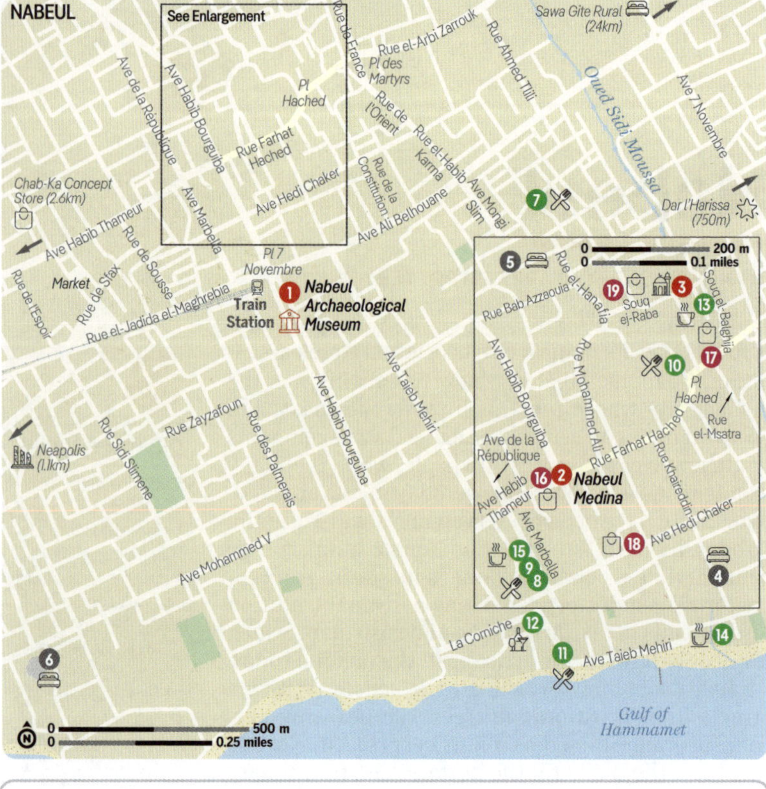

HIGHLIGHTS
1 Nabeul Archaeological Museum
2 Nabeul Medina

SIGHTS
3 Grand Mosque de Nabeul

SLEEPING
4 Dar El Gaied
5 Dar R'Bat
6 Gaïa Hotel

EATING
7 Dar Mrad
8 Le Patio
9 Restaurant Bon Kif
10 Restaurant Le Bonheur
11 Sunset Coffee & Resto

DRINKING & NIGHTLIFE
12 After Work Lounge
13 Cafe Maure Chez Hajji
14 L'Auberge
15 Origin Bakery

SHOPPING
16 Abel Gharbi Poterie de Nabeul
17 Craft Store
18 Nattes de Nabeul
19 Nessege Artisanat & Creation

Ancient Mosaics & Terracotta Treasures

Highlights of Nabeul Museum

Stop in at the **Nabeul Archaeological Museum** *(patrimoinedetunisie.com.tn/en/museums/the-museum-of-nabeul; 8DT)* for some historical background on Cap Bon and the ancient town of Neapolis, the city's precursor.

A top draw here is the collection of splendid 4th-century mosaics, moved to the museum from the House of the Nymphs in the archaeological site of Neapolis. Search out the superb depictions of Poseidon rescuing the nymph Amymon, Chryses pleading with Agamemnon while seated between Achilles and Ulysses, and the three Muses bathing in a fountain.

Other highlights are the terracotta statues uncovered in the Punic-Roman sanctuary of Thinissut. These exquisite life-sized statues of female forms represent the goddess Tanit and include a lion-headed goddess, several sphinxes and a mother-goddess nursing her child. The museum is closed on Mondays.

Walking among Age-Old Stones

Exploring ancient Neapolis

The archaeological site of ancient **Neapolis** *(patrimoinedetunisie.com.tn/en/sites/neapolis; 5DT)* lies on a quiet strip of land between a busy main road and the sea. These are the remains of a Roman city built on the rubble of a Punic settlement established here in the 5th century BCE and destroyed during the Third Punic War (149–146 BCE).

Follow the path leading through a grassy field and then head left to reach the **House of the Nymphs**. In the rectangular site, look for the remains of 4th-century mosaic floors made up of geometrical patterns. These are unfortunately badly damaged, but the Nabeul Archaeological Museum shelters the preserved floors recovered from here. Next find a semi-circular wall of what was once a fountain decorated with a striking mosaic of the head of the Titan Oceanus surrounded by fish and other sea creatures.

Retrace your steps and head towards the sea to reach the ancient **fish salting factory**, the other attraction here. The rectangular vats and circular basins set in the floors were used to store salted fish and garum, a salty fish sauce favoured by the Romans. Also lying here are what's left of handsome mosaic floors in two attractive patterns. The site is closed on Mondays.

The Power of Flowers

The art of flower distillation

Have a go at the age-old tradition of flower distillation at this hands-on workshop organised by **Sawa Taste of Tunisia** *(sawataste.com; from 100DT)*. Artisan Rania Mansour Ep Snoussi welcomes participants to her perfume-infused workspace with an introduction to the seasonal flowers and herbs used to make distillates. She then shares how these are used not only in Tunisian cuisine to flavour dishes and desserts, but also for skin care and medicinal purposes.

After moving to the distillation room, you can see traditional distilling equipment consisting of copper boilers connected with pipes to vast terracotta pots. Watch as the boiling water and steam transform the plant material into vapour, which

BEST SHOPS FOR HANDICRAFTS

Abel Gharbi Poterie de Nabeul: A vast selection of pottery at fixed prices. Look for the pottery-filled courtyard opposite the medina gate on Habib Bourghiba Ave.

Nessege Artisanat & Creation: You'll find Omar Moussa busy at his loom weaving exquisite scarves, *fouta* (cotton bath towels) and other textiles from natural fibres.

Nattes de Nabeul: A treasure trove of all things made of woven rushes or palm leaves sold at fixed prices.

Craft Store: Pocket-sized shop in the covered souq peddling clothing, textiles, pottery and high-quality souvenirs crafted locally.

Chab-Ka Concept Store: Out-of-the-way boutique of jewellery, glassware, sculpture and objets d'art created by Tunisian artists and artisans.

EATING IN NABEUL: OUR PICKS

Dar Mrad: A changing menu of traditional home-style Tunisian fare served in a pleasing setting with indoor and outdoor spaces. *noon-5pm Mon-Sat* €€

Restaurant Le Bonheur: A cheery eatery in the medina decorated with colourful tiles and dishing up plates of couscous and other Tunisian specialities. *10am-10pm* €€

Le Patio: An upmarket restaurant with a contemporary vibe and menu of seafood, steaks and Tunisian cuisine. Alcohol served. *noon-11pm* €€€

Restaurant Bon Kif: A local favourite for its seafood dishes, extensive list of Tunisian wines and delightful covered courtyard. *10am-4pm, 6pm-midnight* €€€

NABEUL: A CERAMICS HUB

Ameni Ebdelli, ceramic artist. *@el_tohfa_marque*

Nabeul has a very long pottery tradition that goes back centuries (p314). Today, there are many potters here working in the traditional style as well as using more modern approaches.

The traditional pottery of Nabeul is characterised by the colours used: red, blue, green and yellow. These are colours found in nature. Then there's the motifs we use. For example, *affset essid*, which translates as 'lion's paw', is a very common motif, as is the fish eye motif.

I studied many methods to work clay and decorate ceramics and like to add a modern touch to my own work. For example, I enjoy neriage, a technique that mixes two types of clay.

condenses into an aromatic water. A round-bottomed bottle called a *feshka* collects the precious drops of floral water.

Spicing Things up with Harissa

A harissa culinary workshop

Roll up your sleeves and try your hand at preparing harissa during this two-hour participative workshop at **Dar l'Harissa** *(sawataste.com; from 100DT)*. In their culinary space dedicated to this much-loved spicy condiment, Imed Ben Attig and Hela Haddad introduce participants to the six main varieties of chillies grown in Cap Bon.

This is followed by insights into the harissa production process. After harvest the chillies are strung into 5m-long garlands and dried in the sun for up to three weeks. They can also be smoked in traditional ovens fuelled with charcoal made of olive or almond wood to add flavour.

Then it's time to get to work with a traditional pestle and mortar, called *haroussa* (or 'crusher') in Arabic, hence the word harissa. In goes garlic, olive oil, salt and the main ingredient: chilli peppers. A second batch is prepared with a mechanical grinder and followed by a taste test to decide which is superior: the modern or the traditional method?

The workshop winds up with a tasting session of Imed and Hela's high-quality artisanal spreads prepared with harissa, plus nuts, olives, fruit and other local ingredients. There's also the option to end this culinary experience with a traditional meal of harissa-infused couscous.

Street-Food Delights

Snacks by the sea

Do like *les nabeuliens* and descend to **La Corniche**, the city's seafront, on summer evenings. Join the throng out for a stroll on the breezy seaside promenade after sheltering indoors from the daytime heat.

The summer evening atmosphere here is festive and this means food is involved. Lining the promenade is a string of vendors frying up Tunisian street-food favourites. Fricassé, *brik* (savoury filled pastry), *bambalouni* (sugared doughnuts) and *ftira* (flat doughnut) are some of the delectable snacks you can sample. Try them all! These are washed down with glasses of hot mint tea or cold soft drinks.

In the winter the street-food scene shuts downs but you can find these fried delights in the evenings at **Sunset Coffee & Resto** at the end of Taib Mhiri St.

DRINKING IN NABEUL: OUR PICKS

Cafe Maure Chez Hajji: A colourful cafe of traditional tiled walls and wooden tables in the heart of the medina. *6am-9pm* €

L'Auberge: Chilled music and the sea-facing patio create the right vibe at this delightful spot for a drink or snack. *10am-1am Mon-Fri, 8am-2am Sat & Sun* €

Origin Bakery: Bite into brownies, jumbo doughnuts or cinnamon rolls washed down with your favourite brew at this trendy cafe. *6am-midnight* €€

After Work Lounge: One of the few bars in the city. Located at Hotel Byzance, there's a cheery decor and happy hour specials. *1.30pm-1am* €€

Beyond Nabeul

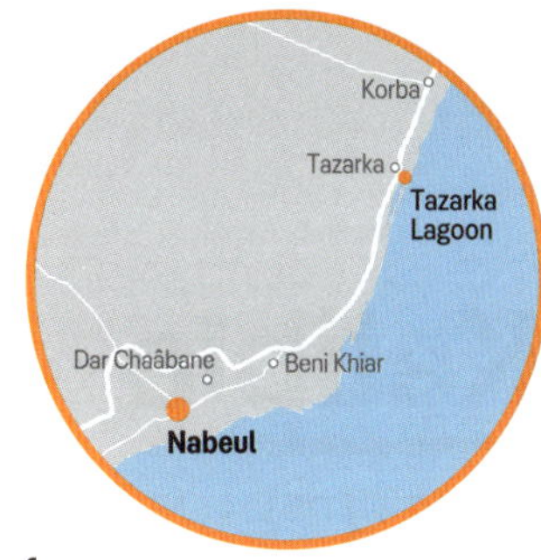

Extending northwards along the coastline from Nabeul lies a string of gorgeous beaches of fine sand indented by shallow lagoons.

If you leave Nabeul behind and travel along the C27 running parallel to the coast, you'll soon pass through Dar Chaabane, a dusty suburb and centre for stonework. Next you'll come to Beni Khiar, a village known for its weaving industry. Close by lies lovely **Maamoura Beach** with the endless soft sands continuing all the way to Tazarka Lagoon. This is the home to a posse of flamingos and many other migratory birds. Further up the coast after Korba stretches a long, thin length of lagoon sandwiched between the main road and the shoreline. These shallow waters are another popular flamingo hangout.

Tazarka Lagoon

TIME FROM NABEUL: **25 MINS**

Flamingos and beachscapes

Tazarka Lagoon is a draw for bird-watchers and nature photographers. Sandwiched between the coastal road and the sea, the lagoon extends about 2km, covering an area of 150 hectares. Though this is a protected area of great biodiversity, it's far from spotless and is often littered with plastic. A local environmental group takes charge with an annual clean-up.

Here you have a good chance to see flamingos throughout the year, but the size of their flocks can vary depending on the migratory season. If the flamingos are not in during your visit, you can spot some of the other 60 species of birds that hang out here. Wading through the warm waters are herons, plovers, black-winged stilts and great cormorants, among others. Clamber up the wooden observation tower for a 360-degree panorama over the lagoon and seascape.

It will take about 90 minutes to stroll along the lagoon and then return to your starting point by tracing the shoreline along a sweep of lovely, sandy beach.

Places

GETTING AROUND

If you plan to travel to other places in Cap Bon, moving around by car is ideal because you can stop off at points of interest along the way. Take care on rural roads, which can be pockmarked with potholes. If you plan to only cover major towns, travelling by louage could be a good option. A regular train service connects Nabeul to Hammamet, while buses are also frequent on this route and to Kelibia.

Kelibia

MAJESTIC FORT | SANDY BEACHES | FISHING PORT

GETTING AROUND

Regular buses and louages travel along the coastal road to Kelibia from Nabeul. Kelibia as a town is a bit spread out, which means it's convenient to have access to a car. This is especially the case if you want to discover the many beaches north of the city centre. While there is also a public bus service operating here, this option doesn't offer a lot of flexibility. Of course there are plenty of taxis zipping around town, ready to take you where you need to go for a very reasonable fare.

TOP TIP

As an alternative to generic hotels, consider staying in a dar (p115), a traditional house of courtyards and charming guest rooms offering bed and breakfast-style accommodation and plenty of old world charm.

You'll spot Kelibia's towering fortress looming in the distance long before you arrive in the city. Repeatedly destroyed and reconstructed, a defensive citadel has stood on this hilltop overlooking the city since the Punic era. This is, after all, a strategic spot on the northeastern corner of the Cap Bon peninsula: just 70km away lies the Italian island of Pantelleria, while Sicily is 140km from here.

Kelibia is also home to an important fishing port, but just northwards of the docks the vibe suddenly transforms. The city's pièce de résistance lies here in the heavenly beaches of ethereal soft white sand. It's like you've just teleported to a chic beach town, with sandy coves stretching before you, one after the other – though unfinished construction projects mar the tableau somewhat. Finally, Kelibia has a fantastic food scene and plenty of cafes where you can kick back and just enjoy the gorgeous sea views.

Monumental Walls & Medieval Towers

A climb to Kelibia Fort

Kelibia Fort *(patrimoinedetunisie.com.tn/en/monuments/the-fortress-citadel-or-borj-of-kelibia; entry 8DT)* looms over the city from its perch on a hilltop overlooking the sea. It's a bit of a climb to reach on foot from one of the footpaths snaking up from Avenue des Martyrs, but you can easily access it by road.

Covering an area of 1.5 hectares, this defensive fort of thick, crenellated walls and squat towers is Tunisia's largest. From its 12th-century ramparts forming the shape of a polygon there are panoramic views across the sea.

While its foundations date from Punic times, the fortress was destroyed and rebuilt multiple times due to its strategically important position on the northeastern corner of Cap Bon. Within its walls you can make out the ruins of a 6th-century Byzantine citadel, as well as a few stone remains of an Ottoman mosque and bathhouse.

HIGHLIGHTS
1 Kelibia Fort
2 Plage de la Mansourah

SIGHTS
3 Ezzahra
4 Hammam Laghzez
5 Kelibia Port
6 Petit Paris
7 Plage de Sidi Mansour

SLEEPING
8 Dar Colibri
see 9 Dar Gino
9 Dar Kenza

EATING
10 Le Goeland
11 Maison Znaidi
12 Mosaïque Resto-Café
13 Restaurant El Mansourah
14 Toro Fish

DRINKING & NIGHTLIFE
15 Café du Fort

Descend the road opposite the entrance to find **Café du Fort**. The vibe here is unfussy and the drink list limited, but the views from its vast terrace of the beaches extending northwards are mesmerising.

Breakfast with Fishers

Early morning at Kelibia port

Kelibia's bustling **port** is one of the most important in Tunisia. It's home to Cap Bon's largest fishing fleet, where 13,600 tonnes of fish are hauled in from the sea each year, representing

EATING IN KELIBIA: OUR PICKS

Toro Fish: Choose your fresh fish from the fishmonger next door and have it fried up. Popular dishes are stuffed squid and octopus couscous. *10am-midnight* €€€

El Mansourah: Delightful upmarket dining spot on a rocky bay with tables perched on wooden platforms at the water's edge. Alcohol served. *8am-midnight* €€€

Le Goeland: Snag a table here at sunset for a meal with a view at this superb restaurant in the fishing port. *7am-midnight* €€

Mosaïque Resto-Café: Another charming eatery in a picture-perfect setting overlooking the water. Head to the upper floor for the best panoramic vistas. *7am-midnight* €€

KELIBIA'S BEST BEACHES

Petit Paris: Just north of the city centre lies this small cove of fine white sand lapped by shallow crystalline waters.

Plage de La Mansourah: Separated by a cape from Petit Paris, another sublime but much bigger curve of impossibly soft white sand.

Plage de Sidi Mansour: Even bigger yet, with an expanse of 200m of the fine powdery stuff. Beware of the strong currents here.

Hammam Laghzez: Another sweep of pristine beach that draws a throng of sun worshippers attracted by the beachside bars and water sports.

Ezzahra: Beachside villas back onto this tranquil expanse of sand so pearly-white you'll think you're on a tropical island.

GIOVANNI RINALDI/SHUTTERSTOCK

Kelibia Fort (p108)

15% of the country's total production. It's no surprise that the national marine fishing school is located here and Kelibia is also known for its shipbuilding industry.

Head to the port in the early morning to watch as the fishers come in and barter their day's catch at the dockside wholesale fish market. The port's resident cats eagerly await their arrival, as do a clutch of early-morning shoppers. Some have their freshly bought fish grilled up immediately on the spot, while vendors are busy here frying up fresh *ftira,* a breakfast favourite.

Sweet Delights: a Taste of Kaak

Kelibia's beloved sweet

Kaak de Kélibia, Kelibia's best-known sweet, is ring-shaped and filled with a delicious paste made of dates. Using fingers or tools, delicate lines or patterns are pressed into the dough before they're slapped onto the sides of a traditional *tabouna* oven to bake.

This tasty treat is prepared at home for special occasions, with each family having a recipe handed down from mother to daughter. Stop for a taste of *kaak de Kélibia* at **Maison Znaidi**, a patisserie on Avenue des Martyrs.

Beyond Kelibia

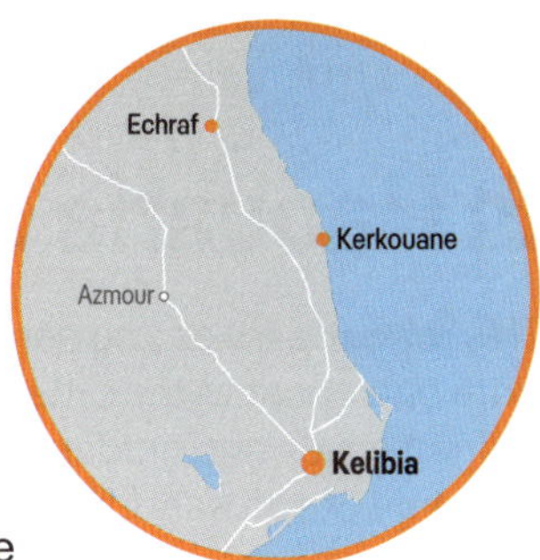

From Kelibia it's easy to reach the fascinating ancient Punic site of Kerkouane and the rugged cliffs of El Haouaria.

Kelibia is the gateway to Cap Bon's windswept northernmost tip at El Haouraria. With rugged cliffs and a rocky coastline, this remote spot has an edge-of-the-world feel to it. Coastal gusts sweep across the dusty landscape, especially in the wet winter months, setting in motion the turbines of the wind farm here.

El Haouraria is also a refuge for many migratory birds thanks to both its climate and its unique geographical location. Every spring tens of thousands of birds travelling between Africa and Europe make a halt here before continuing their journey across the Mediterranean. A falconry festival (Le Festival de l'Épervier) dedicated to sparrowhawks is held here for four days every June.

Places

Kerkouane

TIME FROM KELIBIA: **20 MINS**

Exploring the last Punic city

Occupying an isolated spot on the edge of a rocky shoreline, the **Archaeological Site of Kerkouane** *(patrimoinedetunisie.com.tn/en/sites/kerkouane; entry 8DT)* is exceptional as the only surviving example of a Punic city.

The site itself (closed on Mondays) is a maze of reconstructed walls a metre high outlining perfectly geometric dwellings of rooms and courtyards, some with intact mosaic floors. It's not possible to walk between the walls, but there are several raised viewing platforms allowing for a closer look. Weathered signs in Arabic, English and French offer pertinent details including maps, illustrations and even street addresses. Follow the numbered trail and keep your eyes open for signboards highlighting the main sights.

Search out clues hinting at the ancient city's sophisticated urban planning. This was a fortified city protected by double defensive walls. Streets are arranged in a neat, grid-like pattern and the remains of a sewerage system are visible.

The **House of Tanit** is sheltered by a canopy where a figure of the Punic goddess is traced on a coral-coloured floor speckled with white dots. Peer closely within the walls of the **House with a Central Courtyard** and you'll spot wells and channels for water drainage and a bathroom equipped with a bright red tub – a surprising detail visible in many other dwellings.

Continues on p114

GETTING AROUND

To travel to Kerkouane, you can catch a collective taxi to El Haouaria from the corner of Ali Belhouane and Abou El Kacem Chebbi Avenues and ask the driver to drop you at the turn-off for the archaeological site. From there it's a pleasant 30-minute walk. If you plan to have a look around El Haouraria, you'll need a car as sights are spread out. From Kelibia, louages travel to Nabeul and Tunis.

ROAD TRIP

El Haouaria Highlights

This road trip takes you across the rugged tip of Cap Bon peninsula from one coast to the other and up its highest peak. Nose around Roman caves and hidden coves along the way, stopping off at beaches of soft sand. Then head up into the hills towards the peninsula's culminating point for panoramic views of cliffs and coastlines.

1 The Roman Caves

Start your driving adventure on the rocky western coast where massive stone blocks were excavated during Punic times to build Carthage's monumental buildings and El Jem's celebrated amphitheatre. Horizontal tunnels were cut into the rock of this **quarry**, creating almost a hundred caves. This site is officially closed because of the danger of falling rocks.

The drive: Leaving the coast behind, drive uphill for two minutes towards town.

2 Falconry Centre

This small **centre dedicated to falconry** is run by the Regional Association of Falconers of Nabeul and is worth a stop just for the dreamy sea views. The open-air theatre serves as the venue for the annual falconry festival, while a small exhibition space documents past editions.

The drive: Next, drive for 15 minutes southeast across town towards the eastern coast while taking in the mountain vistas to the north.

STUDIOANGHIFOTO/SHUTTERSTOCK

Coastline with Roman caves

3 Ras Ed Drek Beach

This long strip of **sandy beach** has a forlorn look in the winter but comes alive in summer. Park at the small port at its northern end and set off on foot along the small path running northwards along the coastline. You'll soon come across a series of quiet rocky coves lapped by crystal-clear waters.

The drive: Leaving the port, take the road up into the hills. It heads northwest before swerving towards the east and opening onto panoramic views.

4 El Haouaria Fortress

Perched on the cliffside looms this **19th-century fortress**. From this scenic viewpoint you can take in the sweeping seascape and long expanse of white sandy beaches extending towards Kelibia.

The drive: Drive back to town and then take the road winding north up the mountain. It's about a 25-minute drive to the top.

5 Djebel Abiod

Stop before you reach the telecommunications tower at the mountain's 390m-high **summit**, and follow the path to the left on foot. You'll soon come to a small shelter from where there are dazzling 360-degree views across the mountainscape and the blue waters below. This is a favourite spot with bird-watchers in the spring.

The drive: It's a 10-minute winding drive downwards towards town.

6 Caffe Ristorante Dei Falcon

Conclude your tour with a drink or meal with a view at this upmarket **dining spot**. The large bay windows and outdoor pavilions set among olive trees overlook a gorgeous patch of countryside. Arrive just in time to catch the spectacular sunset.

KERKOUANE: THE LAST PUNIC CITY

Kerkouane was discovered in 1952, and declared a UNESCO World Heritage Site in 1985 for its outstanding value as the only surviving example of a Punic city. Its earliest relics unearthed here date from 6th century BCE, while evidence suggests the city was abandoned during the First Punic War (264–241 BCE). What makes it exceptional is that unlike other Punic cities, it was never reinhabited and built over by the Romans. So far, only about a quarter of the site has been excavated, while a necropolis 1.5km away is yet to open to the public. Many extraordinary artefacts recovered from the tombs as well as the ancient city are on display in the **Kerkouane Museum** on-site, a must visit.

WITR/SHUTTERSTOCK

Archaeological Site of Kerkouane

Continued from p111

Facing the seafront, the **House with a Peristyle** was one of the grandest homes. A few pillars that once supported its peristyle are left standing. The **Punic Temple** made up of three adjoining rooms is in the heart of the city, with the **Priest's House** next door. Look for the **public bathhouse** with benches along its walls, and the **House of the Sphinx**: an illustration suggests what it looked like during Punic times.

Echraf

TIME FROM KELIBIA: **30 MINS**

A millennial olive tree

About 200m from the main road linking Kelibia to El Haouaria, on the edge of the small village of Echraf, stands one of Tunisia's oldest olive trees.

This impressive **age-old olive tree** occupies a grassy clearing next to a white-domed mausoleum. Its thick, gnarled trunk, twisted with age, has a circumference of over 6m, while its tangled branches create a canopy spanning 40m.

A marble plaque declares it dates from the Punic era and testing has revealed the tree is more than 2500 years old. It reportedly still bears fruit, enough to be pressed into a small but precious quantity of olive oil believed to be this ancient tree's elixir.

EATING IN EL HAOUARIA: OUR PICKS

La Daurade: Superb seafood and Mediterranean cuisine with breathtaking sea views. In summer, dine at the water's edge. *9am-midnight* **€€€**

Ristorante Bellariva dalla Lina: An Italian trattoria dishing up generous plates of home-style Italian fare. No alcohol. *12.30-3pm & 7pm-midnight* **€€**

La Sirène: On the menu of this popular family-run restaurant you'll find platters of fresh seafood and home-cooked Tunisian favourites. *9am-11pm* **€€**

Pizzeria Dibeur: For pocket-friendly fast food of pizza, pasta, sandwiches and savoury and sweet crepes cooked up in front of you. *9am-11pm* **€€**

Places We Love to Stay

€ Budget €€ Midrange €€€ Top End

Hammamet

p96

Villa Phoenicia €€ A delightful B&B a three-minute walk from the beach with cosy guest rooms and balconies, terraces and lounges to relax in.

Hotel Royal Azur €€€ Next door to the Bio Azur Thalasso spa; a lavish hotel with spacious sea-facing rooms and suites, four restaurants, four bars, multiple pools and a private beach.

The Orangers Garden €€€ A swish, sea-facing resort of roomy suites and bungalows in palm-tree-filled grounds. Perks include a spa, hammam, swimming pools and private sandy beach.

La Badira €€€ An uber-chic adults-only resort with an all-white minimalist vibe. Some suites boast plunge pools, while on-site extras include a Clarins spa, infinity pool and private beach.

Nabeul

p103

Dar R'Bat €€ A lovingly restored traditional dar near the medina with guest rooms opening onto flower-filled courtyards, a plunge pool and rooftop chill-out space.

Gaïa Hotel €€ Outside the city centre but good value for comfortable rooms with balconies and a minimalist vibe. On-site you'll find a restaurant and bar lounge.

Sawa Gite Rural €€ A quiet rural retreat offering guest rooms on a B&B basis or an entire villa. Join their cooking classes and bread-making workshops.

Dar El Gaïed €€€ Set in lush gardens, this palatial house with many original furnishings features double and triple suites, three outdoor pools and an elegant bar and restaurant.

Kelibia

p108

Dar Colibri €€€ A beautifully decorated B&B combining traditional details with contemporary accents. Perks include a pool, hammam and delightful rooftop terrace.

Dar Kenza €€€ Another beautiful dar done up in a traditional aesthetic offering 12 rooms and four suites, some boasting balconies with sea views.

Dar Gino €€€ A two-minute walk from the beach, this elegant B&B of eight rooms and three suites is set in a lovely traditional dar with a pool.

El Haouaria

p112

Villa Zembra €€€ A sea-facing villa with colourful, cosy rooms and suites and a host of activities on offer including aerial yoga, tai chi and qigong.

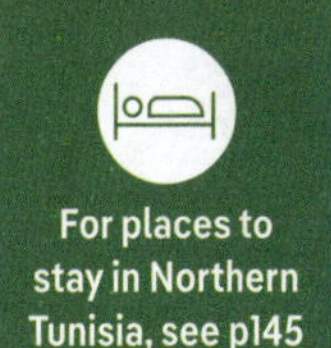

For places to stay in Northern Tunisia, see p145

ZAGHOUDI MAHRAN/SHUTTERSTOCK

Above: Beni Mtir Dam (p136); right: Cap Angela (p129)

Researched by
Paul Stafford

Northern Tunisia

WILD BEACHES AND MOUNTAIN ESCAPES

Head in the opposite direction to the crowds from Tunis to discover ruined Roman towns, hikes through rolling mountainscapes and secluded, sandy coves.

The northernmost realms of Tunisia, beyond the reaches of Carthage and Tunis, are overlooked by all but the most intrepid of overseas visitors. In contrast to the major tourist resorts of the south, there is virtually no development at all along the over 240km (149 miles) of coastline north and west of Tunis all the way to the Algerian border. Even Cap Angela, which marks the northern tip of the African continent, is a secluded coastal gnarl, devoid of fanfare and accessed only by an unpaved road that floods in winter.

This is a much greener version of Tunisia, dominated by off-grid beaches, sprawling lakes and reservoirs, and forest-clad mountains. Outside of the region's major urban centres – the charming fishing port of Bizerte in the northeast and Genoese fort-crowned Tabarka in the northwest (which lie 126km apart by road) – a gentle and undulating wilderness unfurls. There are plenty of opportunities to encounter verdant mountain landscapes around Aïn Draham, Tunisia's main hill station destination, and for wildlife spotting around Lake Ichkeul, Tunisia's only UNESCO Natural World Heritage Site.

Further inland, you'll encounter the fecund farmland of the Medjerda River valley, which has long attracted empires for its fertility. Here, you'll find plenty of fascinating Roman ruins, including Chemtou's former marble quarry, Bulla Regia's unique subterranean mansions, and the remnants of Utica, a former port now located 15km from the sea.

HICHEM KAOUNE/SHUTTERSTOCK

THE MAIN AREAS

BIZERTE
Colourful old port and delicious seafood.
p120

AÏN DRAHAM
Cork oak forests and mountain trails.
p133

Find Your Way

With mighty lakes, the Kroumirie mountains and miles of secluded countryside and coastline in between, parts of northern Tunisia are tough to reach. However, the main towns are well connected to Tunis, making them easier to visit.

Aïn Draham, p133

Explore the evergreen cork oak forests, waterfalls and trails through these Atlas range foothills from a pleasant hill town.

Bizerte, p120

Bizerte's historic core is a delightful, picturesque slice of the Mediterranean with its wooden fishing boats, walled medina and painted waterfront homes.

Mediterranean Sea
Bizerte
Menzel Jemil
Lake Bizerte
Menzel Bourguiba
Raf Raf
Sidi Ferdjani
Lake Ichkeul
Ichkeul National Park
Sejnane
Mateur
Gulf of Tunis
Tabarka
Nefza
Sebkhet er-Ariana
La Marsa
La Calle
Zirba
Tebourba
TUNIS
Yusuf
Aïn Draham
Béja
Oued Medjerda
Ben Arous
Soliman
ALGERIA
Medjez el Bab
Oulad Cheikh Ayed
Bulla Regia
Bou Salem
Grombalia
Oued Medjerda
Jendouba
Ghardimaou
0 20 km
0 10 miles

CAR

Renting a car is by far the easiest way to get around. The best rental services are in nearby Tunis. For the remote mountains and beaches, consider taking a 4WD as the roads are frequently unforgiving, even when paved.

LOUAGE OR TRAIN

Daily trains connect Tunis to Bizerte, Béja and Mateur (an option for Ichkeul). Elsewhere, the omnipresent louages form a broad network that connects most towns and cities. But expect to walk or change to complete most trips.

GIOVANNI RINALDI/SHUTTERSTOCK

Vieux Port (p122), Bizerte

Plan Your Time

Northern Tunisia ticks the boxes for all sorts of itineraries. History buffs, seekers of the great outdoors, beach lovers and gourmets all have something to look forward to.

Dipping Your Toe In

- Use **Bizerte** (p120) as a base to explore the North for a few days. Start in the pretty labyrinth of the city's **kasbah medina** (p120), then take a walking tour of the **Vieux Port** (p123) and sample fresh seafood at one of the many restaurants. The next day, hike **Cap Farina**'s (p125) forest paths from Raf Raf. Finally, take a guided tour of **Ichkeul National Park** (p127).

A Week to Explore

- Hire a car to visit the oft-overlooked corners of northern Tunisia. Head to Bizerte, stopping at the **Utica** (p126) ruins. Then drive west to the pottery makers of **Sejnane** (p129) and the **Genoese fortress** (p139) in Tabarka. Switch the coast for **Oued Zen's mountain trails** (p134) around Aïn Draham. Finally, visit the sunken mansions of **Bulla Regia** (p140).

SEASONAL HIGHLIGHTS

SPRING

The ideal time to see flower-filled meadows. The best temperatures for exploring outdoor archaeological sites.

SUMMER

Concerts at Bulla Regia. **Festival International** in Bizerte. Outdoor pursuits in Aïn Draham's cooler climate.

AUTUMN

The best time for the remote north coast, such as Cap Angela: the weather is still hot but the roads remain dry.

WINTER

Chilly and rainy, with possible snow around Aïn Draham. Thousands of migratory birds flock to Ichkeul.

Bizerte

QUAINT PORT | MEDINA SCENES | DRAMATIC BEACHES

GETTING AROUND

Bizerte's compact old town is walkable, with some limited accessibility (relative to elsewhere in Tunisia) around the Vieux Port for those with mobility restrictions. Local buses 2 and 21 connect Rue Bourguiba with the Corniche. Daily trains run to Tunis from **Bizerte Train Station**, 1.2km southwest of the Vieux Port. The main station for buses to Tunis's Bab Saadoun and Tunis-Carthage Airport is **SRT Bizerte** (aka Zarzouna), located near the P8 road, 1km south of Bizerte Bridge. If you're driving but staying in the Medina, use the paid **Parking Vieux Port** *(7.5DT overnight)* on Rue de la Regence.

TOP TIP

To see Bizerte at its best, visit the Vieux Port at sunset, when the golden light adds its palette to the already pretty display on the water's edge.

Africa's northernmost city, Bizerte, is quite unlike other coastal settlements in modern Tunisia. Despite the pressures of development elsewhere, Bizerte's historic core retains much of its original character. Although popular in the summer months, it remains relatively tourist-free for most of the year. Spend any amount of time around the medina and Vieux Port (Old Port) and you'll leave feeling as though you've experienced a slice of the real Tunisia.

Many domestic visitors come for the beaches fanning out north and south of the historic centre. It's here that you will encounter a modern array of resort hotels. But beyond these, much of the coastline, including Africa's northernmost point, Cap Angela, are notoriously tricky to reach, even in a rental car. Nevertheless, Bizerte is a good base from which to explore this rugged procession of coastline, including Raf Raf, plus the Utica ruins and the UNESCO World Heritage reserve of Ichkeul.

Alleys of White & Blue

Wander Bizerte's mazey medinas

Within the ochre walls of Bizerte's impressive **kasbah** (fortress), the streets and buildings of the city's **kasbah medina** (walled historic city) are tightly packed. The walls date from the 17th-century Ottoman era, although there may have been a settlement here since the Phoenicians, followed much later by a Roman settlement named Hippo Diarrhytus (which sounds like a zookeeper's nightmare).

Although the kasbah's 10m-high ramparts have been closed to visitors for many years, wandering the kasbah medina's higgledy-piggledy maze is the best way to witness local life at its gentlest pace. The only access point is the **Western Gate**, a modest entrance that curves to the left and opens on to the **Kasbah Mosque**, with its stone horseshoe arch doorways and windows. Its marble columns are said to date back

Continues on p123

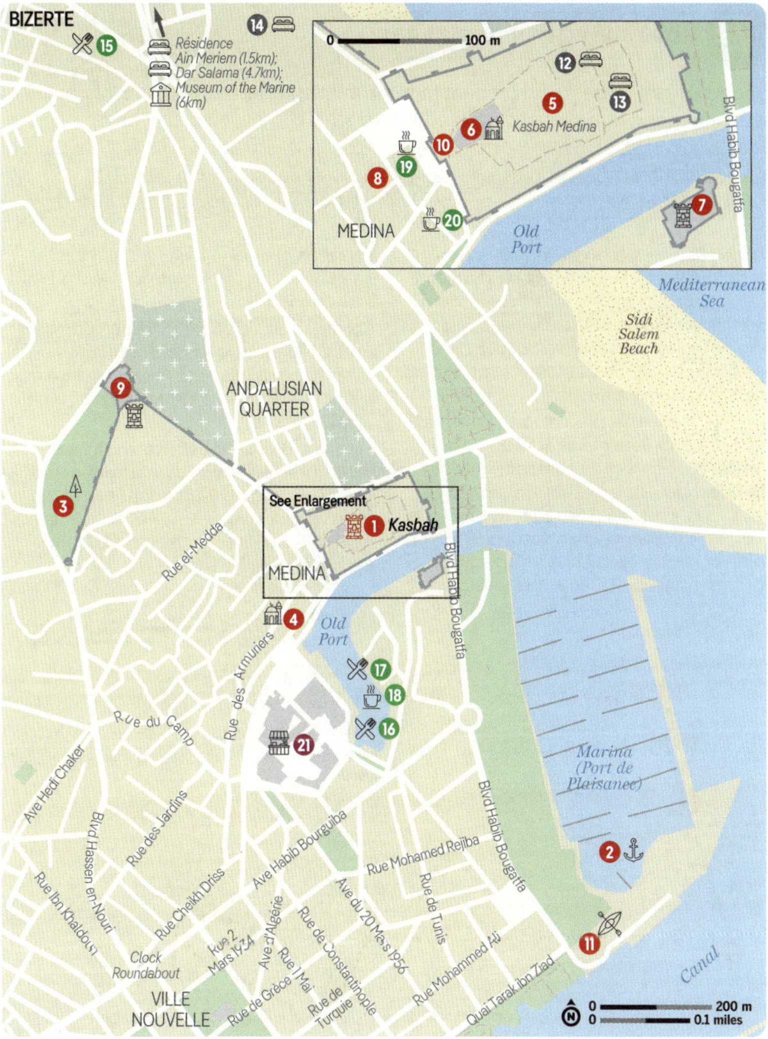

BIZERTE

Résidence Ain Meriem (1.5km); Dar Salama (4.7km); Museum of the Marine (6km)

0 — 100 m

Kasbah Medina
Blvd Habib Bougatfa
MEDINA
Old Port
Mediterranean Sea
Sidi Salem Beach
ANDALUSIAN QUARTER
See Enlargement
Kasbah
MEDINA
Old Port
Blvd Habib Bougatfa
Rue el-Medda
Rue des Armuriers
Rue du Camp
Marina (Port de Plaisance)
Ave Hedi Chaker
Blvd Hassen en-Nouri
Rue des Jardins
Ave Habib Bourguiba
Rue Mohamed Rejiba
Rue de Tunis
Blvd Habib Bougatfa
Rue Ibn Khaldoun
Rue Cheikh Driss
Ave du 20 Mars 1956
Rue 2 Mars 1934
Ave d'Algérie
Rue de Constantinople
Rue 1 Mai
Rue Mohammed Ali
Clock Roundabout
VILLE NOUVELLE
Rue de Grèce
Rue de Turquie
Quai Tarak ibn Ziad
Canal

0 — 200 m
0 — 0.1 miles

HIGHLIGHTS
1 Kasbah

SIGHTS
2 Bizerte Marina
3 Chalbi Belkahia
4 Great Mosque
5 Kasbah Medina
6 Kasbah Mosque
7 Ksibah
8 Medina
9 Spanish Fort
10 Western Gate

ACTIVITIES
11 Sport Nautique Bizertin

SLEEPING
12 Dar El Kasba
13 Dar Warda
14 Hotel Nour Congress

EATING
15 Best Voice
16 Café El Ksiba
see 7 Creative Space Café
17 Le Phénicien
see 11 Le Sport Nautique
18 Pâtisserie Parisienne La Medina
19 Restaurant Ksiba
20 Tea Pot Vieux Port

SHOPPING
21 Marché aux Poissons

FORTS & PORTS IN BIZERTE

Unpack Bizerte's past and present through multicultural architecture, historic landmarks and atmospheric promenades on this old town walking tour.

START	END	LENGTH
Kasbah's Western Gate	Spanish Fort entrance	2.15km; 2 hrs

Follow this route after exploring the kasbah medina (p120), starting at the ❶ **Western Gate** (p120). Turn south and you will emerge at the picturesque ❷ **Vieux Port**, filled with little painted fishing boats and overlooked by pastel-hued homes. Note the sculpture of two dolphins in the centre, an emblem of Bizerte.

Turn left, heading east beneath the kasbah wall through the ❸ **Gate of Ras Al Sass**. Cross the modern bridge, where a small fortification, the ❹ **Ksibah**, faces a larger one across the port. The Ksibah, whose entrance is on the south side, houses the **Oceanographic Museum** *(5DT)*. It's a little bit jarring to explore this historic space when its rooms are stuffed with small fishtanks containing sad looking fish. Head upstairs for panoramic views of the neat, ochre kasbah walls and Vieux Port.

Continue wandering around the port, snapping photos of the many cats, then head northwest through the markets of ❺ **Place Bouchoucha**, before delving into the ❻ **medina** (p121) with its labyrinth of streets.

Emerge at Blvd Saadi Carnot and continue north to a square tower and wall leading uphill. These belong to the ❼ **Spanish Fort** (see right). Paths lead up alongside the wall to the entrance on Blvd Hassan Ennouri, through ❽ **Chalbi Belkahia**, a wooded park.

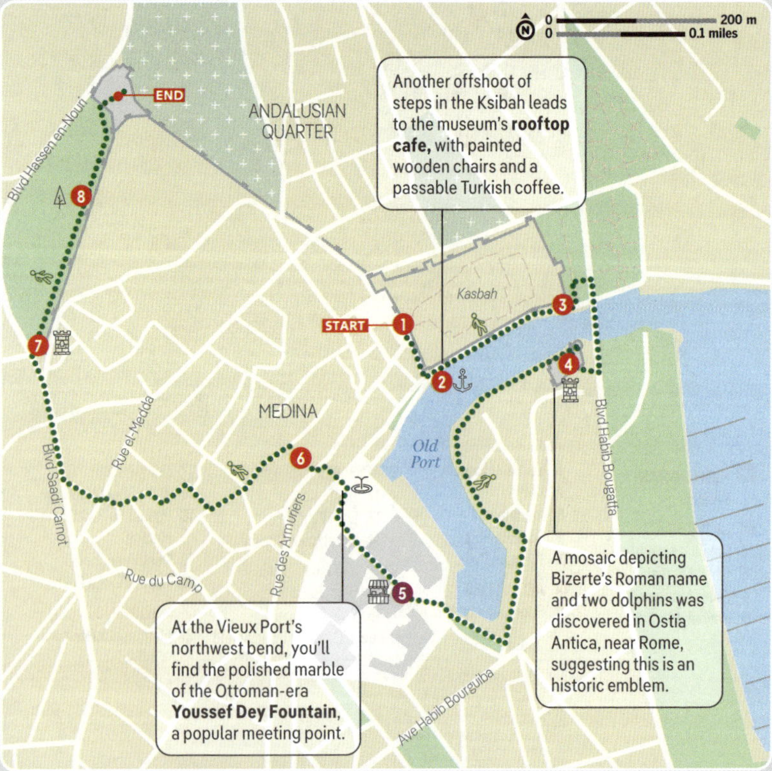

Another offshoot of steps in the Ksibah leads to the museum's **rooftop cafe,** with painted wooden chairs and a passable Turkish coffee.

A mosaic depicting Bizerte's Roman name and two dolphins was discovered in Ostia Antica, near Rome, suggesting this is an historic emblem.

At the Vieux Port's northwest bend, you'll find the polished marble of the Ottoman-era **Youssef Dey Fountain**, a popular meeting point.

Continued from p120
to the Roman era. Take any street from here to head deeper into the warren of cobbled alleys and cul-de-sacs, spanned by archways and fronted by whitewashed buildings with cheery royal-blue window guards and doors. Many of the doors are decorated with black or blue studded patterns. Common motifs include Fatima's hand to ward off the evil eye, a five-pointed star representing the five pillars of Islam, and two dolphins, a symbol of the city since Roman times.

Exit by the same western gate and continue into the compact neighbourhood immediately west of the kasbah, which is also called the medina. Although not contained within walls, the blue and white labyrinth theme continues, and you'll see more glimpses of daily commercial life in the alleys and courtyards. The octagonal minaret of the **Great Mosque**, built in 1652, is the main landmark. Non-Muslims are not permitted inside any of the mosques.

Cannons & Concerts

Look out over the bay

The Spanish (fighting for the Habsburgs against the Ottomans) held Bizerte for a few decades in the 16th century. They started work building a fortress on the high ground immediately north of the Vieux Port, but didn't have time to finish it before the Ottomans retook the city and finished what came to be known as the **Spanish Fort** *(free entry)*, known colloquially as the Andalusian Fort or Fort d'Espagne.

Only the entrance on the north side of the citadel is open. You'll need to show your passport to enter, as it still retains a basic military function. There's a large amphitheatre below where concerts are occasionally still held (along with the **Festival International** in July and August) and you can climb to the top of the battlements for views of the city and beyond to Cap Farina.

Head onto the Med

Boat rides in Bizerte

With all of those boats crowding the **Vieux Port**, it's surprising that there are no official boat tours in Bizerte, especially when you consider that the fish that attract the fishers also attract dolphins, which are still common in the Bay of Bizerte. **Sport Nautique Bizertin** *(snbizertin@gmail.com)*, south of the city's relatively new **Bizerte Marina**, offers kayak and

THE OLD LAND & THE SEA

Tunisia's indelible relationship with the sea is particularly evident in and around Bizerte, which owes its existence to its tactical location on both the Mediterranean and Lake Bizerte. Numerous empires, from the Phoenicians to the French, were attracted by northern Tunisia's fertile lands, protected by these defensible bays and brackish lakes.

In fact, despite Tunisia gaining independence from French occupation in 1956, France held onto their naval base in Bizerte until 1963. They left in acrimony after a Tunisian blockade, followed by deadly confrontations and subsequent UN-led international pressure.

There's still a sizeable Tunisian navy in Bizerte. Many locals will tell you that that's the only reason why the city has evaded the modern developers' blueprints.

DRINKING IN BIZERTE: BEST CAFES AROUND VIEUX PORT

Pâtisserie Parisienne La Medina: Among a popular cluster of cafes just outside the Medina gate. Good pastries, including mille-feuille. *6am-10pm* €

Creative Space Café: Friendly spot occupying the Ksiba's lower floor with waterfront tables. Sign written in Arabic only. *hours vary* €

Tea Pot Vieux Port: Try the baklawa tea, which contains almonds, cashews and hazelnuts. Ask for glass, not polystyrene, cups. *7am-7pm* €

Café El Ksiba: Decent coffee and a great waterfront location with plastic chairs, where you can watch fishers preparing their nets. *6am-midnight* €

A FISHY TAIL

From the net to the plate, fish are the driving force of daily life at the Vieux Port, and Bizerte's seafood is renowned throughout Tunisia. The pretty wooden boats form an artisanal fishing fleet that heads out of the port throughout the day, with the most activity at dawn and dusk. Many of these fishers still use traditional nets and traps, which are much better for the environment than methods used on modern trawlers. They're also the reason why you'll meet scores of feral cats, which hop aboard the moored vessels in search of discarded morsels, all around the port. Watch the catches being hauled in at the **Marché aux Poissons** on the southwest side of the Vieux Port from around 6.30am. Dishes to try include the lobster and *hoot mookli* fried fish.

ANDREAS WOLOCHOW/SHUTTERSTOCK

Spanish Fort (p123)

stand-up paddleboard (SUP) rentals, although dolphin sightings this close to the city are less common. Alternatively, if you speak French, it's sometimes possible to negotiate a hire with one of the fishers, who can take you out on their boat (always make sure you're given a life jacket). Otherwise, ask at your hotel. Jasmine at Dar El Kasba (p145) speaks excellent English.

Model Ships & Morse Codes

Science of sailing the seas

North of the port, a pretty waterfront promenade called the **Corniche of Bizerte** runs for 3km. At its northern edge lies the fascinating **Museum of the Marine** *(hmp.defense.tn/fr/musee-de-la-marine-tunisienne; 5DT)*, run by the Tunisian Navy. There's not always somebody on hand who speaks English, but the displays provide a very insightful look at the importance of ships in the country's history, from the biremes and triremes of the Romans to the modern fleet. The museum, closed on Mondays, also displays a collection of historic seafaring equipment, including Morse code machines and barometers, plus a series of model ships, including a huge galleon in a glass case outside the museum itself.

EATING IN BIZERTE: SEAFOOD

Le Phénicien: Incongruous wooden galleon that's classier inside than it looks. Great tuna *brik* (filled pastry); the catch of the day is pricey. *noon-midnight* **€€€**

Restaurant Ksiba: Try the *couscous au poisson*, especially on a Friday when this dish is traditionally served. Waterfront tables. *9am-10pm Tue-Sun* **€€€**

Le Sport Nautique: One of the fancier establishments in Bizerte known for its shellfish and prawns. *noon-3pm & 7-11pm* **€€€**

Best Voice: Popular brunches, impeccable presentation and a good à la carte selection, including seafood pasta. Arguably Bizerte's best restaurant. *7am-midnight* **€€**

Beyond Bizerte

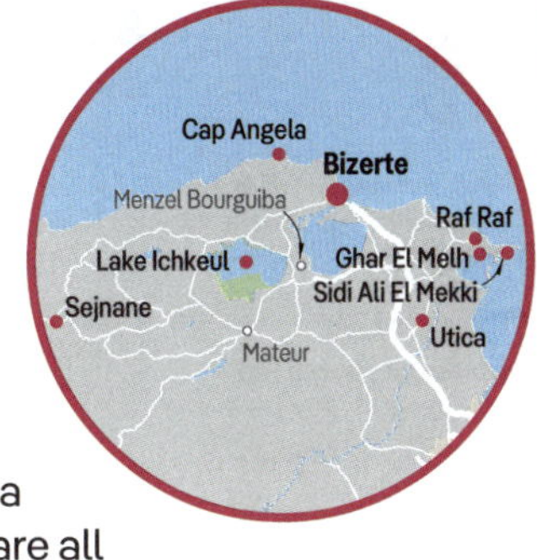

Windswept peninsulas, Roman ruins and a UNESCO World Heritage nature reserve are all within easy access of Bizerte.

The landscape around Bizerte, even away from the coast, is dominated by water. Whether you're visiting one of the coastline's many beaches, the unique and fragile ecosystem of Lake Ichkeul, or the ruins of an old Roman port at Utica, now many kilometres from the Mediterranean, this is a region that has been shaped by its aqueous environment. But that's not to say that the land is flat. Far from it: there are rugged peninsulas offering some great hiking, such as Cap Farina; and, further west, the gently undulating hills and valleys around remote Sejnane, best known for its Amazigh pottery, offer some of the prettiest and greenest vistas in Tunisia.

Places

Raf Raf

TIME FROM BIZERTE: **1HR**

Hiking Cap Farina

The steep-ridged, forest-clad headland of **Cap Farina**, 19km east of Bizerte, juts out into the Mediterranean like a lizard's tail, separating Raf Raf (north) from Ghar El Melh (south). This is a fantastic area for some moderate-level hiking with pretty vistas from the ridgetop. To reach the **trailhead**, pass through Raf Raf until the road meets the forest. There's parking beside the barrier (coordinates 37.180410, 10.226652) if you're coming by car (advisable).

The trail runs through a pine forest rooted firmly in the sandy loam. It's best to stick to the smaller paths either side of the main way to avoid trudging through deep sand. Look for patches of cobblestone, said (perhaps apocryphally) to be vestiges of an original Roman road. The frigate-shaped island nearby is Île Pilau.

To reach the ridgetop, keep right when the path forks, up a hairpinning goat track. From this coastal vantage point, you can look south towards Tunis, with Sidi Ali El Mekki below, and north towards Bizerte. The path is not the easiest to follow at the top, but it eventually drops down to the basic remains of a **Roman temple**. From here, head north to see remnants of a **Roman quarry**, following the low return path back to the car park. The total hike is around 10.3km (6.4 miles). Allow at least three hours and bring water. Alternatively, if you're not driving, you can continue west from the Roman temple to Sidi Ali El Mekki.

GETTING AROUND

Louages to Cap Angela depart from the bus station on the junction between Blvd Saadi Carnot and Ave Hassen Nouri. The **Gare Routière de Bizerte** bus station has services to Tabarka, Aïn Draham, Sejnane and Ras Jebel (for onward trips to Raf Raf). For Ichkeul and beyond, car rental really opens up the possibilities for exploration. Although a few major rental firms have offices in Bizerte, they're unreliable and it's best to rent from Tunis.

THE BEST CAPES & BEACHES AROUND BIZERTE

Raf Raf Plage: Domestically, Raf Raf is a beloved resort destination, thanks to its white sand, deep green forest and stunning azure waters.

Remel Plage: Remel Beach's facilities are now derelict, but from here you can wander east, past the driftwood fishing cabins to two large shipwrecks.

Les Grottes: Features blocks of fossilized coral, eroded by the sea. There are very few caves, despite the name, and a few pretty, sandy coves.

Cap Blanc: If you're driving, take the first, potholed right after Les Grottes to this barren, trail-webbed promontory with pretty coves either side.

Ain Damous Plage: Stunning soft white sand beach, hinting at the barren stretches of coastline between here and Tabarka; 4WD access only.

Sidi Ali El Mekki

TIME FROM BIZERTE: **1HR**

Saints and sunners

Sidi Ali El Mekki is an upmarket beach resort with restaurants and hotels spread along the fine sand without overcrowding it. Nevertheless, in the summer months, it can get very busy here. The village is named after a local Sufi saint, whose **tomb** can be found northeast of the settlement in a whitewashed structure built directly into the headland's rockface. You can also do the reverse of the Cap Farina hike from here.

Ghar El Melh

TIME FROM BIZERTE: **55 MINS**

Forgotten Ottoman village

It could have been so different for **Ghar El Melh**. With not one but three forts, various rulers deemed this village a strategically crucial settlement, starting under Ottoman rule with the Dey of Tunis Usta Murad in 1637. But fate had other plans.

Originally called Porto Farina, the forts of **Borj El Loutani**, **Borj El Wostani** and **Ghar El Melh** are impressive, although opening times are sporadic, if they open at all (your best chance is mornings from Monday to Thursday). The fortifications were destroyed by a British naval expedition in the 17th century and rebuilt, only to be defeated by nature when the Ghar el-Melh lagoon silted up. There's a pretty **Vieux Port** with colourful fishing boats beside Borj el-Loutani.

Utica

TIME FROM BIZERTE: **50 MINS**

Remnants of an ancient port

Formerly an estuary port on the Medjerda River, the ruins of **Utica** *(entry 8DT)* now lie 15km from the sea, surrounded by vineyards and olive groves. According to Roman historian Pliny the Elder, Utica was founded by the Phoenicians as a trading post way back in 1101 BCE, although archaeological digs place the oldest-known ruins at around the 8th century BCE, which would still make it one of the earliest colonial cities in North Africa. Little remains from the Phoenician era, other than a **necropolis**.

The Romans developed the site's main structures, building orderly streets and villas, complete with the usual luxury features such as mosaic flooring, columned courtyards and *triclinia* (dining rooms with seats on three sides). The highlight is the **House of the Cascade**, which features a stunning fishing mosaic, one of the few still left in situ. Beyond this

EATING & DRINKING AROUND SIDI ALI EL MEKKI: OUR PICKS

Cheeky Monkey: Tasty dishes including a great seafood bulgur salad and the occasional marine speciality, such as sea urchins. Open year-round. *hours vary* **€€€**

Lovina Beach Club: Midway along Cap Farina, this neat spot, as with most places in this area, only opens in the summer months. *9am-8pm May-Sep* **€€€**

Café du Vieux Port: Simple place for a tea or bottle of water in Ghar El Melh beside the Vieux Port. No food available. *6am-10pm*

Restaurant Pirate: Tables and hammocks on a rickety boardwalk right over the Ghar El Melh lagoon. The grilled fish is a must. *9am-9pm* **€€€**

ROBERT HARDING VIDEO/SHUTTERSTOCK

House of the Cascade, Utica

small cluster of villas, the rest of the site is little more than an overgrown collection of foundations. Rough-hewn blocks and the stumps of marble columns are all that remain of the **Forum**. The site is often empty, save for shepherds leading their flocks through the ruins.

Utica Archaeological Museum (500m west of the visitable ruins; included in ruins ticket) is divided into a **Punic Room** and a **Roman Room**, with statuary, mosaics and everyday items from both periods on display. The museum is closed on Mondays, but the ruins remain open throughout the week.

Lake Ichkeul

TIME FROM BIZERTE: **45 MINS**

A lake of two faces

Ichkeul National Park, Tunisia's only UNESCO Natural World Heritage Site, is a 12,600-hectare expanse of lake, marshland and the forest-covered bulwark of Jebel Ichkeul (511m).

What makes Ichkeul so unique in North Africa is its lake's seasonal salinity. During the summer, reduced river flow and evaporation means Ichkeul's water level falls below that of Lake Bizerte, a brackish lagoon to the east. Bizerte's saltwater then flows into Lake Ichkeul. During the winter, the six rivers that feed Lake Ichkeul from the south and west then tip the balance back in favour of fresh water.

If that sounds incredibly fragile, that's because it is, and environmental mismanagement has unfortunately upended this delicate balance (see p129). The lake now sees higher than normal salinity year-round and the migratory birds don't come in anywhere near the same numbers any more. Nevertheless, Ichkeul remains one of northern Africa's most important natural spaces.

Because the Tunisian government has made it mandatory to obtain a permit to visit its national parks, visiting Ichkeul requires some advance preparation. It's a frustratingly

NORTHERN TUNISIA'S COAST FROM A DIFFERENT ANGLE

The beaches of northern Tunisia are remote, but many of the islands are practically impossible to reach. This, in turn, has made them some of the best places in the country for **diving** and **bird-watching**. Since COVID-19, guided tours have become scarce, although summer boat trips to the **Cani Islands**, 22km northeast of Bizerte, and the **Galite Islands**, 62km north of Tabarka, are not unheard of. It's worth asking for more information at your local hotel. Similarly, **surfing** is an unheard-of pursuit in northern Tunisia. But that doesn't mean there aren't any decent breaks. If you're keen to surf where few have surfed before, start with **Bel Aqua** *(belaqua.tn)* in Tunis.

BIRDS IN NORTHERN TUNISIA

Park ranger **Jamel May** names his favourite species of bird in Ichkeul.

There are fewer birds here these days, but my favourite are the ones that you can see here throughout the year, such as the **Moussier's redstart** *(Phoenicurus moussieri)*. It's a species that doesn't exist in Europe; it's native to Tunisia and there's a strong population in Ichkeul.

I think the colours of the **purple swamphen** *(Porphyrio porphyrio)*, which lives in the marshes, are magnificent. They are quite shy birds but you can spot them in the reeds by their bright red beaks.

The **European bee-eater** *(Merops apiaster)* is also an incredible bird. They don't just feed on bees, but also eat wasps, dragonflies and other insects.

MARISHA_SL/SHUTTERSTOCK

Ichkeul National Park (p127)

opaque process and is best organised through a guide or tour company. You'll also need your own transport. Louages from Mateur and Menzel Bourguiba can drop you off at the archway entrance, but this is still 9.5km from the Ecomuseum and main trail. Contact local ranger **Jamel May** *(25 702 852)*, an enthusiastic and proud guardian of the park, to help organise a guided tour.

Beyond the ticketed entrance gate, you'll pass some of the homes of the 70 families who were allowed to remain inside the national park. These homes have no running water and the residents still use the **hot springs** that you'll see near the Ecomuseum to wash their clothes and bathe.

The **Ecomuseum**, although a little dated, has some decent information about the flora, fauna and geology of Ichkeul in French and Arabic. You can borrow a telescope here to observe waterbirds in the marshes from a nearby lookout.

Bird-watching and water buffaloes

The marshes, lake shallows, forest and mountain of Lake Ichkeul provide a remarkably broad array of environments, encouraging great diversity and making for some exceptional bird-watching. Winter is the best time to visit, when migratory birds from both northern Europe and southern Africa descend on the park. Greylag geese, white storks, greater flamingos, Eurasian hoopoes and around 180 other species call the region home for all, or part, of the year.

From the Ecomuseum, a 3km there-and-back-again **trail** follows the lake's shoreline, where you'll likely see redstarts, great crested grebes and laughing doves. Look up to the crags above to see raptors such as Bonelli's eagle. March and April are great months to see orchids in bloom. The park's water buffaloes are kept overnight in barns made from buildings of an old mine south of Jebel Ichkeul. You'll likely find them in the fields nearby during the day. They are said to have descended from a pair gifted to Ahmed Bey, ruler of Tunisia, in 1840.

Cap Angela

TIME FROM BIZERTE: **50 MINS**

Edge of a continent

Africa's northernmost tip juts into the Mediterranean Sea with very little fanfare. To reach **Cap Angela**, you can take a louage from Bizerte or drive, although the roads are not paved for much of the way. The last kilometre is particularly treacherous and you're best parking your car and walking through the dunes to the promontory, marked by a small metal sculpture of the continent. There's a pretty beach and a working lighthouse (closed to visitors) nearby.

Sejnane

TIME FROM BIZERTE: **1½ HRS**

Amazigh pottery

In the villages north of the rather humdrum town of **Sejnane** are a series of artisanal potteries where fantastic terracotta homeware and animal figurines are made by the local Amazigh women. Drive through the region and you'll see **roadside stalls** laid out with their works. Very few visitors pass through here, so, you'll be paying very reasonable prices for bespoke, handmade pieces (around 20DT for a plate), many of which are exceptional and fully deserving of their listing on the UNESCO list of Intangible Cultural Heritage. Designs are rooted in the traditional Amazigh aesthetics, but there's room for creativity and influence from the region's other cultures. Contact **Saliha** *(99 945 562)*, whose beautiful designs are inspired by local rural themes. She is happy to show people around her workspace and demonstrate the crafting process in exchange for a purchase. Her kiosk and pottery are at coordinates 37.125878, 9.265796.

ENVIRONMENTAL CHALLENGES

Despite UNESCO support, the subsequent building of dams on three of the six rivers feeding seasonal fresh water to Lake Ichkeul fundamentally altered the national park's ecosystem.

The dams meant the lake's salinity stayed high throughout the year, causing significant declines in fish and waterbird populations.

Peak waterbird communities numbered around 225,000 individuals before the dams, but fell to an average of around 17,500 birds between 2010 and 2020. The number of recorded species declined in that same period.

This human-made devastation of the lake's ecosystem has been compounded by a steady reduction in rainfall attributed to climate change. While there are good people on the ground working hard to protect what remains, poor attitudes towards the environment in Tunisia remain pervasive.

HELP ME PICK:

North Coast Beaches

The coastline of northern Tunisia is remarkably undeveloped. To explore these secluded realms of natural beauty, you'll need to prepare well and, on occasion, be self-sufficient. For more than 240km (149 miles) between Tunis and the Algerian border, with the exception of stretches around Bizerte and Tabarka, the Tunisian coast feels both typically Mediterranean, with its scrubby forest and rocky, turquoise-water bays, and completely wild. With a little effort, you'll be able to enjoy some fantastic, secluded beaches.

Where to go if you love...

Sandy Beach Stays

If you're looking for a Tunisia beach that in no way resembles the overcrowded resorts seen elsewhere, **Plage Cap Serrat** has a good balance of sand and amenities. It's also easy enough to reach with a normal car. **Auberge Le Pirate** (p145) is the best of the few eating and sleeping options. Snorkelling is possible thanks to the clear water here.

Houichette Plage is more secluded but for the herd of goats, while **Dar Lahouichet** is one of the few overnight options, although there is talk of further development along the coastline.

ANISBOUKHRIS/SHUTTERSTOCK

Plage Zouara

Coastal Photography

The drive down to the little promontory known as **El Gléâa** is precarious and you'll need to walk the rest of the way once it gets too sandy, but the cove to the west is known as Little Paradise for a reason. A combination of red rock, ochre sand, turquoise water and dark green shrubbery makes for the north coast's most photogenic spot.

For a more unusual photo, the ruined arches of a Roman building (function uncertain) grace the beach at **Sidi Mechrig**. A relatively new road makes this spot accessible with a normal vehicle from Cap Serrat.

Sea-Breeze Hiking

If you like hiking, many of the remote beaches have a short trail or two leading to a nearby hill or cove. At Cap Serrat, follow the track to the lighthouse of **Mont Cap Serrat** or head inland through eucalyptus groves. You can explore the coastal paths from **El Gléâa**, heading over the dunes to beaches further west, such as **Noura Plage**. Given the lack of amenities, it's wise to pack to be fully self-sufficient.

National Parks

Northern Tunisia's most densely forested coastal stretch is found around one of its least-known national parks: **Jebel Chitana**. There's a beach and some tourist infrastructure, including the elegant **Dar El Cap** (p145) hotel, plus a couple of seasonal restaurants, at **Cap Negro**. From here, numerous trails explore the undulating coastline.

Water Sports

Kayak rental is included with stays at **Dar El Cap** (p145) in Jebel Chitana National Park. You can also rent kayaks and explore the coast from the sea at **Plage Zouara**, accessible along a decent road from Nefza. A number of restaurants here, including **Nautic Base**, have summer kayak rentals.

SLIM ALILECHE/WIKIMEDIA COMMONS

Plage Cap Serrat

HOW TO

When to go Spring and autumn months offer the perfect blend of fine weather and few people. In the summer, these secluded spots can rapidly fill with people.

Booking ahead Guesthouses usually only come with basic amenities and can get booked out well in advance during the summer months. In winter, many are closed.

Getting there In most cases, even the most popular coves and promontories are only accessible via unpaved roads. A 4WD is recommended for most places.

Worth considering There can be quite a lot of rubbish and broken glass, even on remote beaches. Walk on the sand with sturdy, closed-toe footwear.

DIY or Guided Tour?

The answer to this will come down to your appetite for self-guided adventure. It's perfectly feasible to visit all of the beaches along the north coast on your own. Indeed, while a 4WD is highly recommended for reaching practically all of them, the truth is that most locals will brave the journey in their own cars, with the exception of the sandy roads, where a 4WD is mandatory. Whether you choose to use a car or a 4WD will depend on whether or not you're concerned about tyre wear and punctures in a rented vehicle, which are risks given the state of some roads.

As undeveloped as these beaches may be, it doesn't mean there aren't facilities. Many of the beaches now have at least basic accommodation and restaurants from spring to autumn. Nevertheless, bring plenty of water and some non-perishable food, just in case. Plage Zouara is a rare case in which you can get there by louage from Nefza. If you'd prefer not to drive, it might be possible to agree a fee with a taxi driver in Bizerte or Tabarka to take you.

While there aren't any established, pre-organised tours to the north coast beaches, it may be possible to organise something bespoke. For a dependable tour agency, take a look at **Dar El Ain** *(darelain.com)* in Tabarka (p137).

WAR RELICS & WATERFALLS

Explore waterfalls, wildlife and war memorials in the hilly core of northern Tunisia on this wilderness driving tour.

START	END	LENGTH
Entrance of Ichkeul National Park	Dawwar Mraf	112km; 5 hrs (with stops)

Circumvent the southern edge of 1 **Ichkeul National Park** (p127), sticking to the farmland where permits aren't required. Spot waterbirds in the marshes around Joumine River. Next, drive to the disused 2 **Kreloua Mine** and look around for water buffalo. Head south, taking the C56 south out of Mateur, then west on the C64.

Follow the C64 for around 11.5km, then take a right to 3 **Tahint**, a pretty little village at the foot of a craggy outcrop known as Hill 609, the site of a key victory against the Nazis by US troops in April 1943. Get back on the C64 and at the junction with the P11 you'll come to 4 **Sidi Nsir Train Station**, which was the focus of a significant Nazi attack on British troops in February 1943.

Continue west on the C64, then head north through Joumine village on a winding, potholed road into the hills through some stunning scenery to 5 **Oued Zitoun Waterfall**. The water cascades down this precipitous drop in foamy ribbons, though it's dry in summer.

Back in the car, continue west and head north on the C126, then west on the P7 to 6 **Sejnane**. Stop at Sejnane Train Station, where storks nest on the surrounding buildings and infrastructure. Take the main road north out of town to shop for Amazigh terracotta pottery in 7 **Dawwar Mraf** village.

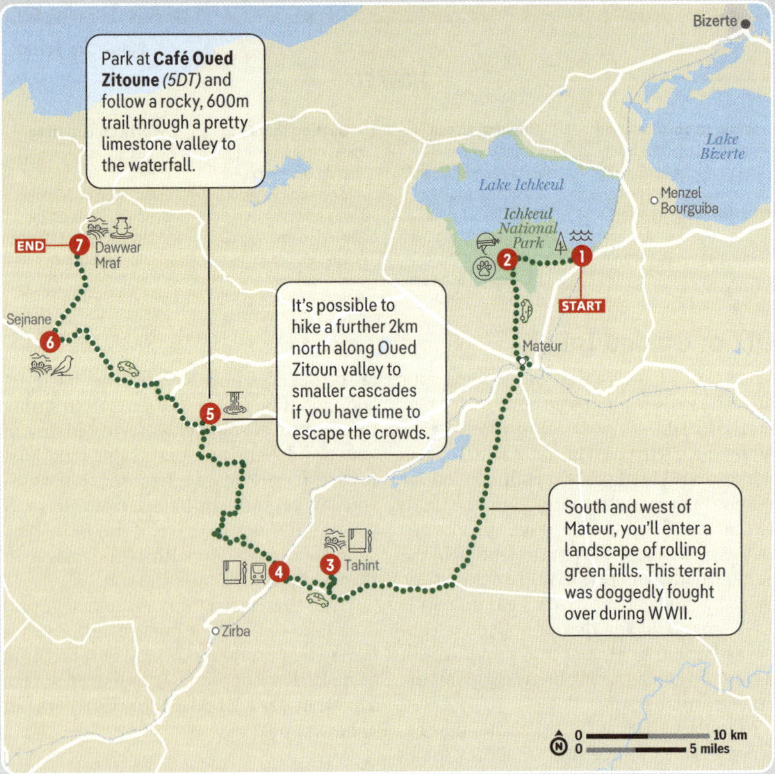

Aïn Draham

HILL-STATION CHARM | NATURE HIKES | MOUNTAIN BIKING

Aïn Draham (aka Ayn Darahim) is a popular hill station. It sits in a fold of the Kroumirie Mountains, a sandstone range that marks the far eastern edge of the mighty Atlas Mountains, with some peaks topping 1000m (3281ft). Here, the slopes are covered in thick, evergreen cork oak forests interspersed with pine, beech and walnut trees; you'll often see people selling bags of walnuts by the side of the road. Snow is not uncommon in the winter months, hence the sloping red-tiled roofs that make the site feel vaguely Alpine, a holdover from the town's time as a French colonial outpost.

The town bustles with visitors throughout the year, particularly at the weekends when it's difficult to book hotels online at short notice. That being said, if you ask around, you'll almost certainly find a room available at one of the many hotels around town.

GETTING AROUND

The drives south to Aïn Draham from Tabarka and north from Firnanah, both along the P17, are the most spectacular scenic drives in northern Tunisia. It is well worth having your own car in this region. In town, the P17 bypasses the main centre. The SRT bus station (with services to Tunis, Bizerte and Tabarka) lies along this road on the northern edge of town. Ave Habib Bourguiba, which connects to the P17 at the north and south of town, runs a hillier, loosely parallel route to the P17 through Aïn Draham's old town centre, where you'll find many of the best restaurants and hotels.

Walks in the Woods

Hiking from Aïn Draham

Apart from the former French Catholic **Aïn Draham Church**, built in the 1930s and now serving as a cultural centre with lovely views, there's not a great deal to see in town. But Aïn Draham is a great base from which to explore the surrounding mountains. Unfortunately, good maps with marked routes are not available. Apps like Wikiloc are your safest bet but are not entirely dependable. But it's still possible to take some simple, self-guided hikes starting in town without the need for a map.

For an easy 4.5-km (2.8-mile) loop hike, head to the Tulip Inn (aka Hotel Nour El Ain; p145) on the north side of town where you can pick up the **Col des Ruines trail** from the car park, behind the hotel. It eventually meets a well-trodden trail that loops around a pine- and oak-clad hill called the Col des Ruines, a name that nods to the abandoned **watch-tower** you'll pass along the way that holds commanding views over the valley.

HIGHLIGHTS
1 Oued Zen

SIGHTS
2 Aïn Draham Church

ACTIVITIES
3 Circuit Eco Touristique Belle Forêt
see 7 Col des Ruines trail

SLEEPING
4 Discovery Eco-Hotel
5 Résidence Panorama
6 Royal Rihana Hôtel
7 Tulip Inn

EATING
8 Al Maghreb Al Amazighi
9 La Fougère
10 Restaurant Mechoui
11 Safsaf

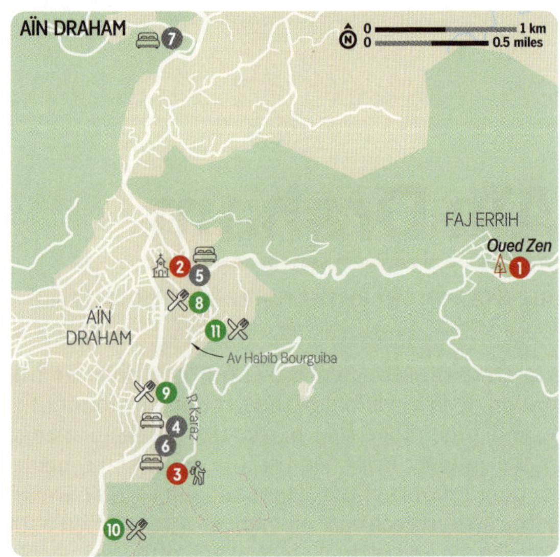

For a slightly longer trail, the **Circuit Eco Touristique Belle Forêt** runs for 7km (4.3 miles) through the forest, starting behind the Discovery Eco-Hotel (p145) on the south side of town. The trail is an oval loop, running north to south along well-established trails.

Tour a National Park

Oued Zen adventures

As Tunisia's greenest region, the **Kroumirie Mountains** are, unsurprisingly, the country's wettest area. In the winter, rains can set in over the mountains for days. Since 2010, the wilderness immediately to the east of Aïn Draham, **Oued Zen**, has enjoyed national park status. The forests, harbouring fauna such as wild boar, genet, mongoose and the endangered Barbary deer, are the pinnacle of the area's natural beauty. There is very little in the way of infrastructure or information, so you'll need a guide. Most major hotels in town, including Royal Rihana (p145) and Discovery Eco-Hotel (p145), can help arrange tours for you from Aïn Draham.

TOP TIP

Although it's generally hard to find good hiking advice or maps in northern Tunisia, the Wikiloc app shows a few decent options. Transtunisia.com has a free app in English and French for self-guided hikes. Use it to walk parts of the Kroumirie route around Beni Mtir.

EATING IN AÏN DRAHAM: OUR PICKS

La Fougère: Try the *brik aux chevrettes* (prawn, potato and egg in pastry). But the main draw is the view from the rear terrace. *7am-11pm* **€€**

Al Maghreb Al Amazighi: Old-school tiled eatery with friendly owners. Great fresh orange juice and flavourful *ojja* (poached eggs). Vegetarian options on request. *7am-10pm* **€**

Safsaf: Bare-bones cafe along Ave Habib Bourguiba best for grabbing a coffee or mint tea. Also has some simple rooms above. *hours vary* **€**

Restaurant Mechoui: Best of the many barbecue restaurants 1km south of town, its grill smoke billowing into the road. *10am-7pm* **€€**

HICHEM KAOUANE/SHUTTERSTOCK

Forest, Aïn Draham

From Mountain Biking to Mushrooms

Eclectic tours around Aïn Draham

There's no shortage of hiking guides based in Aïn Draham, but with most you'll need a good command of French or Arabic. The other option is to use a more established tour company such as Tabarka-based Dar El Ain (p139), whose guides know the region as well as anybody. Their varied, well-curated tours include mountain biking through cork oak forests and mushroom picking in autumn. They also run women-only hikes and family-friendly tours. For bookings, they are more responsive on Whatsapp *(20 002 409)* than via email.

THE FRENCH CONNECTION

Even today, long after Independence, Aïn Draham stills bear the marks of French occupation. Originally used as a military base, the French began turning it into a hill station in the early 1930s, using the cooler mountain climate as an antidote to Tunisia's summer heat. The architecture of sloping roofs, verandas and the occasional church still remain visible, but modern buildings are slowly consuming the view. In 1948, the French built another village, Beni Mtir (p136), for workers who were constructing the first hydroelectric dam in Tunisia. The village retains more of its traditional atmosphere, while the reservoir is one of many hidden imprints of the colonial era upon the landscape.

Beyond Aïn Draham

Drop down from the Kroumirie to visit Tabarka's port and Genoese fort, and the Medjerda valley's remarkable Roman ruins.

Places

The breadth of experiences possible on a day trip from Aïn Draham make the mountain town a fantastic base for exploring this western region of northern Tunisia. To the north, the small Mediterranean port of Tabarka is best known for its Genoese fortress and unusual rock formations. Head south and you'll drop into the fertile Medjerda valley, once known as the granary of Ancient Rome. Its importance to the great Mediterranean empire is evident in the remarkable remnants of a Roman marble quarry at Chemtou and city at Bulla Regia, with its unique subterranean villas. Staying in the mountains, Beni Mtir is an atmospheric alternative to Aïn Draham, with good walks and waterfalls.

GETTING AROUND

Regular buses connect Tabarka with Aïn Draham. Louages and shared taxis depart from the P17 in town for Beni Mtir when full. However, the Roman ruins, located in the middle of remote countryside, are trickier to reach unless you have your own mode of transport. There is some fantastic driving in the mountains, especially on the winding and well-paved P17. Organised tours from Tunis and Tabarka are often the best option if you don't plan to drive.

Beni Mtir & Around

TIME FROM AÏN DRAHAM: **30 MINS**

Waterfalls and reservoir hikes

The rising popularity of Aïn Draham has changed the nature of the place from a peaceful mountain town to a crowded tourist spot, meaning outlying settlements, such as Babouch and **Beni Mtir** (pronounced 'bennim-teer'), have increasingly become the go-to for a more peaceful getaway. The French-built Beni Mtir village sits on the high ground above the reservoir. Many of the original buildings from the late 1940s remain, including the deconsecrated **Beni Mtir Church** and a charming **Centre Ville square**, surrounded by arcaded buildings with black and red window shutters.

The village is the starting point for a number of hikes, including a short 5km loop down to the nearby **Beni Mtir Dam** and back. It's also the start of the **Kroumirie Trekking 50K Trail**, a three-day trek through the mountains to **El Moula Dam**, 10km east of Tabarka. Trail markings and maps were created by **Trans Tunisia** *(transtunisia.com)*. You can use its free app in English and French to place yourself on the mapped trail with GPS along the way. It's possible to walk the first section (13.5km), which loops south through the forest then back up to Beni Mtir Waterfall, in half a day.

Beni Mtir Waterfall is by far the most popular attraction in the area. Busloads of Tunisian tourists descend upon the site on weekends. Wander down the slippery steps, past the tea and walnut vendors, to the rather small and litter-blighted

ANISBOUKHRIS/SHUTTERSTOCK

Beni Mtir Waterfall

falls (which are dry in summer). To get away from the crowds, follow the path along the river in either direction into the peaceful cork oak forest.

Tunisian cheese tasting

With all those sheep and the lingering French influence, it's perhaps surprising that one doesn't encounter much cheese in Tunisian cuisine. But that doesn't mean it doesn't exist. **La Casa Del Formaggio** *(lacasa-delformaggio.com)* is a very rustic, traditional Tunisian mountain farmhouse whose owners make some exceptional artisanal cheeses. Located west of the P17, 3km south of Aïn Draham and down a very bumpy track, the farmhouse has pretty views of the surrounding countryside. You can try and buy a variety of cheddars, plus a great soft cheese called Le Fermier. La Casa Del Formaggio also has a restaurant and there are guest rooms for a peaceful stay in the hills.

Tabarka

TIME FROM AÏN DRAHAM: **1 HR** 

Explore Genoese ruins on a pirate island

The former Barbary Corsair stronghold of **Tabarka** sits on the Mediterranean coast, 14km east of the Algerian border. The small city on a sandy bay is now a popular tourist destination.

PUT A CORK IN IT

The Kroumirie Mountains are rich in a biodegradable natural resource that is in demand around the world: cork.

To obtain it, bark from the cork oaks is harvested in the period between spring and summer, a time when the trees are able to regrow their protective outer layer without suffering too much damage.

The cork, which is durable, water-resistant, elastic and biodegradable, is then sorted, with the best parts turned into bottle stoppers for the wine industry. The rest is used for everything from flooring to furniture.

Wildfires are an increasing concern and poor management is fragmenting the forests, something that the World Wide Fund for Nature (WWF) is working hard to reverse.

EATING IN BENI MTIR & AROUND: OUR PICKS

Cafe Beni Mtir: In a heritage building with red and black shutters. The old Conti hand pump coffee machine still makes a mean espresso. *7am-8pm* €

Green Hills: Tasty wood-fired pizzas in a neat modern restaurant overlooking the dam and reservoir on the northern edge of town. *noon-7pm* €€

Club Des Immigrés: Quirky spot in the forest with some of the best eats in the region, plus resident peacocks. Closed on Mondays. *hours vary* €€

Mazzara Club: Grilled meats and tasty soups are the main fare at this friendly family restaurant midway between Beni Mtir and Aïn Draham. *8am-midnight* €€

STATUES, RUINS & ROCK FORMATIONS WALK

Discover the ruins and rock formations of Tabarka's storied coastline on this self-guided walking tour.

START	END	LENGTH
Statue of Habib Bourguiba	Les Aiguilles	3.9km; 2½ hrs

Begin beside the 1 **Statue of Habib Bourguiba**, Tunisia's first president, who strikes a calm, seated pose here. East and west of the statue is the 2 **Place du 18 Janvier**. Cross the road and into the park heading east (towards the sea). On the left, you will find one of the few surviving memories of Roman Thabraca in the form of **bathhouse ruins**.

Keep walking east, passing the graffiti-covered 'I ♥ Tabarka' sign, then head north to the 3 **Marina**. Take a left at **Le Canari Café** (p142) to the 4 **Statue du Corail**, dedicated to the rare red coral growing offshore, then turn north, following the road (Tabarka Beach should be on your left side).

Soon after the road passes a remnant of the 5 **Genoese defensive wall**, it starts to climb the hill of Tabarka Island. As it switches back, take the paved path on your right. Soon after passing the low ruins of some Genoese shops, the path becomes rougher and rockier, before bending west, uphill to your left, to the foot of the 6 **Genoese Fortress**.

Follow the road back down towards the coral statue, then turn west until you reach the 7 **Violin Statue**. Enter the *corniche* (seafront promenade) and continue to the distinctive rock pinnacles of 8 **Les Aiguilles** jutting out into the bay.

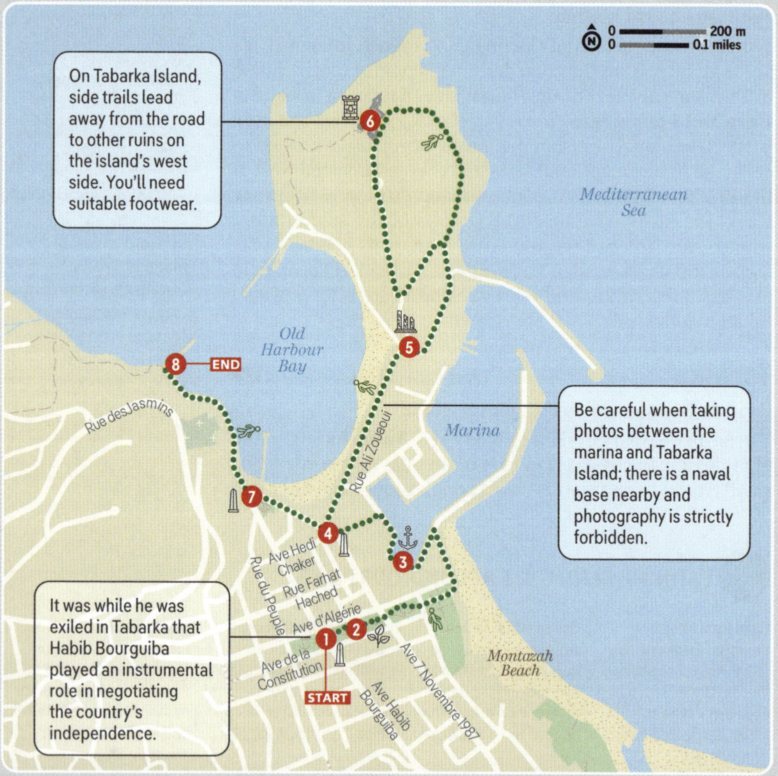

On Tabarka Island, side trails lead away from the road to other ruins on the island's west side. You'll need suitable footwear.

Be careful when taking photos between the marina and Tabarka Island; there is a naval base nearby and photography is strictly forbidden.

It was while he was exiled in Tabarka that Habib Bourguiba played an instrumental role in negotiating the country's independence.

However, it is struggling to rebound from COVID-19 and the subsequent loss or repurposing of some of its major attractions. This includes the city's main historic building, the **Genoese Fortress**, which in 2025 was closed to visitors and had reverted to the control of the Tunisian army, having initially only opened to the public in 2016.

Nevertheless, you can still explore the peninsula on which it sits, plus the many Genoese ruins dotted around it. Known as **Tabarka Island**, this rocky outcrop was connected to the mainland by a causeway while under French rule. Prior to that, the Genoese maintained a fortified presence on the island for around two centuries, starting in the 1540s. Their arrival ended a period when Tabarka served as a stronghold for the Barbary Corsairs, who were pirates under Ottoman rule (p318). It is rumoured that the Genoese received the island as part of a deal with the notorious Khayreddin Barbarossa, in exchange for the release of an Ottoman admiral, Dragut, who was captured and served as an enslaved person on a galley under the Genoese for four years.

Roughly 700m long by 500m wide, the island is easy enough to wander all the way around, following the rough paths that connect the various ruins. Besides the fort, which crowns the high ground to the northern end of Tabarka Island, there is a ruined **church** on the west side and a smaller fort, which is hard to distinguish from the rock it's built on, lower down the slope on the east side.

FORTIFIED COASTS

Tabarka isn't the only coastal city in Tunisia defended by coastal fortifications. Mahdia's **Skifa el Kahla** (p194) and **Ghazi Mustapha Fortress** on Djerba (p266) are fine examples of historic forts.

Boat tours from Tabarka

Tabarka was initially founded as a trading post by the Phoenicians and grew under Roman rule into a key port from which marble, quarried at Chemtou (p143), was shipped around the empire. Today, the Tunisian navy maintains a presence in the port; meanwhile the **Marina** is a focal point of local life, with cafes and restaurants lining the waterfront promenade.

Boat trips aboard the **Sultan 2** and **Hannibal 2** *(20 842 455; 25DT)*, which you cannot miss when they're moored in the marina, head to a cove close to **Maloula Beach**. Both are designed like kitschy pirate ships, with DJs blaring Tunisian pop music from the poop deck. The tour drops anchor along the way, allowing a little time for some **snorkelling** in the relatively clear water before returning. You can hear the boats from far away. For a day trip with a variety of water sports and activities at various local coves, there's a good option run by the Tabarka-based tour company **Dar El Ain** *(darelain.com)*.

Diving the carmine reef

The **red coral** off the shore of Tabarka is what makes Tabarka one of Tunisia's most loved scuba-diving destinations. Known as the red gold of Tabarka, this distinctive coral, like all things beautiful and natural, is under threat. Although the National Marine Reserve status ostensibly protects the

Continues on p142

JAZZ IN TABARKA

As you explore Tabarka, you'll likely come across the sculptures of various instruments placed at traffic junctions. There's a saxophone out past Montazah Beach and a violin on the seafront near Les Aiguilles. Each one is a nod to Tabarka's former role as Tunisia's jazz capital.

Before the COVID-19 pandemic, **Tabarka Jazz Festival** took place each July. Since 2019, there has been a silence between the notes. A local official in early 2025 said that although discussions were taking place at the administrative level, there were still no solid plans to relaunch the festival. Keep an eye out if you plan to travel in July, as things may change.

Byzantine Basilica

TOP EXPERIENCE

Bulla Regia

There's little need for the imagination at **Bulla Regia**, where Roman streets, thermal baths and subterranean rooms are beautifully preserved. The site is best known for its Roman-Amazigh villas, built by wealthy families in Bulla Regia to escape the summer heat. These spaces, which had their own colonnaded courtyards and mosaics, are among Tunisia's most remarkable surviving historic structures. To this date, only 25% of the site has been excavated. Keep that in mind as you explore.

DON'T MISS

- Memmian Baths
- Treasure House
- Byzantine Basilica
- Hunting House
- New Hunting House
- Venus House
- Temple of Apollo
- The Theatre

Roman Road

At the entrance, look out for the **steles** with half-moon carvings, which date back to the town's 4th century BCE origins under Carthage. Continue heading straight until you come to a T-junction. This is the **St Augustine Roman Road**. It connected Carthage to Anneba (Hippo Regia) in Algeria, where St Augustine, an Amazigh bishop, was from. The rooms facing this road on the outside of the Memmian Baths were likely shops serving travellers.

PRACTICALITIES

● patrimoinedetunisie.com.tn/en/sites/the-archaeological-site-of-bulla-regia ● Tunisians/foreigners 5DT/8DT ● 8.30am-5.30pm mid-Sep–Apr, 8am-7pm May–mid-Sep

Memmian Baths

Descend the steps into the **Memmian Baths**, where travellers would have stayed the night. You'll soon find yourself in the vast *apodyterium* (changing room). The *tepidarium* (warm room) is still partially buried. The *frigidarium* (cold room) still has pools on either side with mosaics.

Treasure House

North of the baths, the **Treasure House**, so-named for the 69 Byzantine gold coins discovered here, is the first example you'll see of a villa with a mosaic-covered subterranean room. You can go downstairs here and peer through a window midway down.

Veer northwest to the 6th-century **Byzantine Basilica**. Note the cross-shaped baptismal immersion font flanked by two columns. This was the largest of the Byzantine churches, with a double apse and three naves. A second **church** next door has brilliant mosaics depicting a chalice flanked by peacocks.

The Hunting Houses

A highlight is the nearby **Hunting House**. The upstairs floor has an *impluvium* (cistern) in the main courtyard. Steps here lead underground to the remarkable *peristyle* (courtyard) with eight pillars. Two square columns stand in front of the roomy *triclinium* (dining room) with excellent Amazigh mosaics.

Next door is the **New Hunting House**, with an exquisite hunt scene mosaic. Spot the zebra, panther, rabbits, wild boar and a central section depicting Romans hunting lions.

House of Amphitrite

The mosaics from the upper floor of **Venus House**'s (House of Amphitrite) are in the Bardo Museum (p68), but the subterranean floor still holds Bulla Regia's best in-situ **mosaic**, down the stone steps. A *triclinium* on the left holds the mosaic of two centaurs, one of which is being ridden by Venus. Elsewhere, Cupid rides a dolphin. The fountain in the wall facing the triclinium demonstrates the advanced plumbing involved.

Temple of Apollo

Wander southeast, past many other structures, including **Fisher House** (basement closed since 2008) to the **Temple of Apollo**, named after the large statues of Apollo and Asclepius that were discovered and subsequently moved to the Bardo. The temple faces the **Forum**. This central public space is flanked by the court, market, Capitol and a Roman Basilica.

The Theatre

The **Theatre** held up to 3000 people. The bear mosaic is from the Vandal period. The robed statue at the entrance is headless by design. The head was removable, so that it could be replaced with a likeness of the Roman emperor in power at that time without having to make an entirely new statue from scratch. Concerts still take place here in summer.

BULLA THROUGH THE AGES

Bulla already existed in the 4th century BCE during Carthaginian rule, passing to the Amazigh Numidians in the 2nd century, who added 'Regia' to the name, distinguishing it as an important city for the reigning royals. The combination of Amazigh and Roman architectural ideals created remarkable buildings here. The Vandals, Byzantines, and a series of Arabic dynasties followed, but it's still the Roman-era imprint that is most keenly felt.

TOP TIPS

- For an excellent local English-speaking guide with over 20 years of experience, contact **Amel Ayadi** *(96 014 141)*.
- Although this site is rarely crowded, arrive at opening time in order to experience the ruins to yourself.
- There are some basic info boards around the site in English, French and Arabic.
- The ruins are an excellent place for bird-watching. Egrets often cluster around the Hunting House, plus you'll likely see shrikes, redstarts and serins.
- There are no direct louages to the site, but a taxi from Jendouba should cost no more than 10DT, one-way.

GETTING INTO ALGERIA

Oum Tboul, 14km west of Tabarka, is one of the main land border crossings between Tunisia and Algeria. There is another crossing at **Babouche** (northwest of Aïn Draham), although this crossing is occasionally included in an amber (essential travel only) zone in the travel advisories of many nations.

Although relations between the two nations are largely cordial, you will notice a visible rise in police presence throughout northern Tunisia within 25km of the border and traffic stops are more frequent.

In 2024 a thrice-weekly passenger train service from Tunis to Annaba in Algeria restarted after almost three decades of silent rails. Services stop at Béja and Jendouba en route.

For information about making border crossings further south, see p161.

ANGELO GIAMPICCOLO/SHUTTERSTOCK

Diving, Tabarka

Continued from p139

coral, some harvesting is permitted. However, illegal diving and harvesting has led to a burgeoning coral-smuggling trade due, in part, to the high demand for products made with this scarce and rapidly disappearing coral. Hawkers selling it at the marina are best avoided.

The most sustainable way to experience the coral is to dive the reefs where it grows. The main scuba diving operation in town is **Club Nautique de Tabarka** *(clubnautiquetabarka.tn; dives from 70DT)*, which can even run dives in the winter off-season with advance notice. Dive sites that are most commonly visited include **Roches de Mérous** (Grouper Rocks), **La Grotte aux Pigeons** (Pigeon Cave), a good dive site for beginners with plenty of fish, and the **Tunnels**, which are large enough to pass through freely.

Beaches and tourist zones

To the east of the marina, **Montazah Beach** is a sweeping curve of sand that runs for 3km to the **Zone Touristique**, consisting of half a dozen upmarket resorts surrounded by golf courses. The side closest to Tabarka is usually busy and can get quite engulfedn in litter. It generally gets cleaner the further from Tabarka you go. If you have access to a vehicle, **Barkoukech Beach**, 12km east of Tabarka, is among the prettiest beaches in the area.

EATING IN TABARKA: OUR PICKS

Le Canari Café: Cheery spot with modern decor, the best set-menu platters in town and a fantastic stuffed calamari couscous. *8am-midnight* **€€€**

Restaurant Touta: Look for the royal-blue parasols and seating deck overlooking the water. Unsurprisingly, seafood is a theme across the menu. *11am-11pm* **€€**

Café La Marina: Best for set breakfasts where they serve heaped platters of food. They also have shisha here. *8am-midnight* **€€€**

Pure Nature: Pleasant views of the coastline and good grilled fish are offered at this tranquil spot located 3km west of the old town. *8am-6pm* **€€**

Chemtou

TIME FROM AÏN DRAHAM: **1¼ HRS** 

The lost marbles

In the midst of a hilly, secluded stretch of farm-quilted landscape, you'll find a human-made fissure in the rocky outcrop of Jebel Hairech that holds onto some remarkable yellow, orange and red hues. **Chemtou** (pronounced 'Shem-too') marble was highly prized around the Roman world, including in Rome itself, making this one of the most important historic **quarries** *(Tunisians/foreigners 5DT/8DT)* in North Africa.

A good place to start is the site **museum** (information panels in German, French and Arabic). There are various marble sculptures dotted around, although the highlight is the museum's centrepiece, where blocks retrieved from the Temple of Saturn (a Numidian monument) have been arranged in recreation. Most of the facade has been lost, stolen or sent elsewhere. Head up the stairs to the rooftop for the best view of it.

Marble extraction began under Micipsa, a Numidian king who ruled during the 2nd century BCE. The site became increasingly important under the Romans who, in the 1st century BCE, started using marble as a crucial indicator of power and wealth within state buildings and villas of the elites. The unique colour of Chemtou's marble, created by oxidised calcium carbonate, magnesium and iron, added value.

Over the centuries, an entire town grew to serve the workers and the remnants (from the Numidian, Roman and Byzantine empires) are spread across the surrounding fields. You'll need around three hours to explore it all. From the museum, follow the road uphill, passing the low hill (actually a waste mound from Roman quarrying work) on your right with more modern mining infrastructure in front, to the mountain with great gouges of the **Roman Quarry** in its side, revealing the red and ochre rock.

A path to the right of the quarry leads onto the hilltop, where remnants of old buildings and some rock-cut steps created by the Romans lead to the scant remains of the **Temple of Saturn**. The views of the quarry, aqueduct and the surrounding valley are worth the climb.

Other ruins include a **theatre**, **bathhouse** and a **Byzantine church**, which stand lonely in fields frequented by shepherds and their flocks. Last entry is at 2pm, so try to arrive early. Keep an eye on your country's travel advice as this site, despite being 17km from the Algeria border, is occasionally covered by an amber travel warning. The security situation here, as with at Bulla Regia, may require you to show a passport and provide details of your previous and future itinerary.

ROMAN SHOO-INS

Tunisia is rich with Roman legacy sites, not least of all their additions to **Carthage** (p76) such as the **Baths of Antoninus**. To link up with other ruins near to Bulla Regia, head 60km southeast to the exceptional archaeological site of **Dougga** (p158).

ANCIENT HIGHLIGHTS

Amel Ayadi, guide at Bulla Regia and Chemtou ruins, talks about her favourite aspects of the two Roman sites.

At Bulla Regia, there is a very interesting theatre with a stage and an orchestra, which is still used and has performances in the summertime in July and August at night.

The underground houses are the treasure of Bulla Regia. The Hunting House is one of the very special, very interesting houses excavated with mosaics still in place.

And for anybody who likes to see beautiful mosaics still in place, they must go to the Venus House.

You must also walk up into the quarry of Chemtou, where you can get a closer look at the unusual pinks, yellows and reds of the stone there.

SHADOWS OF WWII

Memories of WWII are littered across northern Tunisia. Many of them created during the war are fading to become a part of the landscape. You might drive past an old trench line or hill containing strategic bunkers and never know.

Northern Tunisia was the scene of a great deal of fighting, particularly in 1943 when the Axis powers launched Operation Ochsenkopf, which claimed thousands of lives on both sides. It's perhaps no wonder, then, that the most prominent memorials of the war are the war cemeteries, filled with the remains of soldiers who never made it home. There are many throughout the country, including at **Medjez el Bab**, **Oued Zarga** and Tabarka (p137) in northern Tunisia.

PAUL STAFFORD/LONELY PLANET

Ruins (p143), Chemtou

Béja

TIME FROM AÏN DRAHAM: **1½ HRS**

War cemeteries

The land around Béja was the epicentre of a lot of crucial battles during WWII, such as the **Battle of Hunts Gap**. Beneath olive and cypress trees, in the sandy loam of Tunisia, are the final resting places of soldiers from Britain, the USA, Canada, France and many other nationalities. They are reminders of a war that took place during the lifetime of less than 1.9% of the Tunisian population; indeed, before many of us were born. **Béja Commonwealth War Cemetery**, which lies 450m north of the train station, holds 309 graves of British soldiers, beautifully maintained by the **Commonwealth War Graves Commission** *(cwgc.org)*.

Places We Love to Stay

€ Budget €€ Midrange €€€ Top End

Bizerte p120

Dar El Kasba €€ Delightful historic family home in the kasbah medina with a central living space and small rooms ranged around the upper floor.

Dar Warda €€ Another pretty kasbah medina accommodation in blue and white. Some rooms even poke above this tight-packed neighbourhood, offering port views.

Résidence Ain Meriem €€€ Resort hotel with a decent pool, bar and restaurant and very spacious, although somewhat worn-out rooms.

Dar Salama €€€ Tucked away in the north end of town, but ideal for those with a car. Rooms are modern and employ traditional design motifs. Pool on-site.

Hotel Nour Congress €€€ One of the Bizerte hotel zone's many underwhelming 'resort' hotels. But this one is in walking distance of the old town.

Sidi Ali El Mekki p126

Cheeky Monkey €€€ A collection of eight bungalows. For a peaceful getaway, go outside of the summer high season. There's a great restaurant on-site (p126).

Cap Serrat p130

Auberge Le Pirate €€ Clean, basic rooms overlooking the beach in this secluded getaway; fresh fish dishes too.

Cap Negro p130

Dar El Cap €€€ Upmarket hotel with an infinity pool and freestanding bathtubs with views of the Jebel Chitana National Park's coastline. Full villa rental only.

Aïn Draham p133

Royal Rihana Hôtel € Slightly worn rooms, off-road parking and a restaurant and bar all under one umbrella in this hunting-lodge-style spot.

Résidence Panorama € Very basic rooms that aren't the cleanest. But choose it if you want somewhere that's cheap and right in the middle of town.

Discovery Eco-Hotel €€ Bright orange neighbour of the Royal Rihana with weathered rooms and a good hiking guide-hiring service; it tends to be frequented by tour groups.

Tulip Inn €€ Also known as Hotel Nour El Ain, the Tulip has seen better days but has a decent indoor pool. As with most hotels in Aïn Draham, you may not be able to reserve without booking through an agent.

Beni Mtir & Around p136

Centre de Camping Outdoors € Wooden bunk cabins in the woods and tents by the reservoir below Beni Mtir village. Also has kayaks for rent.

La Casa Del Formaggio €€€ Pastoral escape in the Kroumirie Mountains in a working farmhouse where cheeses and honey are made.

Tabarka p137

Les Mimosas Tabarka €€ Wrapped like confectionary in green and yellow, this classic old hotel is showing some wear and tear. Still worthwhile if you get a sea-view room.

Marina Prestige €€ Great location one block from the marina in Tabarka. Expect the rather dicey comfort- and quality-to-price ratio common in many Tunisian places to stay.

La Cigale €€€ Although the bar is not high, this is the best hotel in northern Tunisia (outside of Tunis) with good amenities in Tabarka's Zone Touristique.

Villa Belle-Vue €€€ As the name suggests, there are great views of the coast from this hillside apartment that can hold up to eight people.

Thabraca Hotel €€€ Somewhat faded and dated rooms, but still enjoys a fine coastal location and good beach access.

Béja p144

Hôtel Phénix €€ One of the few passable accommodation options in town. This no-frill spot is right in the centre, a couple of blocks from the train station.

Researched by
Owen Morton

Central West & the Tell

ANCIENT RUINS AND BUSTLING MEDINAS

Home to some of Tunisia's finest Roman sites, the central west and the Tell see fewer visitors than you might expect – travellers here can explore ancient ruins without the crowds.

Stretching from the Algerian border in the west to just shy of Tunis, this region encompasses diverse landscapes ranging from desert-like badlands to fertile fields, also including the Tell mountain range. Now home to relatively few people and no major cities, in the Roman era the area was extremely prosperous, acting as the granary of the empire. The number of outstanding Roman remains to be found here today bears witness to the region's importance in the past. Ancient Dougga has a good claim to being Tunisia's best Roman site, and other contenders such as Thuburbo Majus and Uthina are no slouches either.

If exploring the well-preserved and impressive remains of the Roman era doesn't grab you, the region has plenty more to offer. Towns such as El Kef and Zaghouan are home to gorgeous medinas that reward casual wandering, with narrow, glistening white streets bursting with bougainvillea often leading to spectacular Islamic shrines. Zaghouan's Tomb of Sidi Ali Azouz has perhaps the most beautiful tilework to be found in the region, though El Kef's mausoleum of Sidi Bou Makhlouf offers it a run for its money.

West and south of El Kef, the region extends towards the Algerian border. At the time of writing, the UK's Foreign, Commonwealth & Development Office (FCDO) advises against all but essential travel to this part of the region due to ongoing counter-terrorism operations by the Tunisian security forces. We therefore explore impressive Roman sites such as Sufetula and Haidra and the dramatic scenery of Jugurtha's Table in a shorter summary of the area.

ANDREAS WOLOCHOW/SHUTTERSTOCK

THE MAIN AREAS

ZAGHOUAN
Attractive medina and Roman ruins.
p150

EL KEF
Hilltop town with a long history.
p154

For places to stay in central west and the Tell, see p163

LEONID ANDRONOV/SHUTTERSTOCK

Left: Zaghouan (p150); above: El Kef (p154)

Find Your Way

Stretching from just south of Tunis across to the Algerian border, this region covers about 20,000 sq km, about the same size as Slovenia. It's easy to explore in a few days, but a lengthier stay is rewarding.

CAR

With a car, it's easy to get around the region: the roads are largely well surfaced and signposting is good. There's rarely too much traffic, though town centres can get busy and roads can be narrow.

LOUAGE

The major destinations in the region are connected by louage (shared taxis), which can be picked up in towns including Zaghouan, El Kef, Maktar and Testour. For out-of-town sights such as Dougga and Uthina, take a taxi from nearby louage stops.

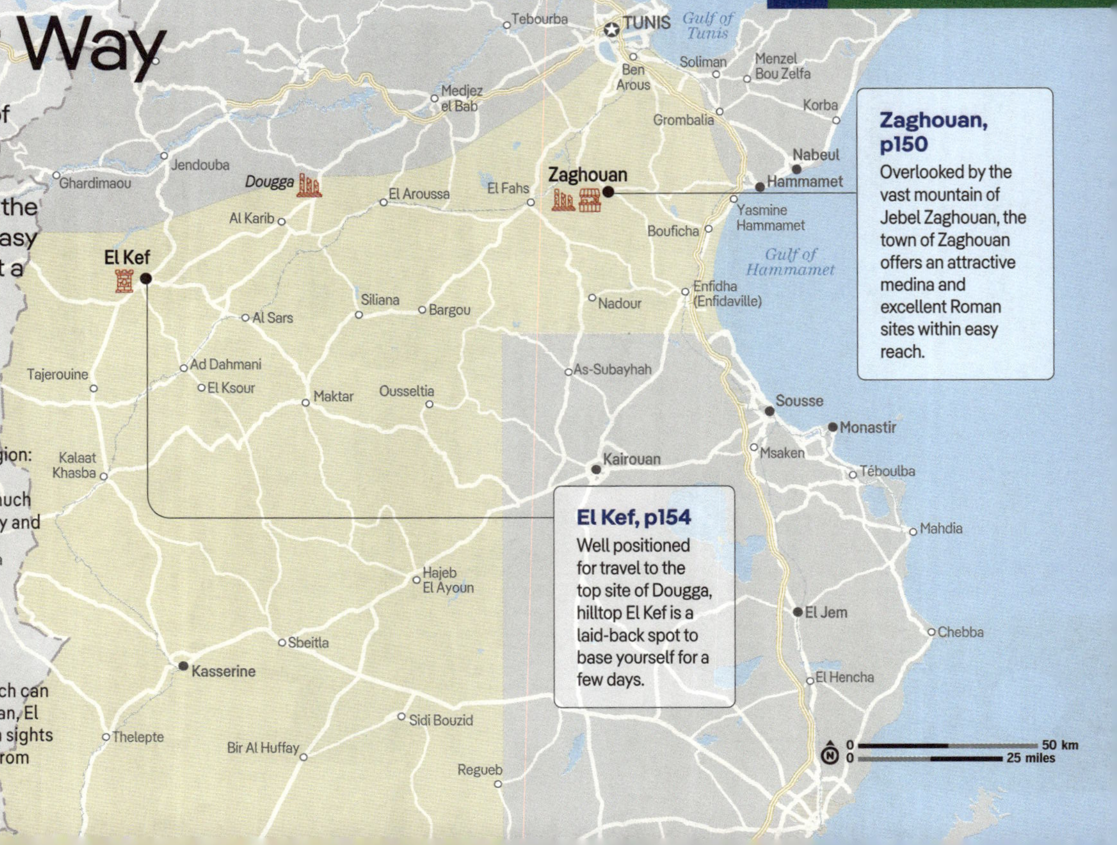

Zaghouan, p150

Overlooked by the vast mountain of Jebel Zaghouan, the town of Zaghouan offers an attractive medina and excellent Roman sites within easy reach.

El Kef, p154

Well positioned for travel to the top site of Dougga, hilltop El Kef is a laid-back spot to base yourself for a few days.

JUAN CARLOS MUNOZ/SHUTTERSTOCK

Doorway of Dar Lachhab and the Capitol (p158), Dougga

Plan Your Time

The main highlights of this region are the outstanding Roman ruins that dot the countryside. Channel your inner archaeologist for a deep dive into the ancient world.

If You Only Do One Thing...

- This area is packed with ancient ruins, but one stands out: the remarkable city of **Dougga** (p158). Make sure that you include it on your trip and allow a good few hours to explore the remains of its beautiful temples and winding streets, as well as the unusual tower of the Libyco-Punic Mausoleum. Dougga can be easily reached from **El Kef** (p154).

Five Days to Explore

- You can explore the region thoroughly yet leisurely. Start in Zaghouan and explore its pretty **medina** (p150), before taking trips out to the Roman sites of **Thuburbo Majus** (p152) and **Uthina** (p151). Travel westward to **El Kef** (p154) via the attractive town of Testour and the excellent Roman ruins at **Dougga** (p158), and enjoy a relaxed wander around the pretty hilltop town.

SEASONAL HIGHLIGHTS

SPRING

The weather is warm, making this a great time to explore the Roman ruins, which are often alive with wildflowers.

SUMMER

The region gets very hot: El Kef bakes, while the ruins offer little shade and limited respite from the sun.

AUTUMN

Temperate weather makes this an enjoyable season for hiking trips up Jebel Zaghouan or Jugurtha's Table.

WINTER

El Kef can get cold, but the region mostly offers pleasant weather, making it a good off-season destination.

Zaghouan

WINDING STREETS | ROMAN RUINS | MOUNTAIN HIKES

GETTING AROUND

Zaghouan's **louage station** is a gravel patch on Ave 14 Janvier, just downhill from the Church of St Helena. Here you can pick up louages to Tunis, Hammamet and Nabeul – ask around for timings. The town centre is easily walkable, and in the medina walking is the only sensible option. The Water Temple is 2km south of the centre, so a taxi may be needed. Uthina and Thuburbo Majus are both about 30 minutes' drive out of Zaghouan, in different directions. Both are easy drives if you have your own wheels; if you don't, hire a taxi for a couple of hours.

Zaghouan is an attractive and low-key town, nestled beneath the bulk of Jebel Zaghouan. It dates back to Roman times, and still retains a couple of examples of Roman architecture at the Arch of Ziqua and the Water Temple – the latter of which was constructed over a spring from which the Romans built an enormous aqueduct to supply water to Carthage, some 80km away. Both are worth a visit, but the real joy of Zaghouan is exploring the gorgeous alleys of its compact medina, which are painted a dazzling white and are bedecked with flowers and occasional spots of lovely tilework. With several very good places to eat and stay, and the excellent Roman sites of Uthina and Thuburbo Majus within easy striking distance, Zaghouan makes an unexpectedly enjoyable place to base yourself for a couple of days.

Wander the Medina of Zaghouan

Temple, tomb and picturesque alleyways

Zaghouan's pretty medina is packed with enticing cafes and water fountains bedecked with beautiful tilework, bougainvillea bursting from the balconies, and some engaging street art. Start at the Roman **Arch of Ziqua** *(free entry)*, then take an alley to your right to climb up towards the Church of St Helena, and wend your way along the main street, rue Sidi Ali Azouz. Don't miss the splendid **Tomb of Sidi Ali Azouz** *(free entry, donations welcome)*, on your right as you ascend the hill, just before you reach an archway. It's often locked, but the caretaker is usually on hand to open up so you can admire the lovely tilework within.

At the southern end of town, just beneath Jebel Zaghouan, is Zaghouan's most substantial Roman ruin, the **Water Temple** *(free entry)*, which dates back to the 2nd century CE. The niches around the edge likely housed statues of nymphs, with a large Neptune in the central shrine. If you're of an energetic bent, you can pick up paths from here that take you to the summit of **Jebel Zaghouan**, an out-and-back hike that takes four to five hours.

HIGHLIGHTS
1 Tomb of Sidi Ali Azouz

SIGHTS
2 Arch of Ziqua
3 Jebel Zaghouan
4 Water Temple

SLEEPING
5 Dar Aida Zaghouan
6 Dar Zaghouan
7 The Bungalow

EATING
see 6 Dar Zaghouan
8 Espace de Loisir La Grotte
9 La Joconde
10 La Vallée

TRANSPORT
11 Louage station

Explore the Ancient Site of Uthina

Amphitheatres and temples

Located about 30km north of Zaghouan off the C36 road, the Roman city of **Uthina** *(patrimoinedetunisie.com.tn/en/sites/the-archaeological-site-of-oudhna; entry 8DT)* was established around 40 BCE and grew in importance over the following centuries, reaching its zenith in the 2nd century CE, when the amphitheatre, Great Baths, and Capitol were built. The town fell into disuse in the early medieval period, but the remains are extensive and reward exploration.

The visitor centre offers a potted history of the site, after which you can take a raised walkway which leads straight to the elegant sandstone **amphitheatre**. After admiring this elegant oval structure, take the dirt path heading southeast, stopping en route at the extensive low-level ruins of a large house, where you'll find some mosaics still in place.

Pick up the rough track leading to the **Capitol** and circle round to the right hand side, admiring the vast bulk of this enormous temple before taking a staircase to ascend into its cool vaulted chambers. From there, climb again to the summit, where six tremendous pillars – one still intact – convey

TOP TIP

It can be challenging to get yourself oriented in Zaghouan, as the various sights are a little spread out, and the best accommodation choice is a short distance out of town to the west. If you're starting at the louage station, you can find your way to the medina by heading uphill.

ROMAN AQUEDUCTS

The countryside around Zaghouan is dotted with fragments of an ancient aqueduct, which lead in a rough trail towards the ruins of Uthina and beyond, eventually reaching Carthage.

Built over just 11 years during the reign of Emperor Hadrian, this 130km-long structure was one of the longest aqueducts in the Roman Empire, transporting fresh water from the spring beneath Zaghouan's Water Temple all the way to the coast. The water carried by this remarkable feat of engineering was used not only for drinking, but also to supply Carthage's enormous Baths of Antoninus, the largest Roman baths complex outside Italy.

The aqueduct suffered damage during multiple conflicts over the centuries, but seems to have mostly survived until the 16th century.

LEV LEVIN/SHUTTERSTOCK

Uthina (p151)

the scale of this huge temple to the triad of Jupiter, Juno and Minerva.

From the Capitol, a gravel track heads downhill eastward, bringing you to the third of Uthina's magnificent Roman public buildings: the **Great Baths**. Not as well preserved as the amphitheatre and the Capitol, they're nevertheless extremely evocative, with higgledy-piggledy blocks of masonry seeming to sprout like mushrooms from the ground.

En route back to the amphitheatre, divert to the right to stop at the **House of the Laberii**, thought to have been owned by Uthina's richest family. Many mosaics from this large residence have been lifted and are now in the Bardo (p68), but several excellent ones remain in situ here, and are well worth visiting.

Ruins of a Roman Town

Visit the site of Thuburbo Majus

Some 30km west of Zaghouan, and just off the C28 road north of the modern town of El Fahs, **Thuburbo Majus** *(patrimoinedetunisie.com.tn/en/sites/thuburbo-maius; entry 8DT)* is an extensive Roman site dating back to around the 4th century BCE, though its heyday came in the 2nd century CE. The ruins are easy to navigate, with most of the remains found alongside the path that runs up from the ticket office.

EATING IN ZAGHOUAN: OUR PICKS

Dar Zaghouan: A big place with set menus of simple, tasty Tunisian food. Eat on the terrace or in the eclectically decorated restaurant. *noon-9pm* **€€€**

Espace de Loisir La Grotte: Popular cafe with faux traditional vibe, best for coffees and milkshakes. Also offers fast food, including crepes and burgers. *9am-11pm* **€**

La Joconde: Excellent restaurant in the centre. Set menus with dishes such as beautifully slow-cooked lamb marinated in rosemary and spices. *9am-4pm Mon-Sat* **€€**

La Vallée: Good coffee and tasty fast food, served on a terrace with gorgeous views of Jebel Zaghouan. *9am-11pm* **€**

You'll reach the site's most impressive monument almost immediately – on your left, topped by four towering pillars, is the **Capitol**, a 2nd-century temple devoted to Jupiter, Juno and Minerva. The wide open space behind it, now strewn with wildflowers, was once the city's **forum**. Around its edges are the remains of smaller temples and public buildings.

Head down the staircase next to the circular Temple of Mercury to rejoin the main path. Ahead of you here are remains of houses, including the House of Neptune, where numerous rich mosaics were found. Some are still in situ, though the most impressive are now in the Bardo (p68).

Proceeding along the main path, you'll pass the ancient market on your left before coming to a staircase on your right descending to a **palaestra** – a public space for athletic training. One of its four grand porticoes is intact, supported by scaffolding, and the inscription along the top can still be read. Behind the palaestra is a **bathhouse**, some of its floor bearing impressive mosaics.

The main path now leads to a second bathhouse, known as the **Winter Baths**. Wander through its rooms to the back, where you'll find a beautiful, large black and white patterned mosaic, set in a spacious chamber with gorgeous pillars in the centre and stone benches around the edges.

Follow the path round to the ruins of two further temples. There's little left of the **Temple of Caelestis** save the arched entrance, though it's plain that it was once a large building. The adjacent **Temple of Baalat** has a bit more remaining, with a staircase up to a platform bearing two small pillars. It's a good spot for a view over the site.

From the Temple of Baalat, a further track leads to a trio of enthusiasts-only monuments. First up are the fairly scanty remains of the Temple of Saturn, behind which on the hill are the still scantier ruins of an early medieval church. Scantiest of all, on the opposite hill, is the mostly unexcavated amphitheatre, of which you can make out its oval shape but see very little of its construction.

THE TRANS TUNISIA TRAIL

The **Trans Tunisia Trekking Trail** *(transtunisia.com)* was established in 2024 as part of an initiative to encourage sustainable tourism across northern Tunisia. Several hundred kilometres of trail have been set up, which are maintained by local communities, and trekkers can undertake the trail as a long-distance route or use sections for shorter walks. There are numerous routes of varying length around Zaghouan, starting from the Water Temple, as well as in surrounding villages including the attractive Zriba Olia. Further west, the trail includes marked routes taking in El Kef, the small but gorgeous Roman site of Althiburos, and the towering bulk of Jugurtha's Table.

EATING IN EL FAHS: OUR PICKS

Restaurant Farah: Friendly, no-frills spot on the main road, serving tasty shawarma sandwiches and pizzas. The best place for a meal in El Fahs. *10am-11pm* €

Ice Dream: Smart, almost hipster, dessert cafe, offering indulgent milkshakes, ice-cream and cakes, as well as some of El Fahs' best coffee. *9am-9pm* €

Issam: Shawarma wraps are the best choice at this popular place, found on El Fahs' main road opposite Restaurant Farah. *10am-11pm* €

Patisserie Hamedi: Male-dominated cafe on El Fahs' main drag, with good coffee, tasty cakes and some savoury pastries. *8am-10pm* €

El Kef

MEDINA STREETS | HILLTOP KASBAH | CHILLED VIBE

GETTING AROUND

The **louage station** on Ave Mongi Slim, about 3km south of the centre, has routes serving much of the north and west, including Tunis, Jendouba and Sbeitla. There are also SNTRI buses serving Tunis from the same spot. The city's **train station** is about a kilometre further south, but sees relatively little traffic. Taxis are easy to pick up from either station to the centre; once you're there, the sights and accommodation are largely clustered together in a walkable, if hilly, radius. If you're driving, you should be able to find parking relatively easily around the main Ave Habib Bourguiba.

El Kef is Tunisia's highest city, located at an elevation of 780m on the face of the mountain Jebel Dyr. It's been settled for several thousand years, and the winding streets of the medina are now home to remains from various eras, ranging from Roman to Ottoman, which reward a couple of days exploring. Beyond the historical sites, it's a lovely relaxed place that's ideal for just stopping and enjoying the slow pace of life – in particular, the attractive square beneath the hilltop kasbah feels like a spot in which you could happily sit and watch the world go by for hours. With the best accommodation options you'll find in this part of the country – including some lovely boutique hotels – and a smattering of decent places to eat, it's a perfect place to base yourself while you visit the superb Roman sites in the surrounding region.

Stroll the Battlements of a Hilltop Fort

The kasbah on the hill

Right at the top of town is the **kasbah** *(free)*, an imposing 16th-century fortress that was built by the Ottoman Turks and subsequently passed through the hands of the French and then the Tunisian military, under whom the site remained in use until 1992. It sits on the site of earlier fortifications, though there's nothing to see of the pre-Ottoman remains.

Enter by the large wooden door and pass a line of cannons, then circle round and cross a drawbridge to access the **inner fortress** through an impressive black and white painted arch. Heading through the vaulted chambers, you'll reach the central courtyard, from which you can climb up onto the walls for fine views over town and across towards the Algerian border. Be careful on the walls – they're well-maintained, but there are steep drops without rails.

HIGHLIGHTS
1 Kasbah
2 Mausoleum of Sidi Bou Makhlouf

SIGHTS
3 Bathhouse
4 Museum of Popular Arts and Traditions

SLEEPING
5 Dar Alyssa
6 Hotel Ramzi
7 Maison Dar Boumakhlouf
8 Maison d'Hôte Casa Zitouna Kef
9 Maison d'Hôte Dar Saida

EATING
see 5 Dar Alyssa
10 Le Petit Bateau

DRINKING & NIGHTLIFE
11 Big Love
12 Café l'Artiste

TRANSPORT
13 Louage Station

Learn about Amazigh Culture

Explore El Kef's best museum

For an insight into the culture of this part of Tunisia, check out the ethnographic displays at the **Museum of Popular Arts and Traditions** *(patrimoinedetunisie.com.tn/en/museums/the-museum-of-traditional-heritage-of-le-kef/overview; entry 8DT)*, just downhill from the kasbah. It holds exhibits covering aspects of local life over the centuries, including an Amazigh tent and plenty of silver jewellery, with explanations of its significance. It's housed in a former *zaouia* (Sufi order headquarters), and the tomb of the Sufi leader Sidi Ali ben Aissa is also found within. At time of writing, the museum was closed for extensive refurbishment, but it is expected to reopen in 2026.

Dip into a Roman Bathhouse

The centre of Sicca Veneria

One of the most important public buildings of Sicca Veneria – as El Kef was known under the Romans – was the **bathhouse** *(free entry)*, the relatively substantial ruins of which

Continues on p157

TOP TIP

El Kef's old buildings – tombs, basilicas, the synagogue – are often locked, with keys held by the tourism organisation **ASM El Kef** *(https://tinyurl.com/asmelkef)*. Unfortunately, at time of writing, ASM had closed: there are hopes for its reopening, but in the meantime it's pot luck whether a caretaker will appear to let you into the various buildings.

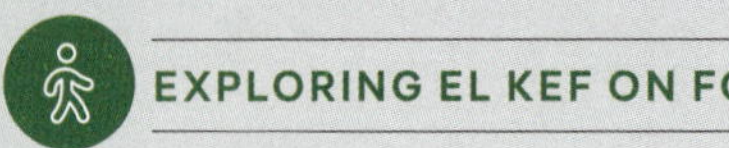

EXPLORING EL KEF ON FOOT

Explore El Kef's historical sites on this rewarding amble through the quiet streets of El Kef's medina.

START	END	LENGTH
Outside the kasbah	Basilica of St Peter	1.1km; 1 hr

Head down the steps from the kasbah to the ❶ **Basilica**, a stolid construction dating from the 4th century CE. Take the steps from the Basilica leading up towards a gleaming white structure, topped with domes and featuring a fine minaret with lovely tilework at the summit. This is the ❷ **mausoleum of Sidi Bou Makhlouf**, the patron saint of El Kef, and was built in the 17th century to house the tombs of him and his family.

Take the narrow alley to the right of the mausoleum's entrance and wander through pretty streets to exit the medina opposite the ❸ **El Kadiria** mosque. This lovely white building has gorgeous tilework around its entrance and on the minaret. Returning to the Sidi Bou Makhlouf mausoleum, stroll downhill through picturesque winding alleys to reach ❹ **La Ghriba** synagogue. El Kef was once a thriving centre for North African Jews, but the population went into decline after WWII. If the synagogue is open, it's worth popping in to take a look at its interesting collection of artefacts.

Finally, descend the steps to the main road, cross it, and take the stepped street downhill, turning right to reach the tour's end point, the ❺ **Basilica of St Peter**. This large church, lacking a roof but otherwise well preserved, dates from the 4th century, making it one of the earliest African basilicas.

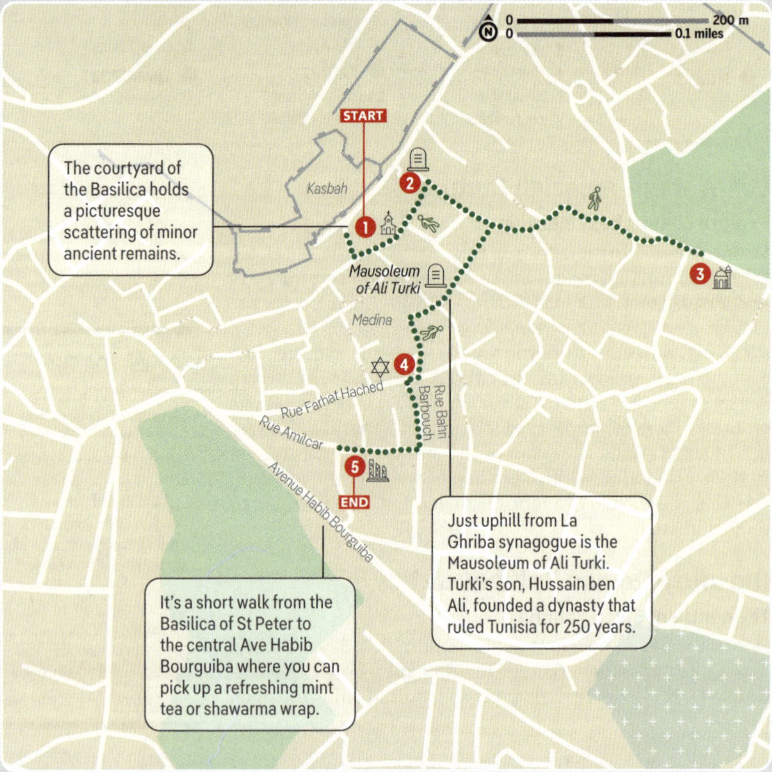

The courtyard of the Basilica holds a picturesque scattering of minor ancient remains.

Just uphill from La Ghriba synagogue is the Mausoleum of Ali Turki. Turki's son, Hussain ben Ali, founded a dynasty that ruled Tunisia for 250 years.

It's a short walk from the Basilica of St Peter to the central Ave Habib Bourguiba where you can pick up a refreshing mint tea or shawarma wrap.

ANDREAS WOLOCHOW/SHUTTERSTOCK

Bathhouse (p155)

Continued from p155

can be found on a pedestrianised street just off the central Ave Habib Bourguiba. Wander among the ruined columns and masonry to descend into the hexagonal hall, which is larger than it initially appears from the outside. The ancient remains here – which were once fed by the waters from the adjacent Ras Al Ain spring – make a lovely foreground for pictures of the nearby gleaming white Sidi Ghreb Mosque.

EL KEF THROUGH THE CENTURIES

El Kef's hilltop location has long made it an attractive place for settlers, offering an easily defensible position with wide-ranging views over the surrounding plains.

Its early history is unclear, possibly having origins as a Phoenician settlement, but it became important under the Carthaginians, who called the site Sicca.

Over the following centuries, the town took multiple names: it was Sicca Veneria to the Romans, Shakbanaria to the Arabs, and finally El Kef to the Ottomans, who arrived in the 16th century.

El Kef was the first Tunisian town taken by the French, who invaded from Algeria in the 1880s, and also one of the first to revolt against colonial rule in the 1950s.

EATING & DRINKING IN EL KEF: OUR PICKS

Dar Alyssa: Some of El Kef's best food can be found at this guesthouse, with set menus of regional specialities, notably lamb with couscous. *5pm-9pm.* **€€€**

Le Petit Bateau: Wood-fired pizzas are served up in this small, traditionally decorated restaurant. The outside terrace is a lively coffee and tea shop. *10am-11pm.* **€€**

Big Love: A modern, female-friendly coffee shop with a great sense of style: striking yellow walls bedecked with fun artworks. Snacky food available. *9am-11pm.* **€**

Café l'Artiste: Welcoming little coffee shop with a hipster vibe and a chilled soundtrack. It's a lovely place to unwind after a day's exploring. *9am-11pm.* **€**

Beyond El Kef

With some of Tunisia's best Roman ruins scattered between attractive small towns, the area beyond El Kef rewards exploration.

Places

El Kef makes a marvellous base for excursions into the surrounding area, which contains some of Tunisia's finest ancient sites. Anyone with the slightest interest in Roman ruins will want to check out Dougga, one of North Africa's best-preserved Roman towns, which lies about 60km northeast. Dougga's central Capitol temple is an especially majestic ensemble. Further remains can be found to the southeast at the impressive site of ancient Maktar, particularly notable for its large forum dominated by a triumphal arch as well as the sizeable bathhouse with in situ mosaics. Further along the road from Dougga towards Tunis is the lovely small town of Testour, which boasts some unexpected Andalusian influence in its attractive Great Mosque.

GETTING AROUND

It's easy to reach the various sights around El Kef if you have your own transport – the roads are asphalted and rarely busy, and signposting is generally good. Public transport is limited to louages: for Maktar, you'll need the route from El Kef to Kairouan, while for Dougga and Testour you should take the louage to Tunis. For Dougga, get off at Teboursouk, from which you'll probably want a taxi for the long uphill slog to the site.

Dougga

TIME FROM EL KEF: **60 MINS**

Monumental temples in a Roman town

The UNESCO-listed **Dougga** ruins *(patrimoinedetunisie.com.tn/en/sites/the-archaeological-site-of-dougga; entry 8DT)* are some of Tunisia's most impressive ancient remains, and you'll want to allow a good couple of hours to explore them. Starting from the car park and cafe, you'll first reach the 2nd-century CE **theatre**, a well-preserved structure that can seat 3500 people. From here, follow the paved Roman path heading west which leads down to the ancient city's centre, the forum, begun around 25 CE.

Although there are the remains of several public buildings around the forum, your attention will be captured by the largest and most intact, the splendid **Capitol**. This magnificent temple was dedicated to the trinity of Jupiter, Juno and Minerva, and was the centrepiece of the forum and the city. Gazing up at the portico, you'll see a carved relief of an eagle, representing the deification of Emperor Antoninus Pius.

Descend the steps west of the Capitol into the lower forum, and follow the path round to the square below. Here, the doorway of the temple known as **Dar Lachhab** provides a marvellous frame for photos looking back at the Capitol. The temple is mostly ruined, but pieces of masonry along the

GONZALO BUZONNI/SHUTTERSTOCK

Libyco-Punic Mausoleum

edges still bear carved inscriptions, and its high walls offer good views over the lower site.

A short way past Dar Lachhab, a paved path bears off to the right, taking you past the ruins of houses and shops spilling down the hillside. It's a hugely evocative path: despite the fact that the town is now in ruins, it's easy to imagine it busy with citizens in its heyday.

At the bottom, the paved route gives way to a dusty track at the edge of a grove of olive trees. From here, slightly to your left, you can see one of the most unusual ruins at Dougga: the pre-Roman **Libyco-Punic Mausoleum**. This lovely structure, resembling a lighthouse and bearing carvings on its four sides, can be reached by a short stroll through the olive trees. You can walk back from here up to the theatre, cafe and site exit.

Testour

TIME FROM EL KEF: **90 MINS**

Explore an Andalusian-influenced town

The lively little town of **Testour**, about half an hour's drive from Dougga, is worth a stop if you're passing by. The centrepiece of its attractive, well-kept medina is the **Great Mosque** *(free entry)*, a yellow-brick structure with a distinctive minaret, which at its top boasts gorgeous tilework and – most unusually – a clock. This almost unique feature is thought to be thanks to the town's Andalusian immigrant community, who arrived here in the 17th century. While in town, it's also worth swinging by the **Habiba Msika Museum** *(78 570 497; free entry)*: you're unlikely to come away any better informed about this local early 20th-century singer, but the tiles on the walls are lovely. Last but not least, be sure to browse the busy shopping street: the town has a good line in **cheese**, and there's excellent street food available.

DOUGGA'S HISTORY

Ancient dolmens on the ridge above the ruins of Dougga attest to its lengthy history, which spans back at least 4000 years.

It appears to have already been a fairly sizeable place when the Carthaginians arrived in the 4th century BCE, and it subsequently passed to the Numidians, under whom it took the name of Thugga. The Numidians sided with Pompey in the Roman civil war in 48 BCE; following Pompey's defeat at the hands of Julius Caesar, their rule over Thugga came to an end.

The Romans took control around 46 BCE, at which time it was renamed Dougga and rapidly expanded, reaching its peak between the 2nd and 4th centuries CE.

It went into decline in later centuries, although people continued to live on the site until the 1950s.

THE FESTIVALS OF TESTOUR

Testour is a lively place that plays host to several festivals throughout the year. The longest-running of these is the **Festival du Malouf**, first established in the mid-1960s. It is held in July and showcases musical performances from local, national, and occasionally international artists, with some events using the Habiba Msika Museum as a rather atmospheric venue.

A relative newcomer to the festival scene is the **Pomegranate Festival**, which kicked off in 2016 as a celebration of the area's rich agricultural produce – in particular (no surprises here) the pomegranate. Held in late October, visitors can enjoy freshly squeezed pomegranate juice while watching musical performances and other cultural events.

EMILY MARIE WILSON/SHUTTERSTOCK

Cheese (p159), Testour

Maktar

TIME FROM EL KEF: 1 HR

Ancient site in the heart of a modern town

The modern town of Maktar contains the ancient site of **Mactaris** *(patrimoinedetunisie.com.tn/en/sites/mactaris-makthar, entry 8DT)*, which was founded by the Numidians in the 5th century BCE and became Roman under Julius Caesar about 500 years later. It remained prosperous under the Byzantines, though went into decline from the 11th century.

Begin your exploration by checking out the small **museum**, which contains mosaics, coins and funerary stelae. Then follow the paved street running slightly leftward which leads up to the forum and the impressive **Arch of Trajan**, at the top of the site.

Downhill from the arch is a large ruin, which was the city's principal **bathhouse**, its immense size and grandeur suggesting that Mactaris was a large and important place. Mosaics still cover many of the floors, including one with a labyrinth design in the largest chamber. From the baths, a path skirts the edge of the site to an attractively overgrown ensemble of ruins, including an open space surrounded by many pillars, which is thought to have been a meeting place for a sort of Roman youth club.

EATING IN TESTOUR & MAKTAR: OUR PICKS

Dar Bessid: Friendly restaurant offering simple but tasty Tunisian dishes, just up the road from the Habiba Msika Museum. *11am-10pm.* €€

Pizza Espana: Popular place serving good wood-fired pizzas, with a perfect spot right on Testour's main square. *11am-11pm.* €

Super Pizza: Cleverly, it doesn't actually do pizza, but the shawarma sandwiches at this central Maktar spot make for very satisfying snacky lunches. *9am-10pm.* €

Café Maktarim: No frills and rather male-dominated, but if you're looking for a quick coffee pick-me-up in Maktar, this is as good a choice as any. *8am-11pm.* €

Along the Western Border

The UK's Foreign, Commonwealth & Development Office (FCDO) advises against all but essential travel to within 30km of the Algerian border and to the Kasserine Governorate, which centres on the city of Kasserine. Within this area are four national parks, which attract the more serious FCDO advisory of warning against all travel: these national parks are named after the mountains of Jebel Chambi, Jebel Mghila, Jebel Salloum and Jebel Sammamma.

The travel warnings in this area have been in place since 2012, when militant jihadists linked to al-Qaeda launched an insurgency, carrying out acts of terrorism in both Tunisia and across the border in Algeria, making their base in caves on Jebel Chambi. The Tunisian security forces responded with an offensive against the jihadists, and ever since the national parks and surrounding areas have seen regular security operations. The national parks remain closed military zones and it is not possible to visit them.

This is a pity, particularly for keen climbers – at 1544m, Jebel Chambi is Tunisia's highest peak, and until the insurgency began, was a popular and reasonably easy hiking route. The surrounding national park is home to a wide variety of wildlife, including Barbary sheep, striped hyenas and Egyptian vultures, as well as the endangered Cuvier's gazelle.

THE ALGERIAN BORDER

Although most travellers cross the border between Tunisia and Algeria at the border crossing of **Oum Tboul** (p142), the border posts of Sakiet Sidi Youssef, El Ayoun and Bou Chebka in this region are all open.

MOUNTAINOUS LANDSCAPES

The scenery in this part of Tunisia is rather stark: it's not desert as such, but in many places it's not far off. It has a somewhat desolate beauty, though, with marvellous views of spectacular, flat-topped mesa formations.

The mountain known as Jugurtha's Table is the most impressive, with a new road winding up almost to the summit, from which there are splendid views of other dramatic formations jutting out from the surrounding plains. It's a lonely experience – few people come up here – but the quiet adds to the sense of being on top of the world.

ANCIENT HISTORY

Although this region is now sparsely populated, in centuries past it was a thriving area.

There are fascinating Roman-era sites here; the most impressive is **Sufetula**. The extensive ruins – in the modern town of Sbeitla – contain a magnificent triumphal arch, outstanding in-situ mosaics, and a splendid trio of temples in the ancient forum.

Nearly as impressive is **Haidra**, a wonderfully desolate site close to the Algerian border which comprises, among extensive low-level ruins, the monumental Arch of Septimus Severus, a huge walled Byzantine fortress, and a little porticoed mausoleum that stands entirely alone in a bare field, its excellent state of preservation seeming all the stranger given its isolation.

Meanwhile, close to El Kef, the ancient Roman bathhouse of Hammam Mellegue is, remarkably, still in use.

Note regional travel advisories on p289.

Travel Warnings

Outside the closed military zones, the region carries an advisory against all but essential travel, largely due to potential cross-border operations by the Tunisian military. It is possible to visit this area, though travellers are likely to encounter police checks at road junctions and roundabouts on a semi-regular basis. At these routine stops, police will want to see passports or other ID, and will ask about travel plans.

Romans to the Byzantines

The area has a long history, evident in the many Roman sites dotting the landscape here. The city of Kasserine may have started life as the Roman settlement of Cilium, while nearby Sbeitla houses the extensive and beautiful ruins of Roman Sufetula. Perhaps the most famous moment in the region's ancient history occurred around 110 BCE, when the Numidian King Jugurtha rebelled against Roman rule, basing himself on the easily defensible flat-topped mountain now known as Jugurtha's Table. Remains of Jugurtha's fortifications atop the mountain can still be seen.

Jugurtha's rebellion failed, but Roman dominance over the area diminished as the empire collapsed. The Roman era was followed by a stint as territory of the Byzantine Empire, which in turn gave way to periods of Vandal and then Arab rule. The ruins of Haidra, close to the Algerian border, are perhaps the best place to see remains from multiple periods: they boast a Roman triumphal arch and an impressive mausoleum, a huge Byzantine fort, and a beautiful Vandal-era church.

Later History

Mirroring the history of the wider country, the region subsequently came under the rule of the Ottomans, the Husseinids, and the French, and a site north of Kasserine saw a significant WWII battle in February 1943. Allied forces, consisting of American and British divisions, had been pushing eastward towards Tunis, but were subjected to a counterattack by the 'Desert Fox', Erwin Rommel, and were forced to retreat a significant distance. The battle proved to be one of the last, and least consequential, Axis victories in North Africa.

The Region Today

In the years since independence, the region's economy – despite Kasserine being a fairly major industrial centre – has struggled. Its nascent tourism industry, centring on Roman ruins such as Sbeitla and the impressive mesa scenery of Jugurtha's Table, has largely collapsed in the wake of the advisories against travel in the area. This is unfortunate, as the area has much to offer: it is to be hoped that the FCDO's travel advice will relax in coming years.

Places We Love to Stay

€ Budget €€ Midrange €€€ Top End

Zaghouan p150

Dar Aida Zaghouan € The centrally located Dar Aida Zaghouan is an attractive little guesthouse with two rooms. Breakfast and dinner are taken in the lovely tiled courtyard.

The Bungalow €€ Somewhat tired but serviceable self-catering holiday apartments close to the Water Temple. There's a decent cafe on site, but no wi-fi.

Dar Zaghouan €€ This large eco-hotel complex on the outskirts of Zaghouan offers traditionally decorated suites and more modern chalets, set in attractive grounds with a good restaurant.

El Kef p154

Dar Alyssa € A welcoming and stylish guesthouse on a quiet street, with six attractively decorated rooms. The courtyard pool is a godsend on hot days.

Maison d'Hôte Casa Zitouna Kef € Friendly and competitively priced guesthouse a short walk away from the town centre, with three simply furnished but comfy rooms.

Hotel Ramzi € Very much no frills but perfectly decent hotel, right in the centre of El Kef. If you're on a tight budget, this is your best choice.

Maison Dar Boumakhlouf €€ A lovely boutique hotel just beneath the kasbah, with exquisite decoration. Evening meals are available and highly recommended.

Maison d'Hôte Dar Saida €€ Welcoming and central hotel with six rooms across three floors of a distinctive building. Breakfast is taken in the traditionally decorated dining room.

For places to stay in central coast and Kairouan, see p207

FABIAN EMANUEL BALINT/SHUTTERSTOCK

Above: Great Mosque (p175), Sousse; right: Medina, Mahdia (p192)

THE MAIN AREAS

SOUSSE
Magical medina and sandy beaches.
p172

MONASTIR
Ancient and modern monuments.
p181

KAIROUAN
Important Muslim pilgrimage destination.
p185

Researched by
Virginia Maxwell

Central Coast & Kairouan

LIVING HISTORY IN VARIED LANDSCAPES

Age-old coastal and inland settlements built around atmospheric, still-thriving medinas where tradition and modernity happily coexist.

This is the sun-soaked Tunisia of postcards and brochures, where architecture and landscapes unchanged for centuries effortlessly meet modern tourist requirements. It is also Tunisia's Islamic heartland, with some considering Kairouan to rank only behind Mecca, Medina and Jerusalem as one of the holiest cities of Islam.

The region's diversity – from religious conservatism to Western hedonism, from five-star beach resorts to traditional fishing villages – is belied by the short commutes it takes to get from one destination to the next. It's easy to get around here, whether it be under your own steam or by using local transport.

One feature that every town and city in this region has in common is a medieval medina. Laden with history but with beating modern hearts, these walled cities-within-a-city are among Tunisia's greatest treasures. They're not the only historical structures to visit, though, as the many and varied dynasties that have ruled this land over millennia have all left their mark. Here, you'll encounter traces of the Phoenicians as well as structures and sites bequeathed by the Romans, Aghlabids, Fatamids and Ottomans. This extraordinary patrimony, which has been acknowledged by UNESCO in World Heritage listings for Kairouan, the Sousse medina and the Amphitheatre of Thysdrus at El Jem, makes the coastal and inland settlements in this part of the country essential stops on any Tunisian travel itinerary.

KRZYSZTOF GACH/SHUTTERSTOCK

MAHDIA
Spectacular coastal location with ancient ruins.
p192

EL JEM
Known for its Roman-era amphitheatre.
p197

SFAX
Coastal city with a sprawling medina.
p201

Find Your Way

Tunisia's central coast is home to the large cities of Sfax and Sousse, as well as a string of towns known for their beach resorts. Inland, set in the semi-arid landscape, are the towns of Kairouan and El Jem.

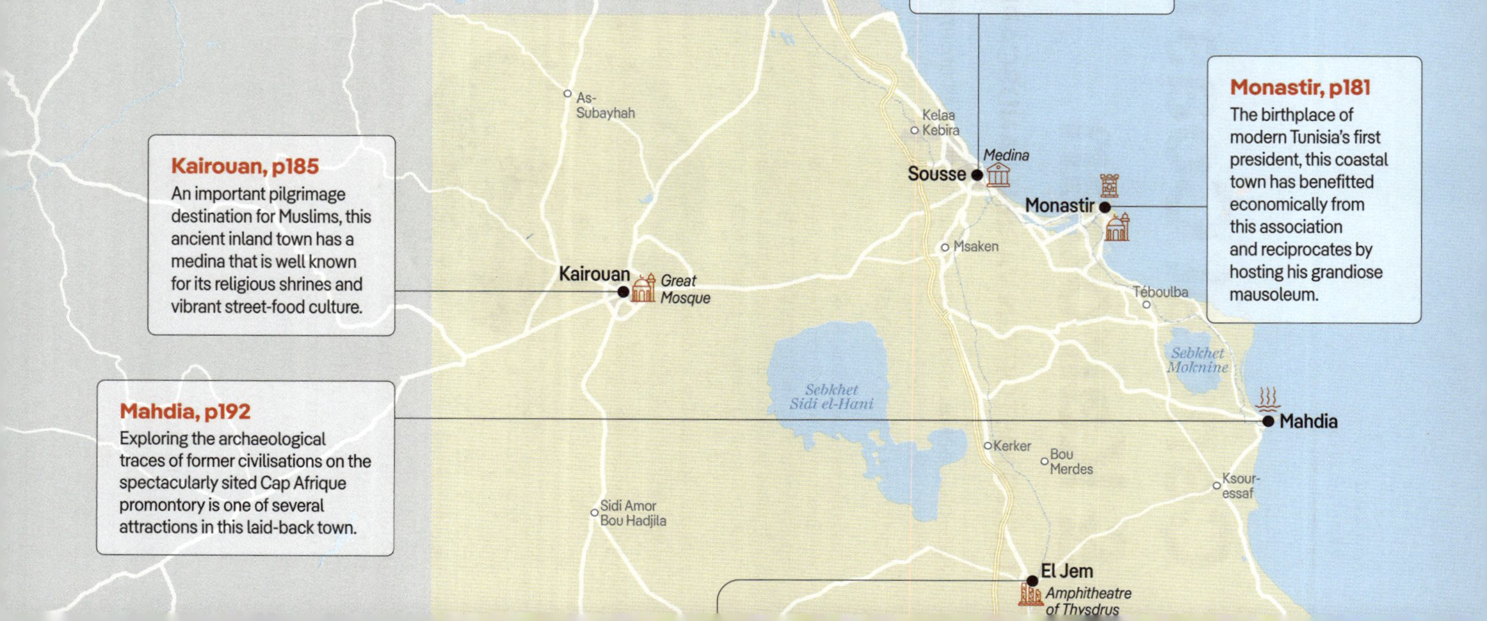

Sousse, p172
An important regional centre with an ancient and rich history, Sousse is known for its World Heritage–listed medina and long, sandy beaches.

Monastir, p181
The birthplace of modern Tunisia's first president, this coastal town has benefitted economically from this association and reciprocates by hosting his grandiose mausoleum.

Kairouan, p185
An important pilgrimage destination for Muslims, this ancient inland town has a medina that is well known for its religious shrines and vibrant street-food culture.

Mahdia, p192
Exploring the archaeological traces of former civilisations on the spectacularly sited Cap Afrique promontory is one of several attractions in this laid-back town.

CAR

Having your own transport makes getting between towns and sites easy, saving long and uncomfortable trips on public transport. Roads are well maintained and destinations are clearly signed. The only disincentive is the lack of parking if you choose to stay in medinas.

BUS

Buses link most major destinations and are the most comfortable public transport option on offer. The big bus companies maintain their vehicles and drivers are generally sensible, which can't be said for many louage (shard taxi) drivers. With one exception (Mahdia), bus stations are located close to town centres.

TRAIN

Sousse, El Jem and Sfax are stops on the SNCFT service between Tunis and Métlaoui. Trains are old, filthy and unreliable. In comparison, the cheap and efficient Sahel above-ground metro links Sousse, Monastir and Mahdia.

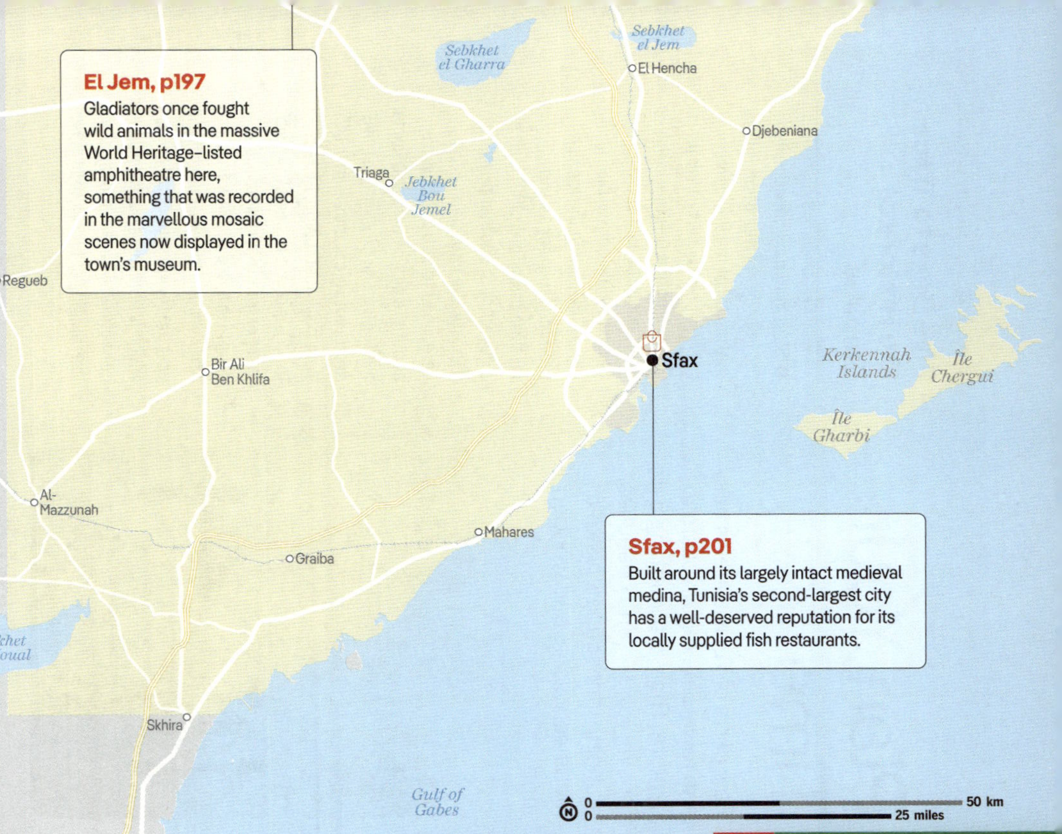

El Jem, p197

Gladiators once fought wild animals in the massive World Heritage–listed amphitheatre here, something that was recorded in the marvellous mosaic scenes now displayed in the town's museum.

Sfax, p201

Built around its largely intact medieval medina, Tunisia's second-largest city has a well-deserved reputation for its locally supplied fish restaurants.

Plan Your Time

Few parts of Tunisia are as easy and rewarding for travellers to explore. There's something here for everyone – sandy beaches, stunning landscapes, historic medinas, wildlife and wonderful food.

ANDY SOLOMAN/SHUTTERSTOCK

Bou Jaffar Beach (p180)

Five Days to Trace the History of Empires

● Start your peregrination in the holy city of **Kairouan** (p185), the capital of the 9th-century CE Aghlabid dynasty. Visit its **Great Mosque** (p186) and its many sumptuously decorated ***zaouias*** (Sufi lodges; p185) before inspecting the locally produced rugs for sale in a **medina mansion** (p190) built by a governor of another powerful dynasty, the Ottomans. From here, head to Sousse to learn about the city's Punic and Roman heritage in the city's impressive **archaeological museum** (p172). Your final destination, **El Jem** (p199), is home to one of Tunisia's most extraordinary sites – the **Amphitheatre of Thysdrus**. After visiting this, be sure to also visit the town's **museum** (p197), which is home to an extraordinary collection of Roman mosaics and the remains of four Roman villas.

Seasonal Highlights

It can be rainy on the coast in winter and hot in summer (especially inland), so the best times to travel here are autumn and spring.

MARCH

The rainy weather abates but accommodation prices and crowds stay relatively low, making spring a tempting time to travel.

MAY

By the second half of the month, the sun can be relied on and the beach beckons. Visiting now or in June is a far more alluring option than joining the ubiquitous crowds in July and August.

JUNE

The summer months are the best if you plan to scuba dive in coastal areas including **Mahdia** (p192), as the water is warm and visibility is good.

A Few Days Relaxing by the Beach

● Base yourself in Sousse, where you can stay in the heart of the historic **medina** (p174) or at one of the many beachfront resorts. Make the most of the local food and drink cultures by spending time investigating the medina's **coffee culture** (p179) and **street food** (p179). At sunset, join the locals promenading along the sandy length of **Bou Jaffar Beach** (p180). Take a day trip to **Mahdia** (p192) to spend time at its beautiful beach and saunter around scenic **Cap Afrique** (p195), where history resonates. Devote the next day to **Monastir** (p181), climbing up the 9th-century watchtower of its ***ribat*** (fort; p181) to marvel at the marvellous panorama of the Gulf of Hammamet that unfolds.

A Week Travelling Your Tastebuds

● This part of Tunisia has plenty to offer food-focused tourists. Start in **Sfax** (p201), where you can feast in restaurants specialising in **fresh fish** (p203), and take a day trip to the **Kerkennah Islands** (p205) to sample its famous octopus caught by the *charfia* method (fishing using palm frond traps; p206). Then head to Kairouan (p185), to enrol in a **spice workshop** (p190), investigate its **street food** (p170) and indulge in the local speciality of ***makroudh*** (syrup-soaked semolina pastry filled with spiced date paste; p191). Finish in **Sousse** (p172), where you can sign up for a **food tour** (p179), snack your way through the **medina** (p174), purchase **artisanal food products** (p178 and relax in a **coffee shop** (p179).

JULY

It's festival season, with both the **Festival International De Sousse** (p180) and the **El-Jem International Symphonic Music Festival** (p199) opening in July and continuing into August.

SEPTEMBER

You may be lucky enough to spot greater flamingos in the **Salines de Monastir** (p184), a wetland reserve just outside Monastir. The best bird-watching seasons in this part of Tunisia are autumn, winter and spring.

OCTOBER

The octopus season opens in mid-October and continues until mid-May in the Kerkennah Islands, so this is the time to head there for a traditional lunch at **Le Régal** (aka Chez Najet; p206) or **Le Pêcheur** (p206).

NOVEMBER

The date harvest is in full swing, meaning that cheap and luscious examples of this beloved local fruit can be sourced in fresh-produce markets. Olives are also being harvested at this time.

HELP ME PICK:

Marvellous Medinas

In the 9th century, Ifriqiya (the Arab-ruled province in North Africa that comprised what is now Tunisia, western Libya and eastern Algeria) was ruled by the Aghlabid dynasty. A succession of emirs bequeathed its capital Kairouan and the settlements of the central coast with walled medinas that have survived the centuries largely intact and are now major attractions for visitors. Managing to thrive despite the threat (and blight) of the ubiquitous modern shopping mall, these medinas stand as the symbolic hearts of their home towns, retaining residential and commercial populations and keeping at bay the fossilisation that so often accompanies mass tourism.

Where to go if you love...

Architecture

Sousse The medina in Sousse is World Heritage listed for good reason. It has retained its 9th century walls, monumental gates, *ribat*, Great Mosque and kasbah, making it the most intact of the coastal medinas.

Kairouan Not only does this medina have a strongly beating residential heart, it also retains many significant buildings constructed by the Aghlabids. These include *zaouias* decorated with fine tiles and plasterwork, mosques (including the fortress-like Great Mosque) and the medina walls. Ottoman-era additions include lavishly decorated mansions now used as hotels and rug shops.

STUDIO/SHUTTERSTOCK

Medina (p188), Kairouan

Sfax Wandering through the medina here is an exercise in time travel, with much of the original building stock and infrastructure little changed since the 9th century. This includes the monumental walls and gates, multiple mosques (including a Great Mosque at the medina's heart), mausoleums and a kasbah.

Street Food

Kairouan There are relatively few restaurants here, but the variety and quality street food makes up for that. Street stands and carts in the medina sell delicious savoury snacks such as *kafteji* (deep-fried vegetables with an egg and potatoes) and *fricassé* (fried, filled bun with harissa; p191), but the most famous medina speciality is the decadently sweet *makhroud* (p191).

Sousse Catering to the shoppers who make regular medina trips and also to the shopkeepers who serve them, the food stands and simple eateries of Sousse's medina are major lures.

Mahdia All hail the famous *chapati* (p195), the inexpensive and tasty flatbread wrap that has every Mahdian in its thrall.

Evocative Accommodation

Sousse The medina here is home to multiple historic dars (traditional houses) that have been passed down through generations of the same family and that now function as guesthouses. Known for their friendly atmospheres and delicious home-style breakfasts, these businesses are major draws.

Monastir It may have the smallest and least intact medina of all the central coast towns, but there is one compelling reason to visit the medina in Monastir – the magnificently renovated and stylishly decorated Dar Benti (p207).

Mahdia The laid-back atmosphere and close proximity to good beaches make Mahdia's medina a good choice for a relaxing visit, particularly as a couple of the best-value dar stays on the coast are found here (p207).

BEARFOTOS/SHUTTERSTOCK

Market, Bab Dhahraoui (p203)

HOW TO

Wear sensible footwear The medinas can only be explored on foot and *ribats* have steep and sometimes crumbling stairs, so you'll need comfortable walking shoes with good grip.

Dress appropriately Keep in mind that the medinas are home to important religious buildings and local families. Women need a headscarf to enter the courtyard of Kairouan's Great Mosque.

Eat sensibly Trust us: in the medinas, the street food is always the best food. Avoid pricey, tourist-focused restaurants.

Book ahead It's always wise to book medina accommodation in advance, particularly on weekends, in summer (especially in Mahdia and Monastir) and during festivals.

Traditional Medina Design

Medinas were laid out according to strict Islamic principles that are thought to have originated in 8th-century Baghdad. Carefully adapted to the rigours of the climate, their deep, narrow streets keep the sun from the centre during the day, and draw in the cool evening air during the night.

Medinas also served a military and defensive purpose, surrounding the city with fortified, crenellated walls and towers, elaborate *babs* or *skifas* (gates) and *ribats*.

The heart of any medina was the city's main mosque. Radiating out from the mosque were the souqs – still the lifeblood of any medina. Closest to the mosque were vendors of the 'noble trades': candles, incense and other objects used in rites of worship. Next were the booksellers, venerated in Muslim cultures, and vendors of leather goods. These were followed by the clothing and textile stalls, furnishings, domestic goods and utensils. Dars (interior-courtyard houses) were set in residential quarters away from the souqs – the size and decoration of the dar depended on the wealth of its owner.

Traders' caravans were usually on the medina's perimeter, so *funduqs* (travellers' inns) were also located there, as were ironmongers, blacksmiths and the other artisans and vendors serving the caravan trade.

Sousse

MEDIEVAL MEDINA | SANDY BEACH | ARCHAEOLOGICAL MUSEUM

GETTING AROUND

Monastir Habib Bourguiba International Airport *(habibbourguiba airport.com)* is linked with Sousse's **Bab Jdid Station** by the cheap and efficient Sahel metro *(sncft .com.tn/banlieue -du-sahel/horaires)*. The **Gare de Sousse** (main train station) is located a short walk northwest of the medina. The **regional bus terminal** is located 1.4km southwest of the medina's El Kebli gate and the main **station for louages** (shared taxis) is on Rue El Masjed El Aksa, south of the medina and the Bab Jdid metro station.

Central Sousse is easily explored on foot; most resorts in the Zone Touristique are a taxi ride away.

The country's third-largest city, Sousse is home to around 170,000 people and a healthy portion of Tunisia's tourist attractions and infrastructure. Chief among these are a remarkably intact medieval medina, a long tranche of sandy beachfront and an impressive archaeological museum.

Set on the Gulf of Hammamet, this part of the coast was settled by the Phoenicians in the 9th century BCE and by the Carthaginians after that (Hannibal based himself here during the second Punic War). When the Carthaginian general was defeated, the residents pledged allegiance to Rome and renamed their city Hadrumetum. After subsequent periods of Vandal, Byzantine and Umayyad rule, the city was colonised in the 9th century by the Kairouan-based Aghlabids, who renamed it Susa and used it as a commercial and military port. It was the Aghlabids who endowed Susa with the monument-rich medina we see today, one that still functions as the lifeblood of the city.

Admire Magnificent Mosaics

Museum in the ancient kasbah

An important element in the UNESCO World Heritage Listing for the Sousse medina (p174), the oldest parts of the city's **kasbah** were constructed by the Aghlabids on the southwestern edge of the medina in the middle of the 9th century. The building, its integrated tower and its ramparts were restored between 2007 and 2012, and new underground exhibition halls were constructed to house the collections of the **Sousse Archaeological Museum** *(patrimoinedetunisie.com.tn/en/museums/sousse-archaeology-museum/overview; entry 10DT)*. Of particular note is the museum's collection of 3rd- and 4th-century Roman mosaics, which is second in size and importance only to the world-famous collection at the Bardo Museum (p68) in Tunis. Most of these mosaics embellished the buildings in ancient Hadrumetum and nearby coastal

Continues on p178

SOUSSE

HIGHLIGHTS
1 Medina
2 Sousse Archaeological Museum

SIGHTS
3 Bab El Gharbi
4 Bou Ftata Mosque
5 Bou Jaffar Beach
6 Dar Essid
7 Great Mosque
8 Museum El Kobba
9 Ribat
10 Théâtre Sidi Dhaher

SLEEPING
11 Dar Antonia
12 Dar Baaziz 3
13 Dar Badiaa
14 Dar Lekbira
15 Hôtel Paris
16 Sousse Pearl Marriott Resort and Spa

EATING
17 Am Bourawi
18 Dar Baya
19 Dell'Arte Spaghetti House
20 L'Escargot
21 Pâtisserie Cherif
22 Restaurant Café Seles
see 15 Restaurant du Peuple
23 Restaurant El Sofra
24 Restaurant L'Espoir

DRINKING & NIGHTLIFE
25 Café El Kasbah
26 Cafe Gharbi Khemais
27 Dar Baba by Tammara
28 Dar Kmar
29 Dar Mariem
30 Fil Zan9a
31 Le Petit Cafe Maure

SHOPPING
32 Bab El Jedid Produce Market
33 Souq El Rebaa

TRANSPORT
34 Bab Jdid Terminal
35 Gare de Sousse

MACIEK GRABOWICZ/SHUTTERSTOCK

Minaret of the Zaouia al Zouqaq

TOP EXPERIENCE

The Medina

Retaining six of its original gates and most of its original walls, the 9th-century medina in Sousse was added to UNESCO's World Heritage list in 1988 in acknowledgement of its importance as a largely intact example of Aghlabid military coastal architecture. This includes a *ribat* that is often described as the oldest example in North Africa, a majestic kasbah and a number of mosques.

DON'T MISS

- Ribat
- Souq El Caïd
- Souq El Rebaa
- Dar Essid
- Bab El Jedid Market
- Great Mosque
- Museum El Kobba

Souq El Rebaa

At the heart of the medina, the covered bazaar known as the **Souq El Rebaa** is geared to tourists these days but retains vestiges of its past glory. It is a good starting point for exploration, as many of the medina's most atmospheric laneways and shopping strips are close by.

Museum El Kobba

Located near the covered bazaar, this former *funduq* (caravanserai) hosts a modest ethnographic **museum** *(adult/child 2/1DT)* that contains old-fashioned mannequin displays of day-to-day life under the Ottomans. The building is thought to have been built in the late 11th century and its most striking feature is a cupola with remarkable zigzag ribbing outside and fluted detailing inside. The museum is open from 9am to 4.30pm Monday to Thursday, 10am to 2pm Saturday and Sunday.

Ribat

This crenellated **fort** *(patrimoinedetunisie.com.tn/en/monuments/ribat-of-sousse/overview; entry 8DT)* is the oldest monument in Sousse's medina. Aghlabid emir Ziyadet Allah I commissioned it in 821 CE as part of his coastal fortifications and it was built on the site of an earlier structure. The *ribat* was garrisoned by devout Islamic warriors who divided their time between fighting and silent study of the Quran in its 35 tiny, cell-like rooms. The internal courtyard is surrounded by porticoes; in the corner is a 35m-high *nador* (watchtower) that functioned as a minaret as well as a point from which messages could be signalled to other forts along the coast. It's possible to climb the *nador*'s narrow spiral staircase to enjoy spectacular views over the medina and to the sea. A prayer hall on the southern side of the 1st floor has an elegant vaulted ceiling. The *ribat* is open from 9.30am to noon and 2pm to 6pm from Tuesday to Sunday between October and March, and from 8am to 7pm from April to September.

Great Mosque

Occupying a prominent location close to the medina's main entrance, this typically austere Aghlabid **structure** *(patrimoinedetunisie.com.tn/en/monuments/the-great-mosque-of-sousse/overview; entry 5DT)* was commissioned by emir Abû al-Abbas Muhammad in 851 CE. Its architect adapted an earlier kasbah, which explains the mosque's turrets and crenellated wall. The mosque's lack of a minaret is also unusual; the tower in the nearby *ribat* is used to call the faithful to prayer. Non-Muslims aren't allowed beyond the central courtyard, which features columned porticos. However, it is possible to view the barrel-vaulted prayer hall from there. The mosque's courtyard is open from 8am to noon and 1.30pm to 3pm from Saturday to Thursday, May to mid-September; from 8am to noon between mid-September and April; from 8am to 11.30am on Fridays and 7am to 12.30pm during Ramadan.

Rue Souq El Caïd

The **Bab El Gharbi** (Western Gate) is located a short walk down the hill from the kasbah. From the gate, the steep and stepped Rue Souq El Caïd, one of the most picturesque streets in the medina, heads down towards the covered bazaar. Wander up or down to find shops, observe artisans at work, taste local street food or enjoy a coffee or mint tea at one of the street's atmosphere-laden cafes.

Dar Essid

Tucked inside the northern ramparts, this privately owned **museum** *(entry 5DT)* allows visitors to gain an understanding of what daily life was like for its 19th-century residents, a well-to-do local official and his family. Enter the small anteroom, which was for greeting strangers, and then proceed to the tiled courtyard surrounded by the family rooms. The extravagant furnishings include Andalusian tiles, objets d'art and European antique furniture in the downstairs rooms.

MINARET MARKERS

The easiest way to navigate the neighbourhoods and winding lanes of the medina is by heading towards its distinctive minarets. To head towards Bab El Kebli, the southern gate, look for the squat white minaret of the Bou Ftata Mosque (p176). To find the *ribat* and Great Mosque, the elegant Ottoman-style octagonal minaret added to the nearby **Zaouia al Zouqaq**, an important Sufi religious complex, is a handy marker.

PLACE DES MARTYRS

The main entrance to the medina is via this large open space, which was formed when Allied bombs destroyed Bab El Bhar (the Sea Gate) and parts of the northern section of the medina's walls in 1943, during the British Eighth Army's final assaults on the Axis battalions that had retreated to Tunisia after their defeat in the Western Desert. The Allied shelling of Sousse was relentless, and much of the city and its port was razed to the ground.

TOP TIPS

- Those travellers who choose to stay in one of the medina's dar hotels overnight will get a true sense of its morning-to-night operation, including early morning market trading and late-night coffee-shop action.
- The best views of the medina can be enjoyed from the *ribat*'s *nador* (watchtower).
- To pause over a coffee, head to Souq El Caïd or to the streets and alleys surrounding the Bou Ftata Mosque.
- To grab a tasty street-food snack, head to the medina's bustling central spine, Rue Laroussi Zarrouk.

The upstairs area, reached by a tiled staircase, is where servants lived and worked. Two roof terraces and a tower can be accessed from this floor.

The museum is open from 10am to 6pm October to March, and from 10am to 7pm April to September.

Bab El Jedid

The medina in Sousse, like many of Tunisia's medieval centres, retains a residential population and sense of community. This means that there are many businesses here catering for the needs of locals rather than visitors. The most important of these is the busy and atmospheric **fresh produce market** at Bab El Jedid on the medina's eastern edge. Walk through to watch the fishmongers expertly filleting the day's catch and arranging it on ice; inspect the piles of locally grown vegetables and fruit; and follow your nose to the stands displaying baskets of aromatic spices alongside buckets of harissa, pickles and olives. The market traders usually start around 7am and operate their stalls until produce is sold out. They don't work on Fridays.

Bou Ftata Mosque

Constructed in the first half of the 9th century, this small **mosque** on the southern stretch of Rue El Maar is thought to be the oldest in Africa. Its squat minaret was added a few centuries later, during the Hafsid period. The mosque was gifted to Sousse by Bou Ftâta, the freedman of Abu Iqal, the Aghlabid emir of Ifriqiya. The triple-arched porch of the mosque carries Kufic inscriptions that include the date of construction. Only Muslim worshippers may enter.

BIESZCZADY_WILDLIFE/SHUTTERSTOCK

Fresh produce market, Bab El Jedid

EXPLORING THE SOUSSE MEDINA

This tour will assist you in navigating the medina's winding alleyways, multiple cul-de-sacs and bustling major thoroughfares.

START	END	LENGTH
Place des Martyrs	Great Mosque	1.7km; 1 hr

Plunge into the medina from ❶ **Place des Martyrs**, heading west past the ❷ **Great Mosque** into Rue el Aghalba. Walk until you reach the fourth alley on the left. Enter this, turn left again at the second alley you come to and walk to the junction of ❸ **Rue Souq El Caïd**, an atmospheric street where you can take a break in a traditional coffee shop and watch artisans working in their tiny ateliers.

Veer left and head downhill into the ❹ **covered bazaar** (Souq El Rebaa), passing the unusual dome of the former *funduq* that now houses the ❺ **Museum El Kobba**. Veer right into Rue Laroussi Zarrouk and walk south along this major thoroughfare, passing its popular pâtisseries and fast-food stands, until you arrive at the historic ❻ **Bou Ftata Mosque**.

Turn left and follow the serpentine alleyway east and then northeast, passing ornately decorated doorways and walking under *mashrabiyas* (projecting upper-storey windows covered in ornate wooden latticework) until you reach the ❼ **Bab El Jedid Market** (see left), joining the shoppers in inspecting the glistening catch of the day and other fresh produce. Continue north to return to the Great Mosque.

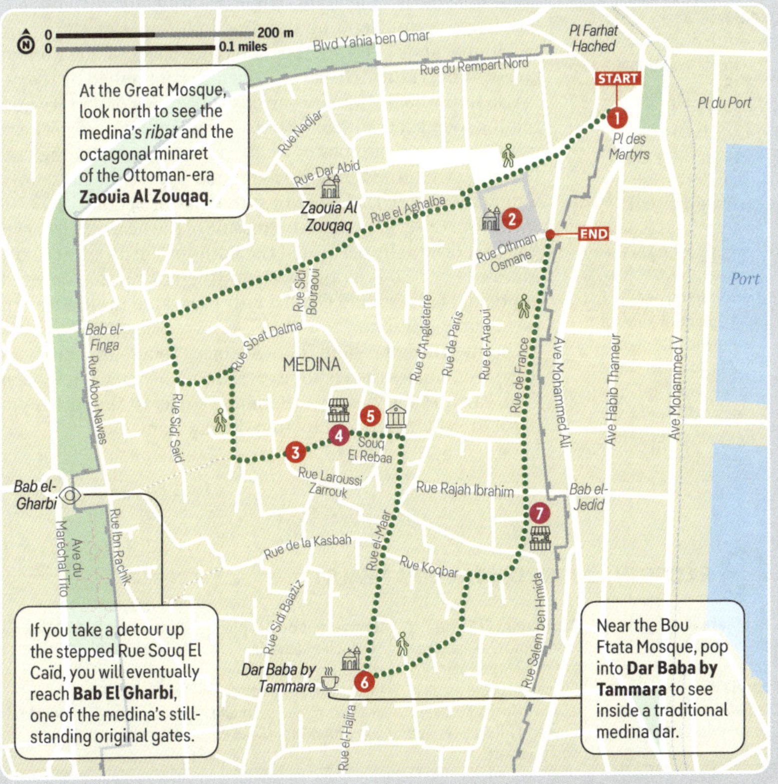

At the Great Mosque, look north to see the medina's *ribat* and the octagonal minaret of the Ottoman-era **Zaouia Al Zouqaq**.

If you take a detour up the stepped Rue Souq El Caïd, you will eventually reach **Bab El Gharbi**, one of the medina's still-standing original gates.

Near the Bou Ftata Mosque, pop into **Dar Baba by Tammara** to see inside a traditional medina dar.

FOOD CULTURE IN THE MEDINA

Jamel Ben Hmida, foodie guide @kamoun.kanoun

More than 10,000 people live in the medina, but most young people are moving to modern neighbourhoods. That is why I want to introduce people to the medina and keep businesses alive. Eating is a good way to do this, as Sousse is famous for its fish dishes and also for traditional dishes such as *khobiza*, which is made from mallow leaves. There are also a lot of dishes that are cooked in medina houses and not presented in the restaurants. I enjoy introducing people to the delicious *kaskrout* (sandwiches) made at **Am Bourawi** and to the super-fresh classic dishes at **Restaurant El Sofra** (see below).

FROM LEFT: KAREN TOMCZAK; KADAGAN/SHUTTERSTOCK

Sousse Archaeological Museum (p172)

Continued from p172

sites such as El Jem, Enfidha, Moknine, Temetra and Uzita. The mosaics depict scenes from daily life – the fishing scenes are particularly charming. Highlights include a richly coloured mosaic of Neptune standing in his chariot, drawn by two hippocamps; and another depicting Bacchus, the Roman god of wine, riding in a satyr-driven chariot pulled by tigers.

Also in the collection are various collections of pottery and tomb goods such as stone steles, urns and ex-votos. These were found in a number of tombs scattered around the city that date from the Punic period. Look out for the museum's famous *Drunken Old Woman* statue in this section.

Also worth seeking out are a mosaic of the head of an ocean god that originally decorated the Baths of Themetra at Chott Meriem near Sousse and a Byzantine-era mosaic-covered baptismal font from El Gaalla, only excavated in 1993 and in excellent condition.

The multilingual labelling (Arabic, French and English) greatly enhances the visitor experience. The museum is open from 9am to 5pm Tuesday to Sunday October to March, to 6pm April to September, and to 4pm during Ramadan.

EATING IN SOUSSE: BEST MEDINA MEALS

Restaurant L'Espoir: Ultra-simple joint serving plates of local specialities such as *lablebi* (spiced chickpea soup). *noon-4pm* €

Restaurant El Sofra: Also known as Chez Fredj, this family-run eatery in the centre of the medina is known for its excellent food and friendly service. *noon-5pm* €€

Restaurant du Peuple: The ladies in the tiny kitchen here conjure up tasty local dishes offered in a well-priced set menu. *noon-10pm Mon-Sat* €€

Restaurant Café Seles: Near Bab El Gharbi, this long-running business is known for its panoramic rooftop. Food is traditional and tasty. *9am-9pm* €€

Take a Food-Focused Walk

Sample local specialities

One of the most satisfying parts of any visit to the medina is the opportunity to enjoy a cheap and cheerful snack or meal. There are plenty of fast-food stands in Place des Martyrs and Rue Laroussi Zarrouk selling *chapatis* (stuffed flatbreads), *brik* (fried savoury pastry stuffed with runny egg and sometimes with tuna or mashed potato), *baguettes farcie* (grilled baguettes with fillings including *shwarma*), *mlawi* (burrito-like stuffed flatbread) and *makloub* (pizza-like bread filled with mayonnaise, harissa and vegetables).

Local foodie **Jamel Ben Hmida** *(jamel.benhmida07@gmail.com; see left)* conducts tours in the medina that introduce participants to savoury and sweet specialities during a food-focused walk. Jamel, who grew up living in the medina, speaks French and Arabic but also works with English-speaking colleagues. A two-hour tour costs €40 per person.

Coffee in the Medina

Relax in a neighbourhood cafe

There are nearly as many coffee shops in the medina as there are pâtisseries (and that's a lot). Most function as community spaces that draw local residents after work and in the evening, although they serve customers all day. Many of the traditional coffee shops are male-only territory, although there are exceptions, one being **Cafe Gharbi Khemais** on Rue Laroussi Zarrouk near the covered bazaar. Foreign visitors tend to gravitate towards the atmosphere-laden **Cafe El Kasbah** and **Le Petit Cafe Maure** on Rue Souq el Caïd; **Dar Mariem** near the Bou Ftata Mosque in the southern part of the medina; and **Fil Zan9a**, a stylish hole-in-the-wall third-wave coffee bar near the Covered Bazaar (look for Restaurant Ali Baba; the coffee bar is close by). All of these cafes welcome both female and male customers; the best coffee is served at Cafe El Kasbah, which serves a thick and strong traditional version that is brewed in hot sand.

Contemporary Culture in Traditional Surrounds

The medina's new-wave businesses

Tradition is held dear by the medina's residents and workers, but in recent years the younger generation has been spearheading a slow change in the type of businesses opening

THE ALL-INCLUSIVE HOTEL PACKAGE

The easy availability of cheap all-inclusive holiday accommodation packages is a major lure for the thousands of foreigners who descend on Sousse, nearby Port El Kantaoui and other coastal beach resorts in summer. Guests are presented with a plastic bracelet at the beginning of their holiday and must wear it for the duration – red may mean that meals, entertainment and all drinks are included in their package; blue might only cover the room and meals. Kids' clubs, playgrounds and wading pools are draws for families, and bars and lounges are popular with older guests in the colder months. Those in Tunisia for a beach break may find these hotels a perfect choice, but travellers here for cultural tourism should stay elsewhere.

EATING IN SOUSSE: OUTSIDE THE MEDINA

Pâtisserie Cherif: The streetside tables at this cafe are highly contested. Offerings include coffee, luridly coloured ice-cream, pastries and gâteaux. *8am-midnight* €

Dar Baya: Close to the beach, this traditional local eatery offers huge servings of delectable grilled fish, couscous, *shakshuka* (spicy egg dish) and stews. *noon-5pm* €€

Dell'Arte Spaghetti House: Opposite the train station, this female-run Italian restaurant offers pastas and salad. Pleasant surrounds but no alcohol. *noon-7pm Mon-Sat* €€

L'Escargot: A local institution, this French restaurant has fusty decor and a menu featuring well-executed traditional dishes. Good wine list. *noon-11pm* €€

BARGAIN HUNTING AT THE FRIPES

Visitors to Tunisia are often surprised by the number of *fripes* (secondhand clothing and shoe markets). Often found in medinas, these street stalls are piled high with used items that have been sent to Tunisia from Europe and sometimes from further abroad. We're not talking desirable vintage items here – these are mass-produced clothes with various degrees of wear that are sold extremely cheaply. There are thousands of *fripes* throughout the country, selling the contents of the many containers that arrive in Tunisia by sea each year. In Sousse, the *fripes* are located just inside the ramparts near Bab El Jebli and the *ribat*.

here. Geared to tourists but far from being touristy, these businesses are usually set in attractive traditional dars and are multi-functional, offering coffee, meals, workshops and artisanal products. The most impressive of these exercises in innovation are Dar Kmar and Dar Baba by Tammara, both located near the Bou Ftata Mosque in the southern section of the medina. **Dar Kmar** *(instagram.com/dar_kmar_sousse)* serves excellent coffee and food in its downstairs space and has a concept store selling artisanal Tunisian products upstairs. **Dar Baba by Tammara** *(instagram.com/darbaba_soussa)* sells homemade artisanal food products such as harissa, runs cooking workshops, programs cinema nights and serves coffee in its central courtyard.

A Slice of Local Life

Promenade by the sea

Named after a 10th-century Muslim holy man whose *marabout* (shrine marking a burial place) is located nearby, sandy **Bou Jaffar Beach** in central Sousse is a popular summer playground. When the sun shines, families picnic, beach shacks sell drinks and ice-cream, children frolic and foreigners sunbathe. Only a few small parts of the strip are claimed by beachfront hotels – their chaises longues and parasols are usually available to nonguests for a small fee.

Swimming here may not be to every local's taste, but promenading here certainly is, especially at dusk. Young couples stroll and enjoy the sunset, noisy groups of teenagers congregate and parents watch over their children as they climb on the low parapet between the path and the sand. Street hawkers set up stalls along the seafront walkway selling ice-cream, sweets and other snacks and do a roaring trade in the warmer weather. In the cooler months, they sell hot mint tea to keep customers warm. It's a perfect microcosm of local life.

Those thinking of taking to the wave-free water here should perhaps reconsider, as in 2024 Tunisia's Ministry of Health advised that two beaches in Sousse were unsuitable for swimming due to high levels of fecal matter in the water. Also note that a lifeguard presence is usually the exception rather than the rule. As a result, most foreign travellers choose to swim in hotel pools rather than the sea.

Attend a Performance under the Stars

Showcase of popular Tunisian music

Held at the open-air **Théâtre Sidi Dhaher** near the kasbah from mid-July to the end of August each year, the **Festival International De Sousse** *(facebook.com/festivalSousse)* is one of the country's pre-eminent cultural festivals. Now in its sixth decade, it focuses on music and hosts big-name local performers as well as the occasional international guest. Recent headline acts have included the wildly popular Mortadha Ftiti, Raouf Maher, Yosra Mahnouch and Zied Gharsa. Tickets cost around 30DT and usually sell out beforehand – ask your hotel if it can obtain tickets for you.

TOP TIP

If using Google Maps in the medina, note that it uses outdated colonial-era names for some major streets. These include Rue d'Angleterre (now Rue Laroussi Zarrouk) and Rue de Paris (now Rue El Maar).

Monastir

MEDIEVAL FORT | PRESIDENTIAL MONUMENTS | BIRDLIFE

Monty Python fans have a compelling reason to visit this small coastal town approximately 20km southeast of Sousse, as its well-preserved medieval *ribat* was used as a set in the incomparable *Life of Brian*. Others may find the town's attractions less than compelling, as its medina is modest in size and was heavily compromised by so-called improvements in the 1960s. These were the initiative of the town's most-famous son, Habib Bourguiba, a leader during the country's struggle for independence and the first president of post-colonial Tunisia. Bourguiba's penchant for self-aggrandisement led to the construction of an eponymous mosque, summer palace and massive mausoleum in his home town, all of which are draws for domestic tourists but of less interest to most international travellers. Though a decent day trip destination for those staying in Sousse or Mahdia, those strapped for time might wish to devote their days to other destinations.

GETTING AROUND

Monastir is home to Habib Bourguiba International Airport, which is linked to the centre of town and to Sousse and Mahdia by the cheap and efficient Sahel metro. The **metro station** and the **bus and louage station** are located in the centre of town, a short walk southeast of the medina. All destinations of interest to travellers can be accessed on foot.

Reminder of Ancient Ifriqiya

Well-preserved Islamic military fortification

The first iteration of Monastir's spectacularly sited ***ribat*** *(patrimoinedetunisie.com.tn/en/monuments/ribat-of-monastir/overview; entry 8TD)* was built by order of Harthimâ ibn A'yûn, the Abbasidian governor of Ifriqiya, in 795-796 CE. However, the fortified structure we see today was largely the work of the Aghlabids, who based its design on that of the *ribat* in nearby Sousse. They also constructed the nearby **Great Mosque**, which has equally severe architecture.

The fort's seemingly chaotic design, with labyrinthine passageways and staircases, is a legacy of the many periods of construction and renovation it has undergone over its long history. The oldest remaining (though heavily restored) sections include a *nador* in the southeast corner; this probably dates from the 9th century. The *ribat*'s walls have been remodelled many times, notably in the 17th century when the cylindrical corner towers were added.

TOP TIP

Don't head to Monastir if you are keen on spending time at the beach – though sandy, the beaches are crowded and usually dirty. Surrounding infrastructure (paths, walls) is in a dangerous state of disrepair.

HIGHLIGHTS
1 Ribat

SIGHTS
2 Bab Brikcha
3 Bourguiba Mosque
4 Great Mosque
5 Mausoleum of Habib Bourguiba
6 Medina

SLEEPING
7 Dar Benti
8 Marina Cap Monastir Appart-Hôtel

EATING
9 Dar Chraka
10 Le Roi du CousCous
11 Restaurant Le Pirate

DRINKING & NIGHTLIFE
12 El Grotte
13 My Favory

TRANSPORT
14 Bus and Louage Station
15 Sahel Metro Station

The internal courtyard is surrounded by galleries containing cell-like rooms that were used as accommodation for defenders. On the 1st floor, the prayer room with its multiple naves and barrel vaults now houses a modest collection of Islamic artefacts, including pottery, coins and wood carvings from the Great Mosque at Kairouan.

There are excellent **views** of the town and the coastline from the ramparts and the top of the *nador*; those suffering from vertigo should tread carefully, and groups with children should be particularly careful as there are few safety barriers.

The *ribat* is open from 8am to 5.30pm October to March, 8.30am to 5.30pm April to September and 8am to 5pm during Ramadan.

A Modest Medina

Monastir's historic town centre

Monastir's cobbled **medina** retains its northern, southern and western historic walls, an Ottoman-era tower and two original gates. Most visitors enter through the 17th-century **Bab Brikcha** (Burgundy Gate), which is located close to the metro station. The **Bourguiba Mosque** in the centre of the medina was built in 1963 and it is accessed via 19 ornately carved wooden doors; only Muslim worshippers may enter. A palm-tree-studded park featuring a golden statue of the young Habib Bourguiba leads from the mosque to the *ribat*, Great Mosque and seafront.

Visit a President's Final Resting Place

Ostentatious presidential tomb

The colourful cupolas and tapering marble minarets of the **mausoleum of Habib Bourguiba** are certainly eye-catching, and the octagonal marble hall containing his sarcophagus is impressive, too. Designed by Tunisian architect Olivier-Clément Cacoub, who was also responsible for the presidential palace in Carthage, the mausoleum was commissioned by Monastir-born Bourguiba and built in 1963, decades before he died. Next to the main hall are tombs of Bourguiba's family members and a small display of his personal items. A staircase on the southern side of the building leads to a 1st-floor interior balcony, from where you can view the tomb's ostentatious interior.

The mausoleum is open from 9am to 4.30pm October to April, to 5.30pm from May to September. Entry is free, but all visitors must be appropriately dressed (shorts not allowed). When the main gate is closed, walk around the fence to the small gate on the northern side.

Tea in the Pirate's Cove

Popular terrace cafe

A short walk from the *ribat*, the **El Grotte** cafe and restaurant sits on the edge of a small harbour where local fishermen keep their boats. It's wildly popular with families and groups of young locals, who congregate on the waterside terrace to enjoy soft drinks and snacks. This is a pleasant spot in which to while away an hour or so over a glass of mint tea, especially as the view ranges over the harbour shacks where fishermen mend their nets.

The cafe is built atop a natural sea cave that legend says was once used by corsairs. Head down the stairs to access this but be careful not to slip on the rocks.

HABIB BOURGUIBA

Often described as the founder of Modern Tunisia, Habib Bourguiba was born in Monastir in 1903 and educated in Tunis.

After studying law in Paris, he returned home in 1927 and became involved in the nationalist movement, co-founding a nationalist political party, the Neo-Destour, which advocated for national sovereignty.

Arrested and imprisoned by the French on a number of occasions, Bourguiba eventually became the de facto leader of the country's nationalist movement, travelling the world to advocate for Tunisian independence. After this was granted in March 1956, he was elected to the newly formed parliament and was appointed as head of government, remaining in this position for three decades.

Bourguiba died in 2000.

EATING & DRINKING IN MONASTIR: OUR PICKS

My Favory: Popular with young people, this cafe on the main seafront road offers cheap drinks and free wi-fi. *7am-11pm* €

Le Roi du CousCous: Longstanding favourite on the edge of the medina, with home-style dishes including fish and royal couscous. *noon-10pm Mon-Sat, to 4pm Sun* €€

Dar Chraka: Frills-free eatery in a secluded medina square serving pastas, escalopes and grills. *hours vary* €€

Restaurant Le Pirate: Look past the kitsch decor at this restaurant in the port compound south of town. It serves good fresh seafood. *noon-4pm & 7-11pm Tue-Sun* €€€

FILM LOCATIONS

There's a simple explanation for why many travellers experience a sense of déjà vu when visiting this part of Tunisia – many well-known films have been shot here, including the following.

Jesus of Nazareth: Monastir and its *ribat* doubled for Jerusalem in Franco Zeffirelli's 1977 TV series.

Monty Python's Life of Brian: Scenes in this 1979 film were shot in Monastir's *ribat*, Sousse's kasbah and El Jem's amphitheatre.

Raiders of the Lost Ark: Steven Spielberg substituted Kairouan for Cairo in his 1981 blockbuster.

Pirates: Roman Polanski shot the galleon scenes of this 1986 film around Sousse.

The English Patient: Mahdia and Sfax doubled for Cairo in Anthony Minghella's 1996 Oscar-winning film.

SKAZARPHOTO/SHUTTERSTOCK

Salines de Monastir

Gawk at Greater Flamingos

Bird-watching over Monastir's wetlands

Travelling from Sousse to Monastir on the Sahel metro, passengers are treated to a wonderful view over the **Salines de Monastir**, a natural salt marsh connected to the sea by two relatively broad channels. Designated as an internationally significant landscape under the Ramsar Convention on Wetlands of International Importance, it is known as a haven for wintering, nesting and permanently resident seabirds, which are attracted by its population of fish and algae. Here, bird-watchers may be able to spot *Tadorna tadorna* (common shelduck), *Himantopus Himantopus* (black-winged stilt), *Recurvirostra avocet* (pied avocet), *Larus cachinnans* (Caspian gull), *Sterna albifrons* (little tern) and – most spectacularly – colonies of *Phoenicopterus roseus* (Greater flamingos), which come here in their thousands to breed.

Despite its perimeter being closed to the public for protection, this richly biodiverse wetland is threatened by pollution from several sources, including tourism, transport and industry.

Kairouan

RELIGIOUS SITES | WALLED MEDINA | STREET FOOD

Many Tunisians believe that seven pilgrimages to Kairouan's Great Mosque is the equivalent of one to Mecca or Medina, fulfilling their spiritual duties to Allah. The mosque is the city's greatest draw both for this reason and for its enormous historical and architectural importance, but it's not the only reason Kairouan is one of the nine Tunisian sites included on UNESCO's World Heritage List. The presence of a number of exquisitely decorated mosques and *zaouias* is a contributing factor, as is its well-maintained medina. The latter is particularly evocative in the late afternoon when the sun creates shadows, highlighting carved doors and other architectural features. Travellers will spend the vast majority of their time in Kairouan inside the medina walls, visiting its monuments, wandering through its bazaars and savouring the various pastries and street foods for which the city is deservedly famous.

GETTING AROUND

Both **Enfidha-Hammamet Airport** *(enfidhahammamet airport.com)* and Habib Bourguiba International Airport in Monastir are around 60km away; car-hire companies have offices at both. Buses travel to/from Tunis, Sousse, Sfax and other destinations; the **bus** and **louage** stations are just outside the northwestern walls of the medina. The medina is flat and its alleyways are well-maintained, making it easy to explore on foot.

Kairouan's Marvellous Zaouias

Historically significant shrines

Pilgrims once congregated in the front courtyard of the **Zaouia of Sidi Sahabi** before joining caravans heading to Mecca. The choice of departure point was deliberate, as this religious complex northwest of the medina is of great historical and religious significance as the burial place of Abu Zama El Belaoui (aka Sidi Sahabi), a companion of the Prophet Muhammad, who was killed in battle in 654 CE. Legend has it that El Belaoui always carried three hairs from the Prophet's beard with him, and the complex is sometimes referred to as the Barber's Mosque.

In the 14th century a *zaouia* was built around El Belaoui's tomb; this was extended and embellished in the 17th century by order of the bey of Tunis, with a mosque and accommodation for pilgrims being added. A minaret and *madrasa* (school for study of the Quran) were added at the end of that century.

Continues on p189

EMILY MARIE WILSON/SHUTTERSTOCK

Great Mosque at dusk

TOP EXPERIENCE

Great Mosque

UNESCO describes Kairouan's **Great Mosque** as being not only one of the major monuments of Islam, but also a universal architectural masterpiece. The mosque is considered to be one of the most holy sites in Muslim North Africa.

DID YOU KNOW?

The first iteration of Kairouan's Great Mosque was constructed only 38 years after the death of the Prophet Muhammad.

History

The mosque is also known as Uqba ibn Nafi Mosque, an acknowledgment of the Ummayad general who founded Kairouan and commissioned the first mosque on this site in 670 CE. The original Ummayad structure was modest in size and was replaced by this significantly larger and more magnificent building by order of the Aghlabid governor of Kairouan, Ziyadat Allah, between 817 and 838.

Exterior

The mosque has a huge footprint – it's approximately 125m long and 75m wide – and the fort-like exterior, with thick, buttressed walls, has a typically unadorned Aghlabid design.

PRACTICALITIES

● patrimoinedetunisie.com.tn/en/monuments/the-great-mosque-of-kairouan/overview ● 12DT (joint ticket) ● 7.30am-2pm Sat-Thu summer; 8am-2pm Sat-Thu winter & Ramadan, to noon Fri

The distinctive three-tiered stepped minaret is the oldest in the Maghreb.

Courtyard

Entry for non-Muslims is via the main gate on Rue Okba Ibn Nafaa (the other eight gates are closed to non-Muslims). Inside, the massive courtyard is lined with porticos formed by a linear series of horseshoe-shaped arches; the large arch on the southeast side signals the entrance to the prayer hall. Designed for water catchment (a sensible strategy in this hot, semi-arid climate), the courtyard's paving slopes towards an intricately decorated central drainage hole that delivers the collected rainwater into the 9th-century cisterns below. The marble rims of the two wells both have deep rope-grooves worn by centuries of hauling water up from the depths.

Prayer Hall

Only Muslims may enter the prayer hall; non-Muslims may peek in from the courtyard.

The main feature inside is the forest of 414 marble and porphyry pillars supporting 17 naves. Like those in the courtyard portico, the pillars were originally Roman or Byzantine, salvaged from Carthage and Hadrumetum (Sousse).

At the far end of the hall, it's just possible to make out the precious 9th-century tiles adorning the *mihrab* (niche showing the direction of Mecca), which is topped by a semidome. These lustrous tiles were imported from Baghdad, along with the wood for the richly adorned 9th-century *minbar* (a pulpit from which the sermon is delivered) next to them; this is thought to be the oldest surviving *minbar* in the Islamic world. The dome in front of the *mihrab* has epigraphic and floral decoration and is generally acknowledged to be a masterpiece of Islamic art.

The painted and carved flat wooden ceilings are decorated with spear-shaped fruit wrapped in symmetrical palm leaves. Elements from a later date include a *maqsura* (screened section for the ruler) to the right of the *minbar;* this was added in the 11th century. The enormous wooden doors date from 1829, and the dome over the prayer-room portico was built around the same time.

The rugs that cover every inch of the prayer hall's floor are made by local female artisans, who donate their work as a gift to Allah.

JOINT ENTRANCE TICKET

The major sites in Kairouan are visited on a single ticket, which can be purchased at the Great Mosque. The ticket (12DT) is valid for the Great Mosque, the Aghlabid Basins and the Zaouias (Mausoleums) of Sidi Sahab, Sidi Abid el-Ghariani and Sidi Amor Abbada. The ticket is valid only for one day and one entry per site.

TOP TIPS

- Visitors must wear modest dress; robes are available at the entrance.
- Women must cover their heads.
- Great views over the mosque and into its courtyard can be enjoyed at Tapis Okba, a rug and souvenir shop opposite.
- The mosque looks wonderful at night, when its walls and minaret are atmospherically lit.

A WALK THROUGH THE MEDINA

Explore the streets of this relatively quiet medina and visit its religiously significant monuments when following this walking tour.

START	END	LENGTH
Bab al-Jalladin	Hotel La Kasbah	1.8km; 1¼ hrs

Enter the medina through ❶ **Bab al-Jalladin** and walk along Avenue Habib Bourguiba. Turn right into Rue Sidi Abid to visit the ❷ **Zaouia of Sidi Abid Al Ghariani**, then pop into ❸ **Société Tapis Allani**, a rug shop occupying a lavishly decorated 18th-century mansion that was once the residence of a Kairouan bey (provincial governor from the Ottoman era) and his four wives.

Next, turn left and follow the winding alleyway until you reach Rue El Khadraouine. Turn right, pass the Thamm Annajjarine Mosque and continue until you reach the 9th-century ❹ **Mosque of the Three Doors**, one of the oldest in Kairouan. Turn left into Rue Moulay Taieb then continue to the top of the street before veering right at the Ibn Khayroun Mosque. Continue northeast along Rue Sidi Bou Omrani and follow this street until its end, turning left to see Kairouan's greatest treasure, the ❺ **Great Mosque**, ahead of you.

Veer left into Rue Sidi Abdelkader and follow the Aghlabid-built walls until you reach Rue Des Aglabiles. Here, turn left to pass through Bab Tunis and return to your starting point or turn right and you will soon come to ❻ **Hotel La Kasbah**, where you will can relax over a drink (alcoholic if you so choose) under the palm trees in its central pool courtyard.

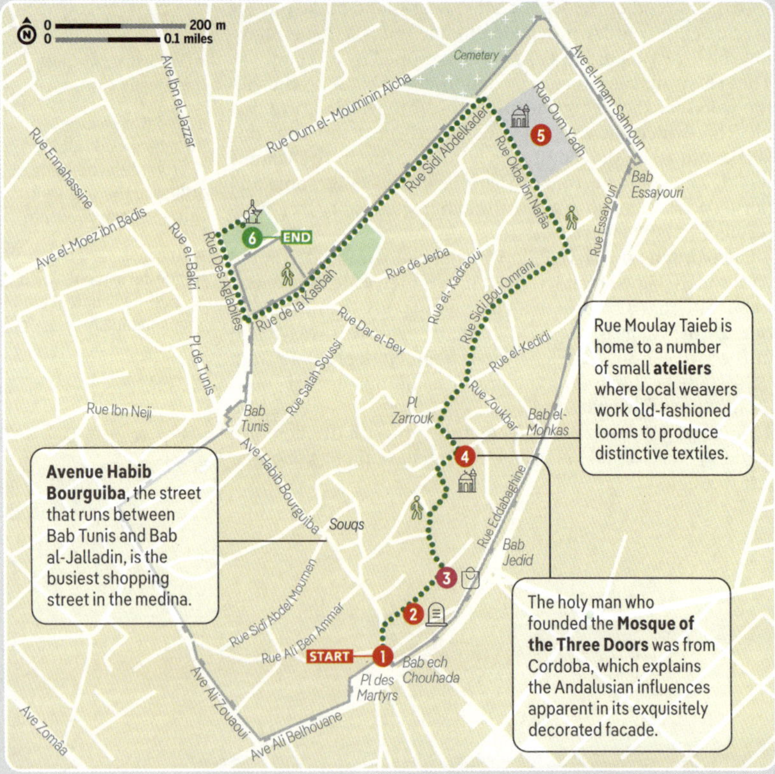

Rue Moulay Taieb is home to a number of small **ateliers** where local weavers work old-fashioned looms to produce distinctive textiles.

Avenue Habib Bourguiba, the street that runs between Bab Tunis and Bab al-Jalladin, is the busiest shopping street in the medina.

The holy man who founded the **Mosque of the Three Doors** was from Cordoba, which explains the Andalusian influences apparent in its exquisitely decorated facade.

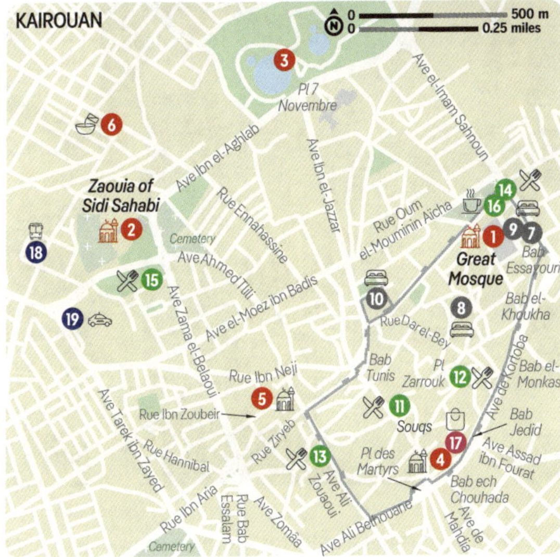

HIGHLIGHTS
1 Great Mosque
2 Zaouia of Sidi Sahabi

SIGHTS
3 Aghlabid Basins
4 Zaouia of Sidi Abid Al Ghariani
5 Zaouia of Sidi Amor Abbada

ACTIVITIES
6 Afawih

SLEEPING
7 Dar Alouini
8 Dar Hassine Allani
9 Dar Lella Habiba
10 La Kasbah

EATING
11 Faouzi Kafteji
12 Go Café
see 11 Jalel Kafteji
13 Pâtisserie Barrack
14 Restaurant El Brija
15 Restaurant Nakcha

DRINKING & NIGHTLIFE
16 Chez Mamie

SHOPPING
17 Société Tapis Allani

TRANSPORT
18 Bus Station
19 Louage Station

Continued from p185

The complex we see today comprises the mosque and *madrasa*, a porticoed front courtyard once used as a stable for horses and a storeroom. The mosque is accessed from the front courtyard, but only Muslims may enter. All visitors can enter the *madrasa*'s internal courtyard, which features Moorish-style arches and exquisite tilework. Access is via two anterooms and a colonnaded passageway. The cupola-crowned mausoleum is accessed off the western corner but is usually closed to the public. The *zaouia* is open from 7am to until 6pm.

Another important *zaouia* in Kairouan is the **Zaouia of Sidi Abid Al Ghariani**, a 14th-century complex just inside the Bab al-Jalladin (Gate of the Leather Workers), the main entrance to the medina. This *zaouia* features horseshoe arches painted in black and white; marble columns with carved capitals; a painted Moorish-style ceiling; and plenty of fine woodcarving, tiles and stuccowork. It was built as a school by a Kairawani scholar called Al Jadidi, whose student Abou Samir Abid taught and was eventually buried here. The *zaouia* is open from 8am to 3pm Saturday to Thursday, to 1pm Friday May to September.

A third significant *zaouia* is that of **Sidi Amor Abbada**, well-known for its seven ribbed cupolas. Built in 1860, it commemorates Sidi Amor Abbada, a local blacksmith and religious teacher. This *zaouia* was closed for restoration at the time of research.

Quality Carpets

Shop for rugs in a governor's mansion

Kairouan is the carpet capital of the country, so if you're in the market for a Tunisian carpet, this is a good place to shop. You'll encounter two basic types of carpet: knotted and woven.

TOP TIP

If a local approaches you in the medina and says that he can take you to a special festival being held nearby for one day only, be warned: this person will almost certainly be employed by a carpet shop with the objective of luring tourists to its business.

THE AGHLABIDS

Ruling ancient Ifriqiyah from 800 to 909 CE, the Abbasid-supported dynasty known as the Aghlabids took the Tunisian Sahel (central-east Tunisia) as their base, ruling the Mediterranean Sea with their powerful fleet, conquering Sicily and establishing Kairouan as their capital. There were 11 Aghlabid emirs before the dynasty's army was conquered by the Fatimids near present-day El Kef.

Today, the coastal *ribats* the Aghlabids constructed, the medinas and Great Mosques they built in strategically important cities such as Susa (Sousse) and Sfax, and their sophisticated and innovative approach to irrigation (illustrated by the still-standing **Aghlabid Basins** cistern system in Kairouan) are reminders of their ambition and power.

NARDA GONGORA/SHUTTERSTOCK

Carpet weaving

The traditional (pre-Islamic) carpet industry was based on the weaving of *mergoums* and kilims. *Mergoums* feature very bright, geometric designs, with bold use of reds, purples, blues and other vivid colours. Kilims use traditional Amazigh motifs on a woven background. Both are reasonably cheap to buy. The *guetiffa* is another type of knotted carpet: thick-pile and normally cream coloured, with Amazigh motifs.

The best-known of the knotted carpets are the classical (Persian-style) Kairouan carpets. This style of carpet-making was first introduced to Tunisia by the Turks. Legend has it that the first knotted carpet to be made in Tunisia was by the daughter of the Turkish governor of Kairouan. Knotted carpets are priced according to the number of knots per square metre, and reputable shops will have an official list of prices on display. On the back of each carpet should be a small, sealed certificate from the Office National de l'Artisanat Tunisien (ONAT) containing the dimensions and type of carpet. ONAT vets all carpets for quality, so it's important to check for this.

A number of rug shops are located near the Great Mosque, but to mix your shopping with some sightseeing, head to **Société Tapis Allani** *(search Facebook for 'Tapis Ali Allani')* near the Zaouia of Sidi Abid Al Ghariani. This business occupies a grand 18th-century residence built by a former bey of Kairouan, with rugs piled in a series of rooms decorated with carved woodwork, painted ceilings, marble latticework, plaster moulding and colourful tiles. The shop is open from 8am to 4pm daily.

Learn the Secrets of Spice Blending

Personalised workshops offered by experts

The Kairouan region is known for its chilli production, and strings of dried chillies swing in the wind at the front of many medina shops, signalling the availability of chillies, spices and pastes. Inside, baskets and tubs are filled with spice mixes such as aromatic *ras el hanout* ('head of the shop'). The blend of this famous product varies from store to store, but usually features cardamom, cumin, coriander seed, clove, cinnamon, nutmeg, mace, black pepper and allspice.

To learn about the spices used in Tunisian food and how to blend *ras el hanout* and other spice mixes at home, book into one of the spice workshops offered by **Afawih** *(afawih.com; 85DT per person)*, a spice company with an atelier and retail outlet in Avenue Touhemi Negra northwest of the medina. Run by entrepreneurial sisters Soulaima and Khadija Omrani, the workshops pass on culinary secrets passed down to the sisters from their grandmother and can focus on mixing spices or preparing harissa. Conducted in Arabic, French or English, the three-hour workshops include lunch as well as an apron and spice mixes to take home.

Kairouan's Favourite Indulgence

Eat and make makroudh pastries

The ***makroudh***, a syrup-soaked semolina pastry filled with slightly spiced date paste, is probably Tunisia's most famous sweet treat. And most Tunisians will admit that the best *makroudh* in the country are made in Kairouan. To sample these diamond-shaped delights, source them from one of the many pâtisseries and *makroudh*-laden street carts in the medina. And if, like many first-time *makroudh* eaters, you are immediately smitten, you may like to book into a *makroudh*-making workshop offered by Halima Barrack, owner and chef at the much-admired **Pâtisserie Barrack** (aka Chez Halima) on Avenue Ali Zouaoui just outside the medina's western wall. **Sawa Taste of Tunisia** *(sawataste.com)*, a recommended company specialising in food tourism, can organise this for you.

STREET EATS

Those who enjoy sampling street foods will find themselves in seventh heaven when in Kairouan's medina due to the ubiquity of stands selling delicious, freshly prepared *kafteji* and *fricassé*. A *kafteji* is a flat bread pocket or baguette stuffed with *mechouia* (paste made with green pepper, tomato, onion, garlic and spices) that's mixed with soft fried egg and harissa and topped with crisp *pommes frites*. A *fricassé* is a small fried bread sandwich stuffed with tuna, mashed potatoes, boiled egg, salad and harissa. Try the *fricassé* stands just inside the Tunis and al-Jalladin gates and the *kafteji* joints underneath the minaret of the Sidi Bouzid Mosque in the Bir Barrouta neighbourhood: **Jalel Kafteji** and **Faouzi Kafteji** are our favourites.

EATING & DRINKING IN KAIROUAN: OUR PICKS

Chez Mamie: Close to the Great Mosque, this cafe with streetside terrace is popular with young locals. *8am-11pm* €

Go Café: Highly recommended female-operated cafe near the Mosque of the Three Doors. Great for meals and (non-alcoholic) drinks. *7.30am-8pm Tue-Sun* €€

Restaurant El Brija: Built into the medina walls, this place is popular with tour groups but also attracts locals. The menu includes pasta and pizza. *8am-10pm* €€

Restaurant Nakcha: In a park opposite the Zaouia of Sidi Sahabi, this popular restaurant and cafe has a pleasant outdoor terrace. *noon-9pm Oct-Apr, to 10pm May-Sep* €€

Mahdia

FATIMID RUINS | TEXTILE SHOPPING | SEA VIEWS

GETTING AROUND

Nearby Habib Bourguiba International Airport in Monastir is linked to the centre of Mahdia by the Sahel metro. The metro also links Mahdia with Sousse and Monastir's centre. The **metro station** is close to the port, a short walk south of the medina. The **louage station** is further south, on Avenue Belhaouane. Buses to Sousse leave from Hiboun, near the Zone Touristique – the metro is far more convenient. Most destinations of interest to travellers can be easily accessed on foot, the only exception being the northern stretch of the Zone Touristique, which is a 10-minute taxi ride from the medina.

Incorporating a narrow peninsula jutting out into the sapphire-blue waters of the Mediterranean, Mahdia is blessed with a truly spectacular setting. It's a wonder, then, that the town manages to stay tranquil for most of the year, avoiding the hordes of tourists who descend on other parts of the coast. This may be due to the fact that the Zone Touristique north of the town centre isn't yet as developed as those elsewhere. Those travellers who decide to spend more than a day here will be rewarded by walks in the small but pretty medina, along the town's long sandy beaches and around the historically resonant Cap Afrique, where traces of Phoenician, Arab, Ottoman and Spanish settlement remain. Walking a loop around this wind-swept promontory with its magnificent sea vistas is one of the central coast's greatest joys.

Take a Bath with the Locals

Bathhouse in the medina

Traditional bath culture is alive and well in modern-day Tunisia, and most cities and towns have at least one hammam (public bathhouse) that is frequented by locals. Some of these hammams have been operating for centuries but others, such as **Hammam El Medina** *(basic bath 10DT, massage 60DT)*, are new, albeit designed to age-old specifications. Enter through the bouganvillea-embellished tiled passageway off the medina's major thoroughfare and you will discover a clean and well-maintained operation notable for its friendly English-speaking welcome and profusion of colourful tilework. Bring swimwear, as this isn't one of those joints where the clients bare all. The hammam is open from 9am to 1.30pm and from 8pm to 10pm for males, and from 2pm to 7.30pm for females.

See Orpheus Charming the Animals

Modest archaeological museum

The ground floor of Mahdia's small and somewhat dusty museum, the **Regional Museum of Mahdia** *(patrimoinedetunisie .com.tn/en/museums/the-mahdia-museum/overview; entry*

HIGHLIGHTS
1 Cap Afrique

SIGHTS
2 Borj El Kebir
3 Mosque of Soliman Hamza
4 Place du Caire
5 Regional Museum of Mahdia
6 Skifa El Kahla

ACTIVITIES
7 Cap Afrique Scuba Diving School
8 Hammam El Medina
9 Subway Dive Center

SLEEPING
10 Dar El Mahdia
11 Hotel Dar Al Madina
12 Iberostar Selection Royal El Mansour

EATING
13 Cafe El Medina
14 Chapati Mounira
15 El Asfour
16 Fratello
17 Le Lido
18 L'Espador
19 Mourad Chapati
see 16 Restaurant Darna

DRINKING & NIGHTLIFE
20 Café Sidi Salem

SHOPPING
21 Mohamed Ismail *fouta* shop
22 Skila

TRANSPORT
23 Louage Station
24 Metro Station

FISHY BUSINESS

Mahdia is one of the largest fishing ports in Tunisia, with many local boats heading out to fish at night. The daily catch is dominated by mackerel and sardines, but *dorade* (gilt-head sea bream) and *mérou* (grouper) are caught from September to December and sea bass (*loup de mer*) is caught between April and June and between September and December. Other fish you might see on local restaurant menus usually come from Italian waters. These include *thon* (tuna) and *espadon* (swordfish). *Poulpe* (octopus) can only be caught from mid-October to mid-May; if you see it on summer menus, it will be frozen or imported.

CHRISTOPHE CAPPELLI/SHUTTERSTOCK

Hammam El Medina (p192) entrance

8DT), is home to three superb mosaics excavated at El Jem: an amazingly lifelike face of a Gorgon (3rd century CE), a delightful depiction of Orpheus charming the animals (late-2nd century CE), and an attractive floral-patterned work. Upstairs, the dimly lit Treasure and Jewellery Room safeguards manuscripts, jewellery, the Trésor de Chebba (109 gold Byzantine coins) and the Trésor de Rougga (268 gold Roman coins). There's also a small ethnographic display upstairs.

Before leaving, ask the ground-floor attendant to unlock the door and gate that allows access to the steep stairs leading to the top of the **Skifa El Kahla** ('The Black Passage'), the medina's massive Fatamid-era fortified gate. There are wonderful **views** over the medina from here.

The museum is open daily from 9am to 4pm, to 3pm during Ramadan.

Watch Weavers at Work

Mahdia's textile workshops

Mahdia has long been famous for its weaving workshops. In the 12th century, geographer and cartographer Muhammad al-Idrisi wrote about the opulence of silk weaving in the town, describing 'clothes of great quality made of a very refined silk fabric'. These skills have passed down through the generations, and today there are still workshops located in the medina. The

EATING IN MAHDIA: OUR PICKS

Restaurant Darna: Popular eatery based in Cafe Fratello opposite the seafront. Order by item or opt for a well-priced set menu. No alcohol. *10am-10pm* **€€**

L'Espador: Mahdia's most glamorous restaurant offers cocktails, a decent wine list, well-cooked meals, live entertainment and a seafront terrace. *noon-midnight* **€€€**

El Asfour: In the Iberostar Hotel, this restaurant serves Mediterranean dishes such as pizza, pasta and steak on two outdoor terraces. Good wine list. *8am-midnight* **€€€**

Le Lido: The location opposite the port isn't attractive, but locals swear by the freshness of the seafood served at this long-operating restaurant. *10am-1pm* **€€€**

most alluring of these is **Skila** *(Instagram @skila.co)* which has two showrooms: one next to Place du Caire in the centre of the medina and another next to the Mahdia Museum. The workshop near Place du Caire is particularly impressive, with working looms downstairs and a spacious showroom upstairs. The weavers, always male, produce gorgeous scarves and wraps using silk, cotton, wool and linen (or blends thereof) – most pieces are the product of around eight hours work. This is an interesting, forward-thinking business that is committed to sustainable and equitable business practices. All fabrics are 100% natural and fair trade standards are adhered to. Items are priced according to their material and the number of colours used; the luxurious silk-cashmere blend is the most expensive. Both shops are open 8am to 5pm daily.

To source a more-affordable woven item, check out the *foutas* (cotton towels) created by Mohamed Ismail at his atelier and **shop** in the street behind Skila's Place du Caire workshop, near the **Mosque of Soliman Hamza**.

Tea in Place du Caire

Busy cafe cluster

Mahdians of every age congregate at the outdoor cafes in this **central medina square**, which is shaded by trees and vines. Join them to enjoy a coffee, tea or cold drink while contemplating the ornate arched doorway and octagonal minaret of the Mosque of Mustapha Hamza, built in 1772 when this square was the centre of the town's wealthy Turkish quarter. There are also some old Mahdian houses with brightly painted doorways to admire.

Evoke the Fatimid City

Explore the Cap Afrique promontory

Fragments of the Fatimid city's original 10m-thick walls dot the shoreline around the narrow tip of the promontory known as **Cap Afrique**. These traces make it easy to imagine the Fatamid-era walled town, which was built on the site of an earlier Phoenician settlement. Both were designed to be protected from seaborne invasion. The ancient harbour from which the Fatimids launched their invasion of Egypt remains in evidence, as do pillars that flanked the entrance and dominated the harbour's defences.

Remnants of a Fatimid palace are being excavated close to the **Borj El Kebir** *(entry 8DT)*, a defensive fort constructed

A LOCAL FAVOURITE

Walking through Mahdia, it's impossible to ignore the number of fast-food stands selling ***chapatis***, a Tunisian riff on the Indian flatbread. The local *chapati* dough is often made using a mix of semolina and whole-wheat flour and after being cooked, the flatbread is stuffed with fillings including tuna, egg omelette, vegetables, *shwarma*, harissa or variations thereof. It is then heated on a flat grill and served as a sandwich-like treat. There are *chapati* stands dotted along the seafront – look for those with queues in front, as these are reliable signals of quality. You'll be looking at around 5DT per *chapati*.

EATING IN MAHDIA: BEST CAFES & FAST-FOOD STANDS

Chapati Mounira: One street back from the seafront, this is probably Mahdia's most-popular *chapati* stand. *7am-1am Mon-Sat* €

Mourad Chapati: Also known as King's Food, this recommended *chapati* stand is located opposite the Iberostar Hotel. *24hr* €

Fratello: On the Corniche, this ultra-popular cafe has a streetside terrace that is a local place to see and be seen. *8am-1pm* €

Cafe El Medina: Overlooking the Great Mosque, this medina cafe offers seating under the lime trees or in its ornately decorated interior. *8am-11pm* €

THE FATIMIDS

An Isma'ili Shia dynasty, the Fatimids took their name from Fatimah, daughter of the Prophet Muhammad, who they claimed as their ancestor. Aspiring to take over from the Abbasids as the leaders of the Islamic world, they conquered large parts of Ifriqiya in 909 CE and established the city of Mahdia in 921, making it their capital and naming it after their caliph, Abdallah al-Mahdi. In 972, they handed over effective control of this part of Ifriqiya to the Amazigh Zirid dynasty and moved to their new conquest of Egypt, basing themselves in Cairo. Traces of the Fatimid settlement can still be seen on Cap Afrique. The Great Mosque we see today is a copy of the Fatimid original.

TOP TIP

If you are keen to visit the beach, head to Mahdia Beach in the Zone Touristique rather than the Corniche Beach closer to town, as the former is usually cleaner and less crowded.

ANDY SOLOMAN/SHUTTERSTOCK

Defence wall ruins, Cap Afrique (p195)

by the Ottomans in the 16th century on the palace site. The fort is open from 9am to 4pm September to April and Ramadan, to 5pm May to September.

Much of the Cap is occupied by a vast cemetery with hundreds of white tombstones gleaming in the Mediterranean sun. When here, be sure to walk a loop around the promontory, admiring the sea views and pausing to enjoy an expertly brewed mint tea at **Sidi Salem**, a cafe teetering on the clifftop below the palace excavations; this is open from 8.30am to 1am daily.

Explore Underwater Shipwrecks

Diving off the Mahdian coast

While not as well known as Tabarka, Cap Bon and Hammamet, Mahdia is a popular scuba-diving destination. During the summer months the water temperature can reach mid-20°C temperatures and visibility is generally good. Local dive outfits, including **Subway Dive Center** *(subway-mahdia.com)* and **Cap Afrique Scuba Diving School** *(instagram.com/cap_afrique_diving_center)*, can take you to dive to the wrecks of WWII ships. Sadly, the schools can't take divers to explore the 1st-century BCE shipwreck of a Roman ship that lies 5km off the coast. This sank on its voyage from Greece to Rome and was discovered by sponge divers in 1907. In the wreck were a marble bust, bronze statues, marble reliefs and other Hellenic works of art. Many of these are now on display in Tunis' Bardo Museum.

El Jem

UNESCO-LISTED AMPHITHEATRE | WORLD-CLASS MOSAICS | ROMAN RUINS

Built on a low plateau halfway between Sousse and Sfax, the town of El Jem was known as Thysdrus in Roman times, when it was a thriving market town set at the junction of the coast's lucrative trade routes. By the 3rd century CE, when its monumental World Heritage–listed amphitheatre was constructed, it was one of North Africa's most important settlements, only superseded by Carthage and Hadrumetum (Sousse). Both the amphitheatre and the wonderful mosaic-filled archaeological museum provide ample evidence of the scope and richness of Roman civilisation in Africa. These days, the semi-somnolent town is surrounded by olive groves, and tourism provides its major source of income. There is no compelling reason to overnight here, as both Sousse and Sfax are only one hour away by road, but a day trip here is highly recommended for all history buffs.

GETTING AROUND

El Jem is a stop on the SNCFT train route between Tunis and Métlaoui, which also includes stops at Sousse, Sfax and Gabès. Note that trains are notoriously unreliable and rarely arrive and depart on time. The amphitheatre and museum are short walks from the **train station**. The **louage station** is on Rue De La Grande Mosquée, just south of the museum. Buses arrive and depart in front of the train station.

View Dionysus' Procession

Magnificent collection of Roman mosaics

Accessed using the joint Ampitheatre/Museum entry ticket, the splendid archaeological **El Jem Museum** *(patrimoinedetunisie .com.tn/en/museums/the-el-jem-museum/overview; joint ticket 12DT)* is one of the best in the country. Built on the site of an excavated Roman villa and mimicking the villa's floorplan, it showcases an exceptional collection of Roman-era mosaics, all richly coloured and in excellent condition.

On entering the building, turn left to find the Room of Orpheus, with its mosaic of the god playing the lyre. Continue to the Dionysiac Procession Room, which is home to the museum's best-known exhibit, a mid-2nd-century CE mosaic featuring the god Dionysus riding a lion alongside his tutor Silenus (on a camel) and an entourage of satyrs and dancing bacchantes. Also here is a delightful mid-2nd-century CE pavement mosaic depicting the Four Seasons. A drunken Silenus reappears in the next room, seated on a donkey.

TOP TIP

A joint ticket (12DT) allows entry to both the Amphitheatre of Thysdrus and the El Jem Museum. It can be purchased at either venue.

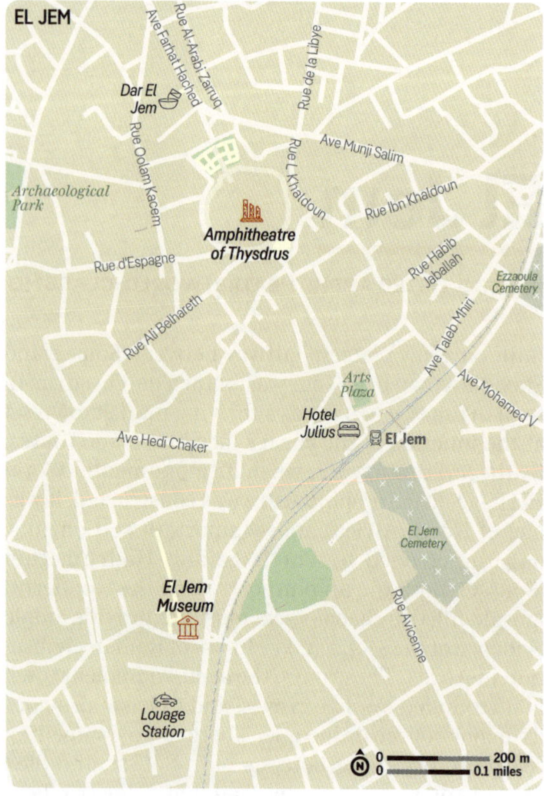

In the rectangular rear room, the standout pieces are a late-3rd-century CE mosaic of an owl that was excavated from a local baths complex and a slightly older scene featuring a nymph riding a sea horse excavated from a villa. A huge mosaic depicting the rape of Ganymede by Zeus' eagle dominates the central courtyard.

At the rear of the museum is a recreation of the House of Africa, a large Roman villa built in 170 CE that was excavated in the 1990s during a search for access to a small adjacent thermal bath and transferred here for display. The house owes its name to an impressive medallion mosaic depicting the Goddess Africa, a moody-looking young woman symbolising the Roman province of Africa (by the hide and two elephant tusks she wears as headgear).

Behind the House of Africa is an area where three Roman villas have been excavated – the House of the Peacock; the House of the Dolphins, which takes its name from a mosaic found in it; and the Sollertianadomus, which reflects an inscription on one of its threshold mosaic.

The museum is open from 8am to 5.30pm October to April, to 6.30pm from May to September.

TOP EXPERIENCE

Amphitheatre of Thysdrus

The original seating capacity of this UNESCO World Heritage–listed amphitheatre (the fourth-largest in the Roman world) is thought to have been around 30,000 – considerably more than the population of the town itself. Built entirely of hefty stone blocks, its facade comprises three levels of arcades that reach a total height of 30m. Inside, most of the supporting infrastructure for the tiered seating has been preserved and a northern section of seats has been reconstructed.

The amphitheatre is generally thought to have been commissioned by the Roman Emperor Gordian III and built between 238 and 250 CE. Stone for its construction had to be hauled all the way from the quarries at the coastal town of Sullectum (modern Salakta), 30km away.

Used for gladiatorial games during Roman times, the amphitheatre later doubled as a last line of defence. The Amazigh warrior-queen Al-Kahina, who united various Amazigh tribes under her leadership to fight against the ongoing Muslim conquest of the Maghreb, is said to have been besieged here by Arab forces at the end of the 7th century.

During the late-17th-century Muradid War of Succession, the bey of Tunis, Mohamed Bey El Mouradi, made an opening in one of the walls to stop the resistance of the followers of his brother Ali Bey, who had gathered inside. Further depredations occurred over the centuries, when the structure was used for functions such as saltpetre production, grain storage and stone supply.

Today, it is possible to climb to the upper seating levels and gaze down on the arena. You can also explore the two long passageways where animals, gladiators and other unfortunates were held before being thrust into the arena to provide entertainment for the bloodthirsty masses.

TOP TIPS

- A cluster of cafes with views of the site can be found behind the amphitheatre.
- In July and August each year, one of Tunisia's pre-eminent music festivals, the **El-Jem International Symphonic Music Festival** *(festivaleljem.tn)*, is staged in the amphitheatre.

PRACTICALITIES

- patrimoinedetunisie.com.tn/en/monuments/the-amphitheatre-of-thysdrus-el-jem/overview
- 12DT (joint ticket)
- 7am-6.30pm summer; 7.30am-5pm winter; 8am-5pm Ramadan

THYSDRUS'S ROMAN VILLAS

In its heyday, El Jem was one of North Africa's wealthiest towns. This was predominantly due to the olive groves that surrounded it. Local landowners became rich through the production and sale of olive oil, and to flaunt their wealth they built large villas lavishly decorated with mosaics. Many such villas have been excavated in the modern town, three of which are located in the rear garden at the El Jem Museum. Sadly, the town's prosperity was curtailed in the early 3rd century CE, after it and the olive groves were destroyed by troops loyal to the Roman emperor Maximinus Thrax, who had been deposed during the infamous Year of the Six Emperors (238 CE) when Gordian I was anointed emperor after an uprising in Thysdrus (El Jem's name at the time).

ANDY SOLOMAN/SHUTTERSTOCK

El Jem Museum (p197)

Create Your Own Mosaic

Tourist-focused workshops and activities

Drawn to El Jem for its extraordinary amphitheatre and mosaic museum? If so, consider factoring in a mosaic workshop at **Dar El Jem** *(dareljem.com)* when you visit. An introduction to the art of mosaics, participants learn basic mosaic-making techniques and create a small example to take home. The dar is unrepentantly tourist-focused, offering Ancient Roman cooking demonstrations and offering a chance to be photographed in a Roman-themed set and drink a beaker of *posca*, a popular ancient Roman drink consisting of water mixed with wine vinegar and herbs.

Sfax

THRIVING MEDINA | FRENCH COLONIAL ARCHITECTURE | FISH RESTAURANTS

A visit to Sfax is an opportunity to experience contemporary Tunisian life unmediated by the demands of tourism. Exploring the largely intact walled medieval medina – perhaps the country's most important after the one in Tunis – provides an insight into how the modern and the ancient can coexist in cultural and aesthetic harmony in today's Tunisia.

Built on the site of the ancient settlements of Taparura and Thaenae, of which no traces have survived, Sfax has been a trading centre for most of its life, and today the city and its surrounds are home to olive-oil production, fish canning and phosphate mining. That said, the local economy doesn't seem to be thriving, and the economic woes that Tunisia has endured over the past decades are clearly apparent here, with infrastructure poorly maintained, cultural institutions such as museums closed, and many of the French Colonial–era buildings that once graced the boulevards of Centre Ville falling into a sad state of disrepair.

Shop with the Sfaxians

A lively medieval medina

Many Tunisians describe Sfax's **medina** as the most authentic in the country, and it's easy to see why. There's hardly a souvenir shop in sight within the still-standing monumental walls, and the narrow thoroughfares are perennially crowded with local shoppers stocking up on cheap clothing, shoes, household goods and other prosaic items. Market areas on the northern edge are noisy, colourful and aromatic places where locals come to buy fresh produce, and tiny workshops on almost every medina alleyway are home to artisans employing centuries-old practices. Elsewhere, modest residences sport iron balconies and painted doors.

The medina dates from the 9th century CE. Its main southern gate, the triple-arched **Bab Bhar** (the Sea Gate, aka Bab El Diwen), is where most people enter. This gate and the

GETTING AROUND

Sfax-Thyna International Airport is located 8km west of the city. The **Gare de Sfax** (main train station) is located just outside the medina's southwestern corner. Trains stop here en route to/from Tunis and Métlaoui, with stops also at Sousse, El Jem and Gabès. The **bus terminal** and main **louage station** are located on Rue Commandant Bejaoui, west of the port.

The only way to explore the medina is by foot, so bring comfortable walking shoes. To get around the rest of the city, taxis are your best bet; these are cheap and plentiful.

TOP TIP

Sfax is one of the few Tunisian cities with a **tourist office**. Operated by the Office National de Tourisme (ONTT), it is located on the port's corniche and open from 8am to noon and 2pm to 5pm Monday to Friday.

HIGHLIGHTS
1 Medina

SIGHTS
2 Bab Bhar
3 Bab Dhahraoui
4 Great Mosque
5 Maison de France
6 Municipality of Sfax Building
7 Museum of Traditional Architecture
8 Sidi Amar Kammoun Mosque & Mausoleum
9 Sidi el Bahri Mosque

SLEEPING
10 Dar Baya
11 Ibis Sfax
12 Les Oliviers Palace

EATING
13 Caféteria Bondin
14 La Renaissance
15 La Sirène
16 Le Bagdad
17 Saffoud Abid

DRINKING & NIGHTLIFE
18 Café Diwan
19 Café Kemour

SHOPPING
20 Fresh Produce Market
21 Souq El Hout
22 Souq Erbaa

INFORMATION
23 Tourist Office

TRANSPORT
24 Bus Terminal
25 Gare de Sfax
26 Louage Station

EATING IN SFAX: OUR PICKS

Caféteria Bondin: Follow the aroma of freshly roasted beans to find this coffee purveyor and cafe. *7am-6.30pm Tue-Sun, to 1.30pm Mon* **€**

Saffoud Abid: Medina favourite known for grilled lamb brochette with salad, bread and spicy sauce. Also runs Le Pêcheur fish restaurant opposite. *10am-3.30pm* **€€**

Le Bagdad: This friendly restaurant in Centre Ville has an old-fashioned ambiance, a well-priced wine list and a fish-dominated menu. *noon-3pm & 7-11 Sat-Thu* **€€**

La Sirène: Though its location in the port is unattractive, this restaurant is known throughout the city for serving ultra-fresh fish. *noon-11pm* **€€**

still-standing walls and ramparts were added in the early 14th century. Near this gate are a number of important religious buildings, including the 17th-century **Sidi Amar Kammoun Mosque & Mausoleum** on the eastern side, which has a particularly elaborate minaret; this can only be entered by Muslim worshippers. On the western side is the permanently closed 19th-century **Sidi el Bahri Mosque**. The latter has unusual engravings on the plinth above the main doorway. Past the mosque, built into the ramparts is **Café Diwan**, a laid-back and atmospheric cafe accessed via a colourful set of steps. It's open from 8am to 7pm Monday to Saturday.

Also built into the ramparts in this southwest corner of the medina is the kasbah, originally built by the Aghlabids as a watchtower and steadily expanded into a *ribat*. Used by the French as a prison, it is now home to the underwhelming **Museum of Traditional Architecture** *(entry 5DT)*, with a few exhibits about restoration projects in the medina. The museum is open from 9.30am to 4.30pm Tuesday to Sunday.

In the centre of the medina is the walled **Great Mosque** (closed to non-Muslims), founded by the Aghlabids in the middle of the 9th century. Its eastern wall is the only section that's visible, as the other sides are hidden by souqs. The elaborate sandstone minaret, a smaller replica of the three-tiered square minaret at Kairouan, was added by the Zirids (Amazigh vassals of the Fatimids) in 988. For a great view of the minaret, head to one of the roof terraces at **Café Kemour**, a traditional coffee shop nestling at its base. This is open from 5am to 5pm every day except Monday.

North of the Great Mosque is the wonderful world of the covered souqs. The main souq running north–south is the **Souq Erbaa** (aka Souq El Rebaa), a cruciform arrangement of vaulted 9th-century passageways crossed by the Souq El Attarine (Spice and Perfume Souq). This part of the medina stood in for the Cairo markets in Anthony Minghella's 1996 film *The English Patient*.

Souq Erbaa emerges on Rue des Teinturiers, where the dyers once carried on their business. It then continues to Rue Abdelkader, which runs inside and parallel to the medina's northern wall, and to **Bab Dhahraoui** (the Northern Gate, aka Bab Djebli), one of the original Aghlabid gates. Just outside the gate are the always bustling **fresh produce market** and **Souq El Hout** (Fish Market).

Follow the Fish-Loving Crowds

Sfax's best fish restaurant

Sfax is home to the largest fishing fleet in Tunisia, so the fish served in its many fish restaurants is fabulously fresh. The best of these eateries are located in the port area and our nomination for the best of all is **La Renaissance** *(98 415 031)*, an opinion we share with most locals if the constant crowds here are any indication. Come here on a Friday or Saturday night, when traditional musicians serenade the diners, copious ice-cold bottles of beer are drunk and tables groan under the weight of multiple plates of freshly cooked seafood. The

HOW LITTLE THINGS CHANGE

In 1148 CE, the independent city-state of Sfax was conquered by King Roger II of Sicily, who ruled it until it was in turn conquered by the Maghrebi Amazigh Almohads in 1156. During the short-lived Sicilian period, the city was visited by the Muslim geographer and cartographer Muhammad al-Idrisi, who served in the court of King Roger.

Recording his impressions in the *Tabula Rogeriana*, an atlas with maps and written descriptions of 70 cities, al-Idrisi described Sfax's walls and protective watchtowers surrounding lively markets where inexpensive, high-quality fruit from the nearby city of Gabès was sold. He also noted that the city had a harbour and benefitted from its fleet's large catches of fish.

His descriptions remain true today, more than 800 years after being written.

THE BARBARY CORSAIRS

Between the 16th and early 19th centuries, the coastal regions of the Maghreb were the hunting grounds of the fearsome pirates and privateers known as the Barbary Corsairs (p318).

Their major ports and areas of power were Algiers, Tripoli, Salé and four coastal cities in Tunisia – Tunis, Susa (Sousse), Bizerte and Sfax. From these bases, the pirates sent their fleets out to capture merchant ships in the Mediterranean and Atlantic. They also raided towns in Europe, capturing locals to enslave.

The most famous of the corsairs was Barbarossa ('Redbeard'), who conquered Algiers in the 16th century and eventually became Grand Admiral of the Ottoman fleet. Barbarossa conquered the whole of Tunisia for the Ottomans and funded its governance from the proceeds of piracy.

CHRISTOPHE CAPPELLI/SHUTTERSTOCK

Place de la République

only problem is the thick fug of cigarette smoke – asthmatics may like to steer clear. The restaurant is open from 11am to midnight daily; dishes are reasonably priced considering their quality. Bookings advised.

Centre Ville's French Colonial Heritage

Moorish Revival architecture

Located immediately south of the medina, Sfax's Centre Ville is home to a number of attractive French Colonial-era buildings. Its focal point is **Place de la République** (aka Human Rights Square), where the 20th-century Moorish Revival-style **Municipality of Sfax Building** is located. This building, which was designed by French architect Rafaël Guy, has many mosque-like characteristics. It once housed the city's archaeological museum, one of the most significant in the country. Sadly, this has been closed for nearly a decade. A second Moorish Revival-style building is immediately north of the municipal building.

Further north up Avenue Habib Bourguiba is a crenellated building that was built as the French Consulate in 1897 and now houses the **Maison de France** (Institute Français). The institute's public entrance is to the rear, accessed from Rue Alexandre Dumas. Also accessed from this point is the institute's garden, which has an inexpensive refreshment kiosk and outdoor seating. It's a hugely popular meeting spot for local students.

Beyond Sfax

Time seems to have stood still on these low-lying islands, which have a traditional atmosphere and markedly slow pace.

Local legend tells us that the Kerkennah island group in the Gulf of Gabès, 23km off the coast of Sfax, is where Odysseus lingered with the sorceress Circe for a year on his voyage home to Greece. More recently, the islands have lured domestic and international visitors to their summer-only beach resorts. This tourism has played an important role in supporting the communities here, as drought has been a major issue since the 1980s and agriculture has all but disappeared. The other local industry, fishing, has been severely impacted by pollution caused by phosphate extraction in Sfax and Gabès, which has led to a diminution in fish stocks. Illegal fish trawling in the surrounding waters has also played a detrimental role.

Places

Kerkennah Islands

TIME FROM SFAX: **23KM; 1 HR**

Cycle the major islands

The group's two major islands, **Gharbi** and **Chergui**, have been connected by a causeway since Roman times. The landscape is desolate due to drought, enlivened only by a scattering of stressed-looking palm and olive trees, saltbush and plantings of prickly pear. The shoreline is slightly more attractive but lacks the long sandy beaches that the central coast is known for. The water is extremely shallow, so not really suited to swimming.

In spring and autumn, cycling here is a popular activity due to the flat terrain, network of dirt paths and pleasant sea breezes – local company **Discover Kerkennah** *(discoverkerkennah.com)* rents mountain bikes from its office just off Remla's main street and also offers guided bike tours. Popular sites to ride to are the **Borj Mellita**, an Ottoman-era watchtower on Gharbi, and the Phoenician archaeological site of **Borj El Hsar** on Chergui.

Bird-watch in the archipelago

The Gulf of Gabès is recognised for its ornithological importance, and a number of migratory species winter in the shallow waters of the Kerkennah archipelago, which is a designated Ramsar wetlands site. These species include *Phalacrocorax carbo* (great cormorant), *Larus genei* (slender-billed gull), *Larus fuscus* (lesser black-backed gull), *Larus cachinnans*

GETTING AROUND

Regular **Sonotrak** *(sonotrak.tn)* ferries travel between the port in Sfax and the island of Gharbi. Tickets for both cars and foot passengers are inexpensive. Taking a car is recommended as public transport is negligible. Alternatively, hire a bicycle in Sfax and take this with you. A local bus meets arriving ferries and travels to Chergui, returning to meet the next ferry; tickets are purchased on board. Taxis and louages can be difficult to find and local drivers levy high charges for all tourists.

TRADITIONAL ISLAND FISHING

Included in Tunisia's UNESCO-auspiced list of intangible cultural heritage, *charfia* fishing is unique to the Kerkennah Islands.

Prompted by the shallowness of the sea around the islands, the *charfia* technique works by embedding palm fronds in the seabed to create a triangular barrier, blocking the path of fish pulled in by the ebb tide and channelling them into capture chambers and finally into a net or trap where they are kept alive until being taken from the water.

Local fishers operate the *charfia* only between the autumn equinox and June to protect local fish stocks (overfishing is a major problem in the Gulf of Gabès) and the *charfias* are rebuilt each year.

JOHN WREFORD/SHUTTERSTOCK

***Charfia* fishing**

(Caspian gull), *Sterna caspia* (Caspian tern) and *Sterna sandvicensis* (Sandwich tern). Local species breeding on the islands include *Falco tinnunculus* (common kestrel), *Cursorius cursor* (cream-coloured courser), *Merops apiaster* (European bee-eater) and *Lanius excubitor* (great grey shrike). Sadly, there are no organised bird-watching tour outfits on the islands. For more information, see datazone.birdlife.org.

Savour Kerkennan octopus

The islands are one of six destinations identified by Tunisia's national tourism office as being important **culinary destinations** *(larouteculinairedetunisie.info)*. The reason for its inclusion is the traditional catch and preparation of locally caught *poulpe* (octopus). Caught in a particular way (see left), the *poulpe* is usually served in a salad, soup, pasta or couscous dish. Unassuming restaurants **Le Régal** (aka Chez Najet) and **Le Pêcheur** in Alataya, on the eastern tip of Chergui, are known for the quality of their *poulpe*. The owner and chef of Le Régal, Najet Werda, occasionally conducts cooking classes (Arabic and French only). Email najet.werda16@gmail.com for details.

To enjoy fresh *poulpe* you'll need to visit between mid-October and mid-May, as octopus fishing is banned in other months. If you choose to come to the islands in winter, be aware that the restaurants aren't always open and ferries can be cancelled due to adverse weather conditions.

Places We Love to Stay

€ Budget €€ Midrange €€€ Top End

Sousse

p172

Hotel Paris € Cheap, clean and frills-free place conveniently located inside the medina ramparts just off Place des Martyrs.

Dar Baaziz 3 € Near the kasbah, this home-style guesthouse offers comfortable rooms and a roof terrace.

Dar Lekbira €€ Beautiful old dar in the centre of the medina with large but relatively basic rooms. Excellent breakfast.

Dar Badiaa €€ In the heart of the medina, this friendly guesthouse has an attractive central courtyard and rooftop terrace. Good breakfast.

Dar Antonia €€€ The most stylish accommodation option in the city, this medina gem has a fabulous roof terrace and on-site restaurant.

Sousse Pearl Marriott Resort and Spa €€€ The beach resort located closest to the medina. Access to the beach is via an under-road tunnel from the pool area.

Monastir

p181

Marina Cap Monastir Appart-Hôtel € A great option for families or those on a tight budget, these concrete cabins overlooking the marina have equipped kitchens, satellite TV and small terraces.

Dar Benti €€€ This exquisitely renovated traditional house in Monastir's medina has facilities including a hammam and a rooftop with small pool and hot tub.

Kairouan

p185

Dar Lella Habiba €€ Located behind the Great Mosque, this guesthouse is the cheapest option in Kairouan worth considering but is overpriced for what's on offer.

Dar Hassine Allani €€ This 18th-century dar in the heart of the medina is looking worn but is one of the more affordable options in the area.

Dar Alouini €€€ Totally rebuilt mansion behind the Great Mosque with underground parking, an indoor swimming pool, rooftop terrace and luxurious rooms. Highly recommended.

La Kasbah €€€ Beloved of tour groups, this reimagined historic fort just outside the medina is notable for its swimming pool and for being one of the few places in the city where alcohol is served.

Mahdia

p192

Hotel Dar Al Madina €€ Impeccably clean, comfortable and well-run guesthouse in the middle of the medina. Room prices plummet in the off-season.

Dar El Mahdia €€ Overlooking the Great Mosque, this arty guesthouse has only three rooms. Guests love the roof terrace with plunge pool.

Iberostar Selection Royal El Mansour €€€ The most conveniently located of the beach resort hotels, with comfortable rooms, helpful staff and a wealth of facilities.

El Jem

p197

Hotel Julius €€ Friendly modern hotel near the train station. Ugly exterior, but upstairs rooms have extraordinary views over the amphitheatre and there's on-site parking.

Sfax

p201

Ibis Sfax €€ Located on a busy street west of the medina, with a restaurant and bar. Rooms are of the stock-standard three-star variety.

Business Hotel Sfax €€€ Popular business hotel in a commercial quarter north of the medina. Rooms are comfortable if characterless.

Dar Baya €€€ Though this is the only medina hotel worth considering, it is ludicrously overpriced considering the standard of the accommodation on offer. Bargain hard.

Les Oliviers Palace €€€ Near the port, this historic business has seen better days, but retains its reputation as the city's most prestigious hotel.

Researched by
Dr Jenny Walker

Matmata & the Ksour

EXTRAORDINARY DWELLINGS – UNDERGROUND AND TOWERING ABOVE

Become a troglodyte for a night in the pit dwellings of Matmata and tour mud-brick fortifications of the Ksour Country by day.

A shaggy-coated goat with beautiful pendulant ears and an inquisitive pair of green eyes gives out a bleat at the bottom of the hill and within moments, another 10 bearded individuals join him. En masse, they look ready to take on an army. In the event, they simply melt into thin air, leaving only their continuing grumbles behind them.

Any Matmata local looking for goats would know, at this point, to tread up to the top of the hill and peer over. The ground around Matmata is riddled with giant holes that have been excavated from the rocky terrain. The holes function as open-air skylights, letting the sun into the town's troglodyte dwellings below. Accessed through underground passages, these cave homes are often described, on account of the 'skylights', as 'pit dwellings'. No place to be walking at night, as the ground opens up without warning, the stroll between pits by day is a fascinating one, allowing for discreet glances over the rim of each buried homestead – complete with reappearing goats.

If Matmata and some of the villages nearby are all about hollowing downwards, the neighbouring Ksour Country is about honeycombing upwards. A *ksar* (*ksour* is the plural) is a fortified granary dating back centuries, and in parts of the semi-arid escarpments around Tataouine almost every Amazigh village has one. Consisting of a conglomeration of arched, mud-built cells, heaped in tiers, these ancient structures are fascinating to visit, especially when combined with a trip to one of the region's ancient hilltop towns.

At the time of research, several governments advise against travel to destinations within 30km of the Libyan border.

PHILIPPE LISSAC/SHUTTERSTOCK

THE MAIN AREAS

MATMATA
Small town famous for its pit dwellings.
p214

TATAOUINE
Provincial hub of the Ksour Country.
p221

For places to stay in Matmata & the Ksour, see p227

ANTON KUDELIN/SHUTTERSTOCK

Left: shepherd near Toujane (p218); above: pit dwelling (p216), Matmata

Find Your Way

The region around Matmata and Ksour Country stretches from Gabès on the coast to Tataouine in the south. Although not a large area per se, it takes a long time to reach and potter around the villages of interest.

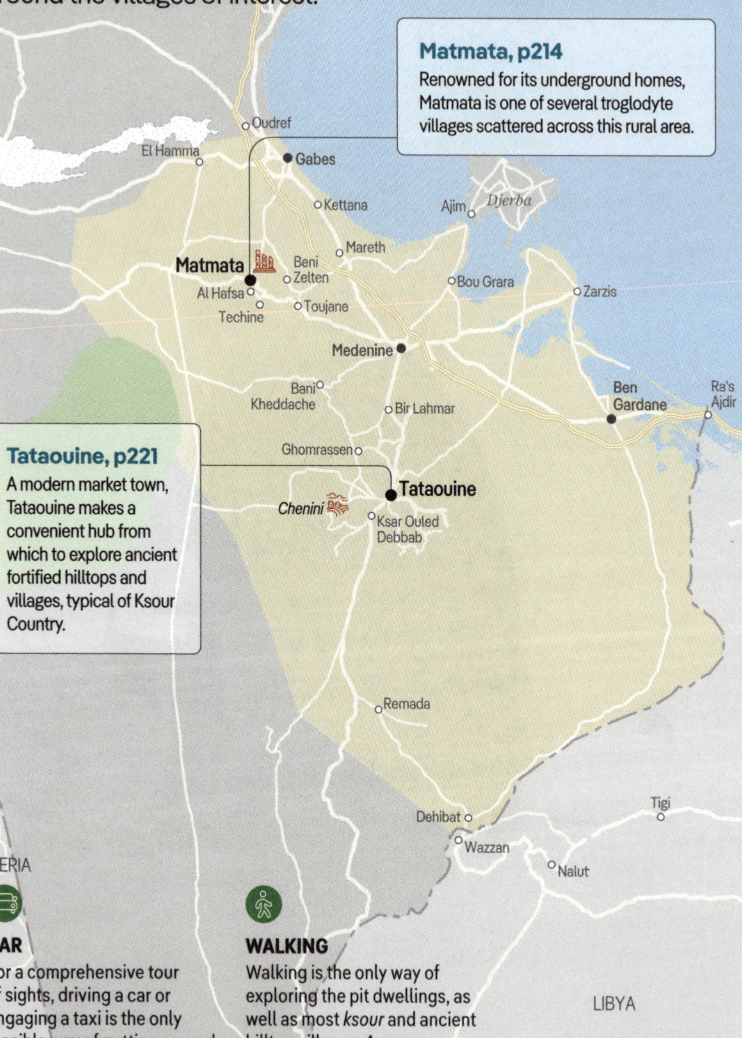

Matmata, p214
Renowned for its underground homes, Matmata is one of several troglodyte villages scattered across this rural area.

Tataouine, p221
A modern market town, Tataouine makes a convenient hub from which to explore ancient fortified hilltops and villages, typical of Ksour Country.

CAR

For a comprehensive tour of sights, driving a car or engaging a taxi is the only feasible way of getting around. A network of small, well-maintained roads connects villages without need of 4WD.

WALKING

Walking is the only way of exploring the pit dwellings, as well as most *ksour* and ancient hilltop villages. Access generally involves steep steps and uneven pathways but the views reward the effort.

Ksar Ouled Soltane (p212)

Plan Your Time

Although it takes several days to visit main sites in and around Matmata and Ksour Country, it's possible to get a flavour of the region on a focused overnighter.

Overnight Trip from Djerba

- From Djerba, take the C116 to **Toujane** (p215), a hilltop village, still partially lived in. Climb up to the C104, enjoying the views. Stay in a troglodyte hotel in **Matmata** (p216) and do the walking tour. Next day, head southeast (C211 and C114) to picture-perfect **Ksar Hallouf** (p227). Detour from the C207 at **Guermassa** (p225) and return to Djerba via **Tataouine** (p221).

Remoter Ksour in Two Days

- From **Tataouine** (p221), spend a day exploring two of the region's best old towns at **Chenini** (p226) and remoter **Douiret** (p212) and treat yourself to a night's stay in **Ksar Ouled Debbab** (p224). On day two, hike up to **Ksar Beni Barka** (p212), a hilltop fortress, and continue to the extraordinary multi-storey *ksour* at **Ouled Soltane** (p212) and **Ezzahra** (p212).

SEASONAL HIGHLIGHTS

SPRING

Tataouine's **Festival of the Ksour** (p225), around March, is an added reason to visit at this mild time of year.

SUMMER

It gets very hot here in summer, making it an effort to explore the sights, which mostly lack shade.

AUTUMN

The perfect time for a visit: the warm, sunny days are ideal for clambering around old fortifications.

WINTER

It's olive harvest time and you can watch the oil being processed by hand. Wrap up warm as temperatures plummet.

Which Ksar?

Choose to visit any of the region's old mud-brick villages, or aim for the *ksour*, with their proliferation of *ghorfas* (long, barrel-vaulted rooms built to store grain), and you are in for an architectural treat. Each of the sights offers a different experience, with some open for accommodation, some in wonderful locations and some where the remoteness is integral to the experience. With an understanding of their best features, it's possible to string together several of these mostly hilltop wonders in a rewarding multiday itinerary.

Where to choose if you love...

Big Statements

Chenini (p226) It's possible to sample both troglodyte living (at Dar Kenza, p227) and a hilltop settlement at Chenini, the most comprehensive and picturesque of all the old Amazigh villages.

Douiret One of the most atmospheric locations for lunch (in a restaurant hidden among the abandoned portion of the village), Douiret can be combined with nearby Ksar Ouled Debbab (p224).

Guermassa (p225) Tucked behind a formidable escarpment, this typical 'bonnet town' is so-called for the way it neatly envelops the entire hilltop. Contrary to first impressions, you don't need a 4WD – access is via meandering road behind the escarpment.

Film Connections

Ksar Haddada (p227) For fans of the Star Wars prequel trilogy, a night's stay at this restored *ksar* is likely to be on the wish list. The elaborate *ghorfas* here were used as the location of enslaved people's quarters in *Phantom Menace*, home of Anakin Skywalker. For an idea of how income from films has helped preserve the architecture, have a peer round the crumbling alleyways off the main courtyards.

Ksar Ouled Soltane Another *ksar* linked to the *Phantom Menace* film shoot, Ouled Soltane has some of the most impressive *ghorfas* of any *ksar* in Tunisia, and should not be missed. Arranged around two courtyards with vertiginous stairs clambering up to the upper storeys, it is particularly photogenic in the late afternoon and early evening when the restored plasterwork turns pink.

Sleep Overs

Ksar Hallouf (p227) Small tour groups often check into this grand *ksar*, worth visiting for the golden afternoon light and an interesting camel-driven olive press.

Ksar Ouled Debbab (p224) Beautifully redesigned as a hotel, this hilltop *ksar* is decorated with bougainvillea – and somewhat incongruous fibreglass dinosaurs.

Ksar Jouamaa Temporarily closed at the time of writing, this *ksar* has impressive corridors of *ghorfas* and is atmospherically lit at night.

Best of the Rest

Ksar Mgabla This somewhat unloved Tataouine *ksar* at least gives an idea of typical *ksour* architecture if transport or budget precludes a visit elsewhere.

Ksar Beni Barka En route to Ksar Ouled Soltane, this little-visited fortified hilltop is crowned with impressive ruins.

Ksar Ezzahra Also on the Ksar Ouled Soltane circuit, this *ksar* rivals its more famous neighbour with two courtyards of multi-storeyed *ghorfas*.

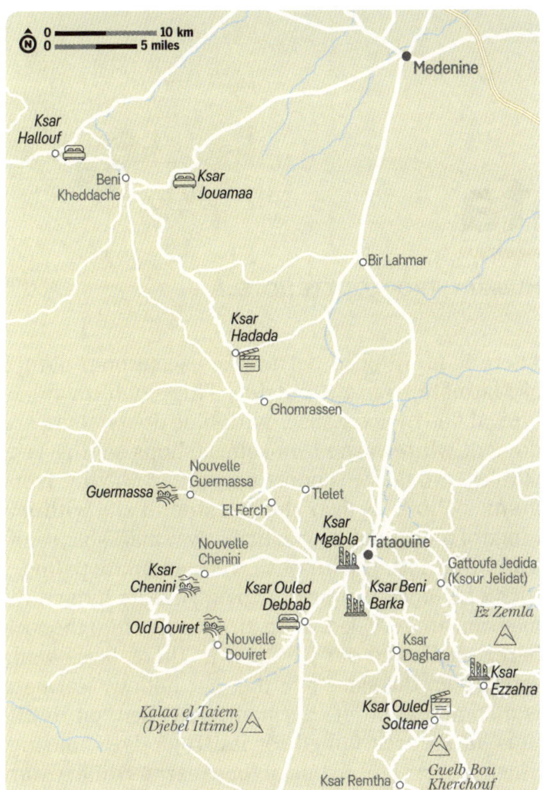

HOW TO

Book ahead If you fancy staying in a *ksar*, bear in mind there are only a limited number of rooms so making a reservation in high season is advisable.

When to go Check availability at *ksar* hotels in low season (midsummer and midwinter) when there may be too few guests to warrant opening up.

What to bring Shade is lacking at all the hilltop sights, so a hat or umbrella is useful. Most of the big hilltop sights have a cafe, but it's best to carry supplies in remoter destinations.

Budget None of the hilltop sights charge an entry fee.

Key Terms

Ksar A communal fortified granary, traditionally built by Amazigh tribes to protect grain, crops and olive oil.

Ksour The plural of *ksar*. *Ksour* date back to the 15th century and are a distinctive part of Amazigh heritage. Most of the best preserved ksour, however, were built along similar designs by Arab settlers after the 16th century.

Ghorfa *Ksour* are comprised of single units called *ghorfas*. These long, narrow, barrel-vaulted rooms, built of stone and gypsum and finished with a mud render, were usually owned by extended families. Extraction of grain during times of scarcity would be regulated by a caretaker – often a local religious leader.

Skifa Most *ghorfas* are arranged around a courtyard secured by a *skifa* (fortified gate), some of which remain in place today.

Tour or DIY?

Tours are possible through Tataouine agents **Savy Travel** *(savytravelservices.com)*, **Gazelle du Sud Tours** *(20 371 516)* and **Agence De Voyages Ksour Tour** *(75 863 633)*. Tours are also offered from coastal hubs and from Douz.

Tours allow for a brief stop at several sights as a day trip and some organise overnight stays in *ksour*. Smaller, specialised trips focusing on cycling and hiking between *ksour* are also possible.

To avoid the crowds and to reach the remoter hilltop villages, self-drive or hire a taxi from Tataouin.

Matmata

PIT DWELLINGS | CAVE MUSEUM | TROGLODYTE HOTELS

GETTING AROUND

It is possible to reach Matmata by louage (shared taxi) via Matmata Nouvelle – a newer town some 16km to the northeast along the C107. Louages connect Matmata Nouvelle with the city of Gabès on the coast.

By car, roads thread throughout the region with even the smallest generally in pretty good condition and with good signposting.

Getting around old Matmata is easy on foot, although there are no paved paths for those hoping to see the pit dwellings from above on a walking route. The flooring of some of the troglodyte sites, including the cave hotels, are uneven and generally involve steps.

There is nothing to betray the exceptional nature of Matmata from the outside. This small town has typical flat-roofed houses with blue doors; there are domed, whitewashed mosques, shops selling vegetables, a bakery, schools and a flag waving from municipal offices near the bus stop. It sits within a range of pretty, but not particularly remarkable, semi-arid hills, dotted with olive trees and date palms.

It's only once you are in town that its hidden dimension are revealed. With an entrance into the rock here, a hollowed out passageway there, brick walls shoring up the sides of a dug-out hollow, Matmata is a combination of caves and so-called 'pit dwellings' in an area famed for its troglodyte housing. Staying overnight in one of these extraordinary warrens of underground rooms is an experience, best complemented by a walking tour with a local guide in the morning.

Going Underground in a Matmata Pit Dwelling

Maison Troglodyte Museum in Matmata

If you want to see how local residents traditionally lived, then the **Maison Troglodyte Matmata** *(entry DT10)* – old Matmata's little ethnographical museum on Shaabet Smaala near Hotel Sidi Driss (p227) – offers a good introduction. A sloping entrance way burrows through the rock leading to the open-to-the-sky 'heart of the house' where a typical bedroom, kitchen and sitting area radiate in spokes around the central pit. There are some interesting old exhibits in each of the rooms such as hand looms, cooking implements and everyday objects, including the extraordinary keys used to secure each cave home.

Tour groups are not uncommon in Matmata, naturally, but it's easy to time your visit to the museum, which opens from 9am to 5pm, for early or late in the day to avoid them. It's not so easy, though, especially on a national holiday, to escape a school trip. When 40 excitable nine-year-olds rush through the

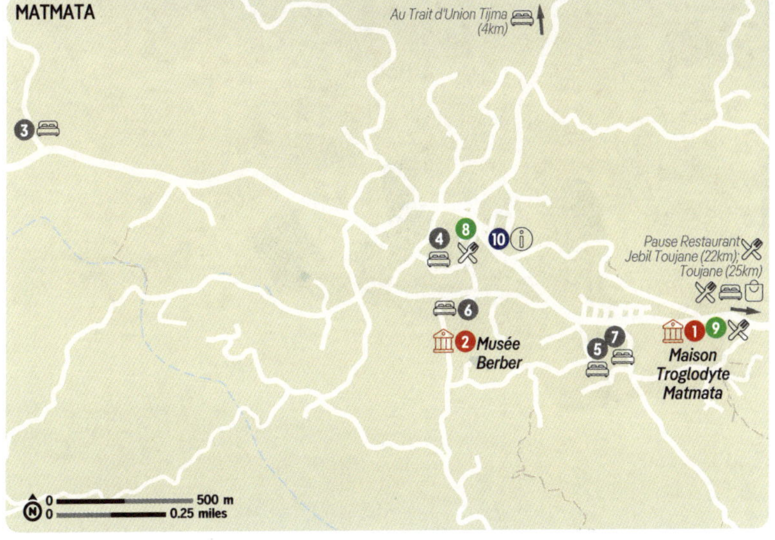

HIGHLIGHTS
1 Maison Troglodyte Matmata
2 Musée Berber

SLEEPING
3 Hôtel Diar El Berber
4 Hôtel Les Berbères
5 Hôtel Matmata
6 Hotel Sidi Driss
7 Touring Club Marhala Hotel

EATING
8 Chez Abdoul
9 Matmata Restaurant Les Troglodyte

INFORMATION
10 Syndicat d'Initiative

underground passage of this showcase of Amazigh heritage, tooting on recorders and blowing tin whistles, it's cacophony amplified, with sound bouncing back through the rock chambers. It's so noisy, even the curators kindly suggest you come back later – or aim for the weekend.

Driving the Escarpment

Matmata to Toujane

The landscape surrounding Matmata is slightly underwhelming, but that all changes as the road (the C104) slips out of town and heads towards the remarkable old village of Toujane, 26km to the east. The drive only takes 30 minutes but makes a good day trip from Matmata with lots of interest en route.

Continues on p218

TOP TIP

To avoid intruding on the privacy of locals while walking around town, it's best to hire a guide. Although you're likely to be approached by would-be guides when you park or get off the bus, it's better to support the activities of the **Syndicat d'Initiative**, near the centre of Matmata.

EATING IN & AROUND MATMATA: OUR PICKS

Pause Restaurant Jebil Toujane: Located along the main road to Toujane, this simple eatery offers impressive views from its escarpment location. *hours vary* €

Chez Abdoul: The couscous dishes are plentiful and tasty here and there's always a warm welcome from the host at this Matmata favourite. *hours vary* €

Matmata Restaurant Les Troglodyte: Perfectly positioned next to the museum, this Matmata restaurant has an attractive terrace shaded by mature trees. *24hrs* €€

Dar Toujane: One of the most atmospheric venues for lunch in the old village of Toujane. Recommended for freshly grilled meats. *6am-11pm Mon-Fri, 24hr Sat & Sun* €€

IGOR GROCHEV/SHUTTERSTOCK

Pit dwelling, Matmata

TOP EXPERIENCE

Going Underground

One of the quintessential experiences of visiting Matmata and the surrounding area is staying overnight in a pit dwelling. There are different ways of doing this, including staying at local guesthouses that offer bed and breakfast or choosing one of the troglodyte hotels in Matmata. Either way, save some time for a guided walk in daylight.

DON'T MISS

- Touring Club Marhala Hotel
- Hotel Sidi Driss
- Maison Troglodyte Matmata
- Musée Berber (Dar Khadija)
- Hôtel Matmata
- Guided Walking Tour
- Local mint, honey and olive oil

Navigating at Night

No matter what your expectations of a troglodyte hotel, it's not likely to be quite like you imagine. Arrive at night and the experience is particularly disorienting.

Take the wonderful **Touring Club Marhala Hotel** (p227), for example. Surprise number one: despite entering a cavernous lobby, the internet works. Surprise number two: at the end of a stone passageway is a circular space where, just as you're calculating how many metres of rock are above you and wondering how a date palm is growing so far underground, you look up to see stars. Surprise number three, unless you're very short, you have to bend over to get through the door but the roof of your room appears to disappear into the night.

PRACTICALITIES

- See p227 for places to stay in Matmata and around. Contact **Syndicat d'Initiative** *(75 240 075)* next to the bus station in old Matmata for a Matmata **tour** *(from DT85)*.

Supper in a Labyrinth

By suppertime, you've just about worked out that you're not staying in a cave exactly, but in a hollowed-out room off a dug-out pit. But another surprise comes at the bottom of a steep flight of stairs, when your internal compass screams 'underground' while the Milky Way floats into view again.

All the troglodyte homes in and around Matmata comprise at least one circular pit, not all of the same depth, that acts as a courtyard for sitting and dining. It's a magical experience sitting in one of these shared spaces at night, in an abstract of shadows, mud-brick stairways and lit crevices that seem to be purpose-made for bonding with strangers.

Sleeping on Stone

Sleeping quarters tend to be pretty basic in all the troglodyte homes, with furniture formed around natural cave features, sometimes including beds of stone and shelves fashioned out of the rock. None are en suite. Given the location, and the fact that there is no source of water in town, only the water collected from erratic rains, it's a miracle there is any plumbing at all, but shared shower blocks have hot water.

View from Above

One special feature of staying in troglodyte dwellings in Matmata is emerging from your cell-like grotto in the morning to find light streaming into the circular pit courtyards. It creates a completely different impression of the space. Equally, no visit is complete without looking down on the accommodation from above.

The only way to do this is to take a walking tour around town. Guides will steer you over rough ground from pit to pit, and as you peer gingerly over the fenceless rim they'll tell you that this form of architecture has been in service for over 600 years.

Formerly there were 500 similar homesteads in town. Now there is only one family living here permanently in the traditional way, although many return each summer to enjoy the constant 25°C temperatures below when it's 45°C above ground.

Other Local Attractions

Two former pit homes are run as private ethnographical museums, **Maison Troglodyte Matmata** (p214) and **Musée Berber** (Dar Khadija), and both are worth the small entry fee.

Run by local residents, they feature traditional dress, handlooms and rugs, and include some unique features, such as the peculiarly huge keys required to secure the premises.

There are other pit dwellings in the neighbouring villages of **Techine** and **Al Hafsah**, with some guides offering the chance to walk the 7km or so between the two.

STAR WARS CONNECTION

Matmata is yet another destination in Southern Tunisia made famous by the Star Wars films, with one of its pit homes serving as the location of Luke Skywalker's childhood home on Tatooine in the original 1977 film, *A New Hope*. With several elaborate pit courtyards connected by underground tunnels, Sidi Driss (p227) was used again in *The Phantom Menace* and *Attack of the Clones*. Today, it's a hotel and retains several of the original set features.

TOP TIPS

- Arrive at your cave accommodation at night when the pit dwellings are at their most atmospheric.
- Work up some courage in the bar at Hôtel Matmata before turning in for the night if you're in any way claustrophobic.
- Avoid walking around off-road at night – pits are everywhere and most have no railing around the rim.
- Make sure you visit Matmata by day as well as at night – looking down on a pit dwelling is a completely different experience to looking up.
- Take a guide when visiting surrounding villages to respect pit-dweller privacy.

PIT-DWELLING CONSTRUCTION

Matmata's underground homes represent a variation on the troglodyte theme. Most cave dwellings either adapt or extend existing cave structures. In Matmata, however, where the earliest pit dwellings are thought to date back to the 4th century, Amazigh communities excavated large circular holes, 10m across, by digging down into the soft limestone. These skilful builders made the pits up to 7m deep and then connected each circular 'courtyard' by tunnelling through the rock.

Cool in summer and warm against winter winds, these unique dwellings were defended from marauders by being hard to spot from the surface. In fact they remained unknown to the wider world until occupying French soldiers came across them in 1943, during WWII.

BIESZCZADY_WILDLIFE/SHUTTERSTOCK

Landscape between Matmata and Toujane (p215)

Continued from p215

Begin with a short diversion to **Techine**, 12km from Matmata. Interesting not only for its troglodyte houses, Techine is typical of the Amazigh villages in the area with pretty, whitewashed houses, stands of oleander and small olive groves.

Back on the main road, the close-knit hills stretch out into a continuous ridge, dotted with shepherds and their dogs. The views from here are spectacular, and several coffee shops, including the Pause Restaurant Jebil Toujane (p215), make the most of their eyries on the escarpment's edge.

At length, the road twists into **Toujane**, one of the few old Amazigh villages still inhabited. Forty-seven families live here, some in traditional dwellings, two of which – Dar Toujane (p215) and Dar Fatma (p227) – offer lunch and accommodation. The village is renowned for its handloomed **carpets**, dyed red with locally grown pomegranates. Guides can show you the artisans at work and the town flaps on a breezy day with their colourful creations, as sold from **Dar Fethi Tarhouni**.

Return to Matmata via the road to **Beni Zelten** – another old village, recently restored. The coffee shop here, housed in a goat-hair tent, is the perfect spot for afternoon tea and another expansive view.

Beyond Matmata

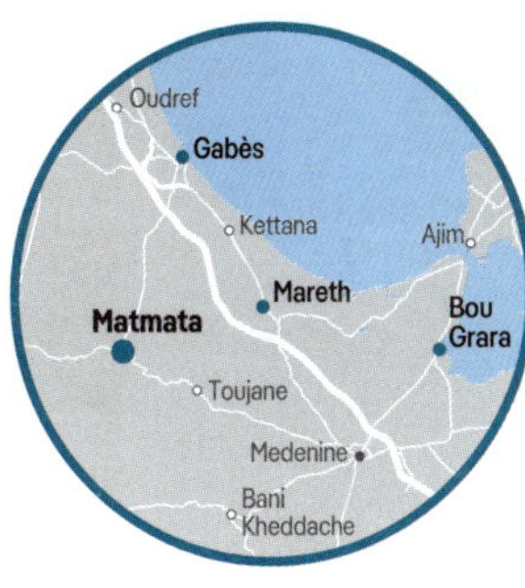

The escarpment landscape around Matmata appears isolated and remote, but is just an hour's drive from major coastal destinations.

Places

While Matmata and the Ksour Country to the south tend to receive most of the regional visitors, there are a couple of reasons to head east towards the coast. Although the big port city of Gabès is unlikely to detain a traveller for long, it does at least have an extensive *palmeraie* (palm grove) that is interesting to explore for those unable to make it to the plantations of the Jerid.

Relatively nearby, there are some well-preserved Roman ruins at Gightis – one of Tunisia's least visited ancient sites, and easily reached from the island of Djerba. Also nearby, for those interested in WWII, is an interesting military museum at Mareth, located at the edge of the coastal plain.

Gabès

TIME FROM MATMATA: **30 MINS**

Visiting the Palmeraie

If you find yourself transiting through Gabès without an immediate onward connection, head for the *palmeraie* of this modern port city. Unusually for a city by the sea, Gabès does little to celebrate its beachfront, but the plantation makes for a pleasant stroll. Stretching inland along the Oued Gabès, the *palmeraie* connects Ghannouche with the oasis village of **Chenini** (not to be confused with Chenini in Ksour Country) – a distance of around 4km. *Calèches* (horse-drawn carriages) are available for a short tour.

The nearby old quarter of town is known as **Grand Jara**. The souqs here sell the *palmeraie*'s giant pomegranates in December as well as herbs and spices. Look for Gabès's famous locally produced **henna** – used for decorating hair, hands and feet.

Mareth

Military Museum at Mareth

For those interested in WWII, the **Mareth Defensive Line Museum** makes an interesting stop between Gabès and Bou Grara. On the edge of town, with bunkers and various ordnance including anti-aircraft guns on display in the grounds, it marks the point where in March 1943 German general Erwin Rommel repelled the UK's Eighth army's advance, leading to the battle of the Mareth Line.

GETTING AROUND

Louages connect Novelle Matmata (a 15-minute ride from old Matmata) to Gabès. The trip takes just 30 minutes. As a major transport hub, Gabès is well served with buses to/from Djerba (four hours), Sfax, Sous and Tunis (six hours).

The quickest way to arrive in the region is to fly to Djerba or take the train from Tunis or Sfax to Gabès. Getting to Gightis, on the Gulf of Bou Grara, is easiest by car.

WHO ARE THE AMAZIGH?

'Berber' is a term you'll hear a lot in the south where many Tunisians proudly claim Berber heritage. While pride is shared in common language roots and cultural practices, not all indigenous peoples of North Africa are happy with the appellation.

Preferring the name Amazigh ('free people' in the Tamazight language), they point out that the term 'Berber' comes from Greek *barbarikos* meaning 'foreign' and was first bestowed by 7th-century Arab invaders to distinguish those who preferred to retain their own language and culture from those who chose to adopt Roman or Byzantine culture.

Referencing difference and division during colonial times, 'Berber' is now something of a pejorative term best consigned, some Amazigh suggest, to history.

SLIMSTYL/SHUTTERSTOCK

Gightis

Bou Grara

TIME FROM MATMATA: 1¼ HRS

The Roman Ruins of Gightis

Stand above the forum at the Roman ruins of **Gightis** *(entry DT5)*, and from the steps of the temple it's just about possible to picture the comings and goings of a busy port with ships out at sea. In place of what is now a wetland of brackish waters where a flock of flamingos comb the shallows, enslaved people would have awaited an uncertain fate beyond the shore while camel caravans unloaded their precious cargo of gold and ivory. The site is open Saturday to Thursday from 9.30am to 4.30 from September to April; and from 8am to noon and 4pm to 7pm from May through August.

Although established by the Phoenicians, it was under the Romans that this coastal entrepôt came to prominence. Much of the masonry scattered around the site dates from the 2nd century, when this part of what is now Tunisia was the southernmost point of Roman Africa. Gightis, with other towns such as Tozeur, formed part of the **Limes Tripolitanus** – a defensive line that guarded the empire's southwestern boundaries against the Amazigh confederations that controlled the trans-Saharan trade routes to the south.

Today, little remains of this stronghold, but the site makes for an atmospheric wander. An hour before sunset, the yellow ochre and salmon pinks of the sandstone resonate strongly under the sun and, with the sea beyond, form a composition that is irresistible for photographers.

EATING IN & AROUND GABÈS: SEAFOOD

Restaurant Fruit de Mer: This popular, semi-open air restaurant near the port is a good place to try *calamari farçi* – squid stuffed with seasoned rice. *11.15am-11pm* **€**

Restaurant LAC: Overlooking the Bou Grara jetty, this fish restaurant serves the catch of the day, fried to perfection and preceded by a good fish soup. *hours vary* **€€**

Restaurant La Luna Italien: Serving generous portions of well-seasoned prawns, squid and fish, this busy, central restaurant gives the menu an Italian twist. *24hrs* **€€**

Restaurant El Mazar: Served in an elegant dining room, this restaurant prepares tasty Tunisian fish lunches but has non-fish options for carnivores. *10am-11pm* **€€**

Tataouine

AMAZIGH VILLAGES | ANCIENT KSOUR | HILLTOP VISTAS

The grand dual carriageways leading out of town to the west and east hint at greater pomp than the town of Tataouine in fact delivers. Without an old medina, and slim on sights now that the museum has closed, the main reason to be in this busy provincial centre is as a base to tour the surrounding old Amazigh villages and *ksour* – the traditional fortified granaries that typify the area. With a couple of good hotels, plenty of cheap eateries and even a Carrefour, Tataouine delivers as a transport hub, a place to regroup and resupply after desert travels or as a first stop en route from the coastal plain to the mountainous interior.

If the name 'Tataouine' sounds familiar, it may be because film director George Lucas adopted it for the desert planet of Tatooine in filming the original Star Wars – a connection still celebrated locally.

GETTING AROUND

Buses from Tunis (eight hours), Gabès, Sfax and Sousse arrive into Tataouine at the long-distance **station**, 1.5km north of the town centre. This station also serves Djerba (Houmt Souk).

Local buses, from Medenine and Ghomrassen, pile into the **station** at the western end of Rue 1 Juin 1955. **Louages to Chenini** (20 minutes) and Douiret leave from nearby.

To visit any of the *ksour* in this area, it's best to rely on a private car or taxi. All the villages are linked by a good network of roads with only a few stretches of graded road to be cautious of.

STUDIOANGHIFOTO/SHUTTERSTOCK

Ksar Mgabla (p212), Tataouine

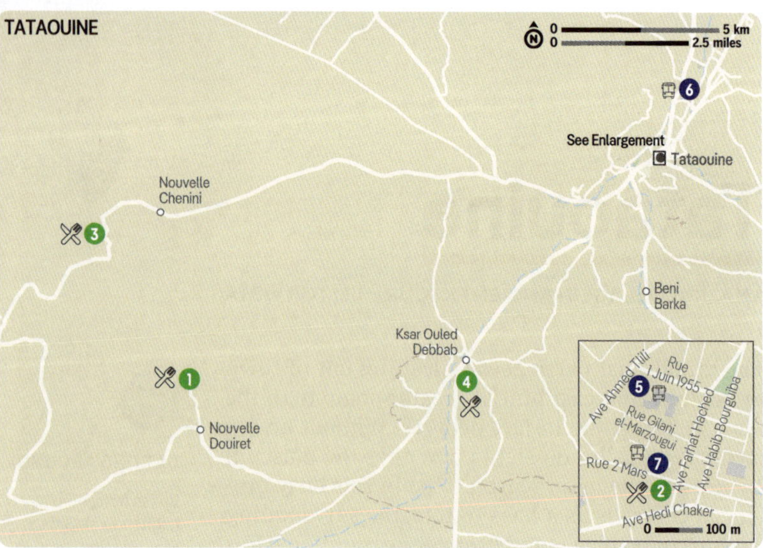

EATING
1 Chez Raouf
2 Corne de Gazelle
3 Restaurant Mabrouk Chenini
4 Restaurant Ouled Debbab

TRANSPORT
5 Bus & Louage Station
6 Long-Distance Bus & Louage Station
7 Louages to Chenini & Douiret

TOP TIP

Pragmatic though it may be to book in for several days at a Tataouine hotel, consider reserving a night or two instead at one of the hotels operating inside the *ksour.*

Horn of Plenty

Sampling local pastries

If you're in town for even the briefest of visits, stop at one of the many bakeries and sample a *corne de gazelle* (p222). Roughly resembling the horn of their namesake, they are packed with chopped nuts, drizzled in local honey and baked in pastry. They're delicious with a strong shot of coffee. Sadly, they're likely to be as close as you come to the real thing – gazelles are seldom seen in the Tataouine hills these days, except occasionally in the desert further south.

EATING IN & AROUND TATAOUINE: OUR PICKS

Corne de Gazelle: This central patisserie bakes up new batches of Tataouine's signature pastry each day which is good news for a picnic. *Hours vary* €

Chez Raouf: Half the fun of eating in this traditional home, in the heart of the old *ksar*, is finding it. The cosy courtyard kitchen serves good soups. *Hours vary* €

Restaurant Mabrouk Chenini: Specialising in Tunisian staples (soup, salad, *brik*, grill) for tour groups, this restaurant is a good lunch stop on a *ksour* tour. *8am-11pm* €€

Restaurant Ouled Debbab: Offering a wonderful hilltop setting for a meal, this attractive *ksar* restaurant is reason enough to consider staying the night. *10am-8pm* €€

TOURING TATAOUINE'S FAMOUS OLD GRANARIES

Spend a day driving a rural loop around some of the region's best *ksour*, following the RL1014 and RL1012. Bring your own refreshments.

START	END	LENGTH
Tataouine	Tataouine	60km; day excursion

Humbly crumbling back to dust, 1 **Ksar Mgabla** (p212), on the edge of Tataouine, makes an atmospheric introduction to the traditional fortified granaries that famously dot the region. Having escaped restoration, it gives an idea of how a *ksar* would originally have looked. Better still, you're more likely to bump into a flock of sheltering sheep here than a rambunctious coach party.

Driving south towards Maztouria, branch off to 2 **Ksar Beni Barka** (p212). Occupying the whole hilltop, it's hard to recognise that this extensive fortification is man-made rather than a natural erosion of the hill's crest. Edging along an unpaved track, park at the mosque and walk to the top for 360-degree views.

Back on the road, passing smaller *ksour*, including squat 3 **Ksar Daghara**, follow signs to 4 **Ksar Ouled Soltane** (p212) – an architectural highlight, with four stories of *ghorfas* wrapped around the two courtyards. Watercolour paintings of the *ksar* made famous as a location for Star Wars help bring income into the village.

Continue to four-storey 5 **Ksar Ezzahra** (p212). Lacking the cinematic connection of its more famous neighbour, this gem of architecture is seldom visited, despite its exceptional exterior staircases. The RL1012 is unpaved for about 2km north of here until it joins the RL994. At the junction, explore the rambling relic 6 **Ksar Jelidat**, as you head back to Tataouine.

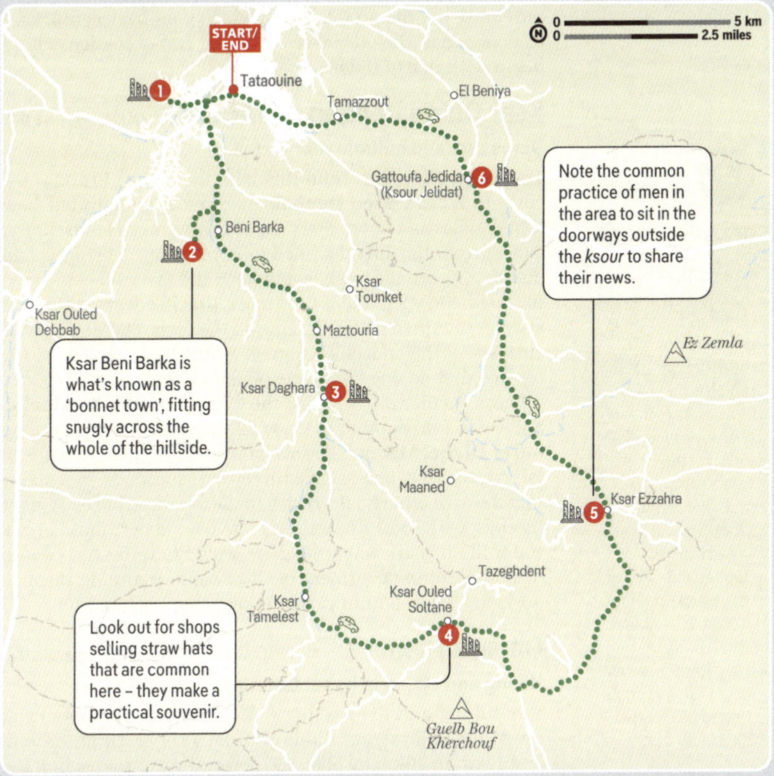

0 5 km
0 2.5 miles

START/END
1 Tataouine
Tamazzout
El Beniya
Gattoufa Jedida 6 (Ksour Jelidat)
Beni Barka
2
Ksar Tounket
Ksar Ouled Debbab
Maztouria
Ksar Daghara 3
Ksar Maaned
Ksar Ezzahra 5
Ez Zemla
Tazeghdent
Ksar Ouled Soltane 4
Ksar Tamelest
Guelb Bou Kherchouf

Note the common practice of men in the area to sit in the doorways outside the *ksour* to share their news.

Ksar Beni Barka is what's known as a 'bonnet town', fitting snugly across the whole of the hillside.

Look out for shops selling straw hats that are common here – they make a practical souvenir.

Beyond Tatacuine

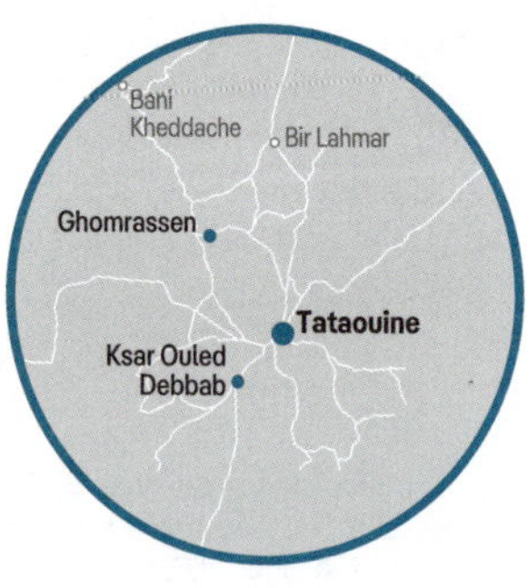

Stay overnight in a *ksar*, visit exquisite Amazigh villages, rest under ancient olive trees and discover two local obsessions.

Places

While the area surrounding Tataouine showcases the most celebrated *ksour*, there are other grand examples further afield, some of which offer overnight accommodation. In addition to these architectural wonders, the region is home to some magnificent old Amazigh villages at Chenini, Douiret and Guermassa. All three are strung along hilltop ridges, but each has a character all its own and a trip to the region isn't complete without visiting at least one.

If you're growing weary of mud-brick artistry, then a stroll in the countryside may help. The region is famous for its light, pure olive oil, the production of which goes back centuries – as do some of the olive trees. And the two obsessions? Let's begin with one of them...

Ksar Ouled Debbab

TIME FROM TATAOUINE: **15 MINS**

Dinosaurs and million-year vistas

Travel just 10km west from Tataouine along the P19 and you'll come to **Ksar Ouled Debbab** – a beautiful, renovated *ksar* that doubles as a hotel. The view of a rosy-tinged landscape at sunset from the lofty, fortified hilltop is alone worth the trip out here, as are the fresh lemon juice and tasty snacks served in the cafe nestled under the arches. Staying overnight in the stylishly adapted *ghorfa* is icing on the cake. There's only one curiosity – the enormous fibreglass dinosaur parked on the terrace that no one has any explanation for.

Travel further north, along the C207 to **Bani Kheddache**, and you'll find another of these jolly monstrosities sitting on top of **Djebel Miteur**. The accompanying signboard helps to fathom the local obsession with replica sauropods. It explains that the area is particularly rich in the fossilised bones of giant reptiles, with some dinosaur remains found here dating back 100 million years when this area would have been a swamp belonging to the continent of Gondwana. Scanning the arid horizon from the hilltop, that takes some imagination.

Ghomrassen

TIME FROM TATAOUINE: **30 MINS**

Hiking and biking in Ksour Country

Five hiking and five cycling routes begin in the provincial town of Ghomrassen. Ranging from 7km to 11km on foot, and 12km to 30km by bike, the non-technical routes link the

GETTING AROUND

As with other destinations in Ksour Country, the easiest way to tour any of the attractions in the region is by taxi or hire car. Taxi drivers charge around €150 for a day trip from Tataouine and will probably suggest a loop around Ksar Ouled Debbab, Douiret and Chenini which picks up three of the best sights of the area. To charter a taxi from Tataouine just to Chenini costs around €10 for the 20-minute trip.

Guermassa

best features of the region, showcasing dinosaur footprints, marine fossils, old olive trees, remote *ksour* and expansive escarpment views.

Ghomrassen itself is an interesting starting point with an old quarter spread along the wadi and a large boulder at the western entrance of town noted for its **petroglyphs**.

One route ends at the spectacular 'bonnet town' of **Guermassa**, spread tightly across the hilltop. Don't despair at the impossibly steep rock face: a 3km detour winds around the back of the cliff and slowly ascends to the village. The cafe here makes a great stop for tea at sunset when sheep the colour of straw on the hillside suddenly turn to gold.

A break from bricks and mortar

It may look barren, but the terrain around Ghomrassen is rich in minerals and olives grow well here. Some very aged specimens are signposted off the road and walking along farm paths to see them is a remedy for *ksar* fatigue.

One such venerable old **olive tree** is found 2km off the road that links Douiret with Chenini. The canopy forms a giant umbrella whose shade supports a whole ecosystem, but its 'trunk' consists of multiple branches. It's humbling to think this ancient wonder was around long before many of the *ksour*.

Another obsession: La Route Cinématographique

And so at length to the second of the two local obsessions – film locations. A national route, **La Route Cinématographique**, is dedicated to four English-language film cults – the Star Wars saga, *The English Patient*, *Indiana Jones* and *Monty Python's Life of Brian* – and four of the dozen named sites of interest are located in Ksour Country.

The most famous of these is **Ksar Haddada** (p227), originally built in 1845 and spread over two floors of 360 *ghorfas*, it appeared in 1997's *The Phantom Menace* as the location of enslaved people's quarters in Mos Espa, the imaginary town on Galactic Planet Tatooine. Today, the *ksar*, a short drive from Ghomrassen, functions as a hotel.

THE ELUSIVE FESTIVAL OF KSOUR

Flowing robes, rhythmic clapping, folk dancing, camels bedecked with colourful sheep-wool rugs – for 39 years the **Festival of the Ksour** in Tataouine has delighted crowds with displays of Amazigh culture. Check with the tourist office and they list the festival in February. Consult the internet and you'll learn that it's a thriving three-day event, held in March. Ask locals and they'll tell you that yes, the festival is an annual fixture – in April.

But before you rush to Tataouine sometime this spring, there's a secret to be shared. The festival doesn't exist! At least, not anymore. Despite no evidence of it since 2018, it had until then amassed nearly four decades of collective memory, so it's one to watch for the future.

TOP EXPERIENCE

Chenini

Only a hint of the exquisite hilltop Amazigh village of Chenini is afforded from the dry wadi bottom that leads through buttress escarpments to the settlement's base. Suddenly the road rounds a bend and the magnificent amphitheatre of aged buildings comes into view. Strolling around Chenini is not to be missed – allow at least a couple of hours to do it justice.

ANISBOUKHRIS/SHUTTERSTOCK

TOP TIPS

- Rather than rushing up the steepest path, follow residents in a more leisurely zigzagging and view the village from multiple viewpoints.
- Beware shortcuts, which often lead to vertiginous dead ends.
- **Douiret**, a similar village (although abandoned), is a 30-minute drive away.

PRACTICALITIES

- Chenini may feel like a giant museum, but it's a living, working village so there are no opening times or entry fee.

A Lived-In Relic

Chenini is a tumble of cave dwellings, each kept private with a fenced courtyard. Unusually, many are still lived in or kept for housing livestock. As such, the village is animated with signs of life – a newly painted door, a carefully tended houseplant, a string of washing. Aim for the 12th-century *kalaa* (hill fort) on the saddle between the two parts of old Chenini, marked by a picturesque mosque and teashop.

Shopping for Rugs

Vendors take pride in explaining the tattoo marks, palm trees and other Amazigh iconography woven into the design of locally made, hand-loomed *kilims*. Buying a rug from Chenini is a good way of making your visit count, contributing to the village's sustainable future.

Looking for Sleepers

Ask for directions to the Seven Sleepers and you may be waved towards **Dar Kenza** (p227) where the owner offers rooms in his cosy troglodyte home. What in fact you're looking for are the tombs of seven Christians and their dog, who, according to legend, fell asleep in a Chenini cave and woke up 400 years later in a world of Islam. Having grown to 4m, the Islamic converts, or so the story goes, were buried in 5m-long grave mounds. The site is a 20-minute walk from Chenini's white mosque.

Places We Love to Stay

€ Budget €€ Midrange €€€ Top End

Matmata
p214

Touring Club Marhala Hotel **€** A fun, wonderfully well-organised and friendly warren of pits and passageways, this is the cave stay of choice.

Hôtel Les Berbères **€** This cave dwelling also has long labyrinthine passages leading to simple cave rooms with shared bathrooms.

Hôtel Matmata **€€** When asked whether there's a bar in this stylish *ksar*-themed hotel, the receptionist responded that the hotel had everything required of a comfortable night's stay – hot water, clean linen, en suite bathroom and a beer!

Hotel Sidi Driss **€€** Doubling as a sight for movie lovers, this pit dwelling was used in the Star Wars franchise and is now a modest hotel.

Hôtel Diar El Berber **€€** Near Matmata, this hotel has built new cave-like rooms in a double-storey complex, offering a sense of troglodyte living but with a few more creature comforts.

Au Trait d'Union Tijma **€€€** An elegant modern take on an aged theme, this stylish troglodyte hotel has lots of attractive furnishings in the village of Tijma.

Toujane
p215

Dar Fatma **€€** At the top end of the main road, this is the most popular place to stay in the pretty village of Toujane.

Trogl'Auberge Chez Bechir **€€** A cave home with a quaint courtyard and grand views of the semi-arid mountain landscape.

Tataouine
p221

Hôtel Mabrouk **€€** The best option currently in Tataouine with pretty gardens and large rooms, and serving an excellent breakfast, located on the road heading north of town.

Hôtel Dakyanus **€€** Just out of town, this hotel offers its own tours and has a fine panoramic view of the escarpment.

Hotel Al Ryan **€€€** This new hotel is in the northern new town, some way out from anywhere useful, but it does at least have large, modern rooms and serves good food.

Ksar Accommodation
p212

Gite de Douiret Chez Rouf **€** Initiated by a community project to bring tourism into the old town of Douiret, this guesthouse offers simple rooms and good meals and is a characterful place to stay.

Dar Kenza **€€** In Chenini, this delightful troglodyte home makes a lovely place to stay, offering tours and giving a warm welcome.

Ksar Hallouf **€€** You'll need to book ahead for this windswept but characterful *ksar* hotel, 14km from Beni Kheddache, as it's popular with small group tours.

Ksar Haddada **€€** Even if you're not a Star Wars fan, you may enjoy staying at this *ksar,* which was renovated as a film set and is now an attractive place to stay.

Ksar Ouled Debbab **€€€** On a hill east of the modern village of Debbab and commanding expansive views, this old *ksar* (p224) offers simple rooms tastefully decorated, and the food is excellent.

Gabès
p219

Hotel Atlantic **€** From the glamorous 1923 facade, you'd never know this hotel was just a budget option with no food and no service – but it does offer a reasonable if tired-looking room for the night.

Hôtel Chems **€€** A large hotel with rooms with sea views, this is part resort and part business hotel near the port. It has a very good restaurant.

For places to stay in the Sahara, see p243

ANGELA N PERRYMAN/SHUTTERSTOCK

Above: camels in the Sahara; right: Ksar Ghilane oasis (p240)

Researched by
DrJenny Walker

The Sahara

INSPIRING DESERT LANDSCAPES, HOME TO NOMADS

Explore the Grand Erg Oriental, a sea of sand rimming the great Sahara, and enjoy the company of fellow adventurers in isolated oasis towns.

Dressed in bow tie, linen shirt and woollen stockings, and sporting a pair of brogues befitting the English Patient, a vintage-styled archaeologist joins others in similar attire in the lobby of a Zone Touristique hotel in Douz. Members of a history reenactment society from the USA, the infectiously enthusiastic group pause for a selfie before boarding the coach for a desert treasure hunt.

This is the fascinating part of being in the desert towns of Douz and Ksar Ghilane, on the edge of Tunisia's portion of the Sahara – they are visitor hubs in the middle of an almost unpopulated region and as such are full of the excitement of people enacting their desert dreams. Evolving to cater to those in transit between the great rolling sand dunes of the Grand Erg Oriental to the south and the cities on the coast, these dusty entrepôts have always been sociable gathering places, offering refuge for travellers in the harshest of environments.

But the erg, with its magnificent sea of dunes and rocky outcrops, isn't just an empty landscape framed by the human eye. It's also home to diverse flora and fauna, elaborately adapted to high temperatures and low rainfall. Learning about the life of the desert (at the Musée du Sahara, on a tour or chatting with semi-settled Bedouin guides during a camping trip) helps build a respect for this fascinating land of extremes.

At the time of research, several governments advise against travel to destinations within 20km of the Algerian border or within 30km of the Libyan border.

BALY PHOTO/SHUTTERSTOCK

THE MAIN AREAS

DOUZ
Friendly travellers' haunt and main Sahara gateway.
p234

KSAR GHILANE
Tiny oasis and popular desert activity hub.
p240

Find Your Way

Accessing the great southern expanse of sand and rock that comprises the Tunisian Sahara is best managed on an overnight or multiday 4WD or camel tour from Douz or Khsar Ghilane. Pre-booking is recommended.

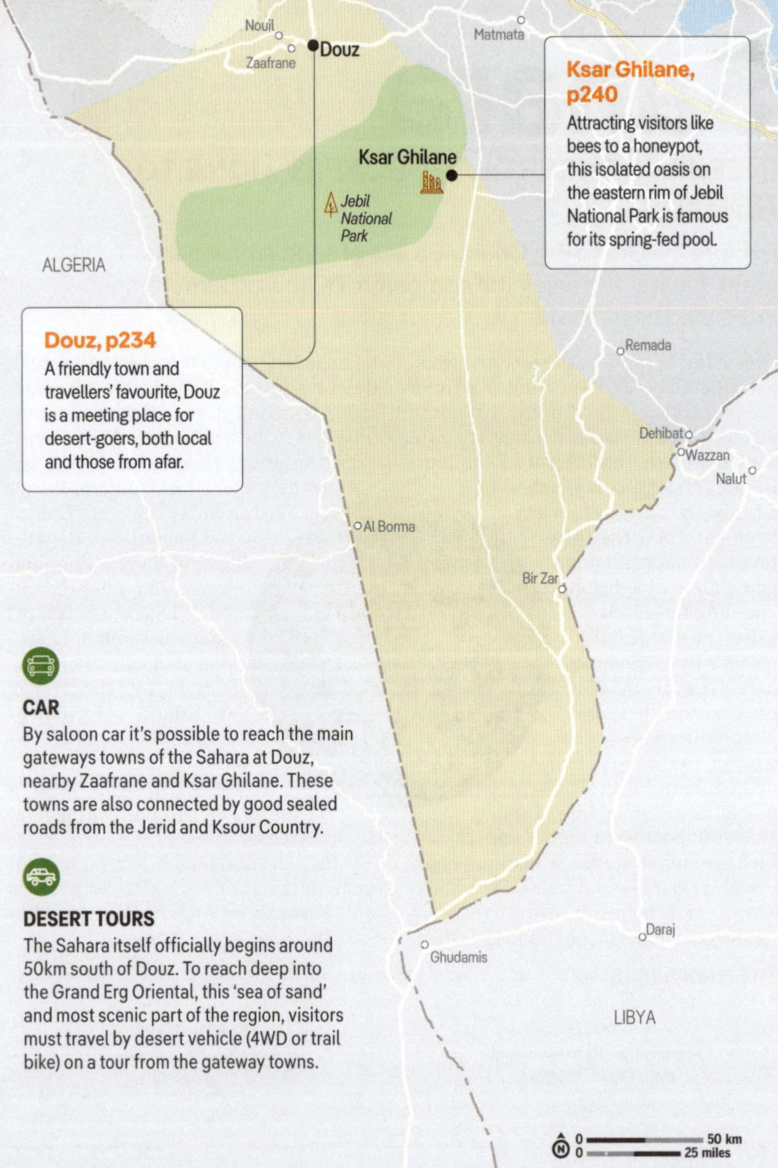

Ksar Ghilane, p240
Attracting visitors like bees to a honeypot, this isolated oasis on the eastern rim of Jebil National Park is famous for its spring-fed pool.

Douz, p234
A friendly town and travellers' favourite, Douz is a meeting place for desert-goers, both local and those from afar.

CAR

By saloon car it's possible to reach the main gateways towns of the Sahara at Douz, nearby Zaafrane and Ksar Ghilane. These towns are also connected by good sealed roads from the Jerid and Ksour Country.

DESERT TOURS

The Sahara itself officially begins around 50km south of Douz. To reach deep into the Grand Erg Oriental, this 'sea of sand' and most scenic part of the region, visitors must travel by desert vehicle (4WD or trail bike) on a tour from the gateway towns.

KRYSEK/SHUTTERSTOCK

Natural spring, Ksar Ghilane (p241)

Plan Your Time

It takes a lifetime to explore Tunisia's Grand Erg Oriental, the great billows of sand that unfold a 90-minute 4WD-ride south of Douz, but a single night under the stars makes a great introduction.

Desert Introduction

- Spend night one in **Douz** (p234), enjoying the travellers' vibe and visiting the **Musée du Sahara** (p234). Organise a camel ride to a local **Bedouin camp** (p232) and spend night two under the stars with your hosts. From Douz, drive the lonely C104 and C211 for a third night in **Ksar Ghilane** (p240) for a dip in the **pool** (p241) and quad bike ride to **Roman ruins** (p242).

Four-Day Immersion

- Orient yourself to desert life at **Douz** (p234), camel-riding at nearby **Zaafrane** (p237), before travelling by 4WD into the Grand Erg Oriental. Stay at a **tented camp** (p243) in Jebil National Park, the heart of the desert, reserving a day to explore. Continue on to **Ksar Ghilane** (p240) through the park by pre-arranged 4WD, or book an overnight camel journey from the camp. Take a taxi back to Douz.

SEASONAL HIGHLIGHTS

SPRING

High season due to blooming of wildflowers if there's been rain; the desert is at its most welcoming.

SUMMER

Soaring temperatures repel all but the most determined of visitors. Don't expect cooler nights.

AUTUMN

With the biggest palm grove in Tunisia, Douz goes from tourist town to date-harvesting centre in October.

WINTER

The **Sahara Festival** (p236) in November is an interesting time to visit. It gets bitterly cold in the desert at night.

HELP ME PICK:

Desert Excursions

Knowing you'd like to see the Sahara is the easy part – choosing which excursion will give you the best experience of Tunisia's corner of this vast desert takes some planning. There are a bewildering number of options to choose from and tour prices vary considerably. Understanding the main kinds of activities available may just help in selecting the right trip to match your interests and budget.

Which trip to choose if you love

An Adrenalin Rush

Careering down walls of sand behind the wheel of a vehicle may look like fun, but it is laced with the real possibility of getting stuck or even turning over. Driving off-road is a skill that takes years to hone. Thankfully, 4WD outfits in **Douz** (p234) organise short desert excursions with highly experienced drivers. This allows for the excitement of entering extreme terrain without the responsibility of courting danger.

If being driven is not your thing, then quad biking is a safer way to get behind the wheel. From **Ksar Ghilane** (p240), dozens of companies line the main road through the oasis, offering 45-minute rides into the surrounding sea of sand with no need to book ahead. Alternatively, trail biking, offered from Douz on overnight tours to **Jebil National Park** (p238), involves a challenging three-hour journey to reach camp.

Off-road in the Grand Erg Oriental (p238)

Cultural Insight

For centuries, nomads have been travelling through the Sahara, inscribing the sands with their culture through the rearing of camels and the herding of livestock. Although the practice of nomadism is a more fluid concept these days, with tribes now at least partially rooted within oases, the Bedouin still celebrate the freedom of life on the move.

If you're interested to learn how the Bedouin have adapted to modern technologies without compromising their desert heritage, then an evening spent in their company is a great experience. Licensed local guides, arranged in **Douz** (p234), **Zaafrane** (p237) and **Ksar Ghilane** (p240), take guests on camelback about an hour into the desert to their camps, bake them bread and cook them dinner, before plodding back in the morning after breakfast.

Soul Searching

The desert has long been associated with human endurance, and for those attracted by the extremities of this unforgiving environment, a trip to **Jebil National Park** (p238) is a must. The park encompasses some of Tunisia's most spectacular erg landscape, with waves of sand ebbing and flowing up to the distant horizon.

Glamping at one of the camps near **Taimbaïn** (p243), a flat-topped mountain with spectacular vistas over the surrounding low dunes, offers a chance to commune with nature during long walks along sandy ridges. Sitting on top of a solitary dune at any time of year makes you appreciative of the company you've left behind.

FROM LEFT: STRUCTURED VISION/SHUTTERSTOCK, PODOLNAYA ELENA/SHUTTERSTOCK

Festival of the Sahara (p236)

HOW TO

When to go Time your visit to coincide with the International Festival of the Sahara (p236) in November when camel and Saluki racing are showcased in Douz.

Book ahead Although you can turn up in Douz and organise a desert trip, it takes at least a day to arrange a multiday camel trip. Book ahead.

What to pack Bring a hat, walking shoes and a sealed bag for your phone (sand!). To avoid sunburn and chafing while camel-riding, wear long trousers.

Before you go Visit Douz' Musée du Sahara (p234) to learn about desert culture and how to identify a camel by its brand.

DIY or Guided Tour

It's possible to get a flavour of the Sahara in a saloon car – but this means tailoring your expectations accordingly. For a start, you can drive to **La Porte du Desert**, a few kilometres south of Douz, and peer through the gateway. Less than a tenth of the Sahara is sand and the view from here, or along the desolate C211 to Ksar Ghilane, is typical – rocky terrain, sparse vegetation and occasional roaming camels.

For most people, though, the desert is synonymous with sand. From Ksar Ghilane, you can park your car on the edge of the oasis and walk into a horizon dotted with low dunes, but taking a guided tour is the only feasible way to reach the more dramatic landscapes of the **Grand Erg Oriental**. This great sea of sand straddling Algeria and Tunisia is best visited on a multiday 4WD trip, but an overnight visit to the Jebil National Park, through **Camp Mars** (p243; *camp-mars.com*) or **Camp Abdelmoula** (p243; *camp-abdelmoula.com*) near Montagne Taimbaïn, makes a great introduction.

You can get behind the wheel of various desert vehicles, but driving unguided into the desert without prior off-road expertise is a recipe for disaster. Go with the experts, such as **Nefzaoua Voyages** (*nefzaoua-voyages.com*) or **Sahha Sahara** (*sahhasahara.com*). Other recommended agencies include **Ghilane Travel Services** (*ghilane.com*), **Zaied Travel** (*zaied-travel.com*) and **Libre Espace** (*libre-espace-voyages.com*).

Douz

SAHARA GATEWAY | DESERT MUSEUM | TRAVELLER VIBE

GETTING AROUND

It's not easy to reach Douz by public transport. Although there's a bus from Tunis to El Faouar (9½ hours), a taxi is then required to complete the 40-minute journey into Douz, making the trip cumbersome. There is no public transport, and the trip between Ksar Ghilane and Douz is expensive by taxi. Car hire represents the most efficient and economical way to reach Douz and get around.

Plenty of taxis run around Douz, the centre of which is comfortably walkable.

Off-road driving in the desert should only be attempted as part of a tour as it takes specific knowledge and skills.

If you had to imagine a town on the edge of the great Sahara, Douz could well be it. There is a genuine buzz of excitement in the traveller-friendly cafes in town, where those who have just returned from an adventure share their stories with those who are eagerly planning their own. There are the 'done-it-all' bikers and 4WD drivers with their 'wheels' ferried over from Europe; special interest groups going in search of the desert's flora and fauna; and, of course, the guides in their blue turbans who've seen it all before and who are keen to do it all again.

The people you don't much bump into at the dusty crossroads of this amiable town are the overlanding backpackers of yore. With the onward routes beyond Tunisia's southern border sealed off in all directions, most people are in town on pre-booked tours. Booking ahead for any trip saves time, but agencies in town also cater to those who prefer to make it up as they go along.

Know Your Tattoos

Learning about Amazigh heritage

As delicate as a flower, or deliberately bold; a cross or a palm tree; a simple spot or a dashed line – each dot of ink represents a piece of tribal heritage, handed down from mother to daughter in the form of facial tattoos. They may not be very much in evidence these days, as the custom has all but run its course, but this extraordinary practice can still be encountered at the **Musée du Sahara** *(75 473 410; entry DT5)* in Douz.

Often mistaken as a mark of possession, similar to the branding of camels (another complex iconography also showcased in the museum), tattoos were in fact about the identification of women with the values of their shared heritage. Each tribe had their own combination of marks – above the eyebrows, at the tip of the nose, on one cheek or below the bottom lip and chin – and the museum does a fine job of setting this cultural practice in the wider context of traditional nomadic life.

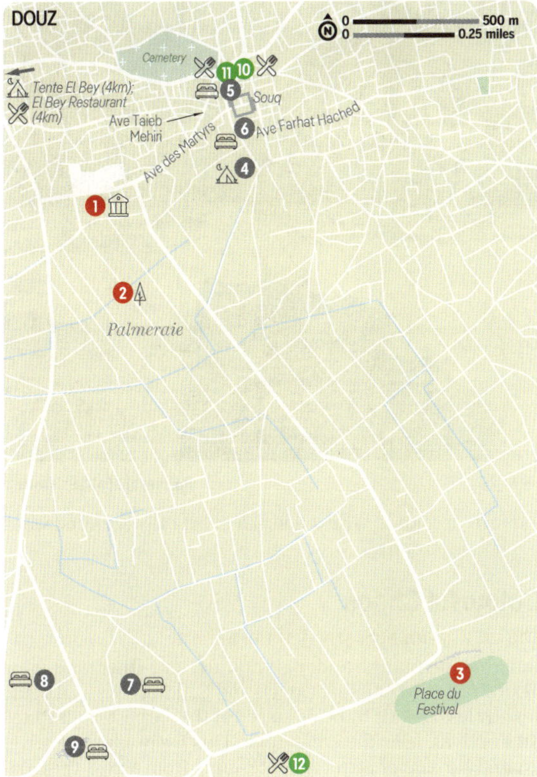

SIGHTS
1 Musée du Sahara
2 Palmeraie
3 Place du Festival

SLEEPING
4 Camping Desert Club
5 Hôtel 20 Mars
6 Hôtel Medina
7 Hôtel Sahara Douz
8 Hôtel Sun Palm
9 Offra Hotel Douz

EATING
10 La Casa
11 Les Palmiers
12 Tej El Khayem

Make it a Date

Sampling fresh dates in Douz' palmeraie

They may be frighteningly calorific and not a good choice for anyone pre-diabetic, but dates are otherwise acknowledged as phenomenally nutritious – so much so that Saharan tribes were able to survive for days on end on a diet of dates, camel's milk and little else.

Douz has the largest **palmeraie** in Tunisia, with some estimates claiming over half a million date palms, allegedly outnumbering residents by 25 to one. But apocryphal numbers aside, there's no denying the importance of dates in Douz. Shops dedicated to their sale crowd out the centre of town, while even the drabbest of streets are made merry in October, when crates are piled high during the annual harvest.

If you happen to be in town at this time, don't miss the chance to sample a fresh date. Bearing little comparison to the dried form, a newly picked date should be sampled when partly ripe so that the sweet flesh can be enjoyed in contrast with the desiccating unripe part. Even if dates are not a favourite, the hand-woven palmfrond baskets used in the

TOP TIP

Although you may be approached to take a trip with an unlicensed guide, it is strongly recommended that any tour is organised instead through a licensed agency. Saving a few dinars may prove costly if your guide has failed to think of your safety before heading out to the dunes.

SAY IT WITH ROSES

In among the Amazigh rugs, leather slippers, faux amber rings and piles of colourful caftans of an oasis souq, an avid shopper won't fail to notice the ubiquitous desert rose. Sporting 'petals' of crystals formed from gypsum, the desert or rock rose occurs naturally in desert environments with a high salt content, and Tunisia's chott landscapes produces some highly elaborate forms.

Growing to up to 10cm across as a single rose, or forming complex clusters, these rock forms are a favourite decoration of oasis homes throughout southern Tunisia. Shopping for a good specimen in Ksar Ghilane, Douz or in the oases of the Jerid helps support local communities who harvest these beautiful works of nature to supplement their income.

BIESZCZADY_WILDLIFE/SHUTTERSTOCK

Palmeraie **(p235), Douz**

harvest, decorated with a flourish of brightly coloured wool, is a good souvenir.

Colourful Chaos

The International Festival of the Sahara

Imagine pennants and palanquins, eye-liner and blue head-dresses, grumbling camels and barking dogs – all made slightly less chaotic by being staged at the purpose-built **Place du Festival**, near the great dune. This lively annual festival around November attracts contestants from across the camel-rearing world in a cultural display that includes camel beauty pageants and Saluki dog races. Don't miss it!

EATING IN DOUZ: OUR PICKS

La Casa: The sides of *kibdeh* (liver) served up with beans makes an unlikely but delicious accompaniment for the pizzas served here. *10am-11.30pm Tue-Sun* €

Les Palmiers: Don't miss eating at this travellers' favourite. Chances are a unique car will draw up outside as you sup your soup among the rallying memorabilia. *8am-11pm* €€

El Bey Restaurant: Tucked away on the edge of town, expect to be greeted by the khol-eyed owner who caters for locals in magical tented spaces. *8am-midnight* €€

Tej El Khayem: If you haven't sampled camel yet, then this tented restaurant offers *gargoulette* – a meat stew made in a clay pot. *6am-midnight* €€€

Beyond Douz

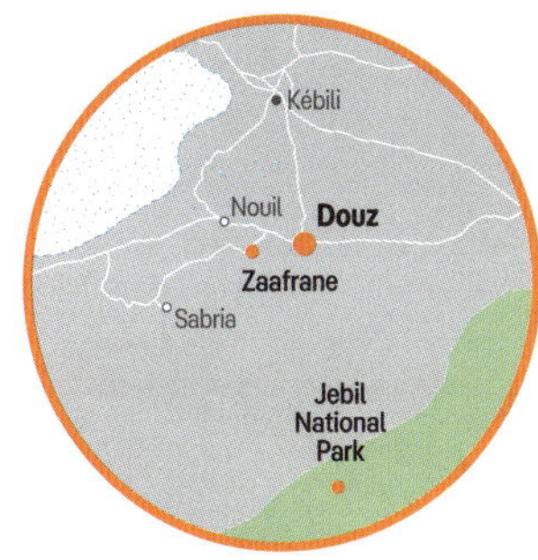

Grapple with infinity in an off-road trip to the Grand Erg Oriental, the sea of sand encompassed by Jebil National Park.

It's not for nothing that Douz is called 'Gateway to the Desert'. In the town centre stands the old souq, an arcaded courtyard shaded by trees with shops selling Amazigh crafts. Punctuating each of the four arcades is an arch through which all manner of goods pour in on a Wednesday evening, and flow out again at noon on Thursday – Douz' market day. Trace the route beyond the four exits and eventually you'll find yourself in the desert.

'Beyond' in Douz, then, means engaging with the desert. This is best accomplished on an overnight 4WD tour or, if time is short, a camel trek to the semi-nomadic encampments along the desert fringe.

Places

GETTING AROUND

Remnants of road entering the desert may be disappointing outbound, but they're likely to be a welcome relief on the return. Paved roads thread as far into the desert as the sands allow, but most don't endure, either crumbling into potholes or becoming scraped into uncomfortable ridges known as 'wash boarding'. Many lie buried under shifting dunes. The only way of navigating the desert, then, is in a 4WD vehicle or by camel – both requiring stamina.

Zaafrane

TIME FROM DOUZ: **30 MINS**

Being led by the nose

If you haven't ridden a camel before, there's an art to it. Thinking of the saddle as an armchair and sinking into it as you might a sofa helps, as does relaxing into the camel's gait instead of fighting against it. But first, you have to mount. This generally means holding onto the pommel of the saddle and letting the camel lurch you back and forward as it stands up. For all but those with camel-riding expertise, it then means surrendering all control to your guide who walks ahead with the nose rope.

After a couple of hours of exercising unaccustomed muscles, you'll be begging to swap places.

The purists baulk at being led, but who cares? The view from the hump is every bit as special and, besides, if a camel bolts, it's a long way to fall. Members of the **Adhara tribe** in Zaafrane make a living from transporting guests to their nearby tented camps aboard these celebrated 'ships of the desert', so, whatever your level of camel-riding mastery, don't let them sail without you.

KRYSEK/SHUTTERSTOCK

Tamarisk trees, Jebil National Park

TOP EXPERIENCE

Jebil National Park

While there's plenty of desert you can see from the road anywhere south of Gabès, none of it can compare with going off-road into the extensive sea of sand that comprises the Grand Erg Oriental. A portion of this vast dune field that straddles two countries falls into Tunisia's **Jebil National Park**. This northern end of the Sahara makes for the quintessential desert adventure.

DON'T MISS

- The excitement of the journey
- Sunset over the erg
- Bread-making the nomadic way
- Sitting around the campfire
- Watching sunrise from a dune
- Sliding down a dune on a sand board

The Brag

Lurching off the track at a 45-degree angle, sand up to the axles and back wheels spinning without forward motion, the only thing being achieved by keeping the foot on the accelerator is a deeper nose dive into the dune. It happens – even to the best of drivers. A slight miscalculation of speed against direction and the sand claims another victim.

If you begin your journey to Jebil National Park at the Palmiers Restaurant in Douz, you're bound to hear just such a story

PRACTICALITIES

- For a list of desert camps within Jebil National Park (which offer 4WD transfers and tours from Douz) see p238.

and plenty like it – firstly because it's so easy to get stuck in soft sand, and secondly because earning a story to tell is integral to the desert experience.

The Journey In

Earning a story to tell is exactly what is in store for those who venture the 60km south from Douz to the flat-topped mountain at **Taimbaïn**. The trip starts innocuously enough on a hard-top road. Then, a few kilometres south, little humps and hummocks of sand start to stray across the tarmac until, at length, the driver is obliged to slalom between miniature dunes and broken road.

Thirty kilometres doesn't sound like much on a smooth piece of highway, but over the corrugated remains of what was once paving, it can feel never-ending. Thankfully, that's when a back-to-basics **tea shop** appears – and a chance for your veteran driver to take a pause before the next stretch.

Swinging off the graded road, suddenly the route passes into what looks like uncharted territory. Contrary to appearances, though, there are clues everywhere: a silver reflector here, a piece of white cloth in the bush there. Using these scraps of landmark, the guides are able to navigate through a curdled muddle of dunes and ridges, rocky flats and sandy ascents into ever-higher billows of sand. It's spectacular and exciting and takes rally-driving concentration – it's not the time, then, to be a backseat driver!

Walking on Wind

'Why', posed a Tozeur landlord, 'do people volunteer to be thrown around for three hours, when they could be bedded down in the desert in one hour?' It's a fair question, but the answer is simple. The scenery near to any of the oases towns is certainly desert and it may even have a sand dune or two, but it's nothing like the experience of arriving at a camp in the golden avenues of dunes encompassed by the national park.

The dunes of the **Grand Erg Oriental** are not the highest (those are to be found further south around Al Borma) but they are spectacularly continuous. Climbing up to the top of a dune in the middle of the afternoon, the waves of sand appear to ripple into infinity. It's not a specious metaphor – the landscape has genuine motion as the wind skims off the top layer of sand and blows it into the neighbouring hollow. As the sun sinks lower in the sky, the sand changes colour and the shadows create a backstory to the day's drama – something to be told and retold around the campfire at night.

DESERT DWELLERS

It may seem inhospitable at a first glance, but Jebil National Park is in fact home to several species of mammal, including gazelles, hares, fennec foxes, barbary sheep and jackals. Established only relatively recently in 1994, the park, which covers all of Tunisia's portion of the Grand Erg Oriental, is designated an Important Bird Area, protecting the houbara bustards, thick-billed larks and desert sparrows.

TOP TIPS

- Check whether your multiday camel trip reaches Jebil National Park – most do not.
- Avoid the summer (May to September) when temperatures are so fierce that it's hard to enjoy any activity.
- For the best photographs, time your shots for an hour before sunset, when the dunes slip from silver to gold.
- Pack an extra layer in winter (October to April) as it gets very cold at night.
- Find out exactly when to expect dawn – sunrise changes quite a bit through the year.
- Protect your phone and camera from sand if it's windy.
- Note landmarks when hiking to avoid getting lost.

Ksar Ghilane

SAHARA GATEWAY | DESERT MUSEUM | TRAVELLER VIBE

GETTING AROUND

Without your own transport, the only way of reaching Ksar Ghilane, 150km southeast of Douz, is on a tour as there is no public transport that serves the area.

By car, it's an easy (if hot and somewhat tedious) drive along the C211 from Douz, but the good news is that good roads lead east to Beni Kheddache and Ksour Country, so you don't have to return to Douz before continuing on.

The oasis and the surrounding *palmeraie* are compact and walkable, and even the sands beyond the oasis are easily accessible on foot, by quad bike and by camel.

You won't be the first to dither at the junction of the C211 and the turn-off to Ksar Ghilane. Having crossed two hours' worth of flat, featureless desert, mostly along a pipeline road that is so straight the Romans could have made it, the prospect of a town here seems at best unlikely. Indeed, it's a brave driver who, passing the pumpless petrol station where 'benzine' is hand-poured through a funnel, commits to the turning and heads west towards the oasis.

Then comes this extraordinary moment when you reach the oasis proper. There are coaches spilling out bewildered passengers, people in swimsuits splashing in the natural springs and ribbons of quad bikes and camels threading into the sands beyond. Hospitable, sociable and commercially driven, Ksar Ghilane is everything you don't expect to see but has in some form or other always proudly been – a constantly evolving desert hot spot.

KRYSEK/SHUTTERSTOCK

Road to Ksar Ghilane

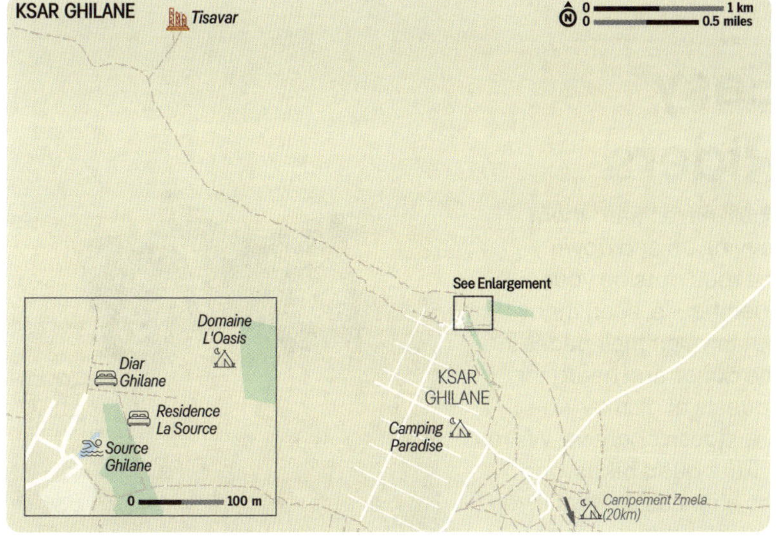

A Dip in Warm Waters

Swimming at Source Ghilane

There's nothing more refreshing than cool water on a hot day, and Ksar Ghilane has a plentiful supply. Water flows from underground springs into a natural pool in the town centre before being channelled into the *palmeraie* beyond.

The water temperature at **Source Ghilane** is pleasant year-round and invites a swim. Surrounded by tamarisks and a circle of cafes and souvenir shops, it's not exactly a hidden gem but it's a treasure nonetheless. Join locals (who tend to swim in shorts and T-shirts) at any time of day and bring your own towel.

TOP TIP

Independent travellers may feel overwhelmed by the mass tourism that has descended on Ksar Ghilane (although 'mass' is a relative term). The trick to enjoying this convivial oasis, though, is to join in rather than opt out – after all, oases have always been about congregations of people, swapping stories and sharing each other's company.

Breaking Bread

Baking the traditional way

Stay at Domain L'Oasis (p243) guesthouse, straddling oasis and desert, and you may wonder about the purpose of the round pit in the garden. All is revealed when the host lights a fire within it and starts to knead flour and water. At length he levers the resultant dough into the embers. When baked, the disc is broken into golden chunks for everyone to share. This is the desert way of enjoying bread and an essential part of a visit to Ksar Ghilane, and the camps near Douz and Zaafrane.

TOP EXPERIENCE

Easy Riders

You'll have heard them revving up and down the road outside your guesthouse, seen them put through their paces in the dunes and heard the squeals of dismay when one doesn't behave. We're talking **quad bikes**, and the chances are that if you haven't ridden one yet, you'll be tempted to do so – and if you have ridden one, you're saving up for the next adventure.

ALGEBA/SHUTTERSTOCK

Quad bike

TOP TIPS

- Choose only the outfits that offer crash helmets.
- Check that your crash helmet fits and wear it, buttoning it under the chin.
- Don't try to take a selfie while driving – if you hit an unseen rocky patch in the sand, you'll need both hands to correct your course.

PRACTICALITIES

- In Ksar Ghilane, there's no need to pre-book a quadbike – just turn up and take off.

Getting Started

If you've ever wanted to give it a go, Ksar Ghilane is a very good place to try quad biking. The dunes beside the oasis are low and easy to negotiate, even for a novice rider. By and large, the guides from the many companies that line the road between Source Ghilane and the desert keep a watchful eye on their reticent wards, and an even closer eye on those who think they are the next quad champion.

The guides start your machine and all you have to learn is that squeezing the right handle moves you forward while the left handle is the brake. Groups of up to 25 bikes head out in a line, following the leader.

Reaching Tisavar

The basic route is to Tisavar, a ruined Roman ksar (traditional fortified granary) around 2km northwest of the oasis. It's not all plain sailing, with shrubs and rocks that require firm steering, but once you hit your stride, and learn to avoid getting too close to the vehicle in front, it's a lot of fun and a great way to cover desert distance quickly.

Note that while quad biking is popular in Tunisia's desert landscapes, there is ongoing discussion of the noise pollution and ecological damage it creates.

Places We Love to Stay

€ Budget €€ Midrange €€€ Top End

Douz – Town p234

Hôtel 20 Mars € This spartan but perennially popular budget hotel, close to the centre of town, is run by helpful, English-speaking management. The courtyard doubles as a travellers' rendezvous.

Hotel Medina € Very close to the souq, this basic budget hotel gets mixed reviews but has an attractive courtyard and serves food.

Hôtel Sahara Douz €€ With an enormous pool, giant canteen-style dining room and bar, this is a tour-group favourite with plenty of places to hide if you're travelling solo.

Offra Hotel Douz €€ Some rooms in this large, resort-style hotel, targetting the local market, overlook the desert, while others are clustered around the pool in bungalows.

Hôtel Sun Palm €€€ One of the better offerings in the Zone Touristique, this castle-like building has plenty of character and some luxury details, including a hammam.

Douz – Camping p234

Camping Desert Club € An attractive camp in the *palmeraie,* this efficiently run outfit serves Italian and Tunisian food and is just a five-minute walk from the souq.

Tente El Bey €€€ A bit pricey for what's on offer, this highly characterful tented camp offers a full Bedouin experience without the inconvenience of actually camping.

Zaafrane p237

Hotel Zaafrane €€ If you want to stay somewhere closer to the dunes than Douz, this recommended guesthouse has simple courtyard rooms and arranges lots of desert activities.

Jebil National Park p238

Camp Abdelmoula €€€ Baking its own bread in the embers of the campfire, this tranquil tented camp is located in a sea of sand with a magnificent view. It offers en suite cabins for those who prefer not to hike to the shared washroom at night.

Camp Mars €€€ If you like to share your desert solitude with like-minded others, this sociable camp is well located near Montagne Taimbaïn, a vantage point from which you'll swear you can spot Niger.

Ksar Ghilane p240

Camping Paradise € A well-kept campsite near the town centre offering half-board in simple tents, the Paradise has a bar and a restaurant within a secure plot.

Residence La Source € A somewhat quirky desert complex, this friendly guesthouse offers simple but spotless rooms, a short stroll from the spring.

Domaine L'Oasis €€ So close to the edge of the low dunes that the sand comes over the wall, this very well run *maison d'hote* has tents and traditional domed rooms and offers excellent food, including handmade bread.

Campement Zmela €€ This excellent camp, in the middle of the Grand Erg Oriental, is a 30-minute drive by 4WD from Ksar Ghilane. It's located right next to a huge dune, has beautifully decked out tents and serves good food.

Diar Ghilane €€ Near to the edge of the *palmeraie,* this guesthouse has an attractive main lodge (albeit a bit noisy) and runs a popular restaurant.

MOHTADI NASRI/SHUTTERSTOCK

Campement Zmela, Ksar Ghilane

Researched by
Dr Jenny Walker

Tozeur & the Jerid

OASIS TOWNS IN AN ARID LANDSCAPE

Discover the aged towns of the Jerid – a fertile strip wedged between two salt lakes.

Waving a baguette as a substitute lightsabre, and wearing a Jedi hoodie, a not-so young Luke Skywalker prances across the sand as the moment is recorded in history – or at least on Instagram. This is Ong Jemal, the 'neck of the camel', and part of the most famous of Tunisia's several Star Wars locations. It was chosen because of the desolate landscape – a whole other world of sand, rock and salt flat, made further alien by the dislocated props from the Hollywood apparatus. It's little surprising that another desert classic, *The English Patient*, was also partly filmed here.

Whether fans of cinema or not, there's no doubting that Tunisians have been quick to understand the imaginative power of a film set, and almost all tours capitalise on the connection. But beyond the cinematic iconography, there's an imaginative power to the landscape here too, with the fertile Jerid and its string of date plantations wedged between the inhospitable pincers of two bone-dry lakes, known as *chott*.

Jerid life is focused in this stripe of green on a string of bustling plantation towns, including Nefta and traveller-friendly Tozeur. Making an excellent base, this ancient brick town has many attractions of its own, as well as allowing for visits to the nearby mountain villages of Jebel El Nebeg.

DASHA PETRENKO/SHUTTERSTOCK

THE MAIN AREAS

TOZEUR
The Jerid's liveliest town and *palmeraie* (date plantation).
p248

TAMERZA
Mountain oasis near the Algerian border.
p256

For places to stay in Tozeur & the Jerid, see p259

LESHIY985/SHUTTERSTOCK

Left: waterfall (p258), Chebika; above: Chott el Jerid (p254)

Find Your Way

The Jerid may be geographically small, but with the surrounding landscapes of salt and rock, it's a region that feels vast. Allow at least four days to explore Tozeur, Nefta and nearby mountain oases.

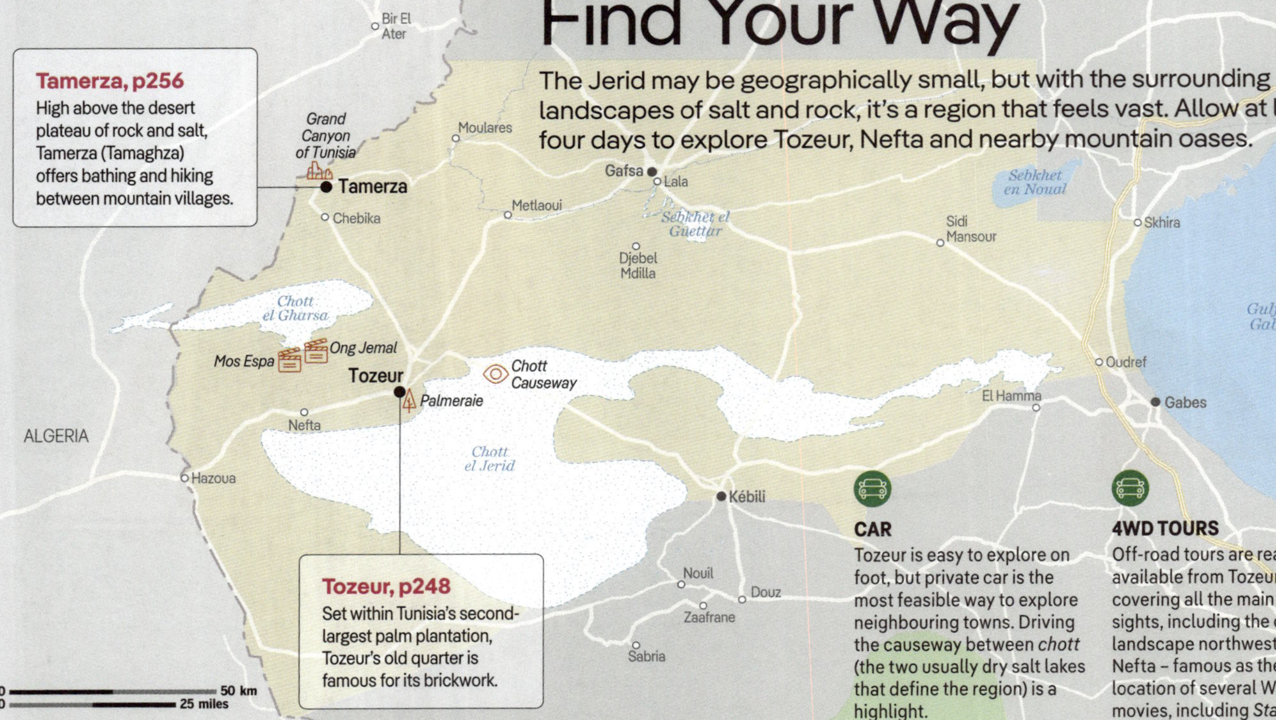

Tamerza, p256

High above the desert plateau of rock and salt, Tamerza (Tamaghza) offers bathing and hiking between mountain villages.

Tozeur, p248

Set within Tunisia's second-largest palm plantation, Tozeur's old quarter is famous for its brickwork.

CAR

Tozeur is easy to explore on foot, but private car is the most feasible way to explore neighbouring towns. Driving the causeway between *chott* (the two usually dry salt lakes that define the region) is a highlight.

4WD TOURS

Off-road tours are readily available from Tozeur covering all the main local sights, including the desert landscape northwest of Nefta – famous as the location of several Western movies, including *Star Wars: A New Hope*.

JESSE33/SHUTTERSTOCK

Mos Espa (p255)

Plan Your Time

Theoretically, you could cover Tozeur and the mountain villages in a weekend. In practice, though, this compact region is less about 'doing the sights' than experiencing life under a date palm.

The Jerid in a Weekend

- Spend two nights in **Tozeur** (p248), exploring the ***palmeraie*** (p248) on the first day and the **old quarter** (p250) on the second. If a third night allows, visit the community projects of neighbouring **Nefta** (p255) and head out for a sunset camel ride around **Ong Jemal** (p255), a poignant Star Wars location. Leave the Jerid via the ***chott* causeway** (p254) – a mesmirising experience of mirage and reflection.

Four Days to Travel

- Combine two days in and around Tozeur with the mountain villages of **Jebel El Nebeg** (p256). While **4WD tours** (p255) are offered here, self-driving in a saloon car allows time to potter in **Chebika** (p258) and to overnight in **Tamerza** (p256). Enjoy an early-morning dip in the waterfalls before tour groups arrive and take a guided hike to **Midès** (p257) through the **Grand Canyon of Tunisia** (p257).

SEASONAL HIGHLIGHTS

SPRING

The Jerid is brushed with a hint of green new growth after a little winter rain. Warm days, balmy nights.

SUMMER

Punishingly hot. Mirages can be spectacular but exploration is a challenge, even under the palms.

AUTUMN

Perfect for visiting: date harvest from October, while November showcases **Sufi** (p255) traditions in Nefta.

WINTER

There might be a little rain and it gets cold. The **Tozeur International Oasis Festival** (p253) is in December.

Tozeur

EXTENSIVE PALMERAIE | BRICK ARCHITECTURE | FAMILY ENTERTAINMENTS

GETTING AROUND

Two airlines fly into **Tozeur-Nefta Airport**, 4km from town, from Paris as well as from Tunis, while long-distance buses connect the town with the capital (seven hours via Gafsa), Kairouan, Sousse and Gabès. Tozeur can less easily be reached by train to Metlaoui from Tunis and onward taxi. Car rental is available through **Hamra**, while tours cover all the local sights of interest.

Tozeur is a walkable town, with taxis and horse-drawn *calèches* for longer distances in the *palmeraie* and shuttling between attractions. The **Zone Touristique**, where many hotels operate, is on the western outskirts of town.

As the location of the second-largest *palmeraie* in Tunisia, Tozeur is largely defined by the velvety-green plantations above which it sits. The lungs of a town often choked with the dust from the surrounding *chott,* the date plantation is cooler in summer and warmer in winter, and its harvest of dates, pomegranates and citrus fruits contributes significantly to the town's economy.

For the traveller, the *palmeraie* makes a peaceful retreat, with several places to stay and to eat in the heart of the oasis. There are also plenty of opportunities for strolling under the palms and some quirky modern attractions to keep the family entertained.

Communities have been thriving on the oasis for centuries and Tozeur has a fine old quarter, Ouled El Hadef (p250), to the east of the bustling new town, that's famous for its elaborate brickwork. Spending time getting lost in its complex of covered alleyways is a highlight of a visit.

Trotting into the Shadows

Calèche ride through Tozeur's palmeraie

An oasis is one thing from above but quite another from underneath. Duck under the canopy anywhere in Tozeur's ***palmeraie*** and a whole other world suddenly comes to life. The light, for one thing, is different, with sunlight pouring through gaps in the palm fronds and spilling onto the ground in a cut-glass diffusion of colour and shape. The heat is another, with the high fronds catching each breeze and channelling it through the undergrowth below.

There are no neat rows of palms here in Tozeur but an organic spread of vegetation. Sprigs of basil hide under citrus trees, pomegranates reach up for the light with their straggly branches, while figs and roses clamber into the sunlight amid the 200,000 date palms.

Although it's possible to walk or cycle between gardens, an hour's horse-drawn visit is even more rewarding. *Calèche*

Continues on p251

HIGHLIGHTS
1 Chak Wak Park
2 Ouled El Hadef
3 Palmeraie

SIGHTS
4 Dar Charaït Museum
5 Eden Palm Farm
see 4 Musée des Arts et Traditions Populaires
6 Sidi Ben Aissa Archaeological & Traditional Museum

ACTIVITIES
7 Au Coeur du Désert
8 Calèches
9 Quad Bike Hire
10 Sahara Lounge
11 Tozeur Bike

SLEEPING
12 Bessila Eco Camping Oasien
13 Dar Natacha
14 Dar Saida Beya
15 Dar Tozeur
16 Diar Abou Habibi
17 Residence Warda
18 Villa Fatima

EATING
see 1 Chak Wak Park Restaurant
19 Les Arcades
20 Restaurant Tozorous
21 Resto Café El Berka

DRINKING & NIGHTLIFE
see 6 Resto Café Essiguifa
see 10 Sahara Lounge

TRANSPORT
22 Bus Station

DISCOVERING THE BEAUTY OF BRICK ON FOOT

Getting lost in Ouled El Hadef is entertaining, but to cover the architectural treasures of Tozeur's old quarter, follow this walking tour.

START	END	LENGTH
Les Arcades	Les Arcades	1.2km; 2 hrs

With the tall brick minaret of Mosque el-Ferdous on your left, cross Ave Habib Bourguiba and enter the 1 **carpet souq**. Covered by a palm-frond roof and housing artisanal shops, the souq opens onto a street of bike repair shops. Turn right by the yellow 'musee' sign, noting the elaborate doorways and lanterns. Peer behind the great brick walls of the passageway at 2 **Resto Café Essiguifa** (p252) and visit the 3 **Sidi Ben Aissa Archaeological and Traditional Museum** (p252), both in traditional courtyard homes.

A covered passageway leads past fine 4 **brickwork arches** into the quaint 5 **medina main square**. Climb up to 6 **Café Berber** for a 'Vue Panoramique' before exiting the square under three ancient marble plaques. Pass under an elaborate 7 **latticed window** to a square with information on Tozeur's distinctive brickwork.

Exit through 8 **Bortal Abderrazak El Hadfi**. Zigzag towards 9 **Sidi Abdeurrahman Mosque** behind a green door (right). At a distinctive blue door (left), in sight of the imposing minaret of the Madrasa of the Bey, turn right and head for the squat minaret of 16th-century 10 **Sidi Bin Ghalleb Mosque**.

From here, slip onto the *palmeraie* road. Turn right after 100m and eventually leave the medina through 11 **Bab El Houlef**. Zigzag into the 12 **covered market** and exit beside Tozeur's 13 **six-tiered brick fountain** with Les Arcades almost opposite.

Many doors have three knockers – one each for women (left), for men (top right) and children (bottom right) – with their own timbre to identify visitors.

The medina's elaborate geometric and geomorphic brickwork, or 'brick mosaic', dates back to the 15th century. Ochre-coloured clay bricks are still hand-moulded and fired in traditional kilns.

The 'bortal', or covered passage, is a key feature of the old medina, providing shade and a place to congregate out of the sun.

Ave Farhat Hached
Ave Ibn Chabat
Ave de Kairouan
START/END
Les Arcades
Rue Hédi Jahallah
Ave Habib Bourguiba
Rue Sidi Ali Ben Taleb
Ave Abdulkacem Chebbi
0 — 200 m
0 — 0.1 miles

Continued from p248
drivers linger on the edge of the oasis ready to take passengers on a 30-minute trot through the palm trees, pausing inside one of the farms to explain date cultivation and the equitable distribution of water.

Strolling along a Timeline

History in 3D at Chak Wak Park

Look beyond Tozeur's *palmeraie* and the eye settles on a forbidding landscape of salt plains and arid rocky desert. It looks like a sea that has retreated, leaving behind a scalped landscape of minimal features. And, in fact, a sea is exactly what the region once was. Evidence of this lies in the marine fossils commonly found in the neighbouring desert that are proof, some suggest, that the Tethys Sea once bordered the ancient continent of Gondwana.

Fast forward a few million years and reptiles stepped into this prehistoric landscape. At **Chak Wak Park** *(76 460 400; entry 15DT)* in the centre of the Tozeur *palmeraie,* there's the chance to learn about their evolution. Looming out of the undergrowth, enormous dinosaur models here preempt displays of human evolution shown through elaborate dioramas and sonorous narratives told in multiple languages (including English).

Something of a Babel on a busy day, but a personal romp through history on a quiet night (the park is open until 11pm), this brainchild of the former mayor of Tozeur is likely to delight anyone of any age for its sheer eccentricity. Equally intriguing is its attempt to gloss the world's major religions and their cherished narratives (including a fetching rendition of Noah's Ark), as well as significant empires and Amazigh traditions.

A Date with a Difference

Date cultivation at Eden Palm

If after trotting around the *palmeraie* you have some unanswered questions about how dates are grown and the part played by the weather (a great topic of conversation among crop sharers), then call into **Eden Palm** *(eden-palm.com),* an open working farm in the middle of the plantation.

Excellent information boards (including in English) describe the processes involved in ensuring a good crop. There's also the opportunity to try some of the many varieties of dates (the Ministry of Agriculture lists 150 grown in Tunisia, only

BEST TOZEUR TOURS

Au Coeur du Désert: Book through this established agency for 4WD tours to the mountain oases and south to Douz and beyond.

Calèches: Board a horse-drawn carriage from Ave Abdelkacem Chebbi for a trot through the palm trees.

Quad Bike Hire: Tour the *palmeraie* or head for the Chott El Jerid beyond by **quad bike** *(30DT per hour),* available from outside Dar Charaït museum.

Sahara Lounge: Engage with the *palmeraie* from the treetops in this adventure park, which includes climbing walls and flying foxes.

Tozeur Bike: Cycle through the *palmeraie* in a mostly traffic-free zone.

EATING IN TOZEUR: OUR PICKS

Resto Café El Berka: In a cosy little corner of the *palmeraie,* this family-run restaurant serves tasty Tunisian dishes. *noon-10pm Tue-Sun* €

Chak Wak Park Restaurant: Reliably open when much else may not be, this *palmeraie* restaurant surprisingly offers wine with a meal. *10am-11pm* €€

Les Arcades: Also known as 'Restaurant de la République', this is the beloved first choice for Tunisian soups and grills beside the old quarter. *11am-11pm* €€

Restaurant Tozorous: An old favourite with a brick-themed dining room, this restaurant serves a fine couscous. *noon-11pm* €

GROWING DATES

Spot the perfect, golden lozenges of fruit dangling from a date palm, and you might think that nature does all the work. In fact, date cultivation is more of a partnership. It takes hard work to ensure a good crop, including hand-dusting the nascent fruit of female trees with pollen taken from male trees, cutting back dead fronds to discourage rodents, and tying down fruit fronds to allow for easy picking.

Although now grown commercially in around 40 countries, date farming originated thousands of years ago in the Middle East and North Africa, and many of the traditions associated with date cultivation, including the complexities of sharing scarce water and community harvesting, are still in evidence today.

LARS FORTUIN/SHUTTERSTOCK

Date palms, Tozeur

four of which are commonly encountered), and to admire the many uses artisans make of all parts of a date palm.

Nights under the Canopy

Staying in the palmeraie

Visiting the plantation by day only gives you half the picture of life under the palm fronds. For a full immersion, nothing beats staying the night in one of the several sleeping options hidden in the oasis (see p259). The sounds change at night with the slightest breeze shaking the canopy, and a chorus of birds competes with the resident roosters at dawn. Cooler in summer and warmer in winter, the plantation feels wholly removed from the busy town at its rim, and its rural rhythms are likely to leave you feeling rested and refreshed.

Saving Tozeur Heritage for Posterity

Visiting an old-quarter ethnographic museum

Even if you're not a fan of museums, the **Sidi Ben Aissa Archaeological & Traditional Museum** *(+216 97 091 083; entry 3DT)* in the heart of Tozeur's old medina is worth making an exception for. Housed in a traditional brick house, restored with French assistance in 2007, this ethnographical museum

DRINKING IN & NEAR TOZEUR: BEST LOCATIONS

Resto Café Essiguifa: Tucked into the courtyard of a beautifully preserved brick house in Tozeur's old quarter, coffee here is served with a warm welcome. *7.30am-11pm*

Sahara Lounge: A leafy garden within the Tozeur *palmeraie,* this venue serves coffee by day and *shisha* to courting couples at night. *9am-10pm*

Café de la Corbeille: Perched above the terraces of La Corbeille, this pit stop in Nefta is popular with tour guides for the view of the *palmeraie. 10am-9pm*

Oasis Pool Bar: At the Anantara Sahara resort, 4.5km from Tozeur and with spectacular views of the *chott,* this bar offers cocktails in stylish gardens. *7pm-midnight*

brings alive the traditions of life in a *medina* home, thanks in large part to the enactments of the caretaker, Souad Kchim, and her husband Mohammed.

Hear strains of an old Amazigh song, echoing around the courtyard? It'll be Souad showing how singing helps distract from the chore of traditional flour grinding. Ululations in the bedroom? It'll be Souad dressing up visitors in traditional wedding finery.

Stay for tea, poured by Mohammed, beside the great clay amphorae once used to store water or olive oil, and admire the courtyard's aged artefacts, saved for posterity.

One-Way Journey from the Beginning of Time

Touring Dar Charaït Museum

Just in case you left Chak Wak Park (p251) wanting more, there's another of the former mayor's esoteric projects at the **Dar Charaït Museum** *(76 452 100; entry 3.50DT),* housed in a lavish re-imagining of an old palace, off Ave Abdulkacem Chebbi. Commencing with a sci-fi rendition of the big bang in a tin passageway that could double as a location for Star Wars, the 'time travel' part of the museum – **Dar Zaman** – is a sequence of dioramas, complete with obligatory dinosaur models, Hannibal crossing the Alps with life-sized fibreglass elephants, and depictions of life after the coming of Islam.

Dar Zaman is something of an Ikea experience, with no opportunity to leave the trail before the exit, so if you've had too much of a good thing in Chak Wak Park, settle instead for the worthy if more predictable museum exhibits in the **Musée des Arts et Traditions Populaires** in the same complex. Allow an hour to enjoy some beautiful textiles and jewellery in the extravagantly decorated palace interior and consider coming in the evening to avoid noisy school visits; the complex closes at 10pm.

Celebrating Heritage

Tozeur's International Oasis Festival

Running since 1938, Tozeur's beloved **International Oasis Festival** is becoming as vintage as the arts and culture it showcases. Celebrating the end of the date harvest (which begins in October), the town also commemorates its multi-ethnic roots that embrace Amazigh, Arab and French traditions. With events that include storytelling, traditional music, camel and horse racing, and opportunities to sample different varieties of dates and other regional food, it's a grand showcase of desert culture.

HOW TO CAPTURE THE AMAZIGH SPIRIT

Souad Kchim, museum curator, guide and poet. *97 091 083*

Stay in a traditional home. Being in a Tozeur house, you'll feel our hospitality and understand what's important to us by what we hang on the walls and cover our floors with.

If you're here in July, **come back in October**! This is when families descend on the *palmeraie* to help in picking the dates. It's a communal activity that involves the whole community.

Buy a rug. A labour of love, it takes four days to make a 2m-by-1m carpet and woven into the pattern are the symbols of our culture.

I may not know the world, but the world comes to us. **Visit our museum** (p252) and you'll be enchanted by the songs of our grandmothers shared in the company of others.

TOP TIP

Browse for rugs, textiles, palm-frond lampshades and baskets of dates along **Ave Abdul Kacem Chebbi** and enjoy the soft-sell approach of friendly vendors over a Tozeur tea.

Beyond Tozeur

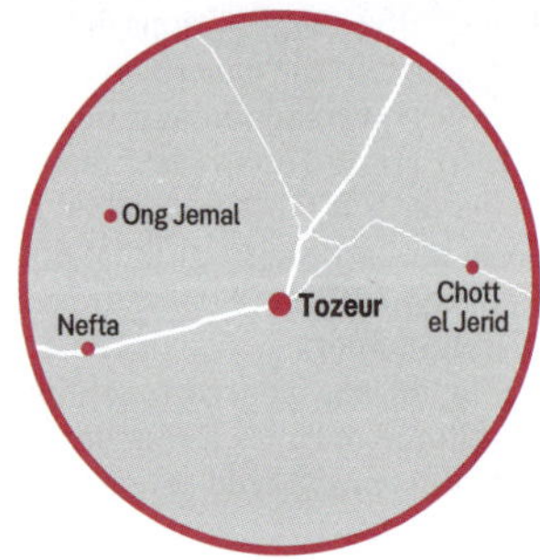

Explore the oasis of Nefta and desolate Mos Espa – a beloved Star Wars location – or take a peak at infinity on the *chott* causeway.

Places

Restless for other worlds, Star Wars hero Luke Skywalker scans the desolate horizon of his home planet and dreams of travelling beyond. It's easy to see why the production team picked Mos Espa as the location for existential musings – the landscape is pared back to basics, a minimal vista of salt plain and dune that glows at sunset.

Wandering around Mos Espa at this time summons up the fertile Jerid's alter ego, but to really engage with time and space, forget about film sets and travel the causeway that splits the Chott El Jerid instead. The road offers a feeble challenge to the engulfing emptiness, and the mind fills in the absence with credible imaginings – in other words, mirages.

GETTING AROUND

Tozeur tour agencies organise 4WD trips to the rock formation at Ong Jemal and the Star Wars set at Mos Espa. These tours can include a visit to Nefta's Corbeille and some off-road driving on the nearby dunes.

It's possible to drive to Mos Espa in a saloon car on a sealed road, which allows for longer at the site. Self-driving is also the best way to visit the *chott* causeway as an outing from Tozeur.

Chott el Jerid

TIME FROM TOZEUR: **40 MINS**

Driving the causeway

If a date plantation is all about the vertical – upright palm trunks, and slices of light falling to the plantation floor – the *chott* is a tribute to the horizontal. There's the arrow-straight road edged with pinkish salt; the great white bar of the dried-out *chott;* and a reflective band of water from freak rains, rimmed by a green stripe of oases, topped by grey escarpment and framed by the sky.

Driving across this landscape of parallels on the elevated ***chott* causeway** is a mesmerising experience as the eye searches in vain for an interruption of form. In the middle, the road appears to run off into infinity and that's when, on a hot day, the dancing begins: a castle, water and people crowding the scene, all shaking in the ribbons of lateral heat.

You may wonder who was foolish enough to make the tracks that run across the broken salt crust in between. But then the dancing begins again and gives you your answer.

It takes about 45 minutes to cross the 50km causeway. Fill up with petrol beforehand, take water and don't trust your eyes – mirages are very common here.

Nefta

TIME FROM TOZEUR: **40 MINS**

Support a community project

For those booked on a tour from Tozeur, a side trip to Nefta is likely to be little more than a pause above **La Corbeille** (a basin-shaped plantation in the middle of town) for a photograph. That's a pity because this oasis town with its own extensive *palmeraie* has much to offer for those with a mind to give it some time.

For a start, the old quarter, albeit smaller than the *medina* of Tozeur, has some excellent examples of geometric brickwork and the town is home to two Islamic shrines, **Sidi Brahim** and **Sidi Merzoug**, testifying to Nefta's important Sufi connections.

La Corbeille, meaning 'basket', is a local attraction for good reason. As a large depression in the landscape some 40m deep and 1km wide that leads into a narrow gorge, it has been cultivated for centuries with date palms and citrus tree. Its terraces make a lovely spot for a stroll above town.

The best way to explore Nefta is through **In Nefta** – a project that is helping to ensure that local communities in town benefit from a tourist visit. The project provides guides and bikes, and facilitates visits to see artisans at work and the sampling of traditional home-cooked meals.

Attending the annual Sufi festival

Sufis regard Nefta as a spiritual home of their mystical branch of Islam and, as the place of burial of two important saints (one of whom is descended from the Prophet Muhammad), the district of **El Bayadha** is an important place of pilgrimage. Each November since 2016, the **Rouhaniyet Festival of Sufi Music** – a celebration of Sufi heritage – has been held in Nefta and a visit during this time is an experience not to be missed.

Ong Jemal

TIME FROM TOZEUR: **40 MINS**

A trip to the movies at Mos Espa

At some point the Star Wars fascination will run out, but until then the franchise can be thanked for keeping a steady flow of visitors to a part of the country hard hit by the post-COVID downturn in tourism.

To see what all the fuss is about, make the 4WD excursion to **Mos Espa** for the film set of the fabled Tatooine spaceport of Mos Eisley; wander round the abandoned buildings and imagine pod racing across the neighbouring **Ong Jemal** – a nearby rock formation accessible only by 4WD. If this all sounds incomprehensible, consider watching *The Phantom Menace* before you go.

Widely available from Tozeur, 4WD tours usually include dune descents and a chance to ride a camel (*around 180DT*).

THE 'IN NEFTA' PROJECT

Mehdi Baccouche, Director of Shanti's 'In Nefta', a community-based tourism project. *innefta@shanti.tn*

Through the In Nefta project's network of local, trained guides, we are able to show visitors our town from a perspective the tourists often miss.

You can hire our bikes and follow one of our four cultural circuits through town or the *palmeraie* beyond, or book a table d'hôte for some home-cooked Nefta specialities.

Check availability in Dar Nefta – our beautifully restored house in the heart of the old quarter, famous for its brick architecture. You can also visit artisans making kilims and palm products in their own homes and learn about the value of their enterprise, or walk through the Corbeille and around town with people who call it home.

Tamerza

MOUNTAIN VILLAGE | WATERFALLS | CANYON HIKING

GETTING AROUND

Although Tamerza is connected by louage with Tozeur and Gafsa, these services are neither daily nor do they connect with Chebika and Midès. Tours cover the three towns in a day trip from Tozeur (about a 50-minute drive), but these are a rushed affair, focusing mostly on a dip in a Tamerza waterfall.

An ordinary saloon car is adequate for reaching all three towns and the Tamerza waterfalls. Self-driving (or taxi) has the added advantage of giving time for photographs along the Chebika and Tamerza road, the P16, with defining views over the Jerid and the *chott* beyond.

It may seem extravagant to single out the small town of Tamerza as a hub for travellers, but in many respects it's the perfect example of a mountain oasis typical of the **Jebel El Nebeg** region. So close to the border that Algerian homes can be spotted from neighbouring Midès, Tamerza (also spelt Tamaghza) has that frontier feel about it, welcoming tour buses by day but happy to retreat to its own routines at night.

Being based in Tamerza allows the few that stay here a rare glimpse of mountain life when the crowds have gone. It also allows a head start on the popular canyon hike to Midès and the chance to have a dip in natural swimming hollows before tours arrive from Tozeur.

To do justice to the three main mountain towns, Tamerza, Chebika and Midès, allow at least two days as the best part of being here is relaxing into the tranquillity of oasis life.

Bathing Beauties

A dip in Tamerza's rock pools

There's something almost baptismal about swimming in arid places. It's not just the refreshment of cold water on a hot day, but also the sense of benefaction involved in each life-giving drop as it issues from the barren rock. Unpredictable, seasonal and affected by drought, the 8m-high **waterfall** at the bottom of Tamerza was reduced, at the time of writing, to a shower of droplets. But higher up the wadi, beside the Cascades Restaurant (p258), the **Cascades Waterfall** was deep enough to bathe in.

Other pools collect in the surrounding network of canyons, offering a similar chance for a dip. Residents are used to people bathing in the beauty of their landscape, but appreciate respect of local norms (eg wearing a T-shirt over revealing costumes) and confining swimwear to the water's edge.

Below the Cascades waterfall, at the southern end of the old quarter, a path leads through a side canyon, above standing

HIGHLIGHTS
1 Cascades Waterfall
2 Grand Canyon of Tunisia

SIGHTS
3 Chebika Ruins
4 Old quarter
5 Waterfall

SLEEPING
see 1 Restaurant & Hotel Cascades

EATING
see 1 Cascade Restaurant
6 Mides Family Resto
see 3 Oasis Cafe
see 1 Restaurant La Tente

pools of water and up to the canyon rim. Ask locally for directions and beware flash floods after rains – the concave walls of the canyon were carved out by such torrents.

Hiking from Tamerza to Midès

The Grand Canyon of Tunisia

With a stout pair of walking shoes, a hat and a guide, it's possible to walk between the two Jebel El Nebeg oases of Tamerza and Midès.

The highlight of this exciting route is passing through a slot canyon where the gap between the canyon walls is so narrow it feels as if the ground has just split apart above you. After about three hours, the route opens out into the wadi bottom of the **Midès Canyon**, known locally as the **Grand Canyon of Tunisia**, from where there's a stiff, but not difficult, hike to the abandoned village clinging to the rim.

It's best to book a guide (through any tour agency in Tozeur) for the 4.5km hike, if only to be clear about possible border sensitivities at any given time.

TOP TIP

Engage local guides in Tamerza, Chebika and Midès. Although the routes through each town are well-established and easy to fathom, the guides give interesting accounts of life in the old mud-brick villages before floods in the 1960s forced their families into concrete homes.

BORDER ADVICE

Although at the time of research the three towns of the Jebel El Nebeg were being routinely visited by tourists, visitors should be aware that their proximity to the Algerian border makes them vulnerable to changing travel advisories.

While the current UK government advice is to avoid Tunisian border zones within a distance of 10km in the area, some other advisories exempt the town of Midès, which is within sight of the Algerian border.

These advisories change to take into account wider political realities and visitors should check their own government advice before making a decision to travel in the area. This is particularly important as going against such advice may invalidate travel insurance.

Tea & Talk in Canyon Country

Panoramic views from Midès

Guides anxious for work in an area with little other than cross-border trade for income are likely to find you before you find them at the old quarter of **Midès**, the most northerly of the three abandoned mountain towns in Jebel El Nebeg. While it's not difficult to find your way around, spending time chatting over a mint tea with one of these polyglots is a very enjoyable way to spend an afternoon.

Fewer visitors bother with the town, so life moves at an even slower pace around here and the guides are keen to share memories of more prosperous times, when the various film crews (most notably of *The English Patient*) brought some glamour and wealth into the community.

The village's location is stunning with the vast s-bend of the so-called 'Grand Canyon of Tunisia' carved out of the vertically walled cliffs below. Avoid walking beyond town without a guide – the white houses to the immediate north are in fact in Algeria.

Walking Towards Water

A circuit around Chebika

You don't need a guide to complete the little circuit of the abandoned town of **Chebika**, but a local perspective certainly helps to understand what was lost when floods swept away the homes of those who lived here. The ruins of the village, a 20-minute drive from Tamerza, make for a poignant reminder of the power of rain in an arid landscape where water quickly gathers momentum over the dry ground to devastating effect.

An obvious path climbs above the village to a fine vantage point above Chott El Gharsa and descends into a beautiful little palm-filled canyon with a natural spring, pool of toads and a picture-perfect **waterfall**. Come early to avoid tour groups. The circuit takes only about half an hour to walk, but it repays a slower pace to enjoy the magic of the spot.

EATING IN JEBEL EL NEBEG: LIGHT LUNCH

Cascades Restaurant: In Tamerza, this delightful restaurant serving a tasty Tunisian lunch has a prime perch above the waterfall in town. *8.30am-11pm* €

Restaurant La Tente: Also in Tamerza, serving grills and snacks, this Bedouin-themed restaurant is a popular pit stop for visitors. *8am-11.30pm* €

Mides Family Resto: On the approach road to the Midès oasis, this small, family-friendly restaurant is locally popular for its large portions of tasty fare. *8am-midnight* €

Oasis Cafe: Overlooking the oasis in Chebika, this cafe is either overwhelmed by tour groups or empty. Either way, it's good for a quick bite. *8am-11.30pm* €

Places We Love to Stay

€ Budget €€ Midrange €€€ Top End

Tozeur Town p248

Residence Warda € It's seen better days, but this simple hotel offers cheap and friendly lodging for those that just want a place to sleep.

Maison d'Hôtes Villa Fatima €€ Run by two retired teachers, this friendly guesthouse offers delicious home-cooked, evening meals – possibly with a beer.

Villa Fatima €€ Housed in a stylishly modernised traditional brick home, this guesthouse is a stone's throw from the old quarter.

Dar Saida Beya €€€ The hamman in this attractive traditional brick home is a welcome addition to this popular guesthouse near the old quarter.

Dar Tozeur €€€ This gorgeous traditional guesthouse is in the heart of the *medina* and expands inwards quite unexpectedly with gardens, a hammam, pools and a cinema room.

Anantara Sahara – Tozeur Resort & Villas €€€ With a hammam and a spa, this is Tozeur's most luxurious residence, with superb views of the desert and beautifully landscaped gardens, 4.5km from town.

Tozeur Palmeraie p248

Bessila Eco Camping Oasien € With gated grounds, this campsite offers pitches for your tent under the palms or cosy and comfortable cabins.

Diar Abou Habibi €€€ The dates are so close to the terraces of these stilted, self-catering lodges in this popular oasis retreat, that you can reach out and pick one.

Dar Natacha €€€ With a menagerie of donkeys, goats and chickens in the garden, and a wealth of interesting artefacts in the guest quarters, there's something to interest all the family here.

Nefta & Tamerza p255, p256

Restaurant & Hotel Cascades €€ Simple rooms arranged around an attractive wadi-side plot in Tamerza make this a tranquil spot to overnight, and the restaurant is excellent.

Hotel Caravanserail €€ No longer quite the des-res it once was, this Oriental-themed resort in Nefta is nonetheless good value for money.

Dar Hi €€€ If not immediately what springs to mind as a desert ecolodge, this concrete hotel in the middle of Nefta has good views overlooking La Corbeille and a good restaurant and thermal pool.

Gafsa

Although offering little reason to stay, Gafsa is nonetheless an important transport hub. The following accommodation options may be helpful if stuck between onward connections.

Jugurtha Palace €€ Although 4km out of town, this is the best (if somewhat grandiose) place to stay in Gafsa; it has a big pool and mountain views.

Hôtel Gafsa Palace €€ A comfortable, business-oriented hotel on the edge of town, this high-rise hotel near the stadium makes a pleasant-enough stop-over.

JENNY WALKER/LONELY PLANET

Diar Abou Habibi, Tozeur *palmeraie*

For places to stay in Djerba, see p277

BTWIMAGES/SHUTTERSTOCK

Above: Houmt Souk (p264); right: pottery (p267), Djerba

Researched by
Isabel Putinja

Djerba

ARCHITECTURAL HERITAGE, TRADITIONAL HANDICRAFTS AND SANDY BEACHES

For a small island, Djerba packs in much more than beaches of golden sand, thanks to its distinctive architecture, exquisite handicrafts and unique cuisine.

Djerba's history is one of diversity and peaceful coexistence. It's home not only to its original Amazigh inhabitants, but also to one of the last communities of the Ibadi sect of Islam and a small Jewish population. Maltese Christians settled here in the early 19th century, followed by sponge fishermen from Greece. The legacy of this multiplicity of religions is reflected in the island's diverse architecture: Ibadi mosques, a dozen synagogues, and Catholic and Orthodox churches.

SKAZARPHOTO/SHUTTERSTOCK

The onset of tourism in Djerba in the 1960s focused entirely on the picture-postcard island idyll of sandy beaches dotted with palms. The northern and eastern coastlines witnessed the mass construction of mammoth resorts designed to contain sun-seeking visitors within their compounds.

Away from the coastline, the island's flat, arid landscape is painted with groves of centuries-old olive trees and orchards of fig and citrus, punctuated by towering palms. Many of Djerba's treasures lie inland, and those looking to get closer to its soul can stay in a traditional *funduq* (caravanserai) or rural *hŭch* (rural family home) as alternatives to beach resorts.

In 2023 Djerba was added to the UNESCO World Heritage list (p272), ushering in new recognition for its cultural and natural heritage. This honour coincides with an evolving approach to tourism that's moving away from the beaches towards the island's bucolic traditions.

THE MAIN AREA

HOUMT SOUK
Charming market town full of history.
p264

Find Your Way

Covering 514 sq km, Tunisia's biggest island is relatively small and easy to explore. Djerba has its own airport – **Djerba-Zarzis International Airport** – and can also be reached by ferry or by road via the Roman causeway.

Houmt Souk, p264

Djerba's main town was a historical trade hub, as evident in its busy markets and souqs. It's also chock-full of attractive heritage architecture.

TAXI

Though buses connect major towns across the island, frequency is limited. However, travelling by taxi is easy and cost-effective. Fares are paid by the meter with night fares kicking in from 9pm.

CAR

Exploring Djerba by car is the most convenient option. Travel distances are short: it takes less than an hour to traverse the island. There are plenty of car hire agencies at the airport or in Houmt Souk.

HICHEM KAOUANE/SHUTTERSTOCK

Guellala Heritage Museum (p274)

Plan Your Time

Besides a beachside break, visitors can venture into the countryside on a bicycle, take a road trip to discover Djerba's architectural heritage or get close to Djerba's handicraft traditions.

Pressed for Time

- A day is enough for Djerba to work its charms. Start in Houmt Souk with a walk through its historical **town centre** (p266) and a **street-food tour** (p268). Next head to **Erriadh** (p271) to take in the eclectic street art of Djerbahood and magnificent **El Ghriba Synagogue** (p271). Round things off with a stop at seaside **Sidi Jmour Mosque** (p273)and a sunset swim.

Five Days to Explore

- Add a day trip to **Guellala** (p274) to meet the island's potters and try your hand at the wheel. Then swing by the **Guellala Heritage Museum** (p274), pausing at its cafe with a view. Head into Djerba's olive groves on a **bicycle** (p269) to see traditional rural homes and weavers' workshops. End your stay with a road trip of Djerba's **UNESCO monuments** (p272).

SEASONAL HIGHLIGHTS

SPRING

Spring days are very warm and even balmy. The tourist crowds are not yet here and the beaches beckon.

SUMMER

Peak temperatures and coastal crowds. Explore in the early morning. Enjoy Houmt Souk's lively summer nights.

AUTUMN

Sunny days are still here, making this quieter shoulder season an excellent time to explore the island.

WINTER

The winter months can be windy and cooler but still very pleasant. This is the best season to plan a bicycle tour.

Houmt Souk

HERITAGE ARCHITECTURE | VIBRANT MARKETS | STREET FOOD

GETTING AROUND

Houmt Souk is a small town with its main sights located within a 1.5km radius. This and the flat terrain make walking an ideal way to get around, but few roads have footpaths. There are plenty of yellow taxis milling around town for longer runs; fares are reasonable and charged by the meter. The **bus station** *(gare routière)* is just off ave Habib Bourguiba in the centre of town, with the louage station just next to it and a taxi rank steps away. Taxis only operate on the island, while louages travel to destinations on the mainland.

TOP TIP

Come to Houmt Souk on a Monday or Thursday morning to experience the colour and hubbub of market day. Its nucleus is the central market with stalls extending across the old town.

Djerba's biggest town and administrative centre has its charms. Don't let the plethora of souvenir shops of Houmt Souk's old town dupe you into thinking you're in a tourist trap. Look around and you'll come face to face with everyday life. Women returning from the market with straw bags full of produce. Men sharing the day's news at the cafe on the square. Children hoisting heavy backpacks heading home from school. Barbers, weavers and tailors busy at work. Street cats lazing in the sun.

As a port city, Houmt Souk was a busy trade hub that welcomed travelling merchants for centuries. Here you can stay at a traditional *funduq* (a medieval travellers' inn transformed into a contemporary boutique hotel) or at a traditional dar tucked in a quiet cobblestone lane.

As a tourist centre and transport hub, Houmt Souk also serves as an ideal base to explore other corners of the island.

Get to Know Djerba

Museum of traditional homes and industries

Get acquainted with Djerba's culture, traditions and inhabitants at the splendid **Djerba Traditional Heritage Museum** *(patrimoinedetunisie.com.tn/en/museums/the-museum-of-the-traditional-heritage-of-djerba/overview; entry 8DT).*

It won't take more than an hour or two to browse the excellent exhibits of detailed reconstructions, models and audio-visual displays organised around seven themes. Here you'll see traditional farming and fishing tools, as well as a detailed model of the typical buildings and structures making up a *menzel,* a Djerban farmstead. Equally fascinating is the model of a traditional underground olive oil mill.

Move on next to the vast collection of earthenware pots and learn about the entire pottery-making process, from extracting and preparing clay to throwing, firing and glazing. Then

Continues on p266

HOUMT SOUK

0 200 m
0 0.1 miles

Mediterranean Sea
Marina Complex
St Nicholas Church
Amphitheatre
Borj Ghazi Mustapha
Blvd de l'Environnement
Rue Mongli Slim
Rue Dargouth Pacha
Blvd de l'Environnement
Ave Taieb Mehiri
Djerba Traditional Heritage Museum
Ave Abdelhamid el-Kadhi
Rue Ibn Charaf
Ave Habib Thameur
Ave Habib Bourguiba
Pl d'Algérie
Ave Ibn Khaldoun
Rue 2 Mars 1934
Pl Sidi Brahim
Rue Jamaa Echeik
Pl Sidi Abdelkader
Covered Souq
Pl Hedi Chaker
Parc des Loisirs Dah Dah
Ave Boumessouer
Rue de la Municipalité
Pl Farhat Hached
Pl Mongi Bali
SOUQS
Pl Bechir Saoud
Rue 20 Mars
Rue Mosquée el Ghorba
Rue Mohammed Badra
Rue Remada

HIGHLIGHTS

1 Borj Ghazi Mustapha
2 Djerba Traditional Heritage Museum
3 St Nicholas Church

SIGHTS

4 Ettrouk Mosque
5 Fondouk Boucheddekh

ACTIVITIES

6 Djerba Insolite
7 Houch Insolite

SLEEPING

8 Dar Lola
9 Hotel Arischa
10 Hôtel Marhala

EATING

11 Brik Belgacem
12 Café Ben Yedder
13 El Fondouk Restaurant Lounge
14 El Hanout
15 Essofra
16 Haroun

DRINKING & NIGHTLIFE

17 BH Baklawa
18 Café Haj Hassen

SHOPPING

19 Dar El Beskri
see 6 Fondouk La Vannerie
20 Village Artisanal

DJERBA ON THE UNESCO WORLD HERITAGE LIST

In November 2023 Djerba was added to UNESCO's World Heritage List, bringing the total number of such sites in Tunisia to nine. This recognition is a nod to the island's unique rural settlements made up of self-sufficient *houma* (neighbourhoods) and *menzels* (family-run farmsteads), as well as to Djerbans' ingenuity at adapting to water scarcity via the use of water collection systems, wells and cisterns.

While the entire island is not a UNESCO site, there's mention of 24 'monuments' – mostly Ibadi mosques but also El Ghriba Synagogue (p271) and St Nicholas Church. Also included are two urban zones: Hara Sghira (Erriadh) and Houmt Souk's historical centre; and five rural zones: Temlel, Khazroun, Sedghiène, Guechéine and Mejmej.

ANDREJ PRIVIZER/SHUTTERSTOCK

Borj Ghazi Mustapha

Continued from p264

admire traditional textiles in a room dedicated to the island's weaving tradition where mannequins flaunt vibrant Djerban garments. There's also a flashy display of intricate gold and silver jewellery work, while the island's Jewish community is put in the spotlight with a video of the annual pilgrimage to El Ghriba. Another not-to-be-missed display is the one showcasing the island's elaborate weeks-long wedding rituals.

Tracking Architectural Highlights

An exploration of old Houmt Souk

Sea-facing **Borj Ghazi Mustapha** *(patrimoinedetunisie.com.tn/en/monuments/ghazi-mustapha-borj-djerba/overview; entry 8DT)* is one of the town's standout landmarks. Djerba's largest fortress has stood watch here since the 13th century, taking its most recent form in the 16th century under the rule of the Turkish governor it's named after. Poke around the internal courtyard to spot the stone remains of its previous avatars. Then climb the ramparts for sweeping sea and city views and a peek into the open-air theatre next door. This sight is closed Fridays.

Walk towards the port to **St Nicholas Church**, one of the island's 24 monuments on the UNESCO list. This Orthodox church of whitewashed walls and sky-blue doors is set in a grove of palm trees and open to visitors every day from 9am to 2pm. Dedicated to the patron saint of fishermen, it was built in 1890 by the Greek sponge divers who settled here, using planks recovered from their boats for the floors. Decorating the iconostasis on the far wall is a collection of beautifully painted icons sporting haloes of gold leaf.

Head towards the town centre and you'll soon spot the circular Ottoman-style minaret of 16th-century **Ettrouk Mosque**, 'the Mosque of the Turks'. The multiple domes punctuating its roof are also eye-catching details.

Just steps away lies the old town and its labyrinth of narrow cobblestone lanes opening onto the hubbub of cafe-lined squares and covered souqs. Hiding behind wide doorways are *funduqs:* age-old caravanserais or two-storey inns set with large square courtyards surrounded by a collection of storerooms. This is where animals and carts were left for the night, while travellers retired to the upper floor. Duck inside Hotel Marhala (p277) to see a beautifully restored *funduq* offering comfortable rooms to modern-day visitors. Nearby is Fondouk Jemni, now tastefully transformed into **El Fondouk** (p268), an atmospheric cafe and restaurant. Stop in for a coffee or lunch in the airy courtyard decked with hanging grass lampshades or browse the design shop.

Meet the Artisans

Watch artisans at work

While wandering the alleys of Houmt Souk's historical centre, tune into the gentle tap tap of jewellery smiths' tools, the humming whir of tailors' sewing machines and click-clack of weavers' looms. These telltale ambient sounds point the way to artisans' workshops.

In the courtyard of **Fondouk Boucheddekh**, you'll find **Fondouk La Vannerie** *(27 365 909),* Mohamed Khacha's rustic atelier, up a short flights of stairs. You'll likely see the artisan busy at his loom weaving rushes into floor mats, or using palm leaves to make Djerba's traditional wide-brimmed hats and shopping bags and baskets, as well as lampshades and placemats.

For the past 400 years, generations of the Tobji family have handcrafted the traditional *beskri,* an ornate garment embellished with intricate motifs woven with silk and threads of gold and silver. Stop in at the family's shop **Dar El Beskri** *(75 622 321)* to see a traditional loom and many exquisite examples of this 4m-long garment worn by Djerban women and used during wedding ceremonies.

It's a short walk from the old town to **Village Artisanal**, a charming building on Ave Habib Thameur. Around a central courtyard are two floors of pocket-sized workshops peddling high-quality handicrafts made of rattan and palm leaf, handmade soaps, traditional jewellery and embroidered clothing.

DJERBA'S HANDICRAFTS

Djerba has a rich handicraft tradition carried on by artisans whose crafts have been handed down from one generation to the next.

Basket weaving: Natural fibres from the palm tree are handwoven into the traditional Djerban hat and the typical shopping baskets you see in the markets.

Rush mat weaving: Rushes are gathered from the shores of salt lakes, dried in the sun and woven by hand into floor mats.

Pottery: You'll see colourful glazed examples in the markets, but Guellala, the island's pottery centre, is known for its terracotta.

Weaving: The weaving of textiles such as cloaks, *foutas* (towels) and *beskri* (women's ceremonial garments) is traditionally reserved for men.

EATING IN HOUMT SOUK: OUR PICKS

El Hanout: Next to St Joseph's Church with a changing menu of Tunisian and European dishes and a delightful rooftop terrace. *hours vary* €€

Brik Belgacem: A pocket-sized local favourite near the central market dishing out hot *brik* (savoury flaky pastry), Tunisian salad and *leblebi* (chickpea soup) in the winter. *hours vary* €

Haroun: Dine on the deck of a pirate ship overlooking the fishing port at this upmarket seafood restaurant. *noon-11pm* €€€

Essofra: The spot for traditional Djerban fare. Delight in Djerban rice and squid couscous in a cheerful decor of rustic furnishings. *12.30-3.30pm & 7-10pm Tue-Sun* €€€

DJERBA'S TRADITIONAL ARCHITECTURE

Djerba's traditional house or *hũch* has a square layout with rooms set around a courtyard. Small towers on each of its corners gives it a fortress-like appearance.

A *menzel* is a farmstead surrounded by protective walls. Within its rectangular plot is a *hũch*, barn, stable, threshing platform for grains, and well system.

Harout is the name for a traditional weaver's workshop, typically a long rectangular room set in the ground with vaulted ceilings and a triangular front.

Common across North Africa, a *funduq* is a rectangular two-storied building with an open courtyard. This was a roadside inn or caravanserai where travelling caravans of merchants could spend the night, rest their horses and store and sell their goods.

Crafting by Hand

Join a handicraft workshop

Houch Insolite *(experience@djerba-insolite.com; workshops from 50DT per person; minimum 2 people)* is a traditional Djerban house transformed into a co-working space and residence for artisans and artists. On offer here are artisanal workshops open to anyone keen to try their hand at one of four traditional handicrafts: rush mat weaving, palm leaf weaving, embroidery, or weaving with recycled materials. The workshops take from 90 minutes to three hours.

A Taste of Djerba

Street-food tour

Get to know Djerba through your taste buds. This two-hour street-food tour by **Djerba Insolite** *(experience@djerba-insolite.com; tours 55DT per person; minimum 3 people)* starts at the fish market where each morning the theatrics of the fish auction get underway as vendors wield strings of fish to be sold to the highest bidder. Next is a stop at the spice shops peddling wicker baskets full of bright red chillies, lentils and pulses, garlic and ground spices.

Then it's on to the food. Sink your teeth into a few Tunisian fast favourites, like a freshly fried *brik à l'oeuf,* a pastry filled with egg and parsley; and *fricassé,* a fried bun spread with harissa and stuffed with potatoes, hard-boiled egg, tuna and black olives. Next move on to *kafteji,* a mash-up of fried green peppers, tomatoes, squash, potatoes and eggs. In winter fill up with *leblebi,* a hearty chickpea soup flavoured with cumin and dollops of harissa and served over chunks of bread. The tour rounds off with a glass of extra-strong and sweet mint tea.

EATING & DRINKING IN HOUMT SOUK: OUR CAFE PICKS

El Fondouk: Hit pause with a drink or meal in the courtyard of this beautifully restored and art-filled *funduq. 8.30am-10pm Mon-Sat, from 9am Sun* €€

BH Baklawa: A delightful open-air cafe on a tiny square decked out with rugs, painted tables, colourful armchairs and hanging grass lampshades. *8am-9pm* €

Café Haj Hassen: A favourite meeting place under the trees for mint tea and people-watching on Place d'Algérie. *6am-10pm Tue-Sun, to midnight Mon* €

Café Ben Yedder: You're lucky if you snag a table at this popular morning spot for coffee and pastries. *6.30am-8pm Mon-Sat, to 1.30pm Sun* €

Beyond Houmt Souk

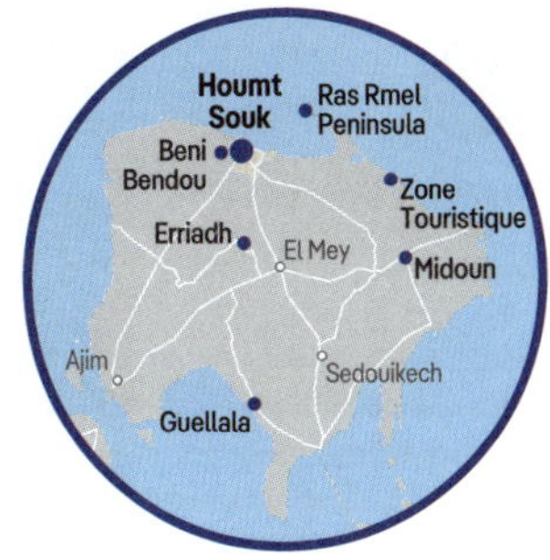

Explore Djerba's sandy shores, venture into the countryside on a bicycle or take a road trip of its heritage sights.

Thanks to Djerba's small size, you can easily set off for anywhere on the island from Houmt Souk. Extending 11km along the northeastern coast from the Radisson Blu Palace Resort to the Taguermess lighthouse stretches the infamous and largely uninspiring Zone Touristique. A long line of colossal tourist resorts extends here, many now abandoned. Though the sweeping sands of **Sidi Hacheni** and **Sidi Mahrès** and other beaches along this stretch are truly lovely, access to some sandy strips are restricted to hotel guests. Beach lovers can test the waters at other much-loved beaches. Try Saguia or Yeti-Lella Hadhria on the east coast, or Sidi Jmour or Cheikh Yahya on the west coast at sunset.

Places

Beni Bendou

TIME FROM HOUMT SOUK: **5 MINS**

Explore cultural heritage by bike

Join cycling enthusiast and founder of **Djerba Cyclo** *(djerba-cyclo.com; 40DT)*, Mahfoudh Laoir, for a two-wheeled tour of Djerba's cultural heritage. This is a chance to leave the arteries of Houmt Souk behind and discover treasures hidden in Djerba's countryside.

There's a halt at **Abou Messouer Mosque**, one of the island's 24 UNESCO-listed monuments, for a close look at this sprawling complex that housed a Quranic school.

Then it's time to go off-road along sandy tracks bordered by neat rows of palms that make way for olive groves. In the winter, families are busy harvesting their olives by hand, spreading nets on the ground to catch falling drupes.

The only buildings here are compact rural dwellings occupied during harvest time and vast *menzels* surrounded by protective hedges of cactus. Almost every plot has its own well system and cistern, though most are no longer in use, while circular platforms are used for threshing.

The two-hour tour concludes with a visit to a weaver busy at the loom in his workshop, the typical triangular front of the *harout* easily recognisable.

GETTING AROUND

Most visitors to Djerba prefer to rent a car and explore the island at their own pace. Dependable and cheap, taxis are also a good option, though sometimes hard to come by in more remote places. Buses connect major towns and are budget-friendly, with limited frequency. During the cooler winter months, cycling is a great option thanks to the island's flat terrain and small size. Many initiatives are increasingly promoting this mode of transport.

DJERBA BY BIKE

Djerba is flat and compact, making it ideal for exploring on two wheels.

Djerba Cyclo (p269) has a fleet of high-quality bicycles and helmets for hire at very reasonable rates. Inquire about their off-road heritage tours suiting cyclists of every age and ability.

SoliBikes *(solibikes.com)*, an initiative of the association Djerba Insolite (p268), also has bicycles available for independent or guided tours. Ask them for their hand bike map, *Djerba à Vélo*, outlining four suggested treks.

Tunisian Journeys *(24 372 803; TunisianJourneys2009@gmail.com)* is a slow-travel company with a focus on authentic local experiences. Get in touch to request a personalised made-to-measure tour on two wheels accompanied by a certified guide.

AUTHENTIC TRAVEL/SHUTTERSTOCK

Ras Rmel

Ras Rmel Peninsula

TIME FROM HOUMT SOUK: **15 MINS**

Dune walking and flamingo-watching

Jutting off Djerba's northern coastline is a 10km-long sandbar known as **Ras Rmel** (the cape of sand). This protected area is designated as a wetland of international importance and is a coveted spot for the pink flamingos flocking here between December and March.

From the **Radisson Blu Palace Resort**, head west along the wide sandy beach to an area of marshland bordering a lagoon. These wetlands are frequented by a host of other migratory birds, including egrets, white spoonbills, great cormorants and grey herons. Continue further to reach windswept dunes bordering wild beaches of impossibly soft sand where fishermen perch on the edge of the turquoise-blue waters.

This area is popular with buggy and quad tours, which can make bird-watching a challenge. Pirate-ship tours blaring loud music also ferry tourists here from Houmt Souk's port during the tourist season. The quieter months of January and February are the best time for keen bird-watchers and nature lovers to make the most of this corner of exceptional natural beauty.

Zone Touristique

TIME FROM HOUMT SOUK: **20 MINS**

A spot of R&R

Get your bounce back with a hammam experience at **C'Votre Spa** *(50 244 370)*. Unwind with a 90-minute session (130DT) starting with a rigorous rub down with an exfoliating

EATING AROUND DJERBA: A TABLE WITH A SEA VIEW

Sunset Beach-Resto-Bar: Casual dining on Sidi Mehrez beach and a long list of cocktails, wine and spirits. *10am-midnight Sun-Fri, from noon Sat* €€€

Hotel Villa Azur: Dine alfresco at this beachside restaurant with a menu of Tunisian delicacies or international favourites. Alcohol is served here. *8am-midnight* €€€

Café Mesk Ellil: Take in the sublime seascape of El Jazira beach while tucking into beautifully plated dishes of seafood and Tunisian cuisine. *noon-midnight* €€

Yacht Club Djerba: Stop in for brunch at this upmarket spot with elegant wood-panelled interiors and a large sea-facing terrace. *9am-midnight* €€

treatment of salt salt or rejuvenating seaweed. This is followed up with a restorative relaxation massage. Also on the menu is a wide range of massages and skin and beauty treatments.

Adventures in the water

Take to the warm sea waters for some fun splashing around in the surf. Staff at beachside hotels and resorts in the Zone Touristique can point you in the direction of local providers of water-sport adventures. These cater to all age groups and skill levels – from banana boat thrills for the kids to kitesurfing for the more intrepid.

Erriadh

TIME FROM HOUMT SOUK: **15 MINS**

Eye-catching street art of Djerbahood

In 2014, the small, dusty town of Erriadh was transformed into an open-air gallery dubbed **Djerbahood** *(djerbahood.com),* when 150 artists from around the world were invited to use the town's walls as the canvasses for hundreds of colourful works of street art. Adding to the aesthetic charm are bursts of bougainvillea framing the ornate doorways of traditional dars and *hũchs.*

Many of the original murals have since faded in the hot North African sun, but this ephemeral art project was renewed in 2022 with many breathtaking new works. It's a delight to ramble the clutch of car-free lanes and see what you come across. Have your camera ready.

Africa's oldest synagogue

El Ghriba ('the stranger' in Arabic) is Africa's oldest synagogue (closed on Saturdays). Show your passport and clear security at the police checkpoint, then head towards the arched gateway.

Once inside, women need to put on a headscarf, while kippas are available for men. The magnificent prayer hall is flooded with natural light reflecting off glass chandeliers suspended from high ceilings. Take a moment to admire the beautiful blue and white tiling, antique wooden benches and bright-blue pillars supporting the arches of the arcade wrapping around the hall.

A donation is requested before entering the inner sanctum. Above the raised wooden bimah hangs the *Ner Tamid,* an ornate lantern reflecting light from the stained glass windows.

FUN IN THE WATER

Kitesurfing: Try this extreme sport at **Kite Adventure** *(kiteaventure.com)* to experience the sensation of flying above the water.

Diving: Explore the underwater world off Djerba's east coast with **Archimede Diving Center** Djerba *(djerbaplongee.fr).* Or go deeper with a beginners or advanced PADI course.

Windsurfing: All ages can get on board with a 10-hour introductory course at **Les Dauphins Djerba** *(wassersport-tunesien.de).*

Kayaking: Experience Djerba's most dreamy sunset spot at **Sidi Jmour beach** from aboard a kayak with **Djerba Insolite** (p268; *djerba-insolite.com*). Book by email: experience@djerba-insolite.com.

Horseriding: Djerba Zitouna Stables' *(djerbazitouna.com)* well-tended horses take experienced riders for a ride along beaches of golden sand, ending with an ocean swim.

EATING IN ERRIADH: BEST CAFES

Cafe Chichbagou: A charming spot on the main square for Turkish coffee or fruit juice served on low tables under a leafy canopy. *hours vary*

Cafe Amour: Pause for a drink and join the cats lazing on the carpeted benches of this delightful little cafe in a blue-walled lane. *8am-10pm*

La Terrasse: Take a break from the street art with a coffee or cool drink on this shady upstairs patio overlooking Erriadh's rooftops. *10am-8pm*

Brik Warda Trabelsi: Stop in for a glass of mint tea and *brik, fricassé* and other fried favourites or Tunisian sweets. *hours vary*

ROAD TRIP

UNESCO Highlights

This road trip takes you across the island on a tour of some of its most outstanding UNESCO-recognised architectural monuments. Most of these are located off the main roads and along rural lanes flanked by palm and olive groves. You'll come across rural *menzels* (traditional farmsteads) and families busy at work harvesting olives during the winter months. It's a 15- to 25-minute drive between stops.

1 St Nicholas Church

St Nicholas Orthodox Church (p266) was built in 1890 by Greek sponge fishermen on a spot where their families prayed for their safe return from sea. Step inside to see exquisite religious icons and floors made of reclaimed wood from fishing boats.

The drive: Leave Houmt Souk and head along the main road towards Midoun.

2 Fadhloun Mosque

The fortified walls of beautifully restored Fadhloun Mosque (p276) hint at its defensive purpose, but it was also a madrasa. Arrive before noon to explore its residential quarters, bakery and 19th-century grain mill.

The drive: Leave the asphalt behind and take the dusty road towards Mahboubine where you can spot traditional *menzels*.

3 Underground Mosque of Sedouikech

Surrounded by olive trees, this mosque is easy to miss. Look for two domes rising out of the ground and a white arch serving as its entrance. Steps descend to subterranean chambers with openings for air and light.

LAUREN KEITH/LONELY PLANET

Underground Mosque of Sedouikech

The drive: Drive south along the C117 to El Kantara where you'll spot the Roman causeway to the mainland. Head west from here.

4 Sidi Yati Mosque

This defensive seafront mosque (p275) was built to keep watch on the southern coast. It shelters the mausoleum of Sidi Yati but is not a functioning house of prayer. A wooden jetty provides a photo point.

The drive: Continue northwards along a paved rural road passing through small settlements.

5 El Ghriba Synagogue

Park by the police checkpoint and clear security before walking a short distance to Africa's oldest synagogue (p271). The whitewashed building hides stunning light-filled interiors full of magnificent blue and white tilework, crystal chandeliers and antique benches.

The drive: A dusty country back road leads through olive groves to the next stop.

6 Welhi Mosque

Boxlike but handsome, this fortified mosque also served as an important madrasa. Its oldest section dates from the 12th century and is hidden underground, reached via a narrow staircase. Embossed on the prayer hall's vaulted ceilings are 17th-century Quranic inscriptions.

The drive: Head northwest along a quiet and scarcely populated rural road.

7 Sidi Jmour Mosque

This 10th-century defensive mosque perched on the west coast has stood watch here for centuries. It's closed to visitors, but climb the steps next to the tower for a glimpse into the courtyard and, in the other direction, a view of the beach dotted with fishing boats. Arrive just before sunset for the perfect conclusion to a road trip.

CONSERVING WATER ON DJERBA

Abdelmajid Kachkouch, project coordinator, Association for the Safeguarding of the Island of Djerba (ASSIDJE) *assidje.tn*

Djerba is located in a semi-arid zone and gets no more than 250mm of rain per year. We expect this to decrease by 20% by the year 2100, while temperatures will increase by 4°C.

For centuries, we've been using rainwater collection systems called *majel* or *fesqiya*. These date from Roman times and consist of conical and cubic cisterns buried underground and used to store fresh water. With support from the World Wildlife Fund, we're working on restoring and rehabilitating these cisterns and encouraging citizens to maintain them in an effort to preserve these traditional rainwater collection methods that have existed for centuries.

Guellala

TIME FROM HOUMT SOUK: **30 MINS**

Pottering around the potters' town

La grande jarre, a tall ceramic amphora declaring the town's status as Djerba's pottery hub, is the centrepiece of Guellala's main roundabout. From here walk in any direction to come across shops peddling their ceramic wares, with displays spilling onto the pavement.

Step through the massive blue doors of **Fondouk Guellala de la Poterie** *(free entry)* into a surprising terracotta wonderland. A vast collection of ceramic pots of all shapes and sizes fills a series of interconnected rooms opening on to a vast courtyard. Here you can watch a demo of how clay is prepared. Look out for a white dome sheltering an underground olive mill. Descend its short flight of stairs to see age-old mill stones and massive amphorae.

Next head across the street to the **Ben Mahmoud Romdhan Museum of Pottery** *(free entry)*, a rustic space with floors of fine sand. Here potter couple Adel and Chedlia Ben Mahmoud graciously welcome visitors to their workspace and small museum. Showcased on floor-to-ceiling shelves are samples of white and red pottery – one is mixed with saltwater and the other with freshwater. A corner is dedicated to a collection of black pottery made with leftover olive grinds.

A museum of Djerban customs and traditions

Guellala Heritage Museum covers a sprawling 4000 sq metres spread across a collection of interconnecting rooms set around bougainvillea-filled courtyards. Most of the exhibits feature life-sized mannequins dressed up in traditional costumes demonstrating Djerban ceremonies, customs and traditions. You'll see these costumed figures reenacting wedding rituals, conducting a circumcision ceremony, and showing off traditional weaving and fishing techniques.

Look out for the interesting displays on Amazigh culture and the 3D models of Djerba's Ibadi mosques. In the courtyard, poke around replicas of an underground olive oil press, weaving workshop and potter's kiln.

End your visit with a glass of mint tea on the terrace of the cafe perched on Djerba's highest point. From here you can take in panoramic views over the countryside and the waters of the Gulf of Boughrara sparkling in the distance.

A hands-on initiation to pottery

Get your palms dirty and try your hand at the wheel at **Poterie Mjahed Faouzi** *(50 057 322; 20DT/hour)*. Adults and children are welcome to join in an introductory pottery session with a master potter. Faouzi starts off with some background on pottery in Guellala and the story of his workshop, before sharing details about the clay extraction and preparation process. Then it's on to the wheel, where he demonstrates the throwing process. Participants can then take a crack at creating bowls, cups and plates. Creations can be taken home once they've had time to fully dry and be fired – a process that takes a few days.

The quirky indoor-outdoor workspace here is an experience in itself. Burrowed amid palm trees are a series of huge age-old kilns half buried in the ground and covered in mounds of hardened clay. These are topped with terracotta pots of all shapes and sizes. Meanwhile, an underground gallery cum shop hides a trove of beautifully decorated pots.

Sidi Yati Mosque and sea vews

About 2km south of Guellala, **Sidi Yati Mosque** *(free entry)* perches on a raised embankment in an isolated spot on the edge of the sea. This Ibadi mosque dates from the 10th century and is one of the 24 monuments on Djerba recognised by UNESCO. As a defensive garrison mosque, its task was to guard the island's south coast.

The mosque is not currently used for worship and visitors can freely venture inside. Step through the arched doorway and you'll find yourself in a rectangular courtyard where the mausoleum of its founder, Sidi Yati, sits in a corner. Look for the prayer room topped with four domes and a stairway leading up the short minaret.

A few steps lead from the mosque down the embankment to a rickety pier extending into the sea. This is a good photo point, but do mind your step and take care to avoid the gaps created by missing wooden planks.

Midoun

TIME FROM HOUMT SOUK: **25 MINS**

Visit an underground olive mill

Learn about Djerba's olive oil heritage and the traditional production process at the exquisitely restored **Fessili Traditional Underground Olive Mill** *(huileriefessili@gmail.com; adult/child 10/7DT)*. This 19th-century mill (closed Mondays) is one of the few remaining underground constructions designed to provide a cool environment ideal for the production and storage of olive oil.

Look for the small square windows cut into the vaulted roofs. Olives dropped through these apertures collected in silo-like chambers below, each one reserved for one family. When you descend the narrow, vaulted stairwell you'll notice the air is noticeably cooler underground.

Natural light floods in through perforated holes in the roof. Two granite millstones lay on a circular platform under the domed ceiling. Once used to crush olives, they were powered by a donkey or camel circumnavigating the platform. Look out for the hydraulic press and massive log that served as its counterweight. Information panels in English, French and Arabic fill you in on each stage of the olive-oil production process.

Flavours of Djerba culinary workshop

Delight in the flavours of Djerba's unique cuisine by joining chef and cultural anthropologist Wajdi Borgi in a **culinary workshop** *(contact@destination-djerba.com; 2½hr session 65-120DT)*. The focus here is on authentic recipes prepared with local seasonal ingredients and strictly no additives.

DJERBA'S MIGHTY MOSQUES

Djerba was a stronghold for Ibadis who built a network of defensive mosques to protect themselves. These were organised according to three lines of defence. Perched directly on the coast in the first line of defence, watchtower mosques served as defensive lookouts. Smoke signals were used during the day to warn of danger, while lighted torches raised the alarm at night.

In the second line, a few kilometres away from the coastline, stand fortified mosques reinforced with thick walls and buttresses. Equipped with storage rooms and cisterns, these were places of refuge in the event of an attack. Countryside mosques located in the interior of the island are smaller in size and made up the third line.

DJERBA'S UNIQUE CUISINE

Wajdi Borgi, culinary anthropologist and cultural mediator

The cultural heritage of Djerba's cuisine reflects the island's isolation as well as its mix of different cultures and communities.

Typical ingredients we love to use include *yazoul* – a type of wild garlic similar to chives. We also cook with a lot of wild chard, which has a very earthy and aromatic taste, as well as wild leek and many types of herbs. Dried fish is a protein source and is used for flavouring.

Rouz jerbi (Djerban rice) is the only dish from North Africa that's a traditional dish prepared with rice. It's always prepared with greens, such as parsley, onion, chard or spinach, and mixed with either meat, poultry or seafood.

In the outdoor kitchen set among olive trees, you'll don an apron and grab a mortar and pestle: only traditional tools are used here. While you're busy chopping and dicing, chef Wajdi shares his passion for food and titbits about Djerba and its cuisine.

In summer you may be cooking up a shakshuka of green peppers, chillies, fresh tomatoes, aubergines, potatoes and eggs seasoned with olive oil, cumin and coriander. In winter, fava beans, green peas and chard are the star ingredients. Djerban specialities include *hsou,* a semolina and vegetable soup; and *kesra,* prepared with dried tomatoes and garlic. Participants can select the dishes they'd like to prepare for a two- or three-course meal.

Crocodiles, art and heritage

Covering 120,000 sq metres of sprawling parkland, **Parc Djerba Explore** *(djerbaexplore.com; adult/child 32.5/21DT)* combines three main attractions. It's closed on Mondays.

At the startling **Crocodile Park**, hundreds of sleepy Nile crocodiles laze in the sun by artificial ponds, only stirring during afternoon feeding time.

Art lovers will appreciate the excellent **Lalla Hadria Museum** where 15 exhibition rooms showcase a beautifully presented collection of pottery, copperwork, textiles, jewellery and other objets d'art from Tunisia and across the Islamic world.

An open-air museum, **Djerba Heritage** puts the spotlight on Djerba's architecture and heritage. Wander through the rooms and courtyards of a full-sized traditional *hũch,* explore an underground olive oil mill, visit a reconstructed subterranean pottery workshop and see a traditional weaver's workshop.

Fadhloun Mosque and Museum

Located on the main road from Houmt Souk to Midoun, 14th-century **Fadhloun Mosque** *(patrimoinedetunisie.com.tn/en/monuments/the-fadhloun-mosque/overview; entry 5DT)* is an impressive example of a defensive mosque that also served as a madrasa. Today, it's still a functioning mosque, but every morning (except Fridays), a section converted into a fascinating museum opens to visitors.

Opposite the entrance, stop at the vast courtyard encircled by low walls: this is the rainwater collection system. Thanks to the sloping floor, water drains through holes into the underground cistern. This precious water was freely available to lodgers as well as nearby villagers.

Just right of the entrance lies a complex of rooms that was once the Quranic school with a residential wing for students and even a bakery. Under a domed ceiling you'll spot the millstone and wheel of a 19th-century grain mill, while the storeroom shelters a collection of terracotta amphora once used to store grains, flour and oil.

Take note of the mosque's stocky defensive walls supported by buttresses and its tall minaret set in a crenellated tower. There's no entry to the vast prayer hall, but do peek through the grilled doorway at its vaulted ceiling supported by arches resting on stone columns.

Places We Love to Stay

€ Budget **€€ Midrange** **€€€ Top End**

Houmt Souk p264

Hotel Marhala € Renovated in 2024, this historic *funduq* (travellers' inn) has a bougainvillea-filled courtyard and 25 minimalist guest rooms. On site is a restaurant and bar.

Hotel Arischa € A centuries-old *funduq* converted into a good-value hotel with 16 rustic guest rooms and a courtyard restaurant serving alcohol.

Dar Lola €€ Tucked in the old town, this welcoming B&B has five colourful double rooms on offer and a rooftop terrace with city views.

Erriadh p271

Dar Dhiafa €€€ This rambling dar features 17 romantic rooms and two-level suites opening on to courtyards. There are also two plunge pools, a restaurant and a bar.

Dar Bibine €€€ Five cosy guest rooms set in a stylishly converted dar, plus a plunge pool, spa and indoor and outdoor chill-out spaces.

Zone Touristique p270

Hotel Villa Azur (p270) **€€€** An intimate two-storey hotel on Sidi Mahrès beach with 16 rooms, all with sea-facing balconies. Perks include a large pool and restaurant serving alcohol.

LAUREN KEITH/LONELY PLANET

Dar Bibine, Erriadh

Traditional Tunisian clothes and jewellery, Tunis (p53)

ENDER BAYINDIR/SHUTTERSTOCK

TOOLKIT

The chapters in this section cover the most important topics you'll need to know about in Tunisia. They're full of nuts-and-bolts information and valuable insights to help you understand and navigate Tunisia and get the most out of your trip.

Arriving

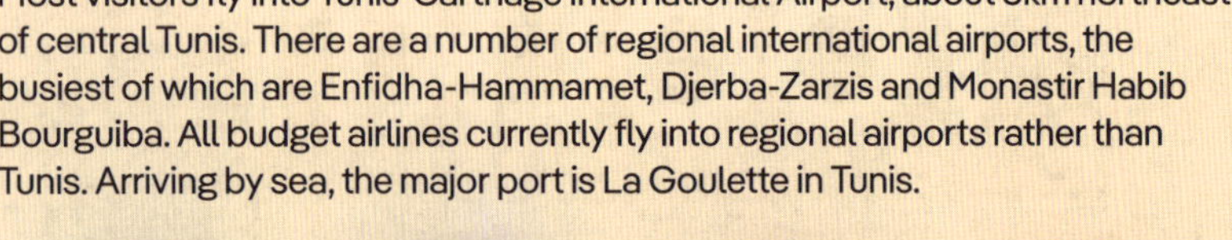

Most visitors fly into Tunis-Carthage International Airport, about 8km northeast of central Tunis. There are a number of regional international airports, the busiest of which are Enfidha-Hammamet, Djerba-Zarzis and Monastir Habib Bourguiba. All budget airlines currently fly into regional airports rather than Tunis. Arriving by sea, the major port is La Goulette in Tunis.

Visas

Citizens of many countries don't need a visa for stays of 90 days or less; check your status with the Tunisian embassy or consulate in your country of residence.

Passport Control

Immigration officers will usually ask where you will be staying on arrival; occasionally they will ask to see proof of this.

Airport Facilities

Arrivals halls have ATMs and currency exchange. You must retain receipts for any currency transactions if you wish to re-exchange local currency when departing Tunisia. ATM receipts don't count.

Wi-Fi & SIM cards

Free wi-fi is available at Tunis-Carthage International Airport, but not at regional airports. Phone companies Orange Tunisia, Ooradoo and Tunisie Telecom have stands in arrivals halls.

Airport & Port Tranfers

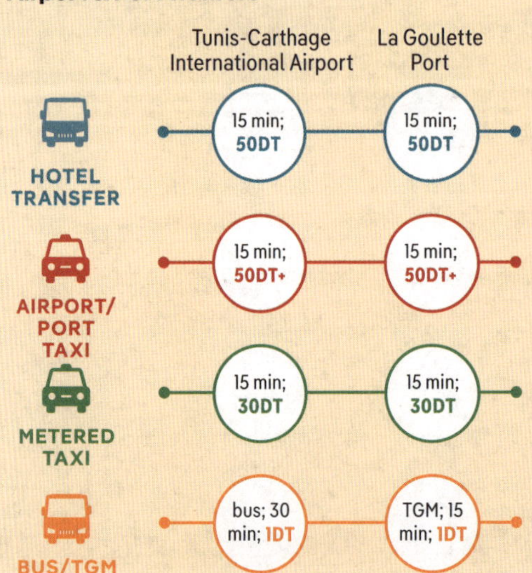

TAXI OPTIONS

The easiest way to get into Tunis from the airport is to arrange a hotel pick-up. This is particularly sensible if you are staying in the medina, as these drivers will take you to your hotel whereas airport taxis will only drop passengers outside the medina's gates. There's also a lot to be said for agreeing on a price beforehand – airport taxis won't use meters and charge extra for bags and at night, or when demand is high. Metered taxis are cheaper again, but you'll need to walk outside the airport's perimeter to flag one down.

FROM LEFT: FUSE/GETTY IMAGES, GEORGE MDIVANIAN/EYEEM/GETTY IMAGES

Getting Around

If travelling long distances (say, from Tunis to Djerba), flying may be the best option. Shorter distances are better travelled by car, train, bus or louage.

TRAVEL COSTS

Car rental
From 90DT/day

Petrol (gas)
2.5DT/litre

Long distance train ticket
4–5DT/hour

Long-distance bus ticket
5DT/hour

Car

Renting a car is the best way to explore the country. Rental agencies have offices at all international airports and in the major cities. Car rental and petrol are cheap; automatic cars are widely available. Roads are generally well-maintained and directional signage is in English and Arabic. Tolls on highways and expressways are uncommon and inexpensive.

Air

Tunisair Express *(tunisairexpress.net)* operates all domestic flights; it is owned by national carrier, Tunisair. Tunisair Express has a reputation for old planes and poor service (flights are rarely on time). The online booking system is problematic – consider using an in-country travel agency. Bus or car are generally much better options when travelling domestically.

TIP

Ride-hailing services including Bolt and InDrive operate in Tunis and Sousse. Note that payment must be made in cash.

LOUAGES: THE LOWDOWN

Louages (shared minibus taxis) are plentiful during the day; they depart when full. Seating is cramped and the driving styles of some drivers can be hair-raising. Every major town has a louage station. Services are colour-coded: a red stripe signifies long-distance, a blue stripe regional and a yellow stripe local/rural. Tickets usually cost the same as a bus ticket.

Bus

National bus company **SNTRI** *(sntri.com.tn)* operates air-con buses that travel from Tunis across the country. Major cities (eg Sousse, Sfax) also have bus companies servicing their areas and nearby destinations. Tickets are cheap and the buses are generally comfortable and punctual.

National Trains

SNCFT *(sncft.com.tn)* operates the main train network. Long-distance trains are old, slow, filthy, uncomfortable and unreliable. Lines link Tunis with destinations including Sousse, Sfax, Gabès, Nabeul, Bizerte and Tozeur. There are two classes of ticket; 1st class is highly recommended.

Other Train Lines

Tunis' TGM light rail connects the city centre with La Goulette, Carthage, Sidi Bou Said and La Marsa. The Sahel Metro connects Sousse with Monastir and Mahdia. Both are cheap, modern and reliable travelling options.

DRIVING ESSENTIALS

Drive on the right

Speed limits
50km/h in urban areas; 90km/h on rural roads; 90-110km on highways and expressways

18

Driving age 18+

Money

CURRENCY: TUNISIAN DINAR (DT)

Credit & Debit Cards

ATMs allowing cash withdrawals are available in cities and most towns. Mastercard and Visa cards are widely accepted. The fee for cash withdrawals is usually around 10–12DT and the maximum withdrawal can be as low as 300DT.

Cash

Make sure that you carry at least some local currency. You'll need this for public transport, taxis, museum entries, fast food and meals in budget eateries.

Changing Money

Bureaux de change can be found in cities and larger towns. These will change euros, US dollars and (sometimes) other currencies. When leaving the country, you can re-exchange any leftover dinars for US dollars or euros as long as you have a receipt from the bureau de change where you made the original transaction. ATM receipts are not accepted.

Tipping

Tipping isn't mandatory in restaurants, but many locals and visitors will tip 10% for good service. It is usual to round taxi fares up at least to the nearest dinar.

HOW MUCH FOR...

Museum entry
approx 10DT

A metro ticket
1–2.5DT

A short local taxi fare
3DT

A local SIM card with data
from 15DT

HOW TO... Bargain

Haggling in tourist-focused shops in Tunisia's souqs is expected, but fixed pricing is the norm in other businesses. If you're keen to try bargaining, start by offering the shopkeeper 50% of his initial price and then see what they counter with. If they eventually offer a price that you are happy with, seal the deal. If not, walk away. It's important to stay good-tempered throughout the negotiation.

LOCAL TIP

Always have a supply of small-denomination notes available for paying taxis, purchasing street food and making other inexpensive transactions, as drivers and vendors often can't or won't change large notes.

COST OF LIVING

A recent worldwide cost of living survey showed Tunis is one of the world's least expensive cities. This will be obvious to anyone travelling here, as transport, food, museum entries and other goods and services are extremely cheap both in Tunis and in the rest of the country. The only exceptions are midrange and top-end hotels, which can still be pricey and often set their charges in euros rather than dinars. That said, this is still an extremely affordable destination for travellers on every budget.

Accommodation

Camping

Agencies in the south, particularly those in Douz, can organise desert camping and glamping experiences for travellers. Ad hoc camping is not really feasible unless you have your own 4WD, as campers are likely to be disturbed by curious locals and/or police anywhere within walking distance of the dunes. A limited number of campsites can be found in the north and on the central coast.

Budget Hotels

Youth hostels are uncommon, with small one- and two-star hotels filling the breach. These are generally clean, if old and run-down. Many offer air-conditioning, private bathrooms, wi-fi and a simple breakfast. As a general rule, budget hotels are located in medinas or near train/bus stations.

Dars

Literally meaning 'house' in Arabic, dars are usually traditional courtyard houses that have been converted into guesthouses. Some dars sit firmly in the budget category; others have undergone full renovations and function as the local equivalents of luxury boutique hotels. For more information about staying in a dar, see p284.

Midrange Hotels

Larger cities and towns offer characterless three- and four-star hotels geared to business travellers and tour groups; many are local franchises of international chains (eg Ibis and Radisson). Often located near commercial centres rather than near tourist sites, these hotels sometimes offer facilities such as on-site parking, bars and restaurants.

HOW MUCH FOR A NIGHT IN A...

Budget dar
From €30 (around 100DT)

Luxury dar
From €90 (around 300DT)

Resort (room only)
From €60 (around 200DT)

Beach Resorts

Tunisia's coastline is littered with resort hotels, generally clustered together in what's known as a *zone touristique* (tourist strip). Most people who stay at these resorts are in Tunisia on an affordable package tour that includes flights, accommodation, meals and drinks. The most popular resorts are at Hammamet, Sousse, Port El Kantaoui, Monastir and Djerba.

HOTEL TAXES

The Tunisian government levies a tax on all hotel rooms that have been classified (ie inspected and awarded an official star rating). Taxes are 1DT per guest per night at two-star hotels, 8DT at three-star hotels and 12DT at four- and five-star hotels. The tax is paid directly to the hotel, with a maximum charge of 10 nights. Children under 12 are exempt from paying the tax.

CLOCKWISE FROM TOP LEFT: MEHANIQ/SHUTTERSTOCK, ENDER BAYINDIR/SHUTTERSTOCK, KRZYSZTOF BUBEL/SHUTTERSTOCK

Staying in a Traditional Dar

One of the many alluring aspects of travelling in Tunisia is the opportunity to stay overnight in a dar, or traditional courtyard house. These *maisons d'hôtes* (guesthouses) are found throughout the country, but are particularly well represented in the medieval medinas of Tunis and the coast. Their hallmarks are central locations, attractive architecture, warm welcomes and wonderful breakfasts.

What is a Dar?

The Tunisian dar is a single- or multistorey house built around a square or rectangular central courtyard. Like Roman villas and Andalusian patio houses, they were developed in response to the local climate, with high walls to block the hot sun from entering living quarters. These high walls also ensured security, privacy and tranquillity: important assets in noisy and crowded environments such as medinas. Light is brought into the house via a courtyard, which is traditionally decorated with colourful tilework and kept cool with plants and water features such as fountains. Grand dars feature arcaded galleries along the sides of the courtyard, which give access to rooms for sleeping, bathing, dining and cooking. There is also usually a formal living room that can be utilised when the weather precludes relaxation in the courtyard. In more modest dars, the rooms are accessed directly from the courtyard, sometimes through intricately carved wooden doors. If they exist, exterior windows on upper floors will often be covered with *mashrabiyas,* wooden screens featuring geometric patterns that ensure privacy and that also catch wind and offer passive cooling in hot climates.

Some modern dar conversions incorporate a new glass ceiling over the courtyard, transforming the space into an all-weather living area reliant on air-conditioning in summer. However, most dars that have been reimagined as hotels or guesthouses retain courtyards that are open to the elements. Some dars also have roof terraces.

In Morocco, the distinction between a dar and a riad (traditional house built around an Islamic-style garden with trees) is often blurred. There are very few riads in Tunisia.

How to Choose

If your destination in Tunisia has a medina, it will almost certainly have dar accommodation on offer. In the budget category, some family homes double as guesthouses. In these establishments, rooms are simple and bathrooms are sometimes shared. Languages other than Arabic may not be spoken, and if one is, it is more likely to be French than English. The consumption of alcohol in the dar may be frowned upon.

In the midrange and top-end categories, the dar usually functions as a business only, with a manager in charge and the owners living elsewhere. Rooms are comfortable and almost always have en suite facilities. Top-end choices may have amenities such as a kettle, safe, hairdryer, and TV with satellite service. These establishments may also have facilities such as a hammam, spa, bar, restaurant or rooftop pool.

Room fit-outs vary wildly in style and degree of comfort. Some dars have high traditional

ARE DARS ACCESSIBLE?

- Many dars are located in the heart of a medina, and medinas aren't particularly accessible environments; for more on this see p287.
- Stairs are a given in almost every dar, and they are often steep and winding. Very few dars have lifts, although there are three notable exceptions: **Dar El Jeld in Tunis** (p90), **Dar Benti in Monastir** (p207) and **Dar Alouini in Kairouan** (p207; pictured). These establishments also have rooms that have been designed for mobility-challenged guests.

SOME OF OUR FAVOURITE DAR STAYS

Budget Gems

- Dar Ya, Tunis (p90)
- Dar Aida Zaghouan, Zaghouan (p163)
- Dar Alyssa, El Kef (p163)
- Dar Baaziz 3, Sousse (p207)

Midrange Treats

- Dar Ben Gacem, Tunis (p90)
- Dar R'Bat, Nabeul (p115)
- Dar El Kasba, Bizerte (p145)
- Hotel Dar Al Madina, Mahdia (p207)

Top-End Indulgences

- Dar El Jeld, Tunis (p90)
- Dar Colibri, Kelibia (p115)
- Dar Antonia, Sousse (p207)
- Dar Benti, Monastir (p207)
- Dar Alouini, Kairouan (p207)
- Dar Tozeur, Tozeur (p259)
- Dar Bibine, Erriadh (p277)

beds that are built into alcoves and these can be difficult to get in and out of. They can also have wooden decorative canopies that are head-banging hazards. Keep this in mind when choosing a room.

Showers in bathrooms rarely have full screens or shower curtains; complimentary toiletries are standard in top-end dars but not otherwise. If there are windows in your dar, these will rarely be double-glazed. Fortunately, though, late-night street noise is minimal in medinas.

Full Medina Immersion

For non-residents wanting a true taste of daily life in a medina, it's almost impossible to beat a dar stay. You'll be able to follow the stream of local residents heading to the produce markets in the morning, join shopkeepers enjoying lunch in a simple eatery, and wind down in a laid-back neighbourhood coffee house in the evening. Instead of traffic noise, the soundtrack to your stay will be the call to prayer and the chatter of children playing in the laneways – it's a true delight.

Breakfast: A Major Draw

Dar breakfasts are always included in the room rate and are almost universally generous and tasty. Each dar will serve a different menu, although treats such as fresh juice and good coffee are standard. Vegetarians are well catered for; vegans may need to settle for bread, jams and fruit. Some dars are known for the quality and generosity of their morning spreads – **La Chambre Bleue** (p90) in Tunis and **Dar Lekbira** (p207) in Sousse are two notable examples.

The Parking Problem

On-site parking at dars is almost nonexistent. Most medinas can only be accessed on foot or by motorcycle, and secure parking around medina walls is hard to come by. There are some exceptions – **Dar Alouini in Kairouan** has an easily accessed on-site underground car park and there are some hotly contested street car parks within the Tunis medina – but if you are self-driving around the country you may need to source accommodation outside the medina walls. Also be mindful that taxis can only drop their passengers at medina *babs* (gates), so you will need to carry or pull your luggage to your dar of choice from that point.

Seasonal Considerations

Few dars have central heating, so many are very cold in winter. Most have air-conditioning units to keep guest rooms cool in summer, but these units can be old and noisy. Breakfast is sometimes served in courtyards that are open to the elements – not great in winter or when it's raining!

Family Travel

Your children will be warmly welcomed in Tunisia. Wherever you're staying, there will be sights, sounds and lots more to excite the young imagination. There are also plenty of child- and teenager-friendly activities on offer, especially in the desert and along the coast.

Baby Equipment

Pavements are generally poorly maintained if they exist at all, so using a pram or stroller is difficult – if you are travelling with an infant, bring a baby carrier or backpack instead. High chairs in restaurants and cots in hotels aren't always compliant with international safety standards. Car seats for children are uncommon; if renting a car, be sure it has seat belts in the back seat that will lock in a child seat.

Kid-Friendly Accommodation

Budget hotels and dars sometimes have steep and dangerous stairs and may not offer cots and high chairs. Rooms rarely have baths. Resorts are well set up for families, offering connecting rooms, kids clubs and menus, babysitting facilities, multilanguage children's TV channels, child pools and play areas.

Baby Supplies

Disposable nappies, infant formula, wipes and sunscreen are available in supermarkets and pharmacies; common medicines are available at pharmacies. Infant foods in jars can be hard to source.

What's on the Menu?

Most Tunisian dishes are lightly spiced and seasoned, so are suitable for palates of every age. Kid-friendly dishes such as pizza and pasta are widely available, as are every parent's major bribery tools: *pomme frites* (French fries) and ice-cream.

TOP FAMILY-FRIENDLY ATTRACTIONS

Ribats

Many coastal towns have retained their medieval *ribats* (forts). These have watchtowers, battlements and other cool features that children love exploring. There are great examples in **Monastir** (p181) and **Hammamet** (p96).

Active Sahara

Camel riding in **Zaafrane** (p237), quad biking in **Ksar Ghilane** (p242), 4WD excursions from **Douz** (p237) or bike-riding through a *palmeraie* in **Nefta** (p255)? Your teenagers will say 'Yes please!'.

Film Locations

Star Wars fans of every age love to emulate Luke Skywalker at **Ong Jemal** (p255).

BEACH OR POOL?

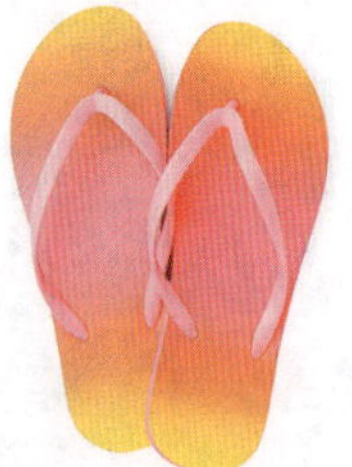

If heading to Tunisia for a summer holiday, be aware that the water at some beaches (eg Sousse) is known to have high levels of pollution. Many beaches don't have lifeguards on duty, either. This is one of the reasons why many resort guests spend their time in the pool rather than the sea.

Resort pools are generally large, clean and overseen by lifeguards, which is particularly important for those travelling with children. Comfortable lounges, poolside food and drink service, grassed areas, sea views and activity programs for children are added incentives.

Accessible Travel

Put simply, Tunisia is a hugely difficult destination for any mobility-, hearing- or visually impaired traveller.

Roads, Paths & Ramps

Pavements and roads across the country are potholed and poorly maintained. Ramps are also usually poorly maintained, if they exist at all. Parked cars inevitably block dropped curbs.

Airport

The international airports have ramps and lifts. If given sufficient notice (minimum 48 hours) airlines can assist mobility-impaired travellers with both boarding and deplaning. Toilets in the arrivals and departures halls are accessible.

Accommodation

As a general rule, the only accessible accommodation is offered at business hotels and at five-star hotels and resorts. Dar stays are very challenging, as rooms are almost always accessed via steep stairs. A few exceptions are listed on p284.

MUSEUM & ARCHAEOLOGICAL SITE ENTRY

Museums and sites overseen by the **Ministry of Cultural Affairs** *(patrimoinedetunisie.com.tn)* usually grant free entry for people with disabilities and one carer.

Public Transport

Public transport in Tunisia is not accessible for those in wheelchairs, or for the elderly and infirm. Hotels may be able to assist with booking a taxi or minibus equipped to carry wheelchairs or walking frames.

On the Beach

Few beaches are accessible for the mobility impaired. One exception is Bou Jaffar Beach (p180) in Sousse, which has a ramp leading from the Corniche down to the sand (but no beach matting).

THE MEDINA CHALLENGE

Exploring Tunisia's marvellous medinas can be difficult for those with a mobility or visual impairment. Cobbled and narrow laneways are often cluttered with rubbish, retail displays and seating, impeding passage. And though most medina lanes are officially pedestrianised, some motorcyclists ignore this rule and expect everyone else to give way.

Although Tunisia has official regulations defining accessibility standards for public buildings, this isn't mandated. Museums and archaeological sites are particularly inadequate in this respect. One exception is the Bardo Museum (p68) in Tunis, which is wheelchair accessible and offers some resources for visually impaired visitors.

RESOURCES

Carthage Magazine *(carthagemagazine.com/tunisia-wheelchair-accessible-travel-guide)* A guide to wheelchair accessible travel in the country.

Lotus Royal Move *(lrmove.net)* Tunis-based company that transports and assists people with disabilities and can provide equipment such as portable ramps.

MED PEDS *(facebook.com/Medpedstunisia)* Mobility-scooter hire in Sousse, Hammamet and Monastir.

Mobility Equipment Hire Direct *(mobilityequipmenthiredirect.com)* British company that can arrange mobility equipment hire including beach wheelchairs in, eg, Hammamet, Nabeul, Sousse and Monastir.

Health & Safe Travel

VACCINATIONS

There are no mandatory vaccinations, but make sure that your standard preventative vaccinations (eg tetanus) are up-to-date. Vaccination against typhoid and hepatitis A and B is also recommended. If travelling from a country where the World Health Organisation warns of Yellow Fever transmission, you may need to show proof that you are vaccinated against this disease before entering Tunisia.

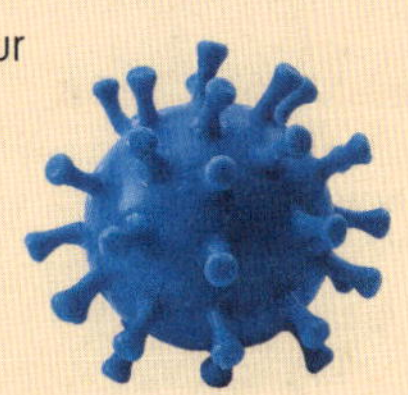

Safe Travel

Be sure to check your home country's Tunisia advice before travelling. At the time of research several governments advised against travel to destinations within 20km of the Algerian border, within 30km of the Libyan border, and in much of the Kasserine and Kef governorates.

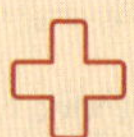

Local Health Care

Major cities and towns have decent health-care clinics and hospitals. The nationwide number for ambulances in Tunisia is 190; be warned that most ambulances are privately operated and charge for their services. The website of the US embassy in Tunisia (tn.usembassy.gov/u-s-citizen-services/local-resources-of-u-s-citizens/doctors/) offers a handy list of suggested medical practitioners and clinics in Tunis.

LGBTIQ+ TRAVELLERS

Tunisia criminalises same-sex sexual activity between men and between women, and LGBTIQ+ people are regularly subjected to imprisonment, discrimination and violence. For more information, see humandignitytrust.org/country-profile/tunisia and facebook.com/damj.tunisie.

Food Poisoning

Occasional bouts of food poisoning (bacterial diarrhoea) can be expected. Treat with rest and plenty of fluids with oral rehydration salts. Stomach disinfectants such as Antinal (nifuroxazide) and Cipro (ciprofloxacin) are available and recommended above Immodium (loperamide), which only treats the symptoms rather than the cause. If symptoms persist more than 72 hours or are accompanied by fever, consult a doctor.

TAP WATER

Though tap water is officially safe to drink, most travellers opt not to do so due to its chemical taste and potential for carrying contaminants.

FROM LEFT: DSGPRO/GETTY IMAGES, VICTOR MOUSSA/SHUTTERSTOCK, NEW AFRICA/SHUTTERSTOCK

Heat Exhaustion

The symptoms of heat exhaustion include headache, dizziness, tiredness and sometimes vomiting. When in the sun (especially in the desert), drink water (ideally with rehydration salts) before you're thirsty, cover your head and wear loose fitting, lightweight clothes that cover your arms and legs. Treatment for heat exhaustion includes drinking water and/or fruit juice, and using cold water and fans to lower your body temperature. Even more serious is heatstroke, which occurs when the body's heat-regulating mechanism breaks down. Treatment is rapid cooling with ice and water, plus intravenous fluid replacement.

Travel Insurance

Travel insurance is highly recommended, particularly coverage of emergency evacuation and adventure activities such as desert trekking, quad biking and camel or horse riding. Make sure that your policy covers all geographical areas in which you plan to travel. The best health care is almost always private and you'll need to show ability to pay prior to treatment and seek reimbursement from your insurance company later.

Dive Insurance

Many regular insurance policies exclude diving, so if you plan to dive while in Tunisia you'll need to take out specific dive insurance. Be sure to confirm that your insurance covers the type of diving you will be doing. A helpful contact is the **Divers Alert Network** *(daneurope.org)*, which offers a variety of plans with worldwide validity for sport divers. At a minimum, check that the plan you choose covers evacuation to a recompression facility, hyperbaric chamber treatment and possibly also search and rescue.

SCAMS & THEFT

Tunisia is remarkably free of the scams that plague travellers in other parts of the world. In some archaeological sites and museums, plainclothes police may ask to see your passport; make sure you ask to see their official identification before handing it over. Pickpocketing and bag snatching is known to occasionally occur, so be on your guard.

ILLEGAL DRUGS

Penalties for drug offences in Tunisia include mandatory prison sentences.

RABIES

Rabies is endemic in North Africa. If a dog or other mammal bites or scratches you, seek medical help immediately.

GOVERNMENT TRAVEL ADVISORIES

- Australia (smartraveller.gov.au)
- Canada (voyage.gc.ca)
- France (diplomatie.gouv.fr/fr/conseils-aux-voyageurs)
- UK (gov.uk/foreign-travel-advice)
- USA (travel.state.gov/content/travel/en/international-travel.html)

Food, Drink & Nightlife

When to Eat

Breakfast: Eaten early. Options range from a croissant and coffee to an *assida* (pudding made with flour or semolina, oil and dates).

Lunch: Usually eaten between noon and 1pm; often a snack from a street-food stall.

Dinner: Served around 8pm in winter, slightly later in summer. The main meal of the day, usually eaten at home. Typically it's salad or soup followed by a substantial main course.

Where to Eat

Cafes: Western-style cafes serve food, but most traditional Tunisian cafes limit themselves to drinks.

Street-food stands: There is a huge range of street-food options, with stands usually specialising in one offering (eg the filled flatbread known as the *chapati*). Some stands offer seating, but others are strictly takeaway.

Local eateries: In medinas and elsewhere, no-frills eateries serve plates of inexpensive home-style food to workers and shoppers at lunchtime.

Restaurants: The only places where alcohol is likely to be served, and inevitably pricey. Tunisians particularly love fish restaurants.

MENU DECODER

Brik: An essential element in *iftar* (fast-breaking) meals during Ramadan, but popular at all times. A deep-fried envelope of pastry that's usually filled with runny egg but can also feature tuna, potato or meat.

Chorba: Beloved local soup with tomato base enhanced by meat or grains such as *frik* (aka freekeh: roasted green durum wheat).

Lablabi: Another local favourite: chickpea soup served with a fried egg, harissa and olives with a dollop of yogurt; popular breakfast dish or mid-morning snack.

Salade méchouia: Ubiquitous salad of finely chopped mixed grilled vegetables, sometimes topped with tuna and/or boiled egg. Often offered as a complimentary starter in restaurants.

Tajine: Nothing like its Moroccan namesake; a frittata-like egg dish with various meat, fish or vegetable fillings.

HOW TO... Eat Vegan & Vegetarian

Despite the country's bountiful supply of locally grown vegetables, it can be difficult to find meat-free dishes here. One major challenge is that canned tuna is often added to dishes whether or not it's mentioned on the menu, so you'll need to firmly state that you want your food without it.

Starters are good bets: *salade Tunisienne* (finely chopped tomatoes, onion and peppers, seasoned with lemon juice, olive oil and mint) is delicious, but don't forget to mention that you don't eat tuna or eggs. *Salade mechouia* and *omni houria* (cooked carrots mashed with garlic and olive oil) are equally tasty.

Egg eaters will enjoy *shakshuka* (eggs baked in a spicy tomato sauce), veggie *tajines* and street-food snacks such as the delectable *kafteji,* a flatbread or baguette stuffed with *mechouia*, a soft fried egg, harissa and crisp *pomme frites* (French fries).

Note that vegetable couscous is often prepared using chicken stock, as is *lablabi.*

FROM LEFT: ANTONIO S/SHUTTERSTOCK, ANDREI KUZMIK/SHUTTERSTOCK

HOW MUCH FOR A...

250ml bottle of beer in bar
10DT

Bottle of local wine
60–100DT

Mint tea
3DT

Small bottle of water
1DT

Express coffee
2DT

Street-food snack
2–4DT

Main dish in local eatery
8–10DT

Main dish in fish restaurant
30–50DT

HOW TO... Drink Like the Locals

The national drink, tea, has two popular varieties: *thé vert* (gunpowder green tea) and a black equivalent confusingly known as *thé rouge* (red tea). The latter is usually heavily sweetened with sugar. Variations include classic North African-style *thé à la menthe* (mint tea), *thé au pignon* (with pine nuts) and *thé à l'almande* (with almonds), in which the almonds react with the tea to create a delectable buttery taste.

Coffee is also widely drunk. The thick, gritty *ahwa arbi* (Turkish coffee), which needs sugar to balance the bitterness. Italian-style coffees include the *express* (espresso), *café direct* (a latte-style coffee) and *capucin* (espresso with a dash of milk foam). These coffees are made with a blend of robusta and arabica beans. Popular coffee chains include Ben Yedder and Bondin.

The most popular alcoholic drink is the locally brewed Celtia lager, but it's also easy to source locally brewed Stella.

The quality of local wine is improving. Producers of note include **Domaine Neferis** (p101) in Cap Bon, which is known for the wines it produces under its Magnifique and Selian labels. The Vieux Magon red produced by **Les Vigneron des Carthage** is also notable.

Alcohol Consumption

Tunisia has the highest level of alcohol consumption in North Africa and the sixth-highest level of alcohol consumption in the Muslim world after Yemen, Uzbekistan, the UAE, Turkmenistan and Turkey.

THE JOYS OF SEASONAL FRUIT

Wander past the fresh-produce stands in a medina or through municipal markets such as the **Marché Centrale** (p71) in Tunis to find out what local produce is in season. Tunisia is blessed with wonderful, sun-ripened fruit and sampling the seasonal bounty is particularly rewarding.

In May, try juicy *bousa'a* (medlar fruit): orange in colour and plumlike in taste. All Tunisian peaches are mouth-wateringly good, but in late June look out for *boutabguia* (aka *pêche de vigne*), a ruby-fleshed variety with an unusual, compact texture. *Mishmish* are extraordinarily delicate apricots; pair them with crunchy, sweet *inzas bouguidma* (meaning 'bite-sized'; miniature pears), which are in season in July.

Fresh *almandes* (almonds), in their green suede-like pods, appear in July and August – crack them open to find a gleaming pale kernel.

Grapes are best in late August – try the fragrant white muscats from around Kelibia or the *razzegoui,* a large white grape, shaded pink. Summer sees roadside stalls stacked with refreshing *della* (watermelon).

From September, blush-red pomegranates join the dessert menu; specify if you want them *sans sucre* (unsugared). The season for local dates, one of the most beloved of all Tunisian crops, starts in October and runs until December. There are many different varieties (the Tunisian MInistry of Agriculture lists 150), but local aficionados swear by the honey-tasting *deglet nour* that are grown in desert *palmeraie* (date groves) in **Tozeur** (p248) and **Nefta** (p255).

Responsible Travel

Climate Change & Travel

It's impossible to ignore the impact we have when travelling; Lonely Planet urges all travellers to engage with their travel carbon footprint, which will mainly come from air travel. While there often isn't an alternative, travellers can look to minimise the number of flights they take, opt for newer aircrafts and use cleaner ground transport, such as trains. One proposed solution – purchasing carbon offsets – unfortunately does not cancel out the impact of individual flights. While most destinations will depend on air travel for the foreseeable future, for now, pursuing ground-based travel where possible is the best course of action.

The **UN Carbon Offset Calculator** shows how flying impacts a household's emissions.

The **ICAO's carbon emissions calculator** allows visitors to analyse the CO_2 generated by point-to-point journeys.

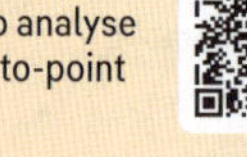

Benefit from Local Knowledge

Sign up for a guided tour of the Tunis medina led by a local resident. These can be organised by **Mdinti** (p60), an initiative set up to support the medina community.

Support Female Entrepreneurs

Based in Cap Bon but covering many other parts of the country, **Sawa Taste of Tunisia** *(sawataste.com)* offers a wide range of female-led culinary experiences, taking visitors into home kitchens for cooking classes and to local businesses for hands-on workshops.

Single-use plastic is a scourge in Tunisia, with plastic bags and bottles littering landscapes across the country (less than 5% of all waste is recycled). Bring a shopping bag and water filter.

Staying in a traditional family dar that has been given a second life as a guesthouse helps to fund building maintenance and allows new generations to retain ownership of family properties.

TRADITIONAL CRAFTS

Souvenir shopping is so much more rewarding if it has the added benefit of supporting traditional local industries. Consider using your purchasing power to snaffle sumptuous handmade silk in **Mahdia** (p194) or traditional ceramics in **Nabeul** (p106).

DRESS APPROPRIATELY

Tunisia is a predominantly Muslim country, and modesty standards can be very different from those in many Western nations. Gauge the local norm before heading out in revealing clothing – some places are more conservative than others.

Support Local Economies

To create employment and support their faltering economies, local communities in rural areas are being proactive, opening guesthouses such as **Gite de Douiret Chez Rouf** (p227) in Douiret.

Share the Love (and Money)

Help to ensure that the local community benefits from tourism by booking an experience with **In Nefta** (p255), a service providing guides and bikes. It also facilitates visits to see artisans at work and sample traditional home-cooked meals.

Explore on Two Wheels

Be kind to our environment and use a bike to explore where possible. **Djerba** (p269) and the **Kerkennah Islands** (p205) are particularly good for this, offering flat terrain and quiet roads.

Seek Out Amazigh Experiences

If travelling in the south, seek out Amazigh-operated tourism experiences. Local initiatives such as the **Musée Berber** (p217) and the **Maison Troglodyte** (p214) in Matmata directly contribute to the economic empowerment of the local Amazigh community.

Shop in Local Markets

Markets around the country sell fresh produce from local producers, supporting rural communities and ensuring that the country retains food security. Shop there rather than in supermarkets, which are supplied by industrial-sized producers.

Water scarcity is a major problem in Tunisia – be considered in your water use.

Many Mediterranean fish species are facing extinction due to over-fishing. Avoid eating under-sized fish.

Ramadan Etiquette

Around 99% of Tunisia's population is Muslim and it's estimated that 92% of this community observes Ramadan fasting – non-Muslim visitors should be sensitive to this and refrain from publicly consuming food, drink and nicotine during daylight hours.

RESOURCES

visittunisiaproject.org/stories
Project focusing on sustainable travel initiatives.

unhabitat.org/tunisia
Information about food security and local treatment of migrants.

wildyness.com
Tunis-based tour agency with a focus on sustainable travel.

FROM LEFT: IEVGEN KOVALEV/SHUTTERSTOCK, BEAUTIFUL LANDSCAPE/SHUTTERSTOCK, JAT306/SHUTTERSTOCK

Women Travellers

Although Tunisian women enjoy more freedom than their counterparts in some other Arab societies, both gender roles and sexual mores remain conservative. Unwanted attention, from constant stares to sexual harassment, is unfortunately common for young women travelling here without male companions, and especially for those travelling solo.

Travelling Safely

Though sexual harassment is legally punishable in Tunisia, many women travellers report being harassed while travelling here, usually in the form of catcalling. The best way to deal with this is usually to ignore the perpetrators, but if you feel it necessary to respond, saying *'hashouma!'* ('shame!') may offer some degree of protection. As in most Muslim countries, dressing modestly – covering at least your shoulders, upper arms and legs – will usually elicit respectful behaviour from local men.

Local bars really aren't the best spots for women to spend time in, as these are emphatically male domains. Also, drink spiking is known to occur. Top-end hotel bars are better bets, as they are more likely to attract female patrons (usually foreigners). Clubs are usually fine if they are patronised by mixed-gender groups of locals – check this out before you enter.

Getting Around

Most local women choose to sit next to other women on buses and louages if possible, and it's a good idea to follow their lead. Note that there are regular complaints about harassment of women on the Tunis metro – avoid travelling on this at night. If by yourself in Tunis or Sousse, consider using ride-share apps such as Bolt and InDrive rather than flagging taxis down in the street, as this gives a degree of protection.

Beach Behaviours

While it is perfectly acceptable to wear a bathing costume at the beach, topless bathing is both culturally inappropriate and illegal. The male sex-worker scene (known in some areas as *bezness*) exists in coastal resorts. Although plenty of foreign women do have genuine relationships with Tunisian men, the goal of many of the men chatting up foreign tourists at the beach is to extort money as well as charm their way into resort bedrooms.

Other Matters

You'll need to have a headscarf to enter sites such as the courtyards of the Great Mosques in Sousse and Kairouan.

Tampons and sanitary pads can be purchased at supermarkets and pharmacies. The contraceptive pill, emergency contraceptive pills (the 'morning after pill') and condoms are available at pharmacies.

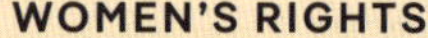

WOMEN'S RIGHTS

Until recently, Tunisia was considered to be one of the most progressive countries in the Arab world when it comes to women's rights. This may be changing, with the numbers of women elected to the national parliament falling dramatically in the past few years (from 31.34% of seats in 2018 to 16.23% in 2023). This isn't the only area of gender equality in which the country is lagging – the 2024 Global Gender Gap Report published by the World Economic Forum ranked Tunisia at at an unimpressive number 115 of the 146 countries it assessed for progress towards gender parity, using the benchmarks of economic opportunities, education, health and political leadership.

KRAKENIMAGES.COM/SHUTTERSTOCK

Nuts & Bolts

OPENING HOURS

Note that all opening hours are shortened during the month of Ramadan and that businesses often stay open later in the summer months.

Banks 8.30am–5pm Monday to Friday

Cafes 8am–11pm

Restaurants Noon–11pm (usually only open for lunch in medinas)

Shops 9am–7pm Monday to Saturday (often closed for Friday prayers)

Smoking

There is a government ban on smoking and vaping in all public places, including public transport and indoor restaurants, cafes and bars. However, this is widely ignored by locals. Hotels accept smoking guests, so specify if you want a non-smoking room.

GOOD TO KNOW

Time zone
Central European Time (GMT/UTC plus one hour)

Country calling code
+216

Emergency number
197 (police)

Population
12.3 million

PUBLIC HOLIDAYS

New Year's Day 1 January

Independence Day 20 March

Martyrs' Day 9 April

Labour Day 1 May

Republic Day 25 July

Women's Day 13 August

Evacuation Day 15 October

Revolution Day 17 December

Islamic holidays including Eid Al Fitr (marking the end of Ramadan), Eid Al Kebir (Eid Al Adhâ; the Feast of the Sacrifice), Muharram (Islamic New Year) and Mouled (aka Mawlid; the birthday of the Prophet Muhammad) are also observed. Dates for these and for the holy month of Ramadan change according to the lunar-based Hejira calendar.

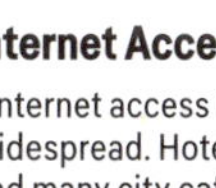

Internet Access

Internet access is widespread. Hotels and many city cafes offer free wi-fi.

SIM Cards

Ooredoo, Orange Tunisia and Tunisie Telecom all sell cheap local SIMS.

Electricity

230V, 50Hz

Type E
220V/50Hz

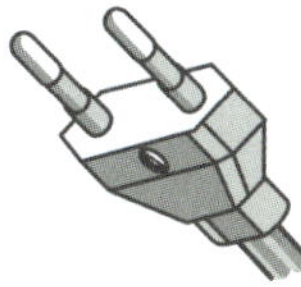

Type C
220V/50Hz

Arabic Language

Arabic is the official language of Tunisia. However, the Arabic spoken on the streets differs greatly from the standard Arabic taught in schools, used in administration, written in newspapers and spoken on the radio. Tunisian Arabic (Derja) is used on these two pages.

Basics

Hello. 'as·sa·laa·ma

Good morning. sbaa·H il·kheer

Good afternoon/evening. ma·saa il·kheer

Good night. tis·baH 'ala kheer (m) tis·baH·i 'ala kheer (f)

Goodbye. bis·sa·laa·ma

Yes. ayy (or na'am – more formal)

No. la

Please. bi·rab·bi (used when asking for something in a shop) tfad·del/tfad·del·loo (to man/ group; used when offering something or inviting someone)

Thank you. y'·ee·shak (m)/ y'·ee·shik (f); y'·ee.shak/y'·ee·shik min gheer mu·ziy·ya (response m/f)

Excuse me. saa·maH·nee (m)/ saa·mHee·nee (f)/saa·mHoo·nee (group)

Sorry. (forgive me) mit·aa·sif (m)/ mit·aa·sif·fa (f)

What's your name? shnu·wa is·mak in·ta (m) shnu·wa is·mek in·ti (f)

My name is ... is·mee ...

How are you? Ish·niy·ha H·waa·lek (m) Ish·niy·ya H·waa·lak (f) Ish·niy·ya H·waal·kum (group)

Directions

Where is ...? ween ...?

What is the address? shnee·ya il·ad·res·sa?

Can you write the address, please? mum·kin tik·tib·lee il·ad·res·sa

Can you show me (on the map)? mum·kin twa·ree·nee (fil·kha·ree·ta)?

Turn left/right. door al·lis·sar/ door al·lim·meen

Time

What time is it? qad·daash il·waqt?

It's (eight o'clock). taw·wa (ith·maan·ya)

yesterday il·baa·raH

today il·yoom

tomorrow ghud·wa

day yoom

Emergencies

Help! 'aw·noo·nee

There's been an accident. fam·ma Haa·dith

I'm lost. ana da·yi' (m)/ana da·y'a (f)

Go away! seeb·ni

Call a doctor! jee·boo·lee it·tab·beeb!

Call the police! jee·boo·lee il·bol·lees!

I've been robbed. sa·ra·qoo·nee

Where are the toilets? ween it·twa·let?

Eating & Drinking

What do you recommend? Wesh ten·saH·neee?

I'm vegetarian. an·na na·baa·tee (m) an·na na·baa·tiy·yeh (f)

I'm allergic to ... 'an·dee Ha·sa·siy·ya lil ...

gluten glu·teen

nuts looz

peanuts kak·wiy·ya

not too spicy mush haar

NUMBERS

1 *waa·Hid* ١

2 *zooz/ith·neen* ٢

3 *thlaa·tha* ٣

4 *ar·b'a* ٤

5 *kham·sa* ٥

6 *sit·ta* ٦

7 *sab·'a* ٧

8 *thmaan·ya* ٨

9 *tis·'a* ٩

10 *'ash·ra* ١٠

DONATIONS TO ENGLISH

Numerous – including alcohol, assassin, coffee, cotton, jar and syrup.

Phrases to Learn Before You Go

Ja·wek be·hi
All good; I understand

Tes·bah 'a·la khir
Have a good night (literally, 'May you wake up to goodness')

Yez·zi
That's enough; please stop doing that.

MSA

Modern Standard Arabic or MSA is the modernised version of Classical Arabic, used in schools, administration and the media – the official lingua franca of the Arab world.

Pronunciation

In the pronunciation guide on the opposite page, the capital H is used to simulate the letter ح which is like the sound made after drinking cold water (ahhh).

The apostrophe is used for the ayn ع which has no English equivalent.

Introduction to Arabic

Muslims say that Arabic is the most perfect language of all, as it's the language in which the Quran was revealed. Religious beliefs aside, the international status of Arabic is impressive: it's one of the world's 10 most widely spoken languages, with over 310 million speakers. Arabic is spoken as the first language across the Middle East and North Africa and is widely used as a second language throughout the Islamic world. It has official status in 25 countries, the Arab League and the African Union, and it's one of the six official languages of the United Nations.

WHO SPEAKS ARABIC?

Arabic is an official language of 23 countries in the Arab world, including Tunisia, Morocco, Algeria, Bahrain, Egypt, Iraq, Lebanon, Oman and the United Arab Emirates.

313 million speak Arabic as their first language

109 million speak Arabic as a second language

French Language

Almost everybody in Tunisia speaks French, so if the thought of getting your mind around Arabic is too much, it'd be good to learn a little French instead.

Basics

Hello. Bonjour. *bon·zhoor*
Goodbye. Au revoir. *o·rer·vwa*
Yes. Oui. *wee*
No. Non. *no*
Please. S'il vous plaît. *seel voo play*
Thank you. Merci. *mair·see*
Excuse me. Excuse-moi. *ek·skew·zer·mwa*
Sorry. Pardon. *par·don*
What's your name?
Comment vous appelez-vous? (pol) *ko·mon voo·za·pay·lay voo*
Comment tu t'appelles? (inf) *ko·mon tew ta·pel*
My name is ...
Je m'appelle ... *zher ma·pel ...*

Directions

Where is ...? Où est ...? *oo e ...*
What is the address? Quelle est l'adresse? *kel e la·dres*
Could you write it down, please? Est-ce que vous pourriez l'écrire, s'il vous plaît? *e·sker voo poo·ryay lay·kreer seel voo play*
Can you show me (on the map)? Pouvez-vous m'indiquer (sur la carte)? *poo·vay·voo mun·dee·kay (sewr la kart)*
Turn left/right. Tournez à gauche/droite. *toor·nay a gosh/drwa*

Time

What time is it? Quelle heure est-il? *kel er e til*
It's (four) o'clock. Il est (quatre) heures. *il e (ka·trer) er*
in the morning du matin *dew ma·tun*
in the afternoon de l'après-midi *der la·pray·mee·dee*
in the evening du soir *dew swar*
yesterday hier *yair*
today aujourd'hui *o·zhoor·dwee*
tomorrow demain *der·mun*
day jour *zhoor*

Emergencies

Help! Au secours! *o skoor*
There's been an accident! Il y a eu un accident! *eel ya ew un ak·see·don*
I'm lost. Je me suis égaré/e. (m/f) *zhe me swee zay·ga·ray*
Leave me alone! Laissez-moi tranquille! *le·say mwa trong·keel*
Call ...! Appelez ...! *a·play ...*
... a doctor un médecin *un mayd·sun*
... the police la police *la po·lees*

Eating & Drinking

A table for two, please. Une table pour deux, s'il vous plaît. *ewn ta·bler poor der seel voo play*
Do you have a menu in English? Est-ce que vous avez la carte en anglais? *es·ker voo za·vay la kart on ong·lay*
What's the speciality here? Quelle est la spécialité ici? *kel ay ler spay·sya·lee·tay ee·see*
I'm a vegetarian. Je suis végétarien/ végétarienne. (m/f) *zher swee vay·zhay·ta·ryun/ vay·zhay·ta·ryen*
The bill, please. La note, s'il vous plaît. *la not seel voo play*

NUMBERS

1 **un** *un*
2 **deux** *der*
3 **trois** *trwa*
4 **quatre** *ka·trer*
5 **cinq** *sungk*
6 **six** *sees*
7 **sept** *set*
8 **huit** *weet*
9 **neuf** *nerf*
10 **dix** *dees*

Glossary

This glossary includes terms and abbreviations you may come across during your travels in Tunisia. Where appropriate, the capital letter in brackets indicates whether the terms are Tunisian Derja (D), Modern Standard Arabic (A) or French (F).

Abbasids – Baghdad-based ruling dynasty (749–1258 CE) of the Arab/Islamic empire
Africa Proconsularis – Roman province of Africa
Aghlabids – Arab dynasty based in Kairouan that ruled Tunisia (800–909 CE)
ain (A) – water source or spring
Allah (A) – Muslim name for God
alloucha (D) – thick-pile, woven, woollen Amazigh rug
Almohads – Amazigh rulers of Spain and North Africa (1130–1269)
Almoravids – dynasty of Amazigh from the Sahara who reigned from 1061 to 1106 in Morocco and the Maghreb, and in Andalusia after 1086
Amazigh – indigenous (non-Arab) people of North Africa
ASM (F) – Association de Sauvegarde de la Médina; organisation preserving the medinas of a number of Tunisian towns
assaba (D) – headband worn by Amazigh women
auberge de jeunesse (F) – youth hostel affiliated with Hostelling International

bab (A) – door, entry, gate
bakhnoug (D) – traditional shawl worn by Amazigh women
Barbary Coast – European term for the Mediterranean coast of North Africa in the 16th to 19th century
basilica – Roman building used for public administration; early Christian church
Berber – outdated term used for indigenous (non-Arab) people of North Africa; Amazigh is the preferred term (see p220)
bey – provincial governor in the Ottoman Empire; rulers of Tunisia from the 17th century until independence in 1957
bezness (D) – the male sex-worker scene
borj (A) – fort (literally 'tower')
boukha (D) – local spirit made from figs
briq (D) – fried pastry usually containing a filling of egg and either prawn or tuna
brochette (F) – kebab
burnous (D) – a traditional Amazigh winter robe in Tunisia, now a loanword in Arabic for warm winter robes generally.

calèche (F) – horse-drawn carriage
caliph – Islamic ruler; originally referred to the successors of the Prophet Muhammad
camionnette (F) – small pick-up truck used as a taxi
capitol – main temple of a Roman town, usually situated in the forum
caravanserai – see *funduq*
casse-croûte (F) – Tunisian fast food; sandwich made from half a French baguette loaf stuffed with a variety of fillings
centre des stages et des vacances (F) – holiday camp
chechia (D) – red felt hat
chorba (A) – soup; also spelt 'shorba'
chott (A) – coast/beach; may refer to a salt lake or marsh
confort (F) – class above 1st class on passenger trains
corniche (F) – coastal road
corsairs – pirates who operated on the North African coast from the 16th to the 19th century
couscous – semolina granules; the staple food of Tunisia

dar (A) – town house or palace
deglat ennour (A) – type of date (literally 'finger of light')
dustour (A) – literally 'constitution' but also name for Habib Bourguiba's political party before independence; see also PSD
dey – the Ottoman army's equivalent of a sergeant; rulers of Tunisia in the 16th century
diwan – assembly (in various Muslim states)
djelba (D) – cotton tunic

eid (A) – festival/celebration
Eid al-Adha (A) – 'Festival of the Sacrifice' marking the pilgrimage to Mecca; sometimes called Eid al-Kebir
Eid al-Fitr (A) – 'Festival of the Breaking of the Fast', celebrated at the end of Ramadan
emir (A) – military commander or prince
erg (D) – sand sea; desert

Fatimids – Muslim dynasty (909–1171 CE) that defeated the Aghlabids and ruled Tunisia from Mahdia from 909 to 969 CE
forum – open space at the centre of Roman towns
fouta (A) – a towel, like that provided in a hammam
funduq (A) – former lodging houses or inns for the travelling merchants of the camel caravans, also known as caravanserai; Arab word for hotel

gare routière (F) – bus station
gargotte (F) – cheap restaurant that serves basic food
gargoulette (F) – clay pot used for cooking; in Djerba these pots are used for catching octopus
ghorfa (A) – a long, barrel-vaulted room built to store grain (literally 'room')
guetiffa (D) – a thick-pile, knotted Amazigh carpet

Hafsids – rulers of Ifriqiyya from the 13th to the 16th century
Hajj (A) – pilgrimage to the holy sites in and around Mecca; the pinnacle of a devout Muslim's life
hammam (A) – public bathhouse; restroom
harissa (D) – spicy chilli paste
harout (D) – traditional Djerban weaver's workshop
hedeyed (D) – finely engraved, wide bracelets made of gold or silver
Hijra (A) – The Prophet Muhammad's flight from Mecca in 622 CE; name of the Muslim calendar
hijab (A) – woman's headscarf
Hilalian tribes – tribes of Upper Egypt who invaded the Maghreb in the 11th century, causing destruction
Hizb al-Nahda – Renaissance Party, the main Islamic opposition party
Husseinites – dynasty of beys who ruled Tunisia from 1705 to 1957

Ibadis – offshoot of the Kharijite sect found only on Djerba, in the villages of the M'Zab Valley in Algeria and in Oman
ibn (A) – 'son of'
Ifriqiyya – Arab province of North Africa, including Tunisia and parts of Libya
iftar (A) – breaking of the day's fast during Ramadan; also spelt 'ftur'
imam (A) – religious teacher or guide; prayer leader for a mosque

jabal (A) – hill or mountain

kahf (A) – cave
kalaa (A) – Amazigh hill fort
kasbah (D) – fort or citadel
kassa (D) – coarse mitten used in the steam room of a hammam
khamsa (A) – hand-of-Fatima motif (literally meaning five)
Kharijites – puritanical Islamic sect that broke away from the mainstream Sunnis in 657 CE and incited Amazigh rebellions from the 8th to the 10th century
kholkal (D) – gold or silver anklets
khutba (A) – weekly sermon in the mosque
kilim (D) – woven rug decorated with typical Amazigh motifs
ksar (A) – (plural *ksour*) Arabic for palace; used in Tunisia to refer to fortified Amazigh stronghold consisting of many ghorfas
ksibah (D) – small fort
ksour (A) – see ksar
kuttab (A) – Quranic primary school

Limes Tripolitanus – defensive line developed by the Romans in southern Tunisia
louage (F) – shared long-distance taxi

madrasa (A) – Quranic school
Maghreb – (adjective Maghrebi) northwest Africa, including Morocco, Libya, Algeria and Tunisia
maison des jeunes (F) – government-run youth hostel
malouf (D) – musical form that originated in Andalusia and was adopted as traditional Tunisian music
murabit (A) – Muslim holy man or saint; sometimes used for a shrine to one
masjid (A) – mosque; literally 'place to kneel (in prayer)'
medina (A) – the old quarter of Tunisian towns and cities (literally 'city')
menzel (A) – fortified family dwelling found on Djerba; home
mergoum (D) – woven carpet with geometric designs
mihrab (A) – vaulted niche in a mosque that indicates the direction of Mecca
minaret – tower of a mosque from which the *muezzin* calls Muslims to prayer
minbar (A) – the pulpit in a mosque
moulid (D) – Maghrebi term for the Moulid an-Nabi, the feast celebrating the birth of the Prophet Muhammad
moussem (D) – pilgrimage to a shrine or tomb of a *murabit*
muezzin (A) – mosque official who calls Muslims to prayer
Muradites – dynasty of Tunisian beys, ruling from the 17th to 18th century

nadhoor (A) – watchtower
Numidians – tribe from present-day Algeria who once controlled Northern Tunisia; founders of the cities of Bulla Regia, Sicca (El-Kef) and Thugga (Dougga)

ONAT – Office National de l'Artisanat Tunisien; government-run fixed-price craft shops
ONTT – Office National du Tourisme Tunisien; government-run national tourist office
Ottoman Empire – former Turkish Empire, of which Tunisia was part; based in Constantinople from the late 13th century to the end of WWI
oud – lute
oued (D) – river; dry riverbed
Ouergherma (D) – 17th-century Amazigh confederation that ruled from Medenine

palmeraie (F) – palm grove; the area around an oasis where date palms, vegetables and fruit are grown
pasha – provincial governor or high official in the Ottoman Empire
patisserie (F) – cake and pastry shop
pension (F) – guesthouse

Phoenicians – great seafaring nation, based in modern Lebanon, that dominated trade in the Mediterranean in the 1st millennium BCE; founders of Carthage
PSD (F) – Parti Socialiste Destourien (called the Neo-Destour Party before 1964); first nationalist party in Tunisia
Punic – relating to the Phoenician culture that evolved in North Africa
Punic Wars – three wars waged between Rome and Carthage in the 2nd and 3rd centuries BCE, resulting in the destruction of Carthage by the Romans in 146 BCE

qibla (A) – direction of Mecca in a mosque, indicated by the *mihrab*
qubbah (A) – dome
Quran (A) – holy book of Islam

Ramadan (A) – ninth month of the Muslim year, a time of fasting
razzegoui (D) – a large white grape that ripens to a pink blush
RCD (F) – Rassemblement Constitutionnel Démocratique; President Ben Ali's ruling party
ribat (A) – fort
rôtisserie (F) – basic restaurant serving roast chicken

Sahel – eastern part of central Tunisia occupying the large, fertile coastal bulge between the Gulf of Hammamet and the Gulf of Gabès
sand rose – crystallised gypsum found in the desert and sold as a souvenir
sharia (A) – Quranic law
sheesha (A) – water pipe used to smoke tobacco; also spelt 'chicha'; also *argileh* or *nargileh*
Shiites – one of two main Islamic sects (see also Sunni); its followers believe that the true imams are descended from Ali Ibn Abi Taleb, the Prophet Muhammad's cousin and son-in-law
sidi (A) – respectful term to refer to an older or more powerful man; in a Maghrebi context it means saint
skifa (A) – gate
SNCFT (F) – Société Nationale des Chemins de Fer Tunisiens; national railway company
SNTRI (F) – Société Nationale du Transport Interurbain; national bus company
souq (A) – market
stela – grave stone
Sufi – follower of Islamic mystical orders
Sunnis – one of two main Islamic sects derived from followers of the Umayyad caliphate (see also Shiites)
syndicat d'initiative (F) – municipal tourist office

Taxiphone – public telephone
Tell – high plains of the Tunisian Dorsale, in central Tunisia
thibarine (D) – spirit made from dates; from the village of Thibar near Dougga
tophet (D) – sacrificial site
tourbet (D) – mausoleum

Umayyad – first great dynasty of Arab Muslim rulers (661–750 CE), based in Damascus

zaouia (A) – complex surrounding the tomb of a saint
zone touristique (F) – tourist strip

STORYBOOK

Our writers delve deep into different aspects of Tunisian life

Detail of Bardo Museum (p68)
BEARFOTOS/SHUTTERSTOCK

A HISTORY OF TUNISIA IN 15 PLACES

Older than you'd think, larger than you'd expect and more amazing than you could imagine, Tunisia is a goldmine of history, both modern and ancient. Unique architectural trends, artefacts of incredible beauty, and exceptional ideologies abound at the crossroads of the Greeks and Phoenicians, the Romans and Carthagians, and the desert and the sea. By Sanad Tabbaa

INHABITED SINCE ANTIQUITY, with the ruins to prove it, Tunisia has risen and fallen in importance countless times across the millennia. It was the staging ground of a grand transcultural exchange between Greeks and Phoenicians – one that ends with the Hellenes adopting the Phoenician alphabet that influences the Latin alphabet we use today – and the epicentre of the Barbary Corsair crisis. Tunisia and its neighbours have exerted significant influence on the currents of world history as we understand it, especially on the history of Western civilisation from the Romans onwards.

Carthage, the historic capital of Tunisia whose ruins lie in modern Tunis, was a city-state that seriously challenged Rome. Later, Tunisia would be the birthplace of the Fatimid Caliphate that would conquer Egypt. More recently, it served as the final staging ground of WWII's North African Campaign. All the while, cultural exchanges flourished between Tunisia and Italy, which are separated by only about 300km. This is all to say that Tunisia's place in Mediterranean history is criminally understated and certainly worth learning about – not only to understand Tunisia, but also to better understand both coasts of the Mediterranean Sea.

1. Matmata Pit Dwellings

UNDERGROUND TROGLODYTE HOMES

When the Sahara dried up some 6000 years ago and game migrated for, literally, greener pastures, some people moved up to the coast and some searched for the nearest river, while others decided to coexist with this new reality. With the desert heat routinely reaching 50°C, it is a true marvel that the troglodyte homes in the Matmata pit dwellings remain cool. Although these traditional dwellings of the Amazigh are not the same as those used in the very distant past, paintings in caves to the south, along the Libyan and Algerian borders, suggest that they weren't all that different.

For more on the Matmata pit dwellings, see page 216

2. Neapolis, Nabeul

THE REMNANTS OF GREECE

While Amazigh culture began to emerge in the south, a grand struggle began along the coast between Greeks and Phoenicians. The ruins of Neapolis – known today as Nabeul – are typical of this exchange. Originally founded by the Greeks, Neapolis (which itself means 'new city' and was a standard name for Greek colonies in antiquity) originally functioned as a trade hub. As Phoenician influence along both sides of the Mediterranean grew, it came under threat and was eventually absorbed by the Phoenician city-states of the area. They, in turn, would be absorbed by Rome.

For more on Neapolis, see page 105

3. Utica

THE PHOENICIAN CONNECTION

The Phoenicians, originating from today's Lebanon, were the region's foremost traders some 3400 years ago. To better facilitate trade between the Egyptians, Mesopotamians, Hellenes and Amazigh peoples, they established colonies all across the Mediterranean coastline, both in Europe and North Africa. Utica is one of these, and its Necropolis is one of the better-preserved examples we have of their culture in North Africa. Though the Phoenicians were united by language, culture and a writing system, they were denizens of independent city-states in a world that was not always friendly to traders.

For more on Utica, see page 126

4. Dougga Mausoleum

PUNIC POWER STRUGGLES

As pressures mounted on the Phoenician city-states of the time, one grew in size, importance and military might around the 5th century BCE: Carthage. By this point referred to as the Punic people (shorthand for the Western Phoenicians who had now developed their own culture along the Mediterranean coast), this group would continue their infighting while developing unique arts, culture and sciences. The Libyco-Punic Mausoleum at Dougga is a salient example of this, because of the uniqueness of its design, as well as the fact that it was spared from destruction by the Romans as it was not aligning with Carthage.

For more on Dougga, see page 158

Mosaic, House of the Nymphs (p105), Nabeul

ANDREAS WOLOCHOW/SHUTTERSTOCK

5. Carthage

RUINS OF THE ONLY CHALLENGER

The story of the end of Carthage is well known, with Hannibal establishing colonies on the European coast, taking war elephants across the Alps to fight the Romans over decades, and losing after a long, bloody war in the Battle of Zama in the 3rd century BCE. Punic Carthage was destroyed and its earth salted. The ruins in today's Carthage in Tunis are those of the Roman rebuilding of the city around 100 years later, after the spectre of the enemy had dissolved into legend. Carthage would swiftly become the third most populous and important Roman city, after Rome itself and Alexandria.

For more on Carthage, see page 76

6. Bulla Regia Byzantine Basilica

THE RETURN TO FORM

Rome fell, as empires do. The Vandals, a Germanic tribe, took over Rome's North African territories, including Carthage, and invaded the capital from the south. Though they left few traces of their 100-year occupation, the reconquest of today's Tunisia by the Eastern Roman Empire, usually called the Byzantines, has a much larger portfolio of ruins. Bulla Regia's Byzantine Basilica, and the ruins around it, are one such memento. Dated to the 6th century CE, it shows a return to form as the Byzantines attempted to hold onto those areas deemed most important to Rome.

For more on Byzantine Basilica, see page 141

7. Great Mosque of Kairouan

THE INTRODUCTION OF ISLAM

Uqbah bin Nafi, a general of the Rashidun Caliphate, then of the Umayyads, led a conquest into Byzantine North Africa. Establishing a base of operations in Kairouan, which he founded, he swiftly conquered the entirety of the Maghreb introducing Arabic and Islam. In 670 CE he established the Great Mosque of Kairouan, a masterpiece of Islamic architecture that has become one of the holiest sites in the religion. Virtually every mosque that has followed in the Maghreb has been inspired by the raw magnificence of the Great Mosque of Kairouan, and for good reason.

For more on the Great Mosque of Kairouan, see page 186

8. Zitouna Mosque

PRAYER AND PHILOSOPHY IN TUNIS

The Umayyads were supplanted by the Abbasids, partly due to accusations of corruption and religiously improper policies of Arab supremacy. While the Umayyads retreated to the Iberian Peninsula, successive Abbasid vassals controlled Tunisia, most notably the Aghlabids from the 9th to the 10th centuries. They built and renovated holy sites, and the Zitouna Mosque in Tunis owes its present form to them. Over the centuries, Zitouna Mosque emerged as a centre of Islamic learning and, eventually, expanded with the Zitouna University, a devoted structure in the 13th century.

For more on Zitouna Mosque, see page 58

9. Cap Afrique

FATIMID BEGINNINGS

A missionary named Abu Abdallah Al Shi'i converted many of the tribes of eastern Algeria and Tunisia to the Ismaili sect of Islam on behalf of a master yet unknown to him in the 10th century. That master, the first Fatimid Caliph, was Abdallah Al Mahdi. After hiding around the area of Iraq or Syria, he came to Tunisia to reap the rewards won by Abu Abdallah and, of course, executed him immediately on arrival. The Fatimids established their first capital at Mahdia, the skeleton of which can still be seen in Cap Afrique, before setting off to conquer Egypt.

For more on Mahdia's Fatimid ruins, see page 195

10. Underground Mosque of Sedouikech

HIDDEN PRAYER PLACES

The Fatimids did not hold power in Tunisia for very long and were replaced by the Almohads, or Al Muwahidin (Unitarians) in the 12th century. Practising an extremely strict and exclusionary interpretation of Islam, they conquered much of the Maghreb and most of the Iberian Peninsula. The Almohads were less interested in Tunisia than in Morocco or the Iberian Peninsula, and as such they did not leave as indelible a mark. That said, the Sedouikech Underground Mosque, a hidden place of prayer for Ibadi worship, is a testament to their failure to crush dissident belief.

For more on the Underground Mosque of Sedouikech, see page 272

11. Ouled El Hadef

HAFSID BEGINNINGS AND POWER STRUGGLES

The Almohads appointed a governor of Tunis in the 13th century who proverbially smelt blood in the water. Having lost much territory in the Maghreb piecemeal, and under consistent threat in the Iberian Peninsula, the Almohads didn't seem as intimidating as they did a century ago. A quick coup made that certain, establishing 300 years of Hafsid rule in the process. Ouled El Hadef, the old quarter of Tozeur, quite vividly takes you back to that era. Ambling around the pale bricks arranged in ever-shifting formations can be breathtaking, and was no doubt even more so in the 14th century.

For more on Ouled El Hadef, see page 250

12. Borj Ghazi Mustapha

OTTOMAN CONQUEST AND THE CORSAIR ERA

Tunis was conquered by pirates in 1534. Khayreddin and his brother, Aruj, both nicknamed Barbarossa in reference to their red beards, conquered the Maghreb from the Hafsids in the name of the Ottoman Empire as part of a governmentally sanctioned pirate outfit, known today as the Barbary Corsairs. For 200 years different sets of Ottoman governors controlled Tunisia. Borj Ghazi Mustapha, an extremely well-preserved castle on the island of Djerba, is one such monument dedicated to the governor at the time. Eventually power settled in the hands of the Husaynid

CHRISTOPHE CAPPELLI/SHUTTERSTOCK

Ouled El Hadef (p250), Tozeur

dynasty, which ruled, at least in name, until the 1950s.

For more on Borj Ghazi Mustapha, see page 266

13. Ennejma Ezzahra

THE STAR OF VENUS IN FRENCH COLONIALISM

The Husaynids fell into the same trap that befell the rest of North Africa: they borrowed money from the French, who used financial leverage to establish a budgetary control commission, then applied military pressure from nearby Algeria to force a protectorate upon the Tunisia. By 1881 pressure had turned into full-scale colonisation. Ennejma Ezzahra ('the Star of Venus'), a palace built by French painter and musicologist Rodolphe d'Erlanger in 1921, is a result of that. Aesthetically, It's a magnificent fusion of French Orientalist sensibilities with Arabesque-inspired art. The process that led to it is less inspiring.

For more on Ennejma Ezzahra, see page 81

14. Carthage Palace

THE FORMER SEAT OF POWER

It did not take France long to establish discriminatory practices that disenfranchised Tunisians, taking away their arable farmland and selling it to French settlers at low prices, while denying Tunisians representation. As protests resulted in jailed activists, it seemed violent conflict was inevitable. *Fellaghas* (bandits) roamed the countryside, attacking French farms, police and lines of communication. The French in 1955, at war with Algeria and Vietnam, decided that they didn't want Tunisia all that much anyway and chose to deal with the prime agitator and later president, Habib Bourguiba. Bourguiba would eat, breathe, work and live in Carthage Palace until 1987.

For more on Carthage Palace, see page 85

15. Sidi Bouzid

THE BEGINNING OF SPRING

Bourguiba retired in 1987, leaving behind a developed, pacifist and pragmatic Tunisia. His successor, Ben Ali, is not remembered as fondly. As corruption became constant, a fruit-cart seller in the poor, small city of Sidi Bouzid set himself on fire, asking, 'How do you expect me to make a living?' His cart had been confiscated due to the lack of a permit, even though the requisite permit did not exist. This act set off the Arab Spring, called the Dignity Revolution in Tunisia. Since then, Tunisia has become a democracy in truth, with multiple different heads of state serving their appointed terms, and moving on. All in all, things are looking up.

MEET THE TUNISIANS

The rich mosaic of civilisations shaping Tunisia's identity over millennia has created a diverse population deeply connected to their land. HANANE ZAHROUNI introduces her people and their cultural heritage.

TUNISIANS ARE A blend of centuries of history, migration and adaptation. As a North African nation with deep Mediterranean and Arab roots, Tunisia has long been a crossroads of civilisations, shaping its people into an open yet distinct community. Our rich ancestry reflects Amazigh (formerly Berber), Phoenician, Roman, Arab, Ottoman and French influences. This diversity is visible in our language, cuisine and traditions, making us both unique and familiar to travellers. We also embody hospitality, resilience and cultural pride.

With a population of around 12 million, Tunisian citizens are predominantly young, with a median age of around 33 years. Their youthful energy fuels social and economic change, with many young Tunisians leading in technology, arts and entrepreneurship. Names carry deep meaning, often influenced by Arabic, Amazigh and Islamic traditions, with many choosing names that reflect religious significance or familial heritage.

Tunisians also have a strong sense of community, with our extended families playing an essential role in daily life. Cafe culture is well known throughout the region, and is ingrained in our everyday life as a space for socialising, debating politics, watching football matches, playing card games like 'Chkobba' and 'Rami' or simply enjoying a break. Many writers, artists and activists attend cafes as places for inspiration. While urbanisation has led to a shift towards nuclear families in cities like Tunis, Sfax and Sousse, traditional customs and values still hold strong in rural areas of Djerba and Gafsa with Amazigh and Bedouin influences. Despite the differences, hospitality is a defining trait. Whether visiting a home or a cafe, you can expect a warm welcome and an offer of sweet mint tea or strong coffee.

Religion is an integral part of life for many Tunisians, with Islam being the predominant faith. You will hear the call to prayer echo across cities as you encounter bustling markets, contemporary art scenes and a growing entrepreneurial spirit. Even so, Tunisia has a long tradition of religious tolerance, and the country's secular approach allows for a blend of faith and modern governance.

Agricultural Gems

Tunisia has 1.9 million hectares of olive groves, a pillar of its economy and culture. It leads in date exports, with the Deglet Nour variety making up 30% of global supply.

Tunisians are proud of their dialect, which is a unique blend of Arabic, French, Amazigh and even Italian influences. While Modern Standard Arabic is the official language, everyday conversations are filled with French phrases and local expressions that shift between regions. The north, influenced by European interactions, speaks a dialect with more French borrowings, while the south retains a closer link to Amazigh and Arabic heritage.

Our resilience defines the Tunisian spirit. The 2011 revolution showcased our drive for change, democracy and progress. Today, we continue to push for innovation in technology, arts and activism, while holding onto the cultural richness that defines us. We are a people shaped by history yet always looking to the future.

Pictured clockwise from top left: Making bread, Tunis (p53); goatherd, the Sahara (p229); woman in traditional clothing, Sidi Bou Said (p81); car mechanic, Tunis (p53)

STORYBOOK

MY TUNISIAN STORY

I was born in Morocco and raised in multiple countries, which makes me a 'Third Culture' kid. My parents, however, were born and raised in Tunisia, in the coastal towns of Hammamet and Hammam-Lif. They always made sure that I visited Tunisia every summer holiday to keep in touch with my roots, my culture and my extended family, while becoming fluent in the language. My family dinner gatherings always included traditional meals like couscous, and weekends meant visiting the beaches and olive tree orchards in the countryside to embrace my heritage.

Although my upbringing brought me an international mindset, I have always felt a strong connection to my Tunisian origin; one that blends North African warmth with Mediterranean openness and makes me part of a diverse community that continues to be united by history and resilience.

EXQUISITE OLIVE OIL

Tunisia's olive oil tradition goes a long way back. Today, it's among the world's top five olive-producing countries. By Isabel Putinja

THE OLIVE TREE has been a part of Tunisia's rural landscapes for millennia. Its countryside is ribboned with vast groves of this evergreen tree, covering over one third of the country. Some age-old olive trees planted during Punic and Roman times still stand today. The millennial olive tree of Echraf at the tip of Cap Bon is just one impressive example.

Beloved Tree & Culinary Staple

The olive is Tunisia's most beloved tree. Many families tend to their own groves of olive trees, harvesting their fruits to be pressed into precious olive oil, an important culinary staple. Freshly baked bread dipped into a bowl of golden olive oil is a favourite breakfast. Olive oil is also an important ingredient in harissa, Tunisia's much-loved spicy condiment, as well as in many Tunisian dishes.

In Djerban culture, the olive tree plays an important role in wedding rituals. Just before dawn, the bride-to-be pays a visit to her family's oldest olive tree as a way of paying her respects to the tree and bidding farewell to her ancestors. Then once a married woman, she receives the blessings of her in-laws before their oldest olive tree and is welcomed into the family.

Tunisia's Olive Cultivars

Tunisia has three main olive-growing regions; 85% of olive trees are found in the arid centre and south, and an important, smaller olive-growing region in the north.

The main olive varieties native to the country are Chetoui, which is mostly cultivated in the northern region, and Chemlali, which is the dominant variety of the south. While Chetoui produces an intense oil with green grassy notes, Chemlali has more fruity nuances. It also represents 80% of national production, while almost 20% of olive oil is made from Chetoui olives.

There are many other homegrown cultivars, including Sayali, Ouslati and Gerboui. Semlali and Zalmati are native to Djerba.

Harvest & Pressing

The harvest season begins once the weather starts to get cooler and the olive drupes (the fruit's flesh) change in colour from green to purple. Many Tunisian families press their own olives into oil, transporting the harvested fruits to their local olive mill.

Traditional mills are still found across the country, using granite millstones and hydraulic presses to extract the oil from the olive drupes. These old-fashioned mills are increasingly being replaced with modern two-phase systems, which ensure a more efficient milling process and a higher quality of olive oil.

Djerba's traditional olive mills were constructed underground to protect the olives from heat and light, and to store the oil in ideal conditions. These are no longer in use, but a few of these subterranean mills have been restored and converted into educational museums.

A Long History of Olive Oil Production

Olive oil has been produced in Tunisia since 8th century BCE, and today olives are one of the country's biggest and most valuable natural resources. This puts Tunisia among the top olive-producing countries, along with Spain, Italy, Greece and Turkey.

Tunisia is also a major exporter of olive oil, with as much as 90% of its stock shipped abroad, mostly to the European Union (EU). For many decades Tunisia has exported its olive oil in bulk to other olive-producing countries in the EU to fill in the gaps created by decreasing yields, often as a result of adverse weather or pests.

Premium Olive Oil

Today, there's an ever-increasing number of Tunisian boutique producers focused on making premium extra virgin olive oil. This is packaged in attractively labelled bottles as a luxury export product bound for consumers in Europe and North America. Many such producers have won accolades for their high-quality oils, including international awards from prestigious olive oil competitions around the globe.

Thanks to the hot and dry North African climate, the vast majority of Tunisian olive groves are naturally organic. This is because high heat keeps pests at bay without the need for insecticides. This organic 'premium' is a natural advantage that puts Tunisia among the top producers of organic olive oil.

On the flip side, low rainfall and frequent drought conditions present a challenge for many olive farmers, who depend on rainwater for the natural irrigation of their groves. This results in unpredictable yields, and in some areas of the country olive trees have not been able to withstand prolonged drought.

Olive Oil Tourism

As one of Tunisia's most famous gastronomic products, olive oil is now being celebrated through cultural tourism initiatives. As olive oil tourism takes hold, producers across the country are opening up their bucolic groves to visitors. Those curious about Tunisian olive oil are welcome to join tours of groves and production units. Following the approach of wine tourism, dedicated on-site tasting rooms offer visitors the opportunity to sample native Tunisian olive oil varieties and purchase bottles of these as edible souvenirs.

Those keen to know more can also get insights into the olive-oil-making process by touring the production facility. Producers boasting on-site olive mills are happy to fill in visitors on the entire tree-to-bottle production chain. Some even offer introductory workshops on sensory analysis, sharing tips on the qualities to look for in an extra virgin olive oil.

Finally, travellers looking to get closer to the ground can head into the groves and take part in an olive harvest and experience this festive family event first-hand.

Pottery, Nabeul (p106)
ANDREAS WOLOCHOW/SHUTTERSTOCK

TUNISIA'S CENTURIES-OLD CERAMICS STORY

Tunisian ceramics aren't just a pretty decorative art – they're also a living testament to a fusion of cultures 3000 years in the making.
By Paula Hardy

WHILE THE GREEKS gave the craft its name – *keramikós* means 'of clay' – ceramic art in Tunisia has been evolving since prehistory, first fashioned by Amazigh artisans into storage jars, cooking vessels, and powerful figurines designed to bestow blessings and to fend off evil spirits.

A Bronze Age Art

There's evidence that the art of pottery in Tunisia dates back to the Bronze Age. The use of clay as a material made sense in a country where there were abundant deposits around Tabarka, Tunis, Cap Bon and Djerba. Certainly, clay has been worked in Sejnane (p129) for at least 3000 years to create household items needed for food preservation, cooking and home decoration. Today, Sejnane's UNESCO-recognised craft, practised solely by Amazigh women, continues to be handed down from mother to daughter, and manufacturing methods remain virtually unchanged. Uniquely, the clay is worked entirely by the hands and feet, then modelled into bowls, jugs, jars and figurines and left to dry in the sun, before being polished with seashells and painted with Amazigh symbols in red ochre and black resin extracted from the mastic tree.

Phoenician Know-How

It was the Phoenicians from Tyre (modern-day Lebanon) who introduced the potter's wheel to Tunisia at the end of the second millennium BCE. This led to the first flourishing of a commercial ceramics industry in Tunisia around Carthage (p76) and Cap Bon (p92), where the Phoenicians also developed some of the earliest mosaic art, composed of ceramic tesserae, which can still be seen at Kerkouane (p111). Large terracotta vessels were needed to store the harvest of grain, olive oil and wine, and ship them to export markets around the Mediterranean.

Thus the pottery industries of Moknine – famous for its large-scale unglazed pots originally used for cooling water before refrigeration – and Guellala (p274) on Djerba were born. You can still visit the semi-subterranean workshops and drying rooms of Guellala, which were famous for the manufacture of terracotta amphorae and ingenious camel jugs that won't spill a drop of water, even when turned over. Like the Sejnane potters, the Phoenicians also fashioned more artistic, non-utilitarian artefacts from clay like the strange, grimacing terracotta funeral masks in the Carthage National Museum (p77), which were believed to be imbued with spiritual power.

Nabeul: Technical Excellence

With Roman colonisation of Tunisia in 146 BCE, ceramics made a leap from porous clay and unglazed terracotta to more sophisticated glazed ware, much of which was produced in Nabeul (Roman Colonia Julia Neapolis), the sister city to Naples. Today, Nabeul (p103) is Tunisia's national ceramics centre, the alleys of its souq lined with workshops selling brilliantly coloured bowls, ewers, jugs, plates, tiles and innumerable other household and decorative items.

The city's location on the Cap Bon peninsula, almost within touching distance of Italy, made it a natural furnace of creativity. The Romans made huge technical progress, introducing glazeware, kilns and moulds to enable mass production, as well as *terra sigillata,* a fineware made from red-slipped pottery and decorated with relief scenes that could be produced on an industrial scale for export around the empire. Visit the Nabeul Archaeological Museum (p104) to see the progress between the unglazed terracotta statues of the lion-headed Punic goddess Tanit and the sophisticated Roman ceramics.

In the Middle Ages, Tunisia was conquered by the Muslim Aghlabids and then the Fatimids, who brought with them polychrome geometric, epigraphic and floral designs (the first in the western Mediterranean) and tin glaze technology, as well as a new passion for wall tiles. These were first used in the Great Mosque of Kairouan (p186), built in 836 CE, starting a craze in the decoration of mosques, palaces, bathhouses and other important public venues. It's accepted that Sicily's polychrome glazewares were directly influenced by contact with Tunisia, and ties were also fostered with Moorish Spain, which had its own long tradition of ceramic production. When Andalusian Muslims were later expelled from the Iberian peninsula following the 1492 Reconquista, many came to settle in Nabeul, bringing their expertise with them.

Qallalin Craze

Tunisia's most exquisite, decorative ceramic tiles are known as Qallalin tiles, after the district in Tunis where they were mainly produced. With their flowing floral patterns and story pictures, they carry the spirit of the Andalusian and Ottoman artistic traditions that Tunisian ceramics readily absorbed. The finest quality tiles – along with vases, jars, pitchers and lamps – were produced in the 17th and 18th centuries and decorate palaces such as Dar Hussein (now home to the Heritage Institute), tombs like those of Tourbet El Bey (p64), and the religious school Madrasa Slimania (p63).

Another significant tile centre is inland Testour (p159), founded in the 17th century when another wave of persecuted Muslims from Andalusia settled in Tunisia after King Philip III's 1609 expulsion orders. Even today, the whole town has a vague Andalusian air about it and the Great Mosque and museum are decorated with Testour's distinct tileware.

A French Flourish

The final influence on Tunisian ceramics came with French colonisation in the late 19th and 20th centuries. Celebrated French ceramists Joseph-Ferdinand and Elise Tissier established their factory in Nabeul in 1898, bringing with them new European techniques and design traditions, which they blended with the ancestral expertise in Nabeul. This prompted a renaissance in Nabeul's ceramic scene, with notable new factories opened by Tunisian Jacob Chemla and Frenchman Pierre de Verclos.

Between them these three factories trained a new generation of Tunisian ceramists, who specialised in high-design, decorative tableware. Some of the most significant artists were Hassana and Hassine Abderrazak, followed by their sons Mohammed and Abdelkader, as well as Hassen Kharraz, and Aleya and Abdelkader Ben Sedrine. If you're looking for a memorable souvenir from Tunisia, you can't go wrong with a handcrafted piece of ceramic. Not only are they beautiful in and of themselves, but they also reflect the spirit of Tunisia, a country that has absorbed and transformed the different aspects of Mediterranean culture into an exquisite art form.

KAIROUAN: CITY OF KNOWLEDGE & FATIMA AL-FIHRI

Kairouan was Tunisia's intellectual heart and a crucial city in Islamic history, influencing education and serving as a learning centre for Africa and Europe. By Hanane Zahrouni

KAIROUAN, A UNESCO World Heritage city, has for centuries been steeped in history and culture. Founded in 670 CE, the city quickly grew to fame as a place for the trade of ideas. Central to its history was Fatima al-Fihri, a Tunisian scholar and proponent of education, and the world's first woman to establish a school of higher learning.

Historical Overview

The first word revealed in the Quran was 'IQRA', meaning 'READ'.

Seeking knowledge and educating oneself, for both men and women, was an ongoing pursuit in the Islamic Golden Age, in line with the Islamic principle that educating oneself is a sacred duty and obligatory for every Muslim man and woman.

As such, when Arab general Uqbah Ibn Nafi established Kairouan, not only Islam but also various scholarly disciplines would spread from the city across North Africa.

Kairouan in the Islamic Golden Age

Kairouan is one of Islam's most important cities, considered by some to be the fourth holiest after Mecca, Medina and Jerusalem. During the Islamic Golden Age, from the 8th to the 13th century, it thrived as an intellectual hub. The Great Mosque of Kairouan (p186) was built in the 9th century and became one of the city's most iconic landmarks; a place of worship where scholars exchanged knowledge and ideas on theology, law and philosophy. Kairouan's location also gave access to key trade routes, which increased the spread of diverse cultures and ideas. The resulting blend of knowledge and innovation would influence the intellectual landscape of North Africa and Europe.

Kairouan's ancient library contains some of the world's oldest Islamic manuscripts and highlights early bookbinding technologies and how those techniques travelled through the medieval world. Thus, the components for intellectual and scientific study became firmly embedded in the country.

The city was not only of great importance to the Islamic World; it also attracted European scholars, especially those from Sicily and Spain, who visited Kairouan to study the works of Muslim philosophers, scientists and mathematicians. This provided an important bridge between the Christian and Muslim worlds, fostering a spark that would later help to ignite the Renaissance.

Kairouan would lead the way in other areas, too.

Women's Education & Fatima al-Fihri

It's vital to remember that struggles for and advances towards women's rights existed throughout history, long before Western feminist movements, and in this regard the arrival of Islam in North Africa marked a turning point. The introduction of Islam brought women the legal rights to inherit property, pursue education, and choose who to marry (or divorce).

With these freedoms, many women flourished in Kairouan and played essential

roles in the city and the wider region, making contributions in trade, education, social welfare and other areas. Among these women were influential scholars and religious leaders who left a lasting intellectual and cultural impact in North Africa.

Fatima Al-Fihri (c 800–880), a Tunisian noblewoman born in Kairouan, stands out as one of the most influential of these female leaders, and one of the most prominent personalities of her era. The daughter of a successful merchant, in 859 she used the wealth inherited from her father to establish a place of worship and learning for the Muslim community in Morocco, naming the mosque Al Quaraouiyine after her city of birth – a tribute to her origin and heritage.

Since then, Al Quaraouiyine has remained one of the longest continually operating centres of higher learning globally, attracting many scholars and students over the years and teaching diverse subjects including the Quran, *fiqh* (Islamic jurisprudence), Arabic grammar, logic, mathematics, astronomy, medicine and philosophy. In 1965, it was incorporated into Morocco's state education system as the University of Al Quaraouiyine.

Fatima's legacy, however, extends much further than the founding of a mosque and school. Her dedication to learning contributed to the intellectual landscape of North Africa, and she showed astounding foresight and commitment to her people by dedicating her wealth to Al Quaraouiyine. It was a decision rooted in her upbringing within the scholarly environment of Tunisia, which had long been a centre of Islamic scholarship.

Thus Kairouan, as a city of intellectual and cultural life, became a vital catalyst for the educational transformation and scholarly exchange of North Africa during the Islamic Golden Age, shaping the academic landscape of the Muslim world for centuries. It, and Al Quaraouiyine, became cradles for the region's brightest minds and attracted renowned scholars from across the globe. Scholars such as the 12th-century cartographer Muhammad al-Idrissi, known for his maps that aided Renaissance European exploration, have been linked to Al Quaraouiyine, as have influential figures including judge Ibn Rushayd al-Sabti, famous explorer Leo Africanus, historian Ibn Khaldun and astronomer Nur ad-Din Al-Bitruji. European thinkers, too, found their way to Al Quaraouiyine's hallowed halls, including Belgian scholar and grammarian Nicolas Cleynaerts. The university marked a new chapter in its long-standing legacy as a pioneer in shaping North African and global scholarship.

Karouan Today: An Educational Legacy

Kairouan's star may have waned over time as other nearby cities, like Cairo, eclipsed it in influence, but Kairouan never truly lost its spark, and it has still not forgotten its role as a city of learning and tradition. A living museum of its learned past, its narrow streets open onto centuries-old madrasas (Islamic schools), libraries and mosques that remain centres of contemplation and study.

Visitors to Kairouan can stop by the Great Mosque to stand beneath its enormous minaret and imagine the generations of scholars who argued philosophy and theology beneath its roof. The Aghlabid Basins, a complex hydraulic system constructed in the 9th century, are evidence of the city's sophistication in engineering and city planning.

Aside from its architectural splendour, Kairouan remains a centre of traditional crafts. It is famous for its handwoven carpets, intricate calligraphy and fine ceramics, all reflecting centuries-old artistic and intellectual traditions. To this day, Kairouan's artisans draw inspiration from the geometric patterns and mathematical theories that scholars in the city's golden age pored over.

From its founding as a city of intellectual exchange to Fatima al-Fihri's inspired establishment of Al Quaraouiyine University in Morocco, the city's profound impacy is undeniable. Today, many travellers worldwide continue to visit the region to understand better the city's impact on the Islamic world and Western society and the development of global knowledge.

Great Mosque (p186), Kairouan

GIMAS/SHUTTERSTOCK

Pirate ship
ISTVAN CSAK/SHUTTERSTOCK

PIRATES OF THE MEDITERRANEAN

By far one of the strangest historical events in modern history, though with extremely wide-reaching effects and consequences, this is the story of the Barbary Corsairs. By Sanad Tabbaa

FIRST OFF, IT'S important to establish a bit of pirate lingo. The difference between a pirate and a privateer is not a question of activity but of legality. A privateer is simply a pirate who's been commissioned by some government or other. The difference between either of those and a corsair is one of history and geography: a corsair was a pirate or privateer who operated in the Mediterranean. These people made their living raiding coastal villages, taking hostages for ransom, selling them into slavery when unpaid, and robbing merchant vessels. This could all be avoided through payment of tribute, on the spot for regular pirates, or to the government for privateers.

In the 16th century the entire Maghrebi coastline was conquered by corsairs.

The Barbarossa Brothers

Khayreddin and Aruj Barbarossa (literally the Redbeard pirates) were brothers and corsairs in the employ of the Ottoman Empire who hailed from the island of Lesbos in today's Greece. Rising from humble origins, they became the Grand Admiral of the Ottoman Navy and the Dey of Algiers, respectively. Their personal activities resulted in a massive power struggle over the North African coastline that persisted for almost a century, and their legacy resulted in a Mediterranean Sea that for nearly 300 years was nigh impossible to cross without paying tribute to the nominal, if not actual, Ottoman beys, deys, sultans and pashas of the Maghrebi coast. They were the first major Barbary Corsairs.

But I'm getting ahead of myself. By the beginning of the 16th century, North African power had been fragmented, with the once-formidable Almohads reduced to a memory. Smaller-scale local rulers, often paying lip service to some great power or other, controlled the rich cities of the Mediterranean coastline that themselves were being eyed by the European powers to the north and the Ottomans to the northeast. The solution presented itself in the form of the Barbarossa Brothers.

Through a few decades of dedicated piracy, the elder brother, Aruj, ended up amassing a significant fighting force, which was nominally aligned with the Ottomans, who tolerated their presence in exchange for one-third of the Barbarossas' spoils. Using this force, he took over the island of Djerba in Tunisia to use as a base for expeditions into the rest of North Africa. In the process, he acquired another nickname,

Baba Aruj, for his work in transferring Muslims and Jews fleeing the Iberian Peninsula to North Africa, and yet another – Gümüş Kol ('Silver Arm' in Turkish) – after losing his arm in battle and having it replaced with a silver prosthetic. From his base in Djerba, Aruj Barbarossa attacked Algiers to liberate it from Spain. Having conquered the city he realized that he was unprepared to repel European aggression on his own. Barbarossa then aligned himself directly with the Ottomans and became the Bey of Algeria for a short time before his death.

After Aruj's death, his brother Khayreddin assumed both his responsibilities and the nickname Barbarossa. More aligned with the piracy side of the family business than he was with governance, Khayreddin conquered Tunis in the name of the Ottomans in 1534. The city exchanged hands, from Ottoman to Spanish to Hapsburg, over the coming decades, eventually falling to the Ottomans in 1574. One Spanish soldier, writing of the insurmountable odds and the Spanish surrender in that final battle, would amass some renown of his own: Miguel Cervantes. Hence, reality proves itself stranger than fiction.

USING THIS FORCE, ARUJ BARBAROSSA TOOK OVER THE ISLAND OF DJERBA IN TUNISIA TO USE AS A BASE FOR EXPEDITIONS INTO THE REST OF NORTH AFRICA.

Djerba (p261)

ANISBOUKHRIS/SHUTTERSTOCK

The Era of the Barbary Corsairs

By the end of the 16th century, the Maghrebi coast was both indisputably Ottoman and the home to the Barbary Corsairs. The local governors of Tunis in today's Tunisia, Tripoli in today's Libya, Algiers in Algeria, and various ports in Morocco derived the majority of their nations' incomes from governmentally sanctioned piracy. The Barbary Corsairs raided vessels aligned with states that didn't, or couldn't, pay tribute, robbing them of their goods and taking hostages for ransom and selling them into slavery if that ransom went unpaid. It's difficult today to imagine the massive effect this had on the merchant vessels in the Mediterranean, but for 300 years the risks of sailing without paying tribute were well known to sailors.

To attempt to understand the significance of this large-scale piracy, one needs only to know about Denmark. By the 18th century, it had become so dangerous to enter the Mediterranean Sea that Danish local churches were systematically collecting funds to pay the ransom of sailors taken hostage by the Barbary Corsairs. By 1715, the state itself established the *slavekasse,* or enslaved people's fund, to pay for the ransoms through a state-sponsored anti-enslvement insurance program.

This state of affairs continued until the end of the 18th century, though by this point the people taken were rarely actually sold into slavery. The hostage business appeared to be more profitable and less prone to unnecessary strife. At the beginning of the 19th century, though, the death knell of the Barbary Corsairs began to sound.

The USA signed the Declaration of Independence in 1776, prompting Britain to withdraw its protections for American merchant vessels from the Barbary Corsairs. Although the Sultan of Morrocco recognised the nascent USA in 1777, signing America's longest unbroken Friendship Treaty in 1786, the governors of Tunis, Algiers and Tripoli were not as welcoming. Barbary Corsairs raided American merchant vessels with impunity until tribute was paid. By 1794, the USA was forced to establish the US Navy specifically to protect its vessels from the corsairs. Initially, though, the costs of maintaining the Navy and its ineffectiveness led the USA to capitulate, paying no less than 20% of its annual budget as tribute to the pirates.

In an effort to prove itself in the international arena and to escape the onerous tribute payments, the USA declared war on the states of the Maghrebi coast. The first of these Barbary Wars ended in a stalemate, forcing diplomatic concessions from both sides in 1805. The war of 1812, though, began after the British encouraged the return of piracy on US vessels; a suggestion warmly embraced by the Barbary Corsairs. This led to a second war with the US Navy, which by then was more developed and ready to deal with the aggression of the pirates. The Second Barbary War ended in only three days. The dey of Algiers, and his Maghrebi allies, promised the Americans frcc, safc conduct through the Mediterranean Sea, renouncing the practice of tribute in 1815.

The Legacy of Piracy

The era of the Barbary Corsairs was nearly at an end. Though Mediterranean state-sponsored piracy was nearly eradicated following the Barbary Wars, it continued in a subdued form for a few more decades. With the Ottoman Empire in a state of decline and the power of the corsairs waning, France saw an opportunity to put the issue to rest once and for all. France invaded Algiers, the hub of the Barbary Corsairs, and established a protectorate in the process, beginning the colonisation of Algeria in 1830. Yes, you read that right. The colonisation of Algeria was conducted under the pretext of fighting pirates.

The loss of funds from tribute and ransom meant that Tunisia could no longer economically compete. Additionally, the humiliating defeats during the era of the Barbary Wars had the Husaynid bey of Tunisia attempt to modernise his country and establish some form of organized military, with officers' schools and infrastructure to match. This led him, and a couple of his descendants, to borrow large sums of money from the French and the British in order to finance these projects. Crucially, this was money that Tunisia couldn't realistically afford to pay back at predatory interest rates. Using the pretext of securing their economic interests, the French used this financial leverage, as well as their military presence in neighbouring Algeria, to establish a budgetary control commission in Tunisia.

Once the budget of the state was no longer locally decided, the French had become the de-facto rulers of Tunisia, and they made this status a legal reality using the pretext of a border skirmish in 1881. And so, the colonisation of Tunisia was complete - due in no small part to piracy.

A MODERN, MULTILINGUAL SOCIETY

Tunisia represents a true melting pot of cultural influences, and nowhere is this more apparent than in the arena of language.
By Paula Hardy

WHILE MODERN STANDARD Arabic is considered Tunisia's only official language, on a day-to-day basis the country's 12 million inhabitants speak Tūnsi (Tunisian Arabic), a language that is still causing controversy over whether it is a distinct language or a divergent dialect of Arabic.

Multicultural Origins

Tunisia's linguistic history is defined by its ability to absorb diverse influences. The oldest language spoken here was Numidian or Lybic-Berber, a proto-Berber Afroasiatic language. When Phoenicians from Tyre (now Lebanon) arrived in 814 BCE and founded Carthage, a new Lybic-Punic bilingualism developed. The Romans added

 Women browsing books, Tunis (p53)

Latin to the mix when they conquered Carthage and colonised the area in 146 BCE.

Classical Arabic arrived in 673 CE with the Islamic conquest of North Africa. It became the main administrative language of the province, although regional variations arose as different tribes, namely the Banu Hilal and Banu Sulaym, emigrated to different regions of the country in the 11th century, while a separate Judeo-Tunisian Arabic dominated in Jewish hubs such as Djerba. The picture was further complicated in the 15th century with the arrival of Arabic-speaking Andalusians following the Spanish Reconquista in 1492, and then by the arrival of Spaniards, Ottomans and Italian immigrants between the 17th and 18th centuries. Finally, the French colonised Tunisia in 1881, making French the official language of the country, although it was only spoken by the educated elite.

By independence in 1956, Tunisia was linguistically fragmented with variations of Tunisian Arabic, Algerian Arabic, Libyan Arabic, French and various Amazigh dialects spoken in different areas of the country. That's why one of the first tasks undertaken by Habib Bourguiba, the first president of Tunisia, was the implementation of free basic education for all Tunisians and the compulsory teaching of Modern Standard Arabic as part of the process of Arabization. Tunisian Arabic, the indigenous local language, was only finally recognised by the government in 2011.

Modern Standard Arabic & French

Modern Standard Arabic and French are taught in Tunisian schools, while public schools offer pupils English classes from the age of 10. That said, an increasing number of Tunisians are learning English simply through contact with tourists and the media. Street signs, official notices and government speeches are in Modern Standard Arabic, while French remains the language of higher education, science and business. Finally, online, most Tunisians converse in Franco-Arabic, which is a mix of Arabic, French and English and uses a Latin script.

The Maltese Connection

Tunisian Arabic is very different from other Arab dialects/languages, and other than their closest neighbours – Libyans, Algerians and Moroccans – most Arabic speakers find it unintelligible. However, the Maltese and Tunisians can understand each other extremely well. While Maltese contains more Italian words than the French vocabulary in Tūnsi, it is also a Siculo-Arabic (or Sicilian Arabic) language remnant from the time when Malta was part of the Emirate of Sicily in the 9th century.

Language & Identity

Depending on context, both French and Arabic can be languages of power and solidarity in Tunisia. There's no doubt that to be educated in Tunisia is to be a French speaker. However, Tunisians may categorise themselves and their language use to contrast themselves not only to Europe and to other urban/rural communities in Tunisia, but also to other countries in North Africa. Both French and Arabic can also be either overtly institutional and official or friendly and comfortable, depending on who is speaking to whom and in which context.

For older Tunisians who went through the educational system in the 1970s and '80s during the height of Arabization, the Arabic language is a symbol of a recovered Islamic identity following years of oppressive French colonialism. However, for younger Tunisians, the trend is towards speaking more English, a global language and the lingua franca of the internet.

Today, Tunisia's language landscape remains as dynamic as ever. There's no doubt that multilingualism is key to economic success, particularly in highly multicultural environments such as the tourism sector. In addition, many young Tunisians aspire to work abroad and are therefore diversifying their language repertoire by learning German, Italian or Turkish. This makes Tunisia a model for the kind of multilingual society that UNESCO states is key for building sustainable, tolerant and respectful societies of the future – a future in which it posits that speaking three languages 'should be the normal range of language knowledge in the 21st century'.

INDEX

D

E

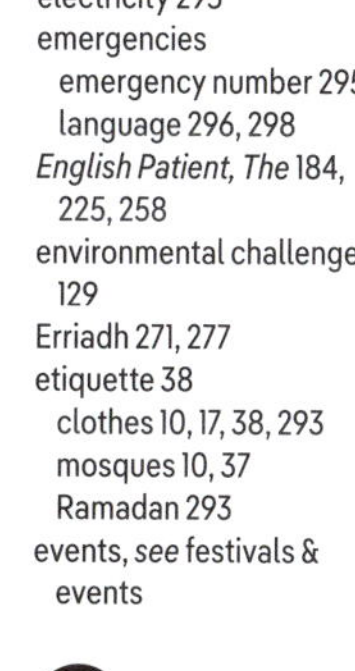

F

Map Pages **000**

With a sturdy pair of walking shoes, a hat and a guide, you can hike from Tamerza to Midès via the Midès Canyon, known locally as the Grand Canyon of Tunisia (p257).

Charming, French-built Beni Mtir (p136), with its red-roofed French architecture, is surrounded by forest. It is the starting point for a number of hikes.

FROM LEFT: MARQUES/SHUTTERSTOCK, HICHEM KAOUANE/SHUTTERSTOCK

Mapping data sources:
© Lonely Planet
© OpenStreetMap http://openstreetmap.org/copyright

THIS BOOK

Destination Editor Zara Sekhavati

Production Editor Barbara Delissen

Image Editor Nicolas D'Hoedt

Cartographers Corey Hutchison, Jennifer Johnston, Daniela Machová, Wayne Murphy, Anthony Phelan

Coordinating Editor Michael Mackenzie

Cover Researcher Daisy Korpics

Thanks Natalie Butler, Kate Chapman, Pete Cruttenden, Charlotte Orr, Kathryn Rowan, Sanad Tabbaa

Paper in this book is certified against the Forest Stewardship Council™ standards. FSC™ promotes environmentally responsible, socially beneficial and economically viable management of the world's forests.

Published by Lonely Planet Global Limited
CRN 554153
6th edition – Dec 2025
First published Jul 1998
ISBN 978 1 83758 676 9

10 9 8 7 6 5 4 3 2 1
Printed in China